THE STRUCTURE OF THE ARTISTIC TEXT

CONTENTS

PREFACE

This translation has two purposes. The first is to make *The Structure of the Artistic Text* accessible to those who do not know Russian or whose decoding apparatus, as the author might say, lacks the sophistication necessary to handle the message. The clues, after all, are not in italics, and even if they were, the problem of deciphering the message would be complicated by the fact that there are several languages, several codes, employed by the author.

The second purpose is to encourage a discussion of Lotman's theories, which are controversial by any count. In the Soviet Union his works, in particular *Lectures on Structural Poetics* and the one under discussion here, have received considerable attention. The comments made are, for the most part, disparaging. While most Soviet critics admit, somewhat begrudgingly, that Lotman has some very interesting things to say about literature, almost all agree that his approach suffers from the same "errors" that the formalists committed. He is accused of subjectivism (Xrapčenko) and excessive schematism (Gončarov). Jurij Barabaš's attitude toward Jurij Lotman and toward structuralism in general is fairly typical: "The principle of the closedness of the aesthetic set, its immanence, its isolation from the world, from man, from meaning, does not simply represent an error on the part of individual authors; it is inherent and organic to the very nature of structuralism and is inherited from formalism" (*Problems of Aesthetics and Poetics,* Moscow, 1972).

Despite this sort of standard criticism levied by the orthodox and the elite, the science of semiotics continues to flourish in the Soviet Union, especially in what has come to be known as the Tartu School. Today, seven years after the appearance of *The Structure of the Artistic Text,* we have every reason to claim that the work represents a sort of watershed in the history of the school, that its publication marks the temporal divide between academic adolescence and maturity.

There is, of course, an extensive pre-history which we cannot ignore if we wish to view the Tartu group in proper perspective. In his recently published *Essays on the History of Semiotics in the USSR (Očerki po istorii semiotiki v SSSR,* Moscow, 1976) V. V. Ivanov traces the movement in Russia to Potebnja, Veselovsky and Šaxmatov. The subsequent evolution of the structural and semiotic approach owed a great deal to the works of the Russian formalists (Šklovskij, Tynjanov, Jakobson) and such fellow travellers as Žirmunskij and Vinogradov. Nor should we underestimate the significance of the Prague Linguistic Circle (Jakobson, Trubetzkoy, Mukařovsky, among others), the works of such out-standing literary historians as Baxtin and Gukovskij, and the studies in folklore by Propp and Bogatyrev, in the scholarly lineage of Soviet semiotics. The history of the movement has yet to be written, and when that task is finally accomplished the list of contributors will undoubtedly be expanded to include figures whom we still regard as peripheral or even antagonistic to the movement. For example, in his *Essays* Ivanov makes a strong case for including Eisenstein, Marr and Meščaninov in the annals of the precursors of Soviet semiotics. Here we can only refer the reader to the scholars mentioned above and to such historical sketches as Ivanov's *Essays,* Erlich's *Russian Formalism* and the descriptions of the Prague Circle in *Sound, Sign and Meaning* (Ann Arbor, 1976).

Clearly the Tartu School is carrying on a tradition that has a fairly long history in the Soviet Union. It is not an aberration, nor is it the sole offshoot of semiotic studies. In fact as a coherent entity it has matured to the point where it represents a bough rather than a branch of the overall trend under discussion. Still it has its own history and it is within that context that we speak of the central role played by *The Structure of the Artistic Text.* The six years preceding its appearance constituted a period of experimentation and preparation initiated by Lotman's *Lectures on Strucural Poetics (Lekcii po strukturnoj poètike,* Tartu, 1964). This was the first in a series of works on sign systems in art and culture (*Trudy po znakovym sistemam*) put out by Tartu University, and it represented the first real attempt by the group to establish a theoretical framework for the application of semiotics to the study of literature and art. It was, however, a series of lectures, not a cohesive system, and in this sense served more or less as a draft of something still unspoken.

The aura of discovery surrounding this first substantive study continued to inform subsequent works in the series. These, in contrast to the pioneering issue, were collections of essays by various authors which explored separate theoretical aspects of semiotics and art and attempted to apply particular axioms of Lotman's incipient system to the study of individual works. Meanwhile the author himself continued to revise, expand and perfect the system undergirding these theoretical forays.

The result was the work that is presented here in translation. The fact that *The Structure of the Artistic Text* (1970) was published in Moscow by Iskusstvo, a press without direct academic affiliations, is itself a clear indication of the lively interest generated by the Tartu School and its activities. On the one hand, the book is quite literally an extension of the *Lectures;* many passages are transposed verbatim from the earlier text. On the other hand it is far more sophisticated. Not only does it expand on the various theoretical principles outlined in the earlier work, it also introduces vital concepts—that of the secondary modeling systems, for example—which are at best only hinted at in the *Lectures.* One can also draw conclusions concerning the sophistication and vitality of Lotman's newly elaborated system by looking at subsequent works by the author and his colleagues. Two years after the appearance of *The Structure of the Artistic Text* Lotman published a series of essays, *Analysis of the Poetic Text (Analiz poètičeskogo teksta*, Moscow, 1972) in which the theories outlined in *Structure* are put to the practical test of specific literary analysis. In his next monograph, *The Semiotics of Cinema* (*Semiotika kino,* Tallin 1973) he applied the same basic theories to the genre of film. The most recent works by Lotman and other members of the Tartu group in the seventh issue of *Trudy po znakovym sistemam* (1976) and other anthologies manifest a growing interest in the application of semiotics to problems of cultural typology. Lotman's current investigation of the cultural sign systems of eighteenth-century Russia (*Kulturnoe nasledie drevnej Rusi*, Moscow, 1976) represents yet another outgrowth of the system set forth in *The Structure of the Artistic Text*, and a further demonstration of its viability.

The broad applicability of Lotman's system is due in large measure to the "moveability" of the metalanguage it employs. Actually what we are confronted with is a composite of metalanguages borrowed from structural linguistics, information theory and semiotics as such. While their respective vocabularies often overlap, we do not always find a corresponding coincidence of meaning. Though the polysemy of the terms makes them extremely versatile, it can be a source of confusion for readers who are unfamiliar with one or more of the metalanguages involved. It would, of course, be presumptuous to impose any sort of glossary on the reader, but we would do well to explore the semantic range of a few crucial words so that those who are not yet on good terms with the metalanguages employed might be better able to decode the author's message.

We might begin with a discussion of the term "language," the most basic and least controversial in the book. At the beginning of Chapter One we are given a general description of natural languages as a "system of communication." That definition is considerably narrowed in the subchapter "Art Among Other Sign Systems," where language is defined in traditional Saussurian terms as merely one aspect of the communication system. This difference would appear to be academic until the term is applied to art. As a monolithic entity art, as language, is identified as a means of communication, and, once again monolithically, as a language in the Saussurian sense of that word, an "abstract system of invariant relation." Clearly a semantic shift is involved here. To say that Russian is a language or a modeling system is not the same thing as saying that art is a language or a modeling system, and not only because the former is a primary and the latter a secondary modeling system. The former may be described as "an abstract system of invariant relations;" the latter is no such thing, any more than, say, "science" is. Lotman's breakdown of the concept of language is implicitly based on a recognition of this fact. Thus he speaks of natural languages (Czech, Russian), artificial languages ("the languages of science, "the languages of conventional signs") and secondary languages. The typological discrepancy that seems to creep in here—myth and art, as examples of secondary languages, are not to each other what, say, Czech is to Russian or the metalanguage of nuclear physics is to the metalanguage of inorganic chemistry— is resolved when the author begins to discuss the functional side of art as an abstract category. Instead of equating art with language he speaks of art as a *generator* of languages. This refinement helps to restore the specificity and differentiation necessary to make the definition workable. Nonetheless part of the burden of definition must be borne by the reader. Is art as such a language? Is literature a language, or cinema, or sculpture? Is a given period or school (Realism, the Baroque) a language? Is a specific genre within these art forms a language? Is a specific text a language? At various points in his work Lotman responds affirmatively to all these questions, and the reader must himself determine what the author means by language in each case: an integral system of communication, a specific sign system of invariant relations, a modeling system that generates artistic works or a modeling system generated by art.

The many levels at work in Lotman's view of language apply in equal measure to his concept of code, for they are most often identified with each other. The term, of course, is borrowed from information theory, where it is defined as "an agreed transformation whereby messages are converted from one representative into another," necessarily implying the initial presence of a language (Colin Cherry, *On Human Communication,* second edition, Cambridge, Massachusetts, 1970). It has become commonplace in structural linguistics to apply the term to natural languages as such, which in itself requires a reformulation of the original definition. Further changes are necessary when the term is applied to art, and unless we are aware of them, the equation may seem suspect.

The major semantic shift in this case occurs when the word "code" is applied to diachronic segments in literature and art. When we are dealing with natural languages we can legitimately discusss and describe the code in its synchronic aspect alone, but when we deal with the "code" of a literary movement, for example, we must describe several synchronic cross sections; in other words, we have to describe it as a diachronic phenomenon, and always keep that diachronic aspect in mind when we try to analyze a given text. Our understanding of the signs and rules of Russian Realism, for example, is based on the deduction of invariant elements observed across a specific temporal spectrum. But these elements are invariant for a given author only if he percives them as part of a system. Lotman himself says that the language of a work of art is "that given which exists before the creation of a concrete text..." If this is so, then

Gogol could not have "encoded" his work into the "language" of nineteenth century Russian Realism because that code did not exist at the time of writing it.

The obvious danger of applying the word code to the set of invariants culled from a group of heterogeneous texts is that the receiver—especially the trained receiver, otherwise known as the literary critic—confuses his metasemiotic description with the semiosis of the author. He constructs a code to decipher a message that is not consciously encoded on that particular level. Lotman handles this problem very neatly by claiming that an artistic text can be interpreted ("decoded") in a virtually infinite number of ways, that it induces the reader to construct codes that are applicable to the message at hand. In other words, the interpretation of an artistic text or group of texts does not demand an "agreed transformation." When this condition is lifted, the word code can be as freely applied to art as to natural languages.

This use of the term is in turn based on one of Lotman's basic tenets, that everything in a work of art is meaningful. Now the multiplicity of artistic codes employed in a given text certainly helps to account for the multiplicity of meanings that arise. It also accounts for the multiplicity of interpretations: the failure to perceive and/or decipher a code present in a text can alter one's perception of the message. The possibility of a virtually infinite number of interpretations does not imply that all elements in the artistic text are consciously encoded, but Lotman nonetheless claims that they are all meaningful because they join together to form a model. "The language of an artistic text in essence is... a model of the universe, and in this sense its whole structure belongs to the sphere of 'content'—it carries information." On the other hand the author says in no uncertain terms that in a text "the presence of extra-systemic elements—an inevitable consequence of materialization—as well as the feeling that the same elements may be systemic on one level and extrasystemic on another, both inevitably accompany art." In order to resolve this contradiction Lotman introduces a degree of relativity in the opposition between code and message, between variant and invariant elements, which would be unacceptable for the description of natural languages. But he is dealing with secondary languages, and therefore he can claim that what is a code on certain semiological planes may be perceived as a message on others, that variants on certain levels of the artistic text are invariants on others, and vice versa.

Another term that frequently appears in the book is "information," and here too some clarificaiton is in order. Lotman provides several definitions, some of them relating to information theory, others based on the meaning of the word in common parlance. Information theory treats information as a statistical concept applicable only on the syntactic level; it is a property of signs, a measure of probability. This is what

Lotman means by information when he is discussing the entropy of an artistic text, the statistical probability of the occurrence of a given sign. It is altogether apropos that the author should warn us that he is dealing with quantitative, not qualitative aspects of information. No confusion arises on this count in *The Structure of the Artistic Text.*

More important for the reader is the distinction between semantic information and statistical information. In the sub-chapter on the entropy of an artistic text the author for the most part restricts himself to a statistical, quantitative definition of information based on Academician Kolmogorov's studies in this area. Elsewhere, however, the author frequently speaks of the quantity of *semantic* information. An artistic text, he says, can transmit and store more information than any other sort of verbal text because its language, the "language" of art, consists of a hierarchy of languages of codes. Hence a story by Čexov, say, stores and transmits as much or more information than a textbook on psychology. Unfortunately no ultimately satisfactory method has been established for mathematically measuring the quantity of semantic information in natural language texts (the Bar-Hillel and Carnap theory would be inapplicable here because it is concerned exclusively with a limited universe of discourse, a pure, artificial language system), and so the author's assumption, inviting as it is, cannot be proved or disproved at this point.

Certain properties which Lotman ascribes to artistic texts would make the task of measuring their semantic information extraordinarily difficult. First, the meaningfulness of a message rests to a large extent on the presumption of the receiver, and therefore the quantity of information it "contains" is not an intrinsic property. Even defining what is and is not an artistic text may depend entirely on the perception or mood of the receiver. How can one measure the semantic difference between the declarative sentence, "You owe me $97.34" and Tom Clark's monostiche "You owe me $97.34"? The best one could do would be to measure the statistical probability of this utterance (or components thereof) in ordinary discourse and in a collection of poems.

Second, the semantic information in a text is in many cases potential, that is, it depends, in Lotman's words, on the level of understanding of the recipient. It would also seem to depend on the reception accorded it by future recipients, if, as the author claims, the total semantic information conveyed by a literary work (he is speaking specifically about *Evgenij Onegin*) includes all past, present and future interpretations of that word. Measuring this sort of information potential would be extremely difficult. Despite these reservations, however, we must concur with Lotman that those very properties which make it difficult to arrive at quantitative conclusions are themselves responsible for the tremendous semantic saturation of the artistic text, and this, perhaps, is the major point that the author wishes to make.

We could continue at length in our discussion of Lotman's metalanguage, pointing out where the terms he borrows correspond with their counterparts in other metalanguages, and where they diverge. Hopefully the comments we have made will suffice in making the reader aware of the terminological complexities that must inevitably accompany an approach of this kind. Lotman would be the first to admit that a metalanguage does not spring fully armored from the head of the scholar; it is forged gradually; each piece must be examined, tested for vulnerability and perhaps even replaced. One of the major purposes of this translation, as we noted earlier, is to encourage that sort of examination and testing.

We have concentrated on the problem of the metalanguage rather than the system itself, not only because this is likely to prove the first stumbling block encountered by the reader, but more importantly because the system of structural analysis outlined rests solidly on the metalanguage it employs. One of the main hopes entertained by structuralists is that they will at last be able to settle on a precise set of terms and strict rules governing their usage. That in itself would represent an invaluable contribution to literary studies. *The Structure of the Artistic Text* is, among other things, a series of experiments designed to test the endurance of a new and at the same time borrowed metalanguage; some of them are conclusive, others are not, but all of them are intriguing.

In order to render the text more comprehensible for those who do not know Russian and are familiar only with the classics of Russian literature, we have furnished a number of notes identifying lesser known authors and explaining certain allusions made by the author and the writers whom he cites. To avoid cluttering the text we have not footnoted references to major Russian authors whose works have been translated into English. The perplexed reader should consult any standard history or dictionary of Russian literature and, if he so desires, make use of some of the very fine translations presently available—Vladimir Nabokov's translation fo Pushkin's *Evgenij Onegin* and Lermontov's *A Hero of Our Time,* Guerney's translation of *Dead Souls,* the Maude translation of *War and Peace,* among others.

No attempt has been made to convey the formal properties (rhyme, meter, sound repetition) of the poems cited by the author. Where these properties are the subject of discussion the Russian text has been reproduced according to the accepted scholarly transliteration alongside the translation.

In conclusion we would like to express our indebtedness to Prof. Sergej Syrovatkin for his assistance in editing the translation, and to Alexander Parnis and Valentina Morderer for their suggestions and support.

R. V.

INTRODUCTION

Art has accompanied man throughout the recorded history of his existence. Occupied with production, struggling to preserve his own life, almost always deprived of his basic necessities, man continues to find time for artistic activity, for he senses that it is indispensable. At various stages in history, voices have been raised to proclaim that art is unnecessary, or even harmful. These voices arose in the medieval church as it struggled with pagan folklore and with the traditions of ancient art; they were heard among the iconoclasts who rose up against the church, and among numerous other social movements of various epochs. At times the struggle against one or another aspect of artistic creation, or against art as a whole, was waged with the support of powerful political institutions. All the victories gained in the struggle, however, have proved to be chimerical; art inevitably rises again, outliving its oppressors. This extraordinary resilience, if one reflects on it, seems quite astonishing insofar as each existing aesthetic conception interprets the necessity of art in its own way. Art is not a constituent of production, and its existence is not conditioned by man's need to continually renovate the means by which he satisfies his material wants.

In the course of its historical development, each society works out particular forms for the socio-political organization inherent to it. The historical inevitability of these forms may be perfectly clear to us; we may be able to explain why a society with no internal organization cannot exist; but it is considerably more difficult to explain why a society without art cannot exist. In place of an explanation people usually point out that societies lacking an art of their own are unknown in the history of mankind (or known only as rare anomalies of a socially teratological nature, confirming the general norm through their rarity). We should bear in mind those factors which distinguish art, in this respect, from other types of ideological structures. By organizing society, certain structures inevitably embrace all its members: each individual, by virtue of belonging to a historical collective, is faced with the harsh necessity of being part of some group, of entering into one of the subsets of a given social set. For example, a man living in eighteenth-century pre-Revolutionary France could belong to one of three Estates in order to function as a political entity; but he had to belong to one of them. But society, while at times imposing very strict limits on art, never compels its members to engage in artistic activity. Ritual is obligatory, the round dance—optional. To profess a religion, to be an atheist, to join some sort of political organization, to have a certain legal status—every society presents its members with a compulsory list of such features.

To be a producer or consumer of artistic "goods" is always optional in society. The fact that one man believes in nothing and another dislikes the cinema (poetry, ballet) constitutes violations of social norms which are by no means equally binding. While indifference to official art was taken as a sign of disloyalty in Nazi Germany, it is clear that nothing was implied regarding the norms which govern man's attitude to art.

Nevertheless through its entire history, art has demonstrated its own vital necessity, although it is obligatory neither from the viewpoint of the immediate needs of life, nor from the viewpoint of mandatory social relations.

It has long been observed that the necessity for art is related to the necessity for knowledge, that art itself is a form of cognition, of mankind's struggle for the truth imperative to its existence. Taken at face value, however, this proposition entails a number of difficulties. If the desired cognition is perceived in terms of logical propositions like the results of scientific investigation, then we must agree that mankind possesses more direct means for obtaining them than through art. And if we hold such a view, we must agree that art furnishes knowledge of an inferior type. Hegel wrote unequivocally:

> As a result of its form, art is also limited to a certain kind of content. Only a certain range and a certain degree of truth can find its embodiment in the form of an artistic work.

This proposition inevitably gave rise to the conclusion that the spirit of contemporary culture

> has apparently risen to a stage higher than that in which art presents the highest form of cognizance of the absolute. The unique character of artistic activity and its manifestation in works of art can no longer fully satisfy our higher needs.[1]

In spite of the fact that Hegel's position was repeatedly criticized— by Belinskij, for example,—it is so integral to the understanding of the functions of art characterized above, that it arises again and again in the history of culture. Its manifestations are varied—from periodically resurrected notions of art's superfluity or obsolescence to the conviction that the critic, scholar or any other person possessing the authority of logical, abstract thought, or with pretensions to that effect, has the right to instruct and admonish the writer by virtue of that fact.

This conviction is manifested in the defects of pedagogical methods applied to the study of literature, methods which try to convince students that a few lines of logical deduction (assuming that they are well thought out and serious) constitute the essence of an artistic work, and that the rest is a matter of secondary "artistic features."

Thus existing conceptions of culture explain why production and its forms of organization must exist, why science is necessary, whereas art

1 Hegel, *Sočinenija*, vol. XII (Moscow, 1938) p. 10.

may be viewed as an optional element of culture. We can determine what influence the non-artistic structure of reality has on art. But if the question, "Why is a society without art an impossibility?" remains an open one, and the reality of historical facts forces us repeatedly to pose the question, then we must inevitably conclude that our conceptions of human culture are inadequate.

We know that the history of mankind could not take shape without production, social conflicts, the struggle of political opinions, mythology, religion, atheism, or without the successes of science. Could it take shape without art? Has art been assigned the secondary role of an auxiliary instrument to which the more substantial needs of the human spirit may or may not have recourse? In Puškin, we find the note, "In one of Shakespeare's comedies the country wench Audrey asks, 'What is Poetry? Is it a true thing?' "2* How does one answer this question? Is poetry really a "true thing," or, to use Deržavin's expression, is it:

> . . . . . . ljubezna,
> Prijatna, sladostna, polezna,
> Kak letom vkusnyj limonad.

> [. . . . . . . pleasing,
> Pleasant, refreshing, useful,
> Like tasty lemonade in summer.j

Unfortunately, a purely emotional response based on a love of art, on habitual association with daily aesthetic impressions, is not ultimately convincing. Too often science must reject convictions whose habitualness and mundane obviousness make up the very essence of our day-to-day experience. How easy it would be for a scholar whose whole experience has been restricted to the sphere of European culture to prove that the music of the Far East could not exist, or could not be considered music. The reverse situation is, of course, equally possible. The habitualness or "naturalness" of an idea is no proof of its truthfulness.

The question of the necessity of art is not the subject of this book and cannot be discussed here in all its aspects. We shall dwell on the subject only to the extent that it relates to the internal organization of the artistic text and to its social functioning.

The life of every creature involves a complex interaction with its surroundings. An organism incapable of responding and adjusting to external influence would inevitably perish. Interaction with one's environment may be viewed as the reception and deciphering of information. Man is inevitably drawn into this intense process: he is caught up in a flow of information, life transmits its signals to him. But these signals will remain unheard, the

---

* "I do not know what 'poetical' is. Is it honest in deed and word? Is it a true thing?" *As You Like It*, Act III, scene 3.–Tr.

2 A. S. Puškin, *Polnoe sobranie sočinenij*, vol. XII (Moscow-Leningrad, 1949) p.178.

information will not be understood, and significant opportunities in the struggle for survival neglected, if man fails to cope with the growing need to decipher this flow of signals and convert them into signs that have the power to communicate in human society. Under these circumstances, it becomes necessary not only to increase the number of diverse messages in the already available languages (natural languages, the languages of the different sciences), but to constantly increase the number of languages into which it is possible to translate the flow of surrounding information, making it accessible. Man needs a special mechanism, a generator of more and more new "languages" to act as a vehicle for necessary knowledge. Creating a hierarchy of languages is a more compact means of storing imformation than endlessly increasing the number of messages in one language, but that is not all.

Certain types of information can be stored and transmitted only with the help of specially organized languages. For example, information of the sort provided by chemistry or algebra demands its own language, specially adapted to a given type of modeling and communication.

Art is a magnificently organized generator of languages of a special type, which render an indispensable service to mankind, attending to one of the most complex aspects of human knowledge, one whose mechanism is even now not completely understood.

The notion that the world around us speaks many languages and that the essence of wisdom is to learn to understand them is hardly novel. Baratynskij, for example, continually associated the understanding of nature with the mastering of its language and used terms of linguistic communication ("said," "read") to characterize the act of cognition:

> S prirodoj odnoju on žizn'ju dyšal:
>   Ruč'ja *razumel lepetan'e,*
> I govor drevesnyx listov *ponimal*
>   I čuvstvoval trav prozjaban'e;
> Byla emu zvezdnaja *kniga* jasna,
> I s nim *govorila* morskaja volna.

> [With nature alone he breathed life:
>   He *understood* the *babble* of streams,
> And *comprehended* the murmur of tree leaves,
>   And felt the sprouting of the grass;
> The *book* of the stars was clear to him,
> And the sea waves *spoke* with him.]

Lack of understanding means forgetting or not knowing a language:

> .... *Xram upal,*
> A ruin ego potomok
> Jazyka ne razgadal.

> [. . . . . The temple fell,
> And posterity *did not unriddle*
> *The language* of its ruins.]

More interesting yet is the case of Puškin's "Verses composed at night, in time of sleeplessness," where the poet speaks of the dark and fretful life that envelopes him and demands to be explained:

> Ja ponjat' tebja xoču,
> Smysla ja v tebe išču. . .

> [I want to understand you,
> I search for meaning in you. . .]

This poem was not published during the poet's lifetime, but first included by Žukovskij in the posthumous *Collected Works* of Puškin in 1841. The last line was replaced with the following:

> Temnyj tvoj jazyk uču. . .

> [I study your dark language. . .]

We are not certain of Žukovskij's rationale, and in contemporary editions this line, which cannot be found in Puškin's manuscripts, is removed, However it is difficult to concede that Žukovksij, in the clear absence of any external reason connected with censorship, replaced Puškin's line with his own "apparently to improve the rhyme" (the opinion of the commentators in the *Complete Works* [1937]). It is wholly possible that Žukovskij, Puškin's constant companion in the 1830's, had reasons weighty enough (though unknown to us) for changing this line, despite his thorough acquaintance with the manuscript. But for us there is something else of importance here: whoever initiated the change—whether Puškin or Žukovskij—found the lines *smysla ja v tebe išču* and *temnyj tvoj jazyk uču* semantically equivalent: to understand life is to learn its dark language. In these and many other instances, we are not concerned with poetic metaphors, but with a deep understanding of the process involved in grasping the truth and, in a broader sense, grasping life itself.

For Classicism, poetry is the language of the gods; for Romanticism it is the language of the heart. The epoch of Realism changes the content of this metaphor, but retains its character: art is the language of life, and with its help reality tells its own story.

The idea of a mute world finding its voice in poetry is encountered in many forms in the works of various poets. Without poetry:

> Ulica korčitsja bez"jazykaja —
> ej nečem kricat' i razgovarivat'. . .
> (Majakovskij)

[The tongueless street writhes—
It has nothing to scream or speak with. . .]

The recurrent comparison of art with language, voice and speech demonstrates that art's bond with the process of social communication—latent or fully realized—is basic to the concept of artistic activity.

But if art is a special means of communication, a language organized in a particular manner (our concept of language derives from the broad semiotic definition: any ordered system which serves as a means of communication and employs signs), then works of art, that is, messages in this language, can be viewed as texts.

This position allows us to formulate the aim of our book. In creating and perceiving works of art, man transmits, receives and retains a special *artistic* form of information which cannot be isolated from the structural properties of the artistic text, any more than a thought can be isolated from the material structure of the brain. In this study we will attempt, at least tentatively, to make a general sketch of the structure of artistic language and of its relation to the structure of the artistic text, of its dissimilarity and likeness to analagous linguistic categories; to explain how the artistic text becomes the medium of a particular thought or idea, and how the structure of a text is related to the structure of this idea.

1. ART AS LANGUAGE

Art is one of the means of communication. Indisputably, it creates a bond between the sender and receiver (under certain circumstances both functions may be combined in one person, as in the case where a man conversing with himself is at once speaker and listener, but this does not alter matters).[1] Does this give us the right to define art as a language organized in a specific manner?

Every system whose end is to establish communication between two or more individuals may be defined as language (as already noted, the case of auto-communication implies that one individual functions as two). The common allegation that language implies communication *in human society* is not, strictly speaking, binding, for, on the one hand, linguistic communication between man and machine, and today between machines themselves, is no longer a theoretical problem but a technological reality.[2] On the other hand, the existence of certain forms of linguistic communication between animals has also ceased to be questioned. In contrast, systems of communication inside an individual (for example, the mechanisms of biochemical regulation or of signals transmitted through an organism's nervous system) are not languages.[3]

In this sense, we can apply the term "language" not only to Russian, French, Hindi and the like; not only to the artificially created systems of the different sciences, systems used to describe particular groups of phenomena (we call these the "artificial languages" or metalanguages of the given sciences); But also to customs, rituals, commerce, and religious concepts. In the same sense, we can speak of the "language" of the theater, cinema, painting, music, and of art as a whole, as a language organized in a particular way.

Once we have defined art as a language, however, we express by the same token certain definite opinions regarding its structure. Every language makes use of signs which constitute its "vocabulary" (sometimes we say its

1 For a classification of various types of text according to the relation of sender and receiver, see A. M. Pjatigorskij, "Nekotorye obščie zamečanija otnositel'no rassmotrenija teksta kak raznovidnosti signala," *Strukturno-tipologičeskie issledovanija* (Moscow, 1962).

2 In his article "Vybor jazyka komand" U. Buxgol'c demonstrates that "the system of commands is an intermediate stage between the programmer's language and the language of elementary operations within the machine." (*Kibernetičeskij sbornik,* 2, sb. perevodov, Moscow., 1961, p. 235.

3 It is also true here that extra-linguistic signal communication between separate organisms, similar to impulses within an organism, is significant for lower animals where the individuality of the species is more clearly expressed in a collective. The role of signs increases as each organism takes on individuality outside the group, although primary communication is not completely suppressed as, for example, in the case of parapsychological phenomena among humans.

"alphabet"—these concepts have identical meanings for the general theory of sign systems). Every language has certain rules for combining these signs, and every language is a hierarchical structure.

Stating the problem in this fashion permits us to approach art from two different points of view. First, it permits us to single out those characteristics which art holds in common with every language, and attempt to describe those characteristics in the general terms of a theory of sign systems. Second, it permits us, in light of the first description, to single out that which is inherent to art as a special language, and which distinguishes art from other systems of this type.

Since we intend to use the concept of "language" in a specifically semiotic sense—a sense which differs substantially from ordinary usage—we should define this term. We understand language to mean any communication system employing signs which are ordered in a particular manner. Languages viewed in this way will be distinguished: 1) from systems which do not serve as a means of communication; 2) from systems which serve as a means of communication, but do not employ signs; 3) from systems which serve as a means of communication and employ signs that are completely, or almost completely, unordered.

The first opposition allows us to set languages apart from those forms of human activity that have no immediate or teleological bearing on the accumulation and transmission of information. The second allows us to introduce the following division: sign communication takes place, on the whole, between individuals, whereas communication without signs occurs between systems inside an organism. It would be more accurate, however, to interpret this contrast as an antithesis of communications on the level of the first and second signal systems, since on the one hand, contact between organisms is possible without the use of signs (a feature of particular significance in lower animals, but retained in man in the form of telepathic phenomena); and on the other hand, sign communication is possible inside an organism. We are referring not only to the auto-organization of man's intellect with the aid of some sign system, but also to those instances where signs invade the sphere of primary signals. A man "charms away a toothache with words." Acting upon himself with the help of words, he bears suffering or physical torment.

If, with these reservations, we accept the proposition that language is a form of communication between two individuals, we ought still to formulate a more precise definition. It will prove more convenient to replace the concept of "individual" with the concept of the sender (addresser) and receiver (addressee) of a message. This will allow our scheme to embrace those cases where language links two mechanisms of transmission and reception, rather than two individuals (for example, a telegraph linked to an automatic recording device). But there is something more important here: it is not uncommon to find the same individual acting as both the addresser and addressee of a message (in mnemonic devices, diaries, note-books). Here information is transmitted not in space, but in time, and serves as a means for the auto-organization of the individual. We should consider this a marginal instance in the network of social communications, but for one problem: it is possible to view a man in isolation as an individual, in which case the scheme of communication A→ B (from addresser to addressee) will clearly predominate over the scheme A→ A' (where the addresser himself is the addressee, but in a different unit of time). But one has only to make "A" stand for the concept "national culture," for example, and the A→ A' scheme of communication will be just as significant as A→ B (and among cultural types the former will predominate). Let us go one step further: let "A" stand for the whole of mankind. Then auto-communication will become (at least within the limits of historically real experience) the sole scheme of communication.

The third opposition sets language apart from intermediate systems such as facial movements and gesture which, on the whole, are the domain of paralinguistics.

The concept of "language" as proposed above will encompass: a) natural languages (for example, Russian, French, Estonian, Czech); b) artificial languages–the languages of science (the metalanguages of scientific descriptions), the languages of conventional signals (road signs, for example), and so on; c) secondary languages (secondary modeling systems)–communication structures built as superstructures upon a natural linguistic plane (myth and religion, for example). *Art is a secondary modeling system.* We should understand the phrase "secondary in relation to language" to mean more than "using natural language as material;" if the phrase had such implications, the inclusion of nonverbal arts (painting, music, and others) would be clearly impermissible. The relationship here is more complex: natural language is not only one of the earliest, but also the most powerful system of communication in the human collective. By virtue of its very structure, it exerts a powerful influence over the human psyche and over many aspects of social life. Secondary modeling systems, like all semiotic systems, are constructed *on the model of language.* This does not imply that they reproduce all aspects of natural languages. Music, for example, is clearly distinguished from natural language by the absence of obligatory semantic bonds, but nowadays we find the description of a musical text as a sort of syntagmatic arrangement completely legitimate (cf. the works of M. M. Langleben and V. M. Gasparov). By singling out syntagmatic and paradigmatic bonds in painting (cf. the works of L. F. Žegin and B. A. Uspenskij) and in cinema (cf. the essays of S. M. Eisenstein, Ju. N. Tynjanov, B. M. Ejxenbaum, and C. Metz) we can discern *semiotic objects* in these arts, systems constructed on the model of languages. Inas-much as man's consciousness is a linguistic consciousness, all types of models erected as superstructures on that consciousness—and art among them—can be defined as secondary modeling systems.

Thus art can be described as a sort of secondary language, and the work of art as a text in that language.

Much of the material presented here will deal with the proof and explanation of this thesis. For the present, we will confine ourselves to a few quotations stressing the inseparability of the poetic idea from the particular structure of the text corresponding to it, from the particular language of art. Consider the following entry from Aleksandr Blok's notebooks (July, 1917):

> It is a lie that thoughts are repeated. Each thought is new because the new surrounds it and molds it. *Čtob on, voskresnuv, vstat' ne mog** (my own line), and *Čtob vstat' on iz groba ne mog*** (Lermontov—I just now recall) are two completely different thoughts. What is common to them is "content," which only demonstrates once again that formless content does not exist in itself and does not carry any weight. [4]

In examining the nature of semiotic structures, we observe that the complexity of a structure is directly proportional to the complexity of the information transmitted. As the nature of the information grows more complicated, the semiotic system used to transmit that information grows more complicated. In a correctly constructed semiotic system (one attaining the goal for which it was created) there is no room for unnecessary and unwarranted complexity.

If there exist two systems, A and B, and both transmit an equal amount of information while expending an equal amount of energy to overcome noise in the channel of communication, but system A is considerably simpler than system B, there can be no doubt that system B will be discarded and forgotten.[5]

Poetic speech is a structure of great complexity. It is considerably more complicated than natural language. And if the volume of information in poetic speech (verse or prose—here the distinction is unimportant) and in ordinary speech were identical,[6] artistic speech would lose its right to exist and, indisputably, would die out. But the case is somewhat different. A complicated artistic structure, created from the material of language, allows us to transmit a volume of information too great to be transmitted by an elementary, strictly linguistic structure. It follows that the information

* That having risen from the dead, he might not rise.—Tr.
** That he might not rise from the grave.—Tr.
4 A. Blok, *Zapisnye knižki* (Moscow, 1965) p. 378.
5 We are not concerned here with the problem of redundancy, which in an artistic structure is resolved in very specific terms.
6 Let us suppose that we are comparing two texts in one language, texts consisting of identical lexemes and syntactical constructions, but one is part of an artistic structure, and the other is not.

(content) given can neither exist nor be transmitted outside this artistic structure. By retelling a poem in ordinary speech, we destroy its structure and consequently present the receiver with a volume of information entirely different from that contained in the original poem. Thus the method of considering the "idea-content" and the "artistic features" separately, a method so firmly established in our schools, is due to a misunderstanding of the nature of art, and is harmful, for it inculcates the reading public with a false notion of literature as a lengthy and ornate method of expounding thoughts which could be expressed simply and briefly. If the idea-content of *War and Peace* or *Evgenij Onegin* could be set down in two short pages, it would be natural to conclude that we should read short textbooks rather than long works. This is not a conclusion pressed on negligent students by bad teachers, but one that follows from the entire pedagogical system of literary studies. This system, in turn, is oversimplified, and for that very reason most distinctly reflects tendencies which are clearly felt in literary scholarship.

The writer's thought is realized in a particular artistic structure and is inseparable from it. Tolstoj has the following to say about the central theme of *Anna Karenina:*

> If I were to say in words all that I intended to express by way of the novel, then I would have to write a novel identical to the one I first wrote. And if critics now understand and express in a feuilleton all that I want to say, then I congratulate them. . . And if nearsighted critics think that I wanted to describe only what pleases me, how Oblonskij dines and what sort of shoulders Karenina has, then they are mistaken. In all, or in almost all that I have written, I was guided by the need to collect my thoughts, linked together to express themselves:. . . but each thought specially expressed in words loses its meaning, is terribly degraded when taken alone without the linkage in which it is found.

Tolstoj was unusually perceptive in his observation that artistic thought is realized through the process of "linkage"—through structure—and does not exist outside this structure; the artist's idea is realized in his model of reality. Tolstoj continues:

> . . . We need people who will show the senselessness of searching for isolated ideas in a work of art, and who will constantly guide readers in the infinite labyrinth of links which constitutes the essence of art, according to those laws which serve as the basis for these linkings.[7]

The statement that form corresponds to content is true in a philosophical sense, but still does not reflect the relation of structure and idea

7 L. N. Tolstoj, *Polnoe sobranie sočinenij v 90 tomax,* vol. 62 (Moscow, 1953) pp. 269-270.

with sufficient precision. Tynjanov pointed out its awkward metaphorical qualities (in relation to art):

> . . . Form + content = glass + wine. But all spatial analogies applied to the concept of form in essence only pretend to be analogies: actually, the static feature intimately associated with spatiality invariably sneaks into the concept of form.8

For a graphic representation of the relation of idea and structure, we might more suitably imagine the bond between life and the complex biological mechanism of living tissue. Life, the main property of a living organism, is unthinkable outside its physical structure; it is a function of this working system. The literary scholar who hopes to comprehend an idea independent of the author's system for modeling the universe, independent of the structure of a work of art, resembles an idealist scholar who tries to separate life from that concrete biological structure whose very function is life. An idea is not contained in any quotation, even one felicitously chosen, but is expressed in the whole artistic structure. The scholar who does not understand this and who searches for an idea in isolated quotations is rather like the man who, having discovered that a house has a plan, begins to break down the walls in search of the place where the plan has been immured. The plan is not bricked up in a wall, but realized in the proportions of the building. The plan is the architect's idea, the structure of the building, its realization. The idea-content of a work is its structure. An idea in art is always a model, for it reconstructs an image of reality. Consequently, an artistic idea is inconceivable outside a structure. The dualism of form and content must be replaced by the concept of "idea" as something realized in a corresponding structure and non-existent outside that structure.

An altered structure will convey a different idea to the spectator or reader. It follows that poems do not have "formal elements" in the usual sense of the word. The artistic text is an intricately constructed thought. All its elements are meaningful elements.

Art Among Other Sign Systems

By examining art as a communication system, one may pose and in part resolve a series of questions beyond the range of traditional aesthetics and literary theory.

The elaborate concept of communication found in the contemporary theory of sign systems allows us to outline the general features of artistic communication.

Any act of communication involves a sender and receiver of information. But this is not enough: the familiar problem of misunderstanding demonstrates that not every message is apprehended. In order for the receiver to

8 Ju. Tynjanov, *Problema stixotvornogo jazyka* (Leningrad, 1924) p. 9.

understand the sender's message, the presence of a common intermediary—language—is imperative. If we take the sum of all possible messages in a single language, we will readily observe that certain elements in these messages are mutually equivalent in certain relations. (In one, for example, a relation of equivalence will arise among the variants of a phoneme; in another, between a grapheme and a phoneme.) It is not difficult to see that differences will emerge owing to the nature of the materialization of a sign or its element, while similarities will arise as the result of identical location within the system. What is common to the different mutually equivalent variants will emerge as their invariant. Thus we arrive at the two different aspects of the communication system: a stream of individual messages embodied in some material substance (in graphic or phonic substance, in the electromagnetic substance of a telephone conversation, in telegraphic signs, etc.) and an abstract system of invariant relations. The distinction in communication system between these two principles, and the definition of the first as "speech" (*parole*) and the second as "language" (*langue*) is Ferdinand de Saussure's contribution. In view of this division, it is apparent that since units of language are carriers of particular meanings, understanding is a process in which a spoken message is identified in the receiver's consciousness with its linguistic invariant. Certain features of the elements of a spoken text (those which coincide with their respective invariant features in the system of language) are singled out as meaningful, and others are dismissed by the receiver's consciousness as irrelevant. Thus, language acts as a sort of code, through which the receiver deciphers the meaning of the message that interests him. In this sense, if we allow for a certain degree of inaccuracy, the division of the communication system into "speech" and "language" in structural linguistics may be identified with the distinction of "message" and "code" in information theory.[9] However, if one conceives of language as "a system of invariant elements and the rules governing their combination"[10] then Roman Jakobson, among other scholars, is correct in asserting that in the process of transmitting information, not one, but in fact two codes are employed, the one for encoding and the other for decoding the message. It is in this sense that one speaks of rules for the speaker and for the listener. The difference between the two became evident when attempts were made to artificially generate (synthesize) and decipher (analyze) a text in a natural language with the aid of computers.

9 See V. V. Ivanov, "Kod i soobščenie," *Bjulleten' ob"edinenija po problemam mašinnogo perevoda*, No. 5 (Moscow, 1957); G. Goldman, *Information Theory* (New York, 1953).

10 Cf. "Since a language consists of rules or norms, it is, in contrast to speech, a system or rather a number of systems," (N. S. Trubetzkoy, *Osnovy fonologii* [Moscow, 1960] p. 9); and "A code consists of an alphabet plus a system of fixed constraints," (Goldman, op. cit., p. 21).

All these questions have an immediate bearing on the definition of art as a communication system.

The first corollary to the general proposition that art is one of the means of mass communication is that in order to receive the information transmitted by art, one must master its language. Let us make one more essential digression. Take a language, say, the language of chemical signs. If we write out all the graphic signs used in the language, they clearly fall into two groups: some—the letters of the Latin alphabet—designate chemical elements, others—signs of equality, plus signs, numerical coefficients—designate modes of conjunction. If we write out all the sign-letters, we get a certain set of names in the language of chemistry which, in their totality, stand for the entire sum of chemical elements known at this time.

Now suppose that we divide the entire designated area into groups. For example, let us describe the whole set using a language with only two names: metals and nonmetals. Or let us introduce any other system of notation, going so far as to distinguish the elements and to designate them by separate letters. Clearly any system of notation reflects some scientific conception for classifying the designatum. Thus every system of chemical language is at the same time a model of a particular chemical reality. We have arrived at the essential conclusion that any language is not only a communicative system, but also a modeling system, or rather, that both these functions are inseparably linked.

This is also true for natural languages. In Old Russian (twelfth century) *čest'* and *slava* are antonyms, but are synonyms in contemporary Russian;[11] in Old Russian *sinij* is sometimes synonymous with *černyj,* sometimes with *bagrovo-krasnyj;* the Old Russian *seryj* has the same meaning as our *goluboj* (in reference to the color of the eyes) and *goluboj* is equivalent to our *seryj* (in reference to the color of animals and birds);[12] in twelfth century texts, the sky is never referred to as *goluboj* or *sinij,* while for an observer of that time the golden color of an icon's background apparently conveyed the color of the sky with total verisimilitude; in the Old Slavic

> Komu sini oči, ne prebyvajuščim li v vine, ne nazirajuščim li
> k'de pirove byvajut'[13]

should be translated:

> U kogo že bagrovye (nalitye krov'ju) glaza, kak ne u p'janicy,
> kak ne u togo, kto vysmatrivaet, gde byvajut piry.*

* Who has red (bloodshot) eyes, if not a drunkard, one who seeks out feasts. . .

11 Ju. Lotman, "Oppozicija 'čest' –slava' v svetskix tekstax kievskogo perioda," *Trudy po znakovym sistemam, III (Tartu, 1967).*

12 B. O. Unbegaun, "Les anciens russes vus par eux-mêmes," *Annali sezione slava,* VI (Naples, 1963).

13 From *Pandekt Antioxa* according to the XI century copy, cited by I. I. Sreznevskij, *Materialy dlja slovarja drevnerusskogo jazyka,* vol. III (St. Petersburg, 1903; rpt. Moscow, 1957) p. 356.

In all these cases we are clearly dealing with completely different models of ethical or chromatic dimension.

But at the same time it is clear that not only "sign-names" but also "copulative-signs" play a modeling role: they reproduce a conception of bonds in the designated object. Thus any communicative system can perform a modeling function and conversely, any modeling system can play a communicative role. Of course, one function may be expressed more strongly than another, or may be scarcely felt at all in concrete social application. But both functions are potentially present.[14]

This is utterly essential for art.

If a work of art communicates something to me, if it serves the goal of communication between sender and receiver, then it is possible to distinguish in the work: 1) a message—that which is transmitted to me; 2) a language—an abstract system, common to sender and receiver, which makes the very act of communication possible. Later we shall see that each of these aspects can be abstracted only in scholarly terms; at a certain stage of study, however, it is absolutely necessary to postulate their opposition in a work of art.

The language of a work of art is that certain given which exists before the creation of a concrete text, and is identical at both poles of communication (later we will qualify this proposition). The message is the information which arises in a given text. If we take a large group of functionally similar texts and view them as variants of one invariant text, removing everything that is "extra-systemic" from our point of view, we arrive at a structural description of the language of the group of texts. V. Ja. Propp's classic work, *The Morphology of the Folktale,* which provides a model of this folklore genre, is constructed in just this way. We can view all possible ballets as a single text (just as we usually view all performances of one ballet as variants of a single text) and, having described it, arrive at the language of the ballet.

Art is inseparable from the search for truth. We must emphasize, however, that the "truthfulness of a language" and the "truthfulness of a message" are fundamentally different concepts. In order to conceptualize this difference, let us take, on the one hand, a statement regarding the truth or falsity of the solution to some problem, or regarding the logical correctness of some assertion; and, on the other hand, a discourse on the truthfulness of Lobachevsky's geometry or of four-valued logic. For each message in Russian or in any other natural language one can pose the question: true or false? But this question becomes meaningless with respect to any language as a whole. Therefore the frequent arguments on the artistic

14 For a detailed discussion of this problem see: A. A. Zaliznjak, Vjač. Vs. Ivanov,, V. N. Toporov, "O vozmožnosti strukturno-tipologičeskogo izučenija nekotoryx modelirujuščix semiotičeskix sistem," *Strukturno-tipologičeskie issledovanija* (Moscow, 1962).

inexpedience, inferiority or even "depravity" of an artistic language (for example, the language of the ballet, the language of Eastern music, the language of abstract painting) contain an error in logic due to confusion of concepts. At the same time it is clear that judgments of truth or falsity must be preceded by a question posed in such a way that one has a clear understanding of what is being evaluated: language or message. Correspondingly various criteria of evaluation will be at work. Culture has an interest in its own peculiar polyglotism. It is no accident that art in its development discards antiquated messages, but with striking persistence retains in its memory the artistic languages of past epochs. Art history abounds in "renaissances," the revival of past artistic languages which are perceived as innovatory.

The distinction of these aspects is also essential for the literary critic (and for any art critic). Here the problem lies not only in the constant confusion of an artistic text's aesthetic value (coupled with constant assertions that what is incomprehensible is bad) with the peculiarities of its language, but also in the failure to consciously analyze the problem to be researched, the refusal to ask what is being studied: the general artistic language of an epoch (its schools, its writers) or a particular message transmitted in that language.

In the latter instance, it would be more advantageous to describe the popular, average, most standardized texts in which the general norm of artistic language is most distinctly revealed. The failure to distinguish these two aspects leads to that confusion which traditional literary criticism has already demonstrated and which it has intuitively tried to escape, demanding that a distinction be made between the "popular" and the "individual" in literary work. Among the early, far from perfect attempts to study the popular artistic norm, we might mention V. V. Sipovskij's monograph on the history of the Russian novel. In the beginning of the 1920's, this question was already formulated as a completely distinct problem. Thus V. M. Žirmunskij wrote that in studying popular literature, "the very nature of the problem obliges one to turn away from the individual and focus on certain widespread tendencies."[15] This question was stated with precision in the works of Šklovskij and Vinogradov.

Once we recognize the difference between these two aspects, however, we note that their relation in artistic communication differs profoundly from their relation in non-artistic communication. The persistent identification of the problem of a language's specificity in some form of art with the problem of the value of the information transmitted through it is too widespread a phenomenon to be considered accidental.

Any natural language consists of signs characterized by the presence of extra-linguistic content of syntagmatic elements whose contents not only reproduce extra-linguistic bonds, but to a significant degree possess

15 V. Žirmunskij, *Bajron i Puškin* (Leningrad, 1924) p. 9.

an immanent formal character. Among these groups of linguistic facts, it is true, there exists a constant interpenetration: on the one hand, meaningful elements become auxiliary, and on the other, auxiliary elements are constantly semanticized (the apprehension of grammatical gender as a sexually meaningful characteristic, the category of animateness, etc.). The process of diffusion is so imperceptible, however, that both aspects are articulated with great clarity.

Art is a different matter. Here, on the one hand, there is a constant tendency for elements of content to be formalized, ossified, transformed into clichés, completely transferred from the sphere of content to the conventional realm of code. Let us cite one example. In his essay on the history of Egyptian literature, B. A. Turaev notes that the murals in Egyptian temples deal with a particular subject: the birth of pharoahs in the form of episodes and scenes recurring in strict order. Here is "a gallery of pictures accompanied by a text and presenting an ancient composition, no doubt assembled for the pharoahs of the Fifth Dynasty, and then officially passed on in stereotyped form from generation to generation." The author observes that "this official dramatic poem in a series of pictures was most eagerly put to use by those whose claim to the throne was disputed,"[16] as for example Queen Hatshepsut; he also relates the remarkable fact that the queen, wishing to strengthen her claim, ordered that her birth be depicted on the walls of Deer-el-Bahr. Only the inscription was altered to correspond to the sex of the queen; the portrayal itself remained strictly traditional and represented the birth of a *boy*. It was utterly formalized; the information lay not in the correspondence of the depiction of the child to the real prototype, but in the fact that an artistic text was or was not placed in the temple, a text whose connection with the given queen was established only by means of an inscription.

On the other hand, the tendency to interpret *everything* in an artistic text as meaningful is so great that we rightfully consider nothing accidental in a work of art. And we will turn again and again to Roman Jakobson's profoundly substantiated assertion on the artistic significance of grammatical forms in a poetic text, as well as to other examples in art where a text's formal elements are semanticized.

Of course the correlation of these two principles will differ in various historical and national forms of art. But their presence and interdependence are constant. Moreover, by admitting that in the artistic work all is message, and in the artistic work everything appertains to the artistic language, we fall into an apparent, rather than actual contradiction.

In light of these considerations, one might naturally ask if it is possible to identify language with the form of the artistic work, and the message with the content, and if this does not invalidate the assertion that structural

16 A. B. Turaev, *Egipetskaja literatura*, vol. 1 (Moscow, 1920) pp. 43-44.

analysis eliminated the dualism of viewing an artistic text in terms of form and content. This identification is unwarranted above all because the language of a work of art is certainly not "form," if we perceive form as something external with respect to content as the carrier of the informational load. The language of an artistic text is, in essence, an artistic model of the universe; in this sense, by virtue of its entire structure, it is a part of "content" and carries information. We have already noted that a model of the universe created by language is more universal than a model of the message which is profoundly individual at the moment of creation. Here it would be apropos to mention that the artistic message creates an artistic model of some concrete phenomenon; artistic language models the universe in its most general categories which, being the most general content of the universe, are the form of existence for concrete things and phenomena. Thus the study of the artistic language of works of art provides us not only with a certain individual norm of aesthetic communication, but also reproduces a model of the universe in its most general outlines. From many standpoints, therefore, the most important information is that which arises when a type of artistic language is selected.

When a writer chooses a certain genre, style or artistic school, he is also choosing the language in which he intends to address the reader. This language enters into the complex hierarchy of the artistic languages of a given epoch, a given culture, a given people, or a given humanity (in the end, the question must be posed in this fashion too). We ought, therefore, to note that the language of a given science is unique to that science and connected with the particular subject and aspect inherent to it. This is an essential property of language and we will refer to it later in our discussion. The recoding of one language into another, which occurs in connection with interdisciplinary problems and in most cases is extraordinarily fruitful, either reveals the objects of two sciences in what had appeared to be one, or leads to the creation of a new field of knowledge with a new metalanguage inherent to it.

Natural language, in principle, allows for translation. It is assigned not to an object but to a group. Within itself, however, it has a hierarchy of styles which allows one to set forth the content of a message from various pragmatic points of view. A language constructed in this fashion models not only a particular structure of the universe, but also the observer's point of view.

The language of art, faced with the dual task of simultaneously modeling both the subject and the object, is the scene of a constant struggle between the notion that there is only one language and the possibility of choice between artistic communicative systems, all of them adequate in some measure. At one pole we find the author of *The Song of Igor's Host* wondering whether he should sing in keeping with the actual events of these times or according to Bajan's scheme; and at the opposite pole we find Dostoevskij's assertion, "I believe that for the various forms of art there exist corresponding series of poetic thoughts, such that one thought can never be expressed in terms of a form which does not correspond to it."[18]

The opposition expressed in these statements is, in essence, imaginary: where there exists only one possible language, the problem of correspondence between the language's modeling essence and the author's model of the world simply does not arise. In this case, the modeling system of the language is not exposed. The greater the potential possiblility of choice, the greater will be the quantity of information carried by the structure of the language itself, and the clearer the revelation of its correspondence with some model of the universe.

Since the language of art models the most general aspects of the picture of the universe, that is its structural principles, in numerous instances it is language which serves as the basic content of a work and can become its message; the text closes in on itself. Such is the case in literary parody and polemics, where the artist defines the type of attitude he takes toward reality and the basic principles of its artistic reproduction.

Thus the language of art cannot be identified with the traditional concept of form. Moreover, the language of art, in utilizing a natural language, transforms the latter's formal aspects into those of content.

In conclusion we should examine one more aspect of the relation of language and message in art. Let us consider two portraits of Catherine II: the ceremonial portrait painted by Levickij, and the informal portrait of the empress in Carskosel'skij Park, the work of Borovikovskij. For the courtiers of Catherine's time, it was extremely important that a portrait resemble the external features so familiar to them. The fact that the same face was depicted in both portraits constituted for them one basic message; the difference in interpretation, the specificity of the artistic language, excited only those initiated into the secrets of art. The interest which these two portraits aroused in the eyes of those who had seen Catherine II is forever lost to us; we are primarily concerned with the difference in artistic interpretation. The informational value of language and message changes in accordance with the structure of the reader's code, his needs and expectations.

The interdependence and mobility of these two principles, however, is clearly manifested in another situation. In tracing the process through which a work of art functions, we cannot help but notice that in perceiving an artistic text, we also tend to sense many aspects of its language as message; formal elements are semanticized, and that which is inherent to the general communication system, by entering into the specific structural integrality of the text, is perceived as individual. In a good work of art everything is perceived as having been created ad hoc. But after the work

18 F. M. Dostoevskij, *Pis'ma,* vol. III (Moscow-Leningrad, 1934) p. 20.

has entered into the artistic experience of mankind, it increasingly becomes the language for future aesthetic communication, and that which was a fortuity of content becomes a code for subsequent messages. Already in the mid-eighteenth century, N. I. Novikov wrote:

> Nor can anyone convince me that Molière's Harpagon was intended as an attack on a universal vice. All criticism of a personal nature with the passage of time is transformed into criticism of a common vice. The justifiably ridiculed figure of Kaščej will eventually serve as the prototype for all usurers.[19]

The Language of Verbal Art

If we employ the concept "language of art" in the sense agreed upon earlier, then clearly literature, as one form of mass communication, must possess its own language. This means it has a closed set of meaningful units and rules governing their combination, rules which allow for the transmission of certain messages.

But literature already deals with one type of language: natural language. How is the "language of literature"[20] correlated with the natural language in which a work is written (Russian, English, Italian, or any other)? And is there in fact a "language of literature," or is it sufficient to distinguish between the content of a work ("message;" cf. the naive reader's question, "What is it about?") and the language of literature as a functional, stylistic stratum of a national natural language?

To clarify this let us pose a trivial problem. Consider the following texts: in Group I, a painting by Delacroix, a poem by Lord Byron, and a Berlioz symphony; in Group II, a poem by Mickiewicz and Chopin's piano pieces; in Group III, the poetic texts of Deržavin and the architectural ensembles of Baženov. Now, as in many studies on the history of culture, we will look upon the texts within each group as one text, reducing them to variants of an invariant type. For the first group, this invariant will be "Western European Romanticism," for the second "Polish Romanticism," and for the third "Russian Pre-Romanticism." It goes without saying that we could describe all three groups as a single text, introducing a second order abstract model of the invariant.

If we set ourselves this task we must naturally provide a communicative system—a language—for each one of these groups, and then for all three together. If we describe these systems in the Russian language, then Russian will be the metalanguage of description (we will disregard the inaccuracy

---

19 *Satričeskie žurnaly N. I. Novikova* (Moscow-Leningrad, 1951) p. 137. Kaščej is a satire on I. Buturlin, Sumarokov's brother-in-law, who is ridiculed in Sumarokov's comedy *Lixoimec* [The Bribe-Taker].

20 From earlier definitions it should be clear that we are using the term "language of literature" not in the sense of the literary language of an epoch, but in a sense parallel to the concepts of the "language of painting," "language of sculpture," "language of the dance," and so on.

of such a description since the modeling influence of the metalanguage on its object is inevitable). But the very language being described, the "language of Romanticism" (or any of its particular sublanguages which correspond to the three groups), cannot be identified with any natural language because it is also suitable for describing nonverbal texts. At the same time, a model of the language of Romanticism derived in this way will also be applicable to literary works and will, on a certain plane, be able to describe the system by which they are constructed (that is on a plane common to verbal and nonverbal texts).

But we must examine the relation between natural language and those structures which are created within verbal artistic constructions and which cannot be recoded into languages of nonverbal art.

Literature speaks in a special language which is superimposed as a secondary system on natural language. Literature is accordingly defined as a secondary modeling system. While literature is not the only secondary modeling system, to view it in the context of other such systems would divert us from the problem at hand.

To say that literature has its own language, one which does not coincide with its natural language but is superimposed on that language, is merely another way of saying that literature possesses an exclusive, inherent system of signs and rules governing their combination which serve to transmit special messages, nontransmittable by other means. Let us attempt to prove this.

In natural languages it is comparatively easy to distinguish signs—the stable, invariant units of the text—and rules of syntagmatics. Signs can be clearly divided into the planes of content and expression; between these there exists an arbitrary relation, one of historical convention. In a verbal artistic text, not only are the boundaries of the signs different, the very concept of the sign is different.

In an earlier work, I wrote that signs in art are iconic and representational rather than conventional, as in language.[21] This statement is obvious with respect to the fine arts; when applied to verbal art, it entails a number of essential conclusions. Iconic signs are constructed on the principle of a causal relationship between expression and content. It becomes difficult, therefore, to take the planes of expression and content and demarcate them in the usual structural linguistic sense of that word. A sign models its content. It is clear that the semantization of the extra-semantic (syntactic) elements of natural language occurs under these conditions in an artistic text. Semantic elements are no longer clearly differentiated; a complex interweaving takes place. What is syntagmatic on one level of the hierarchy of an artistic text proves to be semantic on another.

21 Ju. Lotman, *Lekcii po struktural'noj poetike* in the series *Trudy po znakovym sistemam,* I (Tartu, 1964) pp. 39-44. [Reprinted by Brown University Press (Providence, 1968) —Tr.]

But here we should recall that it is precisely the syntagmatic elements in natural language which mark the boundaries of signs and divide the text into semantic units. Removing the opposition "semantics vs. syntactics" leads to the erosion of the boundaries of the sign. To say that all elements of a text are semantic is to say that the concept of text in the given case is identical to the concept of sign.

In a certain sense, this is true; a text is an integral sign and all the separate signs of the general linguistic text are reduced in the text to the level of elements of this sign.

Thus each artistic text is created as a unique sign with a particular content, constructed ad hoc. At first glance this contradicts the familiar proposition that only repeated elements which constitute a closed set can serve to transmit information. The contradiction, however, is illusory. First, as we already noted, the occasional structure of the model created by the writer is thrust upon the reader as the language of his consciousness. The occasional is replaced by the universal. But that is not all. The "unique" sign turns out to be "assembled" from standard elements, and on a certain level is "read" according to traditional guidelines. Every innovative work is constructed of traditional material. If a text does not sustain the memory of traditional construction, its innovativeness will no longer be perceived.

While it constitutes *one* sign, a text simultaneously remains a *text* (a sequence of signs) in some natural language, and for that very reason maintains its division into words—the signs of a general linguistic system. A phenomenon thus arises which is characteristic for all art: a text is segmented into signs in different ways when different codes are applied.

While general linguistic signs are being transformed into elements of the artistic sign, the opposite process is simultaneously at work. Elements of sign in the system of natural language—phonemes and morphemes— when occurring in a series of ordered repetitions are semanticized and become signs. Thus a text can be read as a chain of signs formed according to the rules of a natural language; as a sequence of signs greater than the individual words in the text, leading to the transformation of the text into a single sign; and as a specially organized chain of signs which are smaller than the word, down to units as small as phonemes.

The rules governing the syntagmatics of the text can be similarly treated. We are dealing not only with the fact that semantic and syntagmatic elements prove to be mutually reversible, but also with the fact that an artistic text is an aggregate of phrases, a phrase, and word, all simultaneously. In each of these cases, the nature of the syntagmatic bonds is different. The first two instances are clear enough; the third requires some amplification.

We would be mistaken in supposing that the coincidence of the borders of a sign with those of a text eliminates the problem of syntagmatics. A text viewed in this way can be broken up into signs and correspondingly can be organized syntagmatically. But the syntagmatics will not be that of a chain, but of a hierarchy; the signs will fit together like *matreški*, with each doll inserted into another.

A syntagmatics of this sort is wholly practical for the construction of an artistic text. While this may be unusual in linguistics, culture readily provides historical parallels—the structure of the universe, for example, as seen through the eyes of the Middle Ages.

For the medieval thinker, the universe is not a sum of essences, but an *essence;* not a phrase, but a word. But this word is a hierarchy of separate words, enclosed, as it were, within each other. Truth does not lie in quantitative accumulation, but in profundity (one should not read many books or many words, but should try and grasp the meaning of one word; not accumulate more knowledge, but try to interpret the old).

It follows that verbal art, though based on natural language, is so based only to transform natural language into its own secondary language, the language of art. This latter is itself a complex hierarchy of languages, mutually correlated, but not identical. The theoretical possibility of many readings in an artistic text is related to this. So too, obviously, is the semantic saturation of art, a saturation impossible in any other non-artistic language. Art is the most economical, compact method for storing and transmitting information. But art also has other properties wholly worthy of the attention of cyberneticians and perhaps, in time, of design engineers.

Since it can concentrate a tremendous amount of information into the "area" of a very small text (cf. the length of a short story by Čexov and a psychology textbook) an artistic text manifests yet another feature: it transmits different information to different readers in proportion to each one's comprehension; it provides the reader with a language in which each successive portion of information may be assimilated with repeated reading. It behaves as a kind of living organism which has a feedback channel to the reader and thereby instructs him.

The means by which this is achieved is of interest not only to those involoved in the humanities. It is sufficient to conceive of a mechanism constructed analogously and issuing scientific information to understand that the disclosure of art's nature as a communication system can effect a revolution in methods of storage and transmission of information.

On the Plurality of Artistic Codes

Artistic communication has one interesting feature: among the usual forms of communication only two types of message relationships are found at the input and output locations of the channel of communication: coincidence and non-coincidence. The latter is equivalent to error and arises as a consequence of "noise in the channel of communication," the various types of circumstances which impede transmission. Natural languages insure themselves against distortions through the mechanism of redundancy, their unique semantic safety margin.[22]

The role of redundancy in an artistic text does not concern us at the moment. What interests us here is that large intermediate zone which lies between the comprehension and non-comprehension of an artistic text. Differences in the interpretation of works of art are common and, despite general opinion, do not arise from attendant and easily obviated causes, but rather are organic to art. It should at least be apparent that the aforementioned property of art, its ability to correlate with the reader and provide him with just the information he needs and is prepared to receive, is related to the possibility of diverse interpretation.

Here, it is of primary importance to consider one theoretical distinction between natural languages and secondary modeling systems of an artistic type. Linguistic scholarship has recognized the validity of Roman Jakobson's position on the division of rules which govern grammatical synthesis (the grammar of the listener). A similar approach to artistic communication reveals its great complexity.

The fact is that in numerous instances the receiver must not only decipher a message with the help of a particular code, but must determine the "language" in which the text is encoded. Here we distinguish the following occurrences:

I. a) The receiver and sender use a common code. The common nature of the artistic language is unconditionally assumed, and only the message is new. This is characteristic of all artistic systems belonging to the "aesthetics of identity." In every case the situation of performance, the thematics and other extra-textual conditions cue the audience to the only possible artistic language of the given text.

b) The reception of contemporary, popular, stereotyped texts is a variant of a). A code common to sender and receiver is also at work. But while in the first instance this is a condition of artistic communication and is emphasized by all possible means, here the author seeks to disguise this fact and lends the text misleading features of another stereotype or replaces one type of cliché with another. Before receiving the message the reader must select from the artistic languages at his disposal that one in which a text or part of a text is encoded. The very selection of one of a number of familiar codes creates additional information. The quantity of information, however, is negligible, since the range of choices is always comparatively small.

II. It is another matter when the listener tries to decipher the text using a code different from the one that the creator uses. Here two types of

22 For a description of redundancy in natural languages see: H. A. Gleason Jr., *An Introduction to Descriptive Linguistics* (New York, 1958) chapter 19. A popular account of the problem of redundancy from the perspective of information theory is given by W. Ross Ashby in *An Introduction to Cybernetics* (New York, 1956) pp. 9-16.

relationships are also possible.

a) The receiver imposes his own artistic language on the text, whereupon the text is recoded (which occasionally involves even the destruction of the structure created by the sender). The information which the receiver seeks to receive is still one message in a language already known to him. In this instance an artistic text is treated as though it were non-artistic.

b) The receiver attempts to perceive the text according to familiar canons, but through trial and error is convinced of the necessity of creating a new code, one as yet unknown to him. A series of interesting processes now occurs. The receiver enters into a struggle with the language of the sender and may be defeated. The writer forces his language on the reader who adopts it as his means for modeling life. In practice, however, in the process of assimilation the author's language is more often distorted and creolized with languages already in the arsenal of the reader's consciousness. Here a crucial problem arises. This creolization has its own laws of selection. In general the theory of the mixing of languages, essential to the study of linguistics, is bound to play a major role in the study of a reader's perception.

There is another interesting case: the relation between the accidental and the systemic in an artistic text has a different meaning for sender and receiver. In receiving an artistic message whose text obliges him to work out a code for deciphering that message, the receiver constructs a model. In this way systems may arise which will organize the fortuitous elements of a text and give them meaning. Thus the quantity of meaningful structural elements may increase in the passage from sender to receiver. This is one aspect of the complex, little-studied ability of an artistic text to amass information.

The Magnitude of Entropy
In Author's and Reader's Artistic Languages

The problem of correlating the synthetic artistic code of the author and the analytic code of the reader has yet another aspect. Both codes are hierarchical structures of great complexity.

The matter is rendered still more complex by the fact that one concrete text can submit on various levels to different codes (for simplicity's sake we will not discuss this relatively frequent occurrence).

In order for an act of artistic communication to take place at all, the author's code and the reader's code must form intersecting sets of structural elements. For example, the natural language in which the text is written must be comprehensible to the reader. Non-intersecting parts of the code form that province which is distorted, creolized, or by any other method reorganized in the passage from writer to reader.

We would do well to point out that attempts have recently been made to calculate the entropy of an artistic text, and hence to determine the amount of information. It should be noted that confusion occasionally arises in popularized works between the quantitative concept of the amount of information and the qualitative concept of the value of the information. These, however, are profoundly different phenomena. The question, "Is there a God?" allows for the possibility of two choices. Selecting a dish from the menu of a good restaurant allows for the exhaustion of significantly greater entropy. Does this demonstrate the greater value of the information received in the second procedure?

It is apparent that all information entering into a man's consciousness is organized according to a particular hierarchy, and the calculation of its quantity has meaning only within the levels of the hierarchy, for only under these conditons can the uniformity of constituent factors be observed. The manner in which these hierarchies of values are formed and classified is part of the typology of culture and cannot be dealt with in the present discussion.

Thus in attempting to calculate the entropy of an artistic text, we should not confuse: a) the entropy of the author's and of the reader's code; b) the entropy of various levels of the code.

This problem was first raised by the academician A. N. Kolmogorov who has made an exceptional contribution to contemporary poetics. A number of Kolmogorov's theories were developed by his pupils and, on the whole, have determined the course of linguostatistical studies in contemporary Soviet poetics.[23]

Kolmogorov's school first set out to establish a strictly formal definition of basic concepts of prosody. Then a broad range of statistics was gathered to study the probabilities of the appearance of certain rhythmic figures in a non-poetic (non-artistic) text as well as variations within the basic Russian meters. These metrical calculations invariably yielded two parallel sets of characteristics for the basic background and deviations from that background (general linguistic norm as background and poetic speech as an individual occurrence; the average statistical norms of the Russian iamb and the probability of the appearance of individual varieties, etc.). Consequently it became feasible to evaluate the informational possibilities of varieties of poetic speech. In contrast to the prosodic studies of the twenties, investigations of this sort raised the question of the content value of

23 See A. N. Kolmogorov, "Ritmika poèm Majakovskogo," *Voprosy jazykoznanija,* No. 3 (1962); A. N. Kolmogorov, A. V. Proxorov, "O dol'nike sovremennoj russkoj poezii, *Voprosy jazykoznanija,* No. 6 (1963); A. N. Kolmogorov, A. V. Proxorov, "O dol'nike sovremennoj russkoj poezii (a statistical description of Majakovskij's, Bagrickij's and Axmatova's *dol'nik*)," *Voprosy jazykoznanija,* No. 1 (1964). Kolmogorov's approach to poetic language is summarized in the following surveys: V. V. Ivanov, "Lingvistika matematičeskaja," *Avtomatizacija proizvodstva i promyšlennaja elektronika,* vol. 2 (Moscow, 1963) and I. I. Revzin, "Soveščanie v g. Gor'kom, posvjaščennoe primeneniju matematičeskix metodov k izučeniju jazyka xudožestvennoj literatury," *Strukturno-tipologičeskie issledovanija* (Moscow, 1962).

metrical forms, and at the same time steps were taken to measure this content value through the methods of information theory. Naturally this led to the study of the entropy of poetic speech.

Kolmogorov concluded that the entropy of language (H) is composed of two quantities: semantic capacity (h_1)–the capacity of language to transmit semantic information in a text of a given length; and the flexibility of a language (h_2)–the possibility of transmitting the same content by several equivalent means. Here h_2 is clearly the source of poetic information. Languages where $h_2 = 0$, for example, the artificial languages of science which in principle exclude the possibility of synonymity, cannot serve as material for poetry. Poetic speech imposes a series of constraints on the text, such as prescribed rhythm, rhyme, lexical and stylistic norms. Having measured that part of the capacity to carry information expended on such constraints (the part is represented by the letter β), Kolmogorov formulated a law by which poetic creation is possible only so long as the amount of information expended on limitations does not exceed the flexibility of the text $(\beta < h_2)$. In a language where $\beta \geq h_2$, poetic creation is impossible.

In applying the methods of information theory to the poetic text, Kolmogorov made it possible for artistic information to be measured in exact terms. We should note the scholar's extraordinary caution–he repeatedly warned against excessive enthusiasm over the still rather modest results of poetic studies based on the methods of mathematical statistics, information theory, and ultimately cybernetics:

> The majority of examples in works on cybernetics concerning the computer modeling of processes of artistic creation are strikingly primitive (the compilation of melodies from four or five note segments based on twenty or thirty melodies fed into the computer, and so on). In non-cybernetic literature, the formal analysis of artistic creation has long been on a high level. Information theory and cybernetics could make a large contribution to these studies. But real progress in this direction demands that cyberneticians take a greater interest in the humanities and learn more about them.[24]

Kolmogorov distinguishes three basic components of entropy in the verbal artistic text: the variety of content possible in the given length of the text (exhausting the variety creates general linguistic information); variety in the expression of the same content (exhausting this variety creates artistic information proper); and formal constraints placed on the flexibility of a language, which diminish entropy of the second type. These distinctions are of fundamental importance.

The state of structural poetics today, however, allows us to assume that the dialectical relations among these three components are considerably

24 A. M. Kolmogorov, "Žizn' i myšlenie kak osobye formy suščestvovanija materii," *O suščnosti žizni* (Moscow, 1964) p. 54.

more complicated. We should note first that the conception of poetic
creation as a choice of one possible variant in the exposition of prescribed
content, with due regard for certain limiting formal rules (and this is
precisely the notion which most often is the basis for cybernetic models of
the creative process) is somewhat oversimplified. Even if we suppose that a
poet creates according to this method (which does not occur very often),[25]
while the entropy of a language's flexibility (h_2) is exhausted for the
creator of the text, the matter may be completely different for the receiver.
Expression becomes content for him; he perceives the poetic text not as one
of several possibilities, but as the sole, unique text. The poet *knows* that he
could have written differently; for the reader there is nothing accidental in a
text taken as artistically perfect. The reader, by his very nature, assumes
that nothing else could be written than that which has been written. The
entropy h_2 is perceived as the entropy h_1, as a broadening of the sphere of
what can be said in the confines of the text. The reader, sensing the
necessity of poetry, sees it not as the means for saying in verse what might
be communicated in prose, but as a manner of setting forth a particular truth
unformed outside the poetic text. The entropy of a language's flexibility
turns into the entropy of the variety of poetic content. And the formula
$H = h_1 + h_2$ acquires the form $H = h_1 + h'_1$ (the variety of general linguistic
content plus the specifically poetic content). Let us attempt to explain this.

We understand that Kolmogorov's model is not designed to reproduce
the process of individual creation which, of course, proceeds intuitively
and along paths both numerous and difficult to determine. Rather, his
model provides only a general scheme of those reserves of language which
make for the creation of poetic information. Let us try to interpret this
model in light of the indisputable fact that the addresser's approach to the
structure of a text is of a different type from the approach taken by the
addressee of an artistic message.

Let us assume that a writer, in exhausting the semantic capacity of a
language, formulates a thought, and owing to the exhaustion of the language's
flexibility, picks out synonyms to express the thought. The writer really is
free to replace words or parts of a text with others semantically coincident
with the originals. We need only look at writers' rough drafts to see words
being replaced by synonyms. From the reader's perspective, however, the
picture is different: the reader considers the text placed before him (if we
speak of a perfect work of art) as the only possible text; "you can't throw
a word out of a song." For the reader the substitution of a word in the
text is not a variant of the content but new content. Carrying this tendency
to its logical extreme, we can say that for the reader there are no synonyms.

25 A study of various poets' manuscripts demonstrates that writers rarely
compose a connected, extended prose text defining the content of a poem which is
then transposed into verse, although there are isolated instances of this (cf. Puškin's
plans for poems).

In return, the semantic capacity of a language is significantly increased for him. Things can be said in verse for which there are no means of expression in non-verse. The simple repetition of a word makes the word unequal to itself. Thus the flexibility of a language (h_2) turns into additional semantic capacity, creating a special entropy of "poetic content." But the poet is also his own audience and can write verse while being guided by the consciousness of an audience. Here, then, the possible variants of a text cease to be identical for him as content; he semanticizes phonology and rhyme; the consonances of word suggest the variant of the text to be chosen; the development of the plot acquires an independence and seems no longer subject to the author's will. The reader's point of view—perceiving all details of the text in terms of content—triumphs. The reader, in turn, can rise to the "authorial" perspective (this often occurs in cultures where poetry is disseminated on a mass scale and the reader himself is a poet). He begins to appreciate virtuosity and tends toward $h_1 - h'_2$ (the general linguistic content of a text is also perceived merely as a pretext for overcoming poetic difficulties).

In an extreme case, any word in poetic language may become a synonym for any other. Take this line written by Cvetaeva: *Tam net tebja—i net tebja* [You are *not* there—no, *you're* not (there)]. Here *net tebja* is not a synonym, but an antonym of its own repetition. But Voznesenskij's *spasite* [save] and *spasibo* [thank you] become synonyms. The poet (like all artists) does more than "describe" some episode, one of many possible plots which when combined constitute a universe—the whole universal set of themes and aspects. This episode becomes a model for an entire universe; it fills this universe with its own uniqueness, and all the other possible plots which the author did not choose are not stories about other corners of the world, but models of the same universe. That is, they are plot-synonyms of the episode realized in the text. The formula takes on the form: $H = h_2 + h'_2$. But just as the essentially distinct "grammar of the speaker" and "grammar of the listener" coexist in the consciousness of each carrier of speech, so the viewpoint of the poet penetrates the reading audience, and that of the reader penetrates the consciousness of the poet. It would even be possible to chart an approximate scheme of types of attitudes toward poetry in which some modification of the initial formula prevails.

For the author there are in principle only two positions: his own and that of the reader or spectator. The same is true of the audience which can assume only one of two positions: its own or that of the author. Consequently all situations possible here can be reduced to a matrix of four elements.

Situation No. 1. The writer is in the position $H = h_2 + h'_2$; the reader, $H = h_1 + h'_1$. The addressee (the reader or critic) divides a work into "content" and "artistic devices;" he places the most value on the non-artistic information contained in an artistic text. The writer views his task as an artistic one; the reader sees the writer primarily as a journalist and evaluates his work according to its orientation, to the journal where the work appears (cf. the way Turgenev's *Fathers and Sons* was received in connection with its publication in *Russkij Vestnik*) or according to the author's social position apart from the given text (cf. the way Fet's poetry was received by the progressive youth of the 1860's following the appearance of his reactionary articles). A clear instance of this situation is the "utilitarian criticism" of Dobroljubov.

Situation No. 2. The writer is in the position $H = h_2 + h'_2$; the reader, $H = h_2 + h'_2$. This situation arises in epochs with a refined artistic culture (for example the Renaissance, and certain epochs in Eastern culture). Poetry is widely disseminated: almost every reader is a poet. Poetic competitions and matches are held (as in antiquity and in medieval European and Eastern cultures). The reader becomes an aesthete.

Situation No. 3. The writer assumes the position $H = h_1 + h'_1$; the reader, $H = h_1 + h'_1$. The writer regards himself as a naturalist supplying the reader with facts that are truthfully described. A factual, documentary literature develops. The writer gravitates toward the essay form. "Artisticness" is a pejorative epithet equivalent to "preciosity" and "aestheticism."

Situation No. 4. The writer is in the position $H = h_1 + h'_1$; the reader, $H = h_2 + h'_2$. Paradoxically, the writer and reader have changed places. The writer views his work as a document, a factual account, while the reader remains aesthetically inclined. In an extreme case, the norms of art are imposed on life: gladiators battle in the Roman circus; Nero judges the burning of Rome by the laws of dramatic tragedy; Deržavin, according to Puškin, hangs one of Pugačev's followers "out of poetic curiosity." (Cf. Leoncavallo's opera *I Pagliacci* where spectators perceive a real tragedy as a display of histrionics.) Puškin writes:

> Xolodnaja tolpa vziraet na poeta,
> Kak na zaezžego figljara: esli on
> Gluboko vyrazit serdečnyj, tjažkij ston,
> I vystradannyj stix, pronzitel'no—unylyj,
> Udarit po serdcam s nevedomoju siloj,—
> Ona v ladoni b'et i xvalit, il' poroj
> Neblagosklonnoju kivaet golovoj.

> An unfeeling crowd gazes on the poet
> As on a roving mountebank: if he
> Gives profound expression to a heartfelt,
>   heavy groan
> And verse achieved thru suffering shrill
>   and cheerless

Strikes the heart with mysterious
strength,
The crowd claps its hands and offers praise,
or now and then
Shakes its head in disapproval.

All of the above situations are extreme cases and are perceived as doing violence to an intuitive norm governing the reader's attitude toward literature. They interest us as the very basis of a dialectic governing the writer's and the reader's view of the literary text, and in their extremes clarify its structural nature. The norm is something different: the systems of the writer and reader differ, but in mastering literature as an indivisible cultural code, each combines both approaches in his consciousness, just as anyone mastering a natural language combines in his consciousness linguistic structures that both analyze and synthesize.

But an artistic text is the end product of the exhaustion of different entropy for addressee and addresser, and consequently carries different information for each. If we do not consider those interesting changes in the entropy of a natural language determined by the quantity β (this will be treated below), we can express the formula for the entropy of an artistic text in this manner: $H = H_1 + H_2$ where $H_1 = h_1 + h'_1$ and $H_2 = h_2 + h'_2$. But H_1 and H_2, roughly speaking, ultimately embrace the entire lexicon of a given natural language, which explains the fact that by comparison an artistic text conveys considerably more information than a non-artistic text.

2. THE PROBLEM OF MEANING IN AN ARTISTIC TEXT

There exists an extremely widespread prejudice that structural analysis attempts to divert attention from art's content, its social and moral concerns, for the sake of purely formalistic study, the statistical calculation of "devices," and the like. Glancing through a work with a sufficiently high degree of formalization, the unprepared reader forms the impression that the live body of a work of art is being dissected simply in order to place certain of its aspects in abstract categories. And since the categories themselves are defined in strange, unfamiliar terms, a feeling of anxiety involuntarily arises. Everyone sees his own bugbear: to some it is "murdering to dissect," to others the propagation of "pure art," perfidious and devoid of ideological content. The most amusing thing is that these two accustations are often hurled simultaneously.

Sometimes because of honest misunderstanding, and sometimes in the heat of polemics that go beyond the limits of objective scientific disputes, critics observe that both the formalists of the 1920's and contemporary structuralists advocate the study of art as a closed, immanent system.

The assertion that the structural, semiotic study of literature ignores questions of content, meaning, the social and ethical value of art and its ties with reality is based on a misunderstanding.

The very concept of the sign and the sign system is inseparably linked to the problem of meaning. In human culture, the sign functions as an intermediary. The goal of semiotic activity is the transmission of a given content.

A method whose primary concern is semiosis cannot ignore the problem of meaning. The essence of the semiotic approach is expressed in the questions of the "meaning" of meaning, the nature of the act of communication and its social role. But good intentions and the repetition of well-worn truths will not suffice if we are to understand the content of art, its role in society and its connection to the non-artistic aspects of human activity. Hardly anyone today would dispute the fact that a society's way of life determines the face of art. But does the repetition of this truism really compensate for our inability to explain how a text by Dostoevskij differs from one by Tolstoj? And why identical conditions give rise to different works of art?

Why then, from a structuralist point of view, must a work be studied as a synchronically closed structure, and why is an immanent analysis of the text the natural result? Do not structuralists thereby ignore the non-aesthetic meaning in a work?

Consider the following example. Before you is a book that contains very important truths written in an unknown language. You are not a linguist, you are not particularly interested in linguistic problems, and the study of language in itself does not intrigue you. What draws you to the book? The desire to know its contents. You will be right, of course, in saying that nothing but the contents is of any concern to you. This is the natural approach of anyone dealing with a sign system.

But if someone expressed a desire to know the contents of the book without understanding the language in which it is written, he would naturally be informed that this was impossible. In order to receive a message, a man has to master the language in which it is written, and once he decides to do this, he has to abstract himself from the contents of the sentences at hand and study their form. Foreign language textbooks are not noted for profound thoughts; their purpose is to teach a language as a system that can serve to transmit any content. If this is formalism, Mitrofan's * assertion that "door" is an adjective, because

> . . . it's adjoined. For six weeks now the door by the pantry
> ain't been hung, so just for now it's a noun.

should be regarded as part of a struggle against this insidious approach. These words do not, as is often assumed, reflect Mitrofan's stupidity, but common sense which does not recognize abstractions and seeks to resolve problems from the perspective of essence rather than method. This is even more clearly seen in Prostakova's notorious instructions for the division of three hundred rubles into three equal shares: "He's talking nonsense, my dear. You found the money. Don't divide it with anyone. Take it all, Mitrofanuska. Don't bother with this idiotic science." Rather than laughing at Prostakova, we should analyze her words. Is she right? No doubt she is if we view the problem from the perspective of common sense instead of trying to master the formal rules of arithmetic (we will not pass judgment on the morality of Prostakova's pronouncement: from the viewpoint of a mathematician, that is a pervert accustomed to looking at the correctness of the operations being carried out rather than the "essence" of a phenomenon, the altruistic response, "Give everything away, Mitrofanuska, don't bother with this egoistic science," would be no less absurd). Cyfirkin is not teaching Mitrofan how to act morally, usefully, or profitably, but how to divide whole numbers. Arithmetic or grammar may be taught in various ways, but we cannot deny that in order to master these disciplines we should, at a certain stage, treat them as immanent, closed structures of knowledge.

This does not imply that once a language has been studied as an immanent system it will no longer be used to receive messages with content. Our interest in the content will be so great, and our mastery of the language's

---

* Mitrofan and his mother, Prostakova, are characters from Denis Fonvizin's play *The Minor* (1782). Here the author plays on the similarity between the Russian *prilagatel'noe* ("adjective") and *priložit'* ("to attach") —Tr.

formal mechanism so automatic, that we will forget this and only recall that we are using a definite mechanism when we communicate with foreigners and children, that is when this apparatus breaks down.

Thus the immanent study of a language is an essential means of getting at the *content* of a written message.

Immediately we are faced with two aspects of a general question: what is the nature of the internal, immanent (syntagmatic) construction of an artistic text, and what kind of meaning does it carry, that is, what is the nature of its semantic bonds with external phenomena?

Before we consider this problem, another question should be posed. What is the meaning of "artistic meaning?" This question is more difficult to answer than might appear at first glance. Indeed, what does it mean to "have meaning?" Following Shannon's lead, B. A. Uspenskij defines meaning as the "invariant in the reversible operations of translation."[1] This would seem to be the most precise definition of meaning as a concept. Let us examine some special aspects of this in secondary modeling systems.

The problem of meaning is basic to all sciences employing semiotics. The ultimate goal in studying any sign system is to define its contents. A person investigating secondary modeling systems is particularly aware of this: it is senseless to study culture, art or literature as sign systems without considering the problem of content. We cannot help but note, however, that the *content* of sign systems is the most difficult aspect to analyze (assuming that one is not satisfied with purely intuitive concepts of meaning). Here it would be helpful to give a more precise picture of the nature of the sign and its meaning.

The fact that a sign is part of a system is basic to its structural definition. In fact, a far simpler interpretation has gained considerable currency. The sign is frequently defined in atomistic terms. The unity of signifier and signified is emphasized considerably more often than the fact that a sign necessarily enters into more complex systems. But the first is only a manifestation of the second. When the aspect of the sign connected with the plane of expression is examined, the systemic nature of the sign is more often emphasized. The possibility of recoding one system of expression into another (a sound system into a graphic one, for example) is an obvious fact which does not contradict the notion that the materiality of a sign is realized above all through the creation of a relational system. Accordingly, on the plane of expression, the existence of isolated, atomistic, extra-systemic signs is simply not possible.

We must recognize, however, that both a sign and its content can be conceived of only as structural chains linked by certain relations. The essence of any element of content cannot be discussed outside of its relation to other elements. A fact which cannot be compared with any

1 B. A. Uspenskij, "O semiotike iskusstva," *Simposium po strukturnomu izučeniju znakovyx sistem* (Moscow, 1962) p. 125.

other and which cannot be classified is not part of a language's contents. It follows that meaning arises when there are at least two chain structures. In familiar terms, we can define one of them as the plane of expression and the other as the plane of content. When one element is recoded into another, different element, a correspondence is established where one element in its own system is seen as equivalent to the other in *its* system. The contact point at which chains of structures intersect can be called a sign; the second chain, the one with which correspondence is established, is the content, and the first is its expression. Hence the problem of content always involves the problem of recoding.[2] It is true that the division of the two planes of content and expression is somewhat conventional (Hjelmslev expresses a similar idea) since the establishment of equivalence between the elements of two different systems is the most frequent, although not the sole way in which meaning is formed. We can point to semiotic systems which aspire to universality but which in principle do not allow for the substitution of meanings from other structural series. Here we are dealing with relational meanings which arise when one element is expressed through others within the same system. This is a case of what might be termed internal recoding.

We should note in passing that such an approach weakens the previously absolute opposition of the planes of expression and content, making them in principle reversible. Of course the goals of communication make special demands on each of these planes and in fact make their bond unidirectional. But theoretically such limitations do not exist. Thus in a language lesson the teacher, speaking to students who do not know English, points to a table and says, "Table." Here things become the signs of a metalanguage, and words are their content.

A secondary modeling system is a structure based on a natural language. Later the system takes on an additional secondary structure which may be ideological, ethical, artistic, etc. Meanings in this secondary system can be formed according to the means inherent to natural languages or through means employed in other semiotic systems. It would be helpful, therefore, to discuss some of the theoretically possible methods of creating meaning, and to find out which ones are applicable to concrete historical literary material, and how those methods are implemented.

Meaning is formed through internal recoding. Semiotic systems are possible in which meaning is formed, not by the convergence of two chains of structures, but immanently, within one system. One example of this sort of recoding is the simple algebraic formula: $a = b + c$. Obviously sign "a" has a definite content. This does not arise out of some connection

2 On the relation between the problem of meaning and recoding see: V. M. Toporov, "O transformacionnom metode," *Transformacionnyj metod v strukturnoj lingvistike* (Moscow, 1964); V. O. Rozencvejg "Perevod i transformacija," ibid.; Ju. A. Šrejder and M. V. Arapov, "Semantika i mašinnyj perevod," *Problemy formalizacii semantiki jazyka. Tezisy dokladov I MGPII* (Moscow, 1964); Roman Jakobson, "On Linguistic Aspects of Translation," *On Translation* (Cambridge, 1959).

with systems fixed outside the equation. We can ascribe an external meaning to "a"—making it stand for some number, for example; but if we do not make this substitution, these signs will still have meaning. Their meaning will be relational: it will express the relation of some elements in the system to others. The content of "a" is "b + c." In a general semiotic sense it is quite possible to conceive of systems whose signs have this sort of content. Mathematical expressions fall into this category, as does absolute music. Of course the problem of a musical sign's meaning is complex and always involves bonds with extra-musical conceptual and emotional elements, but these bonds are far more optional than those in language, and we can imagine, however conditionally, a strictly musical meaning formed by relations of sound series without extra-musical bonds.[3] When meaning is formed by the correlation of a series of elements (or chains of elements) within a structure, we can speak of *plural internal recoding*.

Meaning is formed through external recoding. This is a more common occurrence, for it is present in natural languages. Equivalence is established between two chain-structures of different types, and between their individual elements. Equivalent elements form pairs which combine in signs. We should stress that structures of different types prove to be equivalent. Although it is difficult to establish the fundamental difference between such types of recoding as the deciphering of content and the translation of a phonic form into a graphic form or translation from one language into another, it is still obvious that the greater the distance between structures made equivalent to each other in the process of recoding, the greater the disparity in their nature, the richer will be the content of the very act of switching from one system to the other.

The convergence of two series is the most widespread instance of the formation of meanings in natural languages. We may define it as *paired external recoding*.

In secondary modeling systems, however, we also encounter *plural external recoding*—the convergence of not two but many independent structures; here the sign no longer constitutes an equivalent pair, but a bundle of mutually equivalent elements drawn from various systems.

We might note that in paired external recoding the planes of expression and content (if we ignore the question of their reversibility) more or less naturally stand out. The remaining instances (internal recoding and plural

3 In this respect one can quarrel with the classification of art proposed by M. Wallis in his informative article "Swiat sztuk i świat znaków," *Estetyka:Rocznik II* (Warsaw, 1961). The author divides the arts into semantic and non-semantic types, categorizing music and the nonrepresentational arts, including contemporary architecture, as non-semantic. Correctly stating that signs should convey ideas about "objects other than themselves," the author goes on to assert that the structures of Corbusier or the preludes of Chopin are not signs (p. 39), that is they have no meaning. It would seem more accurate to speak not of the absence of meaning in such artistic structures, but of the relational nature of these meanings.

external recoding) do not in essence yield to such an interpretation.

All the types of meaning formation discussed above are present in varying degrees in secondary modeling systems. Immanent relational meanings are particularly evident in those secondary semiotic systems which lay claim to universality, an exclusive world outlook, to the systematization of all human reality. Literary Romanticism is a clear example of an artistic secondary modeling system where internal recoding dominates.

If we take a concept like "genius" or "great spirit" as it occurs in the system of Romanitcism, we can easily determine its content once we have defined the relation of the concept to others in the system. Let us point out some of the oppositions which reveal the content of this idea. The antithesis "genius–the crowd" is superimposed on the oppositions "greatness–pettiness," "singularity, exclusiveness–banality, mediocrity," "spirituality–materiality," "the creative spirit–animal nature," "revolt–submission," and so on. All the left-hand members of these paired oppositions, on the one hand, and all the right-hand members, on the other, are variants of an archemeaning which gives us some idea of the content of this concept within the structural framework of the Romantic consciousness. We can define its meaning more precisely, however, if we recall that in the system of Romantic thought "genius" enters into other antitheses. Among them, for example, is the opposition of "genius" to the concept of a free, beautiful nation faithful to its traditions (here "genius" is placed in oppositions such as "egoism–altruism," "willfulness–belief in traditions and the heritage of ones ancestors," "an unfeeling heart–the power of emotion," "rationalism–the life of the heart," "disbelief–religious faith") or to the ideal feminine image (resulting in such oppositions as "tragic ruin–harmonious preservation," "ugliness as an expression of disharmony–beauty," "belonging to a world of tragic evil–the good," and so on). As we see, the archetype[4] of the concept "genius" is extremely varied. Nonetheless they enter into one system and consequently all these archetypes are perceived as variations of one archetype of a higher rank and among the variants a relation of equivalence is established. Thus meaning takes shape. In this way we can arrive at a fairly clear notion of the concept "genius" by studying its relation to other concepts in the system and its relation to the system as a whole. From the Romantic viewpoint, however, there is no need to go outside the system. Within the Romantic consciousness, in principle, the problem of the objective meaning of concepts in the language of another system of thinking does not arise. But in a Realistic artistic system the way the meaning of a concept within the system (of ideas or style) is correlated with its meaning outside the system immediately takes on paramount importance. This

---

4 The term "archetype" (and other such terms as "archeseme," "archestructure," etc.) is coined by analogy to N. S. Trubetzkoy's term "archiphoneme," and is used here to mean the totality of distinctive features common to two elements on a given level of a neutralized binary opposition.

meaning surfaces through the process of external recoding, wherein the possibility of switching over from one system of ideas or style into another is demonstrably revealed. Puškin, already viewing the Romantic structure through the eyes of a Realist, sought to expose the meaning behind the Romantic stylistic system by recoding it into another stylistic register:

> On myslit: "Budu ej spasitel'.
> Ne poterplju, čtob razvratitel'
> Ognem i vzdoxov i poxval
> Mladoe serdce iskušal;
> Čtob červ prezrennyj, jadovityj
> Točil lilei stebelek;
> Čtoby dvuxutrennij cvetok
> uvjal ešče poluraskrytyj."
> Vse èto značilo, druz'ja:
> S prijatelem streljajus' ja.

> He thinks, "I will be her savior.
> I will not suffer the seducer
> With the fervor of his sighs and praise
> To tempt her youthful heart:
> The worm, vile, venomous,
> To gnaw at the stalk of the lily;
> A flower, two mornings old,
> To wither still half open."
> All that this meant, friends, is:
> I'll shoot it out with my pal.

Lenskij's romantic phraseology is the expression and the author's speech its objective content. The structure of the non-Romantic narrative is perceived here not as one of several possible modes of expression,[5] but as content, as the structure of reality itself.

The situation is more complicated when the author does not juxtapose two styles, implying that one of them is false, unnatural and pompous, and the other honest and truthful; when he seeks instead to fathom the essence of reality, having understood the limitations inherent to any coding system. Meaning arises from the equalizing of diverse elements, the establishment of equivalence among several very dissimilar primary semantic systems. Repeated recoding makes it possible to construct a semantic kernel common

5 The same can be said of the passage:
> Pokoitsja v serdečnoj nege,
> Kak p'janyj putnik na nočlege,
> Ili, nežnej, kak motylek,
> V vesennyj vpivšijsja cvetok.

> [He reposes in heartfelt bliss,
> Like a drunken wayfarer in his night's lodging,
> Or more tenderly, like a butterfly
> Who sips from a spring flower.]

to the various systems, one which is perceived as meaning that reaches beyond the confines of sign structures and enters the world of the object.

Hence we must stress that the plurality of external recoding means different things in different structures. In some it can take a series of subjective systems and construct their objective invariant—reality. *A Hero of Our Times* is constructed in this fashion. The author provides many subjective points of view which, when projected against each other, reveal a common content—reality. But the opposite is also possible, as in Tieck's comedies, for example, or in some of Pirandello's plays: repeated recoding confirms the absence of objective reality. Reality disintegrates into a large number of interpretations in such a system; it is imaginary. The author sees reality as a sign whose content consists of endless interpretations.[6] In the first case the interpretation is the sign, and reality the content; in the second reality is the sign and interpretation the essence, the content.

We should not forget that theoretically disparate systems of meaning formation often coexist in real secondary modeling systems. In the same system, for example, we can distinguish meanings that arise as a result of internal and external recoding. Thus in analyzing Rousseau's ideas we can try to elucidate the content of isolated concepts or the system as a whole, revealing how these concepts are related to a structure present in reality. We can study, for example, the objective economic meaning of Rousseau's ideas, how his ideas related to the way certain forces in society operated in his day. We can try to determine the meaning of Rousseau's ideas (remembering that we are not trying to determine the meaning of words, but of ideas expressed through words), by comparing them with the ideas found in other structural series—we can take Rousseau's concept of "the people" and compare it with the corresponding notions of Voltaire, Mably, Radiscev, and Hobbes among others. Or there is another option: we can try to determine the meaning of an element by elucidating its relation to other elements within the same system. We arrive at this kind of immanent meaning if we study how Rousseau's idea of "the people" relates to his definition of "man," "reason," "morality," "power," "sovereignty," and so on. True, the immanence of meanings here is not as unconditional as it is, for example, in a mathematical proposition, for in elucidating the relational semantic content of these terms we cannot ignore the many meanings they have outside the system of Rousseau's *Weltanschauung*. But extra-systemic meaings, though inevitably present, are not in this case primary, and at times they can even cause errors.[7]

6 Cf. Aleksandr Blok's instructions in his play *Balagančik* [literally *The Puppet Show*, often rendered as *The Fairground Booth*—Tr.] "Jumps out the window. The distance, seen through the window, turns out to be drawn on paper. The paper tears. Harlequin has fallen head over heels into emptiness."

7 The same is true when the reader has lost a sense of the author's system and involuntarily switches the text into another structure that is more comprehensible to him. A common mistake is the assumption that in the lines *Vosstan'te, padšie raby*

All these considerations are essential in determining the nature of content in secondary modeling systems. We can illustrate this by analyzing certain aspects of Lermontov's style.

Lermontov's Romantic Lyrics form a consistent mono-stylistic structure due to the all-embracing nature of Romantic subjectivism. The world of the authorial "I" is the only existing world and is correlated neither with the real world nor with the world of some other individual. As the Romantic views things, there is no possibility of equivalence between his poetic world and reality—the world as observed by another, more prosaic person. The Romantic system as a whole cannot be recoded (from the perspective of the Romantic). As a whole, it is the only existing system and constitutes the universe of the given poet; consequently it does not have semantic meaning (expression in another system). At the dawn of Russian pre-Romanticism A. M. Kutuzov sympathetically quoted the following lines by Jacob Boehme: "Angels and devils are not far from each other; but just as the angel who has been in Hell is in Paradise and does not see Hell, so too a devil who has been in Paradise is in Hell and does not see Paradise."[8]

In a system built according to such principles, meanings arise owing to the relations of elements within the system, not those of another system. Thus the harmonious inner world of the heroine of a romantic poem is the antithesis of the tragic distress experienced by the hero: her kindness is set in opposition to his demonism, her belief to the abyss of his disbelief, her love to his hatred, and her beauty—often—to his ugliness. Thus the heroine has neither an independent character nor independent meaning. She complements the hero: she is his ideal, his Other (therefore sexual differentiation is sometimes quite unnecessary, and in translating Heine's "The Pine," Lermontov removed this differentiating feature: his pine and palm trees are both feminine).[9] The meaning of the elements arises in their relation to each other.

The same may be said for the semantics of the Romantic landscape. The stylistic unity of Lermontov's Romanticism has much to do with this fact.[10]

["Rise up, fallen slaves"] from the ode "Liberty," Puskin is inciting the peasants to an uprising; this occurs because the words *vosstanie* ["insurrection"] and *vosstat'* ["to rise up"] are shifted from the structural opposition "rhetoric vs. popular speech [*prostorecie*]" (the counterpart to the word "rise up," which singles out its meaning as *podnimites'* ["get up"]) in the structural opposition "revolution vs. reform" or "revolution vs. preservation of the status quo" (the counterpart of the latter would be "act within the limits of the law" or "put up with it"). Clearly, replacing Puskin's system with any other leads to the distortion of meaning.

8 *Trudy po russkoj i slavjanskoj filologii*, vol. VI (Tartu, 1963) p. 319.

9 A. Majkov and Tjutčev translate the opposition differently ("cedar vs. palm"), resolving the gender problem in their own fashion. Cf. L. V. Sčerba, *Izbrannye raboty po russkomu jazyku* (Moscow, 1957) pp. 97-100.

10 We are deliberately ignoring the fact that any secondary modeling system uses a language (and accordingly is based on dual signs) and will examine only those meanings which arise on a supra-linguistic level and are part of the secondary system proper.

When writers went beyond the limits of Romantic consciousness, they required a new approach to the problem of meaning. The objective meaning of signs and structures became an issue. Lermontov began to admit that the same phenomenon could be seen from two perspectives. This led to works where the same content was expressly retold in various semantic keys and stylistic tonalities. Such ambiguity is typical for the narrative poem *Saška:*

> Luna katitsja v zimnix oblakax,
> Kak ščit varjažskij ili syr gollandskoj.

> [The moon rolls through the winter clouds
> Like a Varangian shield or Dutch cheese.]

Ščit varjažskij [a Varangian shield] and *syr gollandskoj* [Dutch cheese] are equivalent because they have a common meaning on the level of reality (moon). (We might note not only a lexical, but also a grammatical, stylistic antithesis here: the solemn inflexional suffix "ij" and the conversational suffix "oj.") The relation between them does not reflect the same lowering of style that we saw in the passage from *Evgenij Onegin* quoted above. There the Romantic style is presented as something false and pretentious (no wonder Belinskij defined Romanticism as "the age of phraseology," and Lermontov pointed out the antithesis between "false glitter" and the "truth of a noble voice") which is opposed to the simple truth. The correlation between the two is unidirectional, recalling the relation of content and expression in language. In *Saška* the system is different. We confront two equally valid points of view, neither of which constitutes the meaning; rather it is their relation to each other which gives rise to meaning. The relation between chain structures here is not unidirectional, but reciprocal. This sort of bonding is underscored by the presence of a stable device: the introduction of strophes which are parallel in content, but stylistically in clear opposition:

> On byl moj drug. S nim ja ne znal xlopot,
> S nim čuvstvami i den'gami delilsja;
> On bral na mesjac, otdaval črez god,
> No ja za to ni malo ne serdilsja
> I postupal ne lučše v svoj čered;
> Pečalen li, byvalo, totčas skažet,
> Kogda že vesel, sčastliv—glaz ne kažet.
> Ne raz ot skuki on svoi mečty
> Mne poverjal i govoril mne *ty;*
> Xvalil vo mne, čto pročie xvalili,
> I byl moj večnyj vizavi v kadrili

* * *

On byl moj drug. Už net takix druzej. . .
Mir serdcu tvoemu, moj milyj Saša!
Pust' spit ono v zemle čužix polej,
Ne tronuto nikem, kak družba naša,
V nemom kladbišče pamjati moej.
Ty umer, kak i mnogie, bez šuma,
No s tverdost'ju. Tainstvennaja duma
Ešče bluždala na čele tvoem,
Kogda glaza somknulis' večnym snom;
I to, čto ty skazal pered končinoj
Iz slušavšix ne ponjal ni edinyj.

[He was my friend. He gave me no trouble,
I shared my feelings and my money with him;
He borrowed it for a month and returned it in a year,
But that didn't annoy me in the least,
I didn't behave any better myself.
If he was sad, he'd speak up right away,
If he was cheerful and happy—he wouldn't show up.
More than once out of boredom he confided
His dreams to me and was a little too familiar.
He praised the same things in me that others did
And always was my partner in quadrilles.]

* * *

[He was my friend. I'll never find his equal. . .
May your heart be at peace, dear Saša!
Though it sleeps in a foreign land,
Undisturbed by anyone, like our friendship sleeps
In the mute graveyard of my memory.
You died as many do, without fuss
But with equanimity. Enigmatic thoughts
Still drifted across your brow
When your eyes closed in eternal repose;
And no one who was listening understood
What you said before you passed away.]

One more example:

Moskva—ne to: pokuda ja živu,
Kljanus' druz' ja, ne razljubit' Moskvu.
Tam ja vpervye v dni nadežd i sčast'ja
Byl bolen ot ljubvi i ljubostrast' ja.

* * *

Moskva, Moskva! . . . ljublju tebja kak syn,
Kak russkij—sil'no, plamenno i nežno!
Ljublju svjaščennyj blesk tvoix sedin. . .

[Moscow is different: as long as I live
I swear, friends, I'll never stop loving Moscow.
There in days of hope and happiness
I first was sick with love and lust.]

[Moscow, Moscow! . . . I love you like a son,
Like a Russian—deeply, fervently, tenderly!
I love the sacred luster of your gray hair. . .]

The above examples indicate that the stratum of "Romantic" style (*ščit varjažskij*) is not only an object of ridicule and parody. Neither stratum represents meaning in its pure form; rather, meaning arises as a result of their projection against each other.

Such a structure reflects a complicated image of reality. The concept of reality as being apparent through ordinary, simple observation is reworked so that reality comes to be viewed as the mutual intersection of various points of view; this allows us to go beyond the limits of any one viewpoint. No one stylistic layer carries information, but rather the intersection of many contrasting styles (points of view) provides an "objective" (suprastylistic) meaning. The style of *A Hero of Our Times* is a brilliant example of this sort of construction. Lermontov constantly uses the device of recoding, demonstrating how something observed from one point of view looks from another. Reality is shown as a mutual superimposition of aspects. Thus the character of Pečorin is presented through the eyes of the author, Maksim Maksimovič, Pečorin himself and other personae. Each one's judgments are limited, beginning with Maksim Maksimovič, who believes that the English "made boredom fashionable" since "they were always inveterate drunkards." But each judgment contains that element of truth which is revealed in its intersection with other judgments.

A complex system of recoding provides the stylistic base of *A Hero of Our Times;* this system reveals the external similarity of various points of view and the distinction between those that are similar. The Romantic antithesis between the Caucasian ("the exotic") and the Russian ("the commonplace") ethos is structurally cancelled out by an affirmation of the unity of the common man's (the naive) point of view. This is structurally revealed in the ease and naturalness with which the untranslatable idioms of the language and customs of Caucasian tribes are recoded into forms familiar to the Russian national consciousness:

"Hey, Azamat, you won't keep your head on your shoulders for long. It'll be *jaman** with your head!" I told him.

The author's question, "How do they celebrate a wedding?"—is directed at Maksim Maksimovic and signals an expectation of the exotic, but the answer deliberately translates ethnographic singularity into the style of

Jaman—a Turkic word meaning "bad "—Tr.

ordinary, everyday life and accentuated Russianisms:

Da *obyknovenno*. Snacala mulla procitaet im cto-to iz Korana, potom darjat molodyx.

"Oh *in the usual way*. At first the mullah reads them something out of the Koran, then they give presents to the young ones."

The words *obyknovenno* ["the usual way"] and *molodye* ["the young ones"] provide the stylistic key to the entire picture, one depicting the complete reversibility of concepts. The feasting Circassians are a *čestnaja kompanija* [boon companions], the *akyn** is *bednyj staričiška* [a miserable little old man] who *brenčit na trexstrunnoj. . . zabyl po-ixnemu. . . nu, da vrode našej balalajki* ["strums on a three-stringed. . . I forget what they call it. . . anyway, something like our balalaika"]. The Circassian dances are recoded into the form of a rural Russian dance: *Devki i molokye rebjata stanovjatsja v dve šerengi, odna protiv drugoj, xlopajut v ladoši i pojut* ["The girls and the young men stand in two rows opposite each other, clap their hands and sing"].[11] It is most revealing that Maksim Maksimovic fully understands the world of the mountain people (*Xotja razbojnik on, a vse-taki byl moim kunakom* ["though he was a brigand, all the same he was my *kunak**"]). Speaking of Kazbič, who killed Bèla's father, he explains, *konečno, po-ixnemu. . . on byl soveršenno prav* ["Of course, according to their laws. . . he was completely in the right"]). Pečorin does not understand them at all. Pečorin's ideas can not be recoded in Maksim Maksimovič's system. To the latter, Pečorin is "a very strange fellow."

> Having fulfilled my duty, I sat down beside him on the bed and said, "Look here, Grigorij Aleksandrovič, you must admit that it was not a nice thing to do."
> "What wasn't nice?"
> "Why, your carrying off Bèla. . ."
> "Suppose I like her?"
> Well what could one say to that? I was nonplussed.[12]

In "Princess Mary" Pečorin's relations with those around him are very complex. Various aspects of his character are projected onto various personae. Lermontov clearly forces heroes of contrasting character to use the same phrases:

> Pečorin: "The wives of local officials. . . are used to encountering an ardent heart under a numbered army button and a cultivated mind under a white army cap in the Caucasus."[13]

* *Akyn:* a Turkic word meaning a singer of folk songs—Tr.
* *Kunak:* a friend or guest for whom traditionally one must do anything—Tr.

11 M. Ju. Lermontov, *Polnoe sobranie sočinenij v 6-ti tomax,* vol. VI (Moscow-Leningrad, 1957) p. 210. Italics are mine.
12 Ibid., p. 219.
13 Ibid., p. 261.

Grušnickij: "And what's it to them whether or not there is a mind under a numbered regiment cap and a heart under a thick army coat."[14]

Pečorin (parodying the speech of a Russian barin's daughter): ". . . in two years or so she will marry an ugly man out of submissiveness to her mother, and will start persuading herself that she is miserable, that she loved only one man. . . but that Heaven did not wish their union because he wore a soldier's coat, although under that thick gray coat there beat a passionate, noble heart."[15]

A special system of relations is established between Pečorin and Grušnickij: identical expressions reveal the difference in their characters. The difference, however, cannot alter the fact that they say the same things, and consequently, that they are equivalent in some respect. We are given the opportunity of seeing Pečorin through the eyes of Grušnickij and Grušnickij through the eyes of Pečorin. Around Pečorin we find a whole system of personae who, as it were, translate his essence into the language of another system, and thereby reveal this very essence. The whole gamut of types of consciousness is here, from those most alien to those which are identical. The formula "different, but the same" can also be viewed as a particular instance of recoding (with zero alteration), a way to make a system manifest to oneself. Pečorin's diary plays the same sort of role by expressing the other side of his personality. So does Doctor Werner. While Pečorin and Grušnickij are so different that the author can have them deliver similar speeches, Pecorin and Werner are so much alike that all their verbal encounters are unavailing: the senseless remarks which they exchange are merely signs of the complete identity of their unspoken thoughts:

> We would often get together and discuss abstract matters with great seriousness, until we noticed that we were putting each other on. Then, after looking meaningfully into each other's eyes, like Roman augers did, according to Cicero, we began to laugh, and when we had laughed our fill, we would part company, satisfied with our evening.

Or, for example:

> Werner entered my room. He sat down in an armchair, set his cane in a corner, yawned and announced that it was getting hot outside. I answered that the flies were bothering me, and we both fell silent.[16]

There is a series of appraisals regarding Pečorin: "he was a decent fellow," "a little strange," a man with whom "one must certainly agree;" "am I a

14 Ibid., p. 265.
15 Ibid., p. 277.
16 Ibid., p. 270.

fool or a villain?;" "apparently, mother spoiled me when I was a child:" "a strange fellow," "a dangerous man;" "there are moments when I understand the vampire!. . . yet I am reputed to be a decent fellow;" "some say he's a decent fellow, others a scoundrel;" a wandering officer "travelling on official government business;" "a hero of our times." But at the same time, we receive information both about the systems in terms of which the hero is described, and about the way these systems relate to the described object (Pecorin).

We observe that a structure whose meaning is formed as a result of the reciprocal recoding of many system-chains allows the greatest freedom to move beyond the limits of each concrete system. This corresponds to the nature of meaning in certain types of realistic art.

Recoding is orgainically related to the problem of equivalence. This problem is particularly significant because the equivalence of elements on various levels is one of the basic organizing principles of poetry and, in a broader sense, of artistic structures in general. It can be traced on all levels, from the lowest (tropes, rhythm) to the highest (the compositional organization of the text). But the complexity is largely due to the fact that the very concept of equivalence in secondary modeling systems of an artistic type is different from the concept of equivalence in structures of a primary (linguistic) type. In the latter case those elements which are synonymous in relation to a common denotatum, to the semantic system as a whole and to any of its elements, those elements which behave identically in identical environments and as a consequence are mutually interchangeable, are semantically equivalent. We must bear in mind that we more frequently encounter semantic equivalence confined to a certain plane, than that full semantic equivalence which is, in any event, the business of the translator, and not of the man carrying out semantic transformations within the limits of one language. Consider the words *est'–žrat'* ["to eat"–"to stuff yourself"] and *spat'–dryxat'* ["to sleep"–"to be dead to the world."] On the level of a message indifferent to stylistic coloring, the words in the first pair (and in the second) are equivalent. But if the message includes, for example, information regarding the attitude of the speaker toward the activity of the object, then the words are not equivalent. And finally in a message where style is the dominant, the first and third and the second and fourth words would form equivalent pairs.

The equivalence of semantic units in an artistic text is realized in a different way: it is based on the juxtaposition of lexical (and other semantic) units which on the level of the primary (linguistic) structure may be recognized as non-equivalent. Moreover the writer often tries to take the most divergent meanings with different types of denotata as the basis for artistic parallelism. Thereupon a secondary (artistic) structure is constructed in which these units are made parallel to each other, and this in turn is a signal that in the *given* system we should view the units as equivalent.

Something occurs which is directly opposed to the phenomenon of semantic equivalence in language, but which is possible only on the basis of a firm knowledge of linguistic communication.

The equivalence of semantic elements in an artistic structure does not imply that they are all identically related to the denotatum, to other elements of the semantic system of a natural language, or to their common environment. On the contrary, all these relations can be different on a linguistic level. But since an artistic structure *establishes* a state of equivalence between these *diverse* elements, the receiver begins to assume the existence of another semantic system, one differing from the general linguistic semantic system, and to assume that within this system these elements are all related in the same way to the semantic environment. This is how the special semantic structure of a given artistic text is created. But there is more to the process than that. The equivalence of nonequivalent elements forces us to assume that signs which have different denotata on the linguistic level have a common denotatum on the level of a secondary system. Thus *syr* ["cheese"] and *ščit* ["shield"], while having different denotata on a linguistic level, have a common denotatum—*luna* ["the moon"]—in Lermontov's poetic text. Moreover it is evident that *luna* as a general linguistic denotatum cannot be designated by the signs *syr* and *scit,* let alone simultaneously. Only the moon as an element in a universe created by Lermontov can be designated in this manner. So we must reject the traditional notion that the world of denotata in a secondary system is identical to the world of denotata in a primary system. A secondary modeling system of the artistic type constructs its *own* system of denotata, one which is not a copy, but a model, of the world of denotata with their general linguistic meaning.

In classifying various types of meaning, we should distinguish two ways in which equivalence is established between chain-series in sign systems: recoding within the sphere of semantics, and recoding within the sphere of pragmatics. *Ščit varjažskij ili syr gollandskoj* ["A Varangian shield or Dutch cheese"] should be viewed as an instance of semantic recoding, for here the semantically different elements are made equivalent.[17] Pragmatic recoding takes place when the same object is treated in stylistically different ways. It is not the model of the object which changes, but rather one's attitude toward it; that is, a new subject is modeled.

Here is an example of pragmatic recoding:

> Nasmeškoj gor'koju obmanutogo syna
> Nad promotavšimsja otcom.
>
> (Lermontov, "Duma")

17 But if we construe this example as the manifestation of a style modeling not two different pictures of reality in order to penetrate "real" extra-semiotic reality, but two possible authorial attitudes to the same real world, then we can consider this as pragmatic recoding.

My—produkty atomnyx raspadov.
Za otcov produvšixsja—
                    rasplata.
        (Voznesenskij, "Otstuplenie v ritme rok-n-rolla")

[The way a deceived son bitterly mocks
His father who has squandered his wealth.
                              ("Meditation")]

[We are the products of atomic disintegration.
Payment
        for fathers who were cleaned out.
                ("Digression in Rock and Roll Time")]

Promotavšiesja otcy ["fathers who have squandered their wealth"] and *produvšiesja otcy* ["fathers who have lost heavily"] obviously coincide, both as object-concept and object-denotatum. But there is a change in pragmatics. In Voznesenskij's poem artistic meaning of a semantic type is formed through a series of complex sound oppositions within the text (*rasplata—raspadov* ["payment—disintegration"] , *produkty—produvšixsja* ["product—who have lost heavily"]); its pragmatic meaning is revealed to a certain degree through extra-textual comparison with Lermontov's lines.[18]

In this sense the earliest example in Russian literature of the formation of new meanings of the pragmatic level can be found in *The Song of Igor's Host* where the author wonders whether he should construct his narrative "in keeping with the events of these times" or "according to Bojan's scheme." The examples he gives of the way Bojan might have described the campaign of Igor Svjatoslavič in song, and his own contrasting style are both revealing.

We should emphasize, however, that semantic and pragmatic recoding in an artistic text can be distinguished, for the most part, only on an abstract level. As a rule, we are usually faced with complex combinations of both systems. Moreover in some structural bonds the convergences may be semantic and in others the same convergences can be pragmatic.

All this confirms the fact that if we view the content of an artistic text only on the level of linguistic communication, we overlook a complex system of meanings fashioned by the artistic structure itself.

The classification of meanings in a secondary modeling system of the artistic type through the establishment of equivalences among semantic

18 It should be noted that the equivalence of the correlated poems by Lermontov and Voznesenskij is achieved not only through their common meaning on the semantic level, but by their functionally similar position in a system of two different styles. "Fathers" in the poetry of Voznesenskij is not equivalent to "fathers" in that of Lermontov, but in both instances we are dealing with words that designate something lofty, related by blood, and traditionally revered. *Promotavšiesja* ["having squandered"] and *produvšiesja* ["cleaned out"] are functionally synonymous, for they express the idea of bankruptcy in a form as outrageous as possible within the confines of a *given* stylistic system.

elements could prove useful in constructing a structural theory of tropes and, on a wider scale, of artistic meanings in general, while distinguishing between semantic and pragmatic types of recoding could prove useful in discussing the problem of stylistics in light of semiotic ideas.

Meanings formed as a result of external recoding can be defined as paradigmatic, and those formed as a result of internal recoding as syntagmatic. Later we will return to these important principles for the formation of artistic meanings. For the moment, let us consider one way in which they are correlated. Systems constructed *only* on the basis of syntagmatic meanings, or *only* on the basis of paradigmatic meanings are impossible in real artistic texts. Most often one type of meaning *predominates*. The stricter the organization of one of these systems, the more loosely the other will be constructed within the given structure. Thus absolute music is constructed on an extremely strict syntagmatic basis. The principal element of meaning is the relation of segments of the text to their textual surroundings. In return, the semantics of each element—its relation to any extra-musical series—represents that free structural reserve which is ordered by the listener during the process of perception. The stricter the order of textual segments, the looser the relation of the text's musical elements to extra-musical ideas.

In a structure of the opposite type—the nineteenth century psychological novel, for example—basic meanings are formed through external recodings (the paradigmatic system). The sequence of episodes or any other textual segments creates particular meanings. But we have only to paraphrase the story and we will immediately see that it is much easier to alter the syntagmatics of the textual segments than to alter the paradigmatics. It is much easier to confuse the order of chapters in *War and Peace* than the relationship between Pierre and Andrej Bolkonskij.

It is significant that when we turn to genres with a stricter syntagmatic structure, such as detective or adventure novels, the rigidity of paradigmatic organization becomes noticeably weaker.

But if we take a text like a lyrical poem and view it as one structural segment (assuming that the poem is not part of a cycle), then the syntagmatic meanings—for example, the relation of the text to other works by the same author or to his life—form the same kind of structural reserve that semantics does in music.

3. THE CONCEPT OF THE TEXT

The Text and Extra-textual Structures

It is difficult to define the concept of the text. First and foremost we should reject the identification of the text with the integrality of a work of art. The prevalent view that the text as a certain mode of reality is opposed to concepts, ideas, and thought processes of any sort, where something too subjective or unstable is seen, is not very convincing despite its outward simplicity.

A work of art, which is a particular model of the universe, a message in the language of art, simply cannot exist apart from that language, just as it cannot exist apart from all the other languages of social communication. It meaning is extremely distorted for the reader who is trying to decipher the work with the help of arbitarary, subjectively chosen codes; but it has no meaning whatsoever for the man who would like to deal with the text totally apart from all its extra-textual relations. The entire sum of historically determined artistic codes which make a text meainingful is related to the sphere of extra-textual relations. And these relations are quite real. The concept "Russian language" is no less real than "a text in the Russian language," though the latter is a reality of a different sort, and the methods for studying it will also be different.

The extra-textual bonds of a work can be described as the relations between the set of elements fixed in the text and the set of elements from which any given element in the text is selected. The use of a certain rhythm in a system which does not allow for other possibilities, its use in a system which allows for one alternative, and its use in a system which provides five equally probable methods for constructing verse from which the poet can pick one, obviously give us completely different artistic constructs, though the materially fixed aspect of the work, its text, remains unchanged.

We should stress that the extra-textual structure is just as hierarchical as the language of a work of art as a whole. A given textual element located on various levels of the hierarchy enters into different extra-textual relations. That is, it will have different entropic value on each level. For example, if we define a certain text as a work of Russian poetry, there is an equal probability that any one of the meters natural to Russian verse will be used. If we narrow the chronological borders of the extra-textual construct we have chosen as our context and categorize the piece as "a work written by a Russian poet of the nineteenth century," or if we do the same with genre ("the ballad," say), the probabilities will change. But a text belongs in equal measure to all these categories, and we should bear this in mind when determining its entropy.

The fact that a text is associated with a given genre, style, age, author, and so on, changes the entropy value of its isolated elements; this fact not only forces us to view extra-textual connections as something wholly real, but also indicates certain ways for measuring this reality. We should differentiate extra-textual connections on the level of the artistic message. We have already cited examples relating to the former. Examples relating to the latter can be seen in cases where the non-utilization of some element, its meaningful absence, the "minus device," becomes an organic part of the graphically fixed text. Such, for example, is the omission of strophes (which are marked by numbers) in the final draft of *Evgenij Onegin;* Puškin's replacement of the final line of his poem"Napoleon" with the line fragment *mir opustel. . .* ["the world became deserted. . ."] and all the other instances where he introduces unfinished constructions into the finished text; the use of non-rhyme where the reader expects a rhyme, and so on. The way an unused element, a minus device, is related to the structure of reader expectation, and the way the latter, in turn, is related to the probability that a textually fixed element will be used in a given constructional position, also makes the information carried by the minus device a wholly real and measurable quantity. This question is part of a much larger problem— the structural role of the *zéro-problème,*[1] the sematic significance of pause, the measurement of the information carried by artistic silence.

In order to measure that information, as we have already seen, a meaningful element or a certain number of meaningful elements synonymous within the confines of the given construct must be located in the position occupied by the minus device in a text of a given length, that is, must be located in the code structure which corresponds to the minus device. In this way the artistic text necessarily enters into a more complex extra-textual construction and together they constitute a paired opposition.

The question is complicated by still another factor: extra-textual structures change the degree of probability of some of their elements, depending on whether these elements are related to the "structures of the speaker" or to the "structures of the listener," to the author's structures or to the reader's, with all the consequences that this complication entails in art.

The Concept of the Text

The following definitions might conveniently serve as the foundation of the concept of "text."

1. *Expression.* A text is set down through the use of signs, and in this sense it is opposed to extra-textual structures. For literature this means, first and foremost, that text is expressed through the signs of a natural

1 See M. Frei, *Cahiers Ferdinand de Sassure,* XI, p. 35; Roland Barthes, *Le degré zéro de l'écriture* (Paris: éd. Gonthier) pp. 151-152; Z. Lissa, "Estetyczne funkcje ciszy i pauzy w muzyce," *Estetyka, Rocznik II* (1961).

language. Expression, in contrast to non-expression, forces us to view a text as the realization of a system, as its material embodiment. In terms of the Saussurian antinomy of language and speech the text always belongs to the province of speech. Correspondingly, a text always has non-systemic as well as systemic elements. True, the principles of hierarchism combined with the multiple intersection of structures may make what is extra-systemic from the viewpoint of one substructure appear systemic from the viewpoint of another, and the recoding of a text into the language of the audience's artistic perceptions can in principle transfer any element from the non-systemic to the systemic class. Nevertheless, the presence of extra-systemic elements—the inevitable consequence of materialization—together with the feeling that the same elements can be systemic on one level and extra-systemic on another, are necessary concomitants of the text.

2. *Demarcation.* It is inherent to the text. In this respect a text opposes, on the one hand, all materially embodied signs not entering into its composition, in accord with the principle of inclusion—exclusion. On the other hand, it resists all structures not marked by a boundary—for example, the structure of natural languages and the limitlessness ("open-endedness") of their speech texts. In the system of natural languages, however, there are also constructions in which the category of demarcation is clearly expressed; these include the word and, in particular, the sentence. No wonder these are particularly important in the construction of an artistic text. In his time, A. Potebnja spoke of the isomorphism of the word and the artistic text. As A. M. Pjatigorskij has shown, a text possesses an indivisible textual meaning, and in this respect can be viewed as an integral signal unit. To be "a novel," "a document," or "a prayer" is to realize a certain cultural function and to transmit a certain integral meaning. Each of these tests is defined by the reader according to a certain set of features. Therefore transferring a feature to *another text* is one of the essential methods for forming new meanings (a textual feature of a document is imparted to a work of art, and so on).

The concept of boundary manifests itself in different ways in different texts. It may be the beginning and end of a text with a structure unfolding in time (later we will discuss the specific modeling role of the "beginning" and "end" in texts of this type), the frame of a painting, the footlights in the theatre. The demarcation of structural (artistic) space from non-structual space is basic to the language of sculpture and architecture.

The hierarchism of the text, the fact that its system can be broken down into a complex construct of subsystems, entails that the series of elements which belong to the internal structure serve as boundaries in subsystems of different types (the boundaries of chapters, strophes, lines, hemistiches). The boundary which tells the reader that he is dealing with a text and which calls up in his consciouness the whole system of corresponding artistic codes is located in a structurally strong position. Since some of these elements are signals of one boundary, and others are signals of several boundaries coinciding in the text (when the end of a chapter is the end of a book, for example), and since the hierarchy of levels allows us to speak of the dominant position of certain boundaries (the boundaries of a chapter hierarchically dominate the boundaries of a strophe, the boundaries of a novel dominate the boundaries of a chapter), certain demarcation signals can play a structurally commensurable role. On a parallel level, the saturation of a text with internal boundaries (the presence of enjambments, strophic and astrophic constructions, division into chapters, and so on) and the marking of external boundaries (the degree of marking here can be reduced to the point where the text looks as though it were mechanically broken off as in Sterne's *A Sentimental Journey*) also provide a basis for classifying types of textual construction.

3. *Structure.* The text is not a simple sequence of signs lying between two external boundaries. Inherent to the text is an internal organization which transforms it on the syntagmatic level into a structural whole. In order, therefore, to recognize a certain aggregate of phrases in a natural language as an artistic text, we need to be convinced that they form a secondary structure on the level of artistic organization.

We should note that the properties of structure and demarcation are interrelated.[2]

The Hierarchism of the Concept of Text

We should stress that in speaking of the material expression of a text, we have in mind one highly specific property of sign systems. It is not "things" themselves, but the relations of things, which are the material substance in sign systems. This is likewise manifested in the artistic text, which is constructed as a form of organization, as a system of relations between constituent material units. Correspondingly, additional structural bonds—relations between system types—can be established between the various levels of the text. A text is divided into subtexts (the phonological level, the grammatical level, and so on) each of which can be viewed as an independently organized text. Structural relations between these levels become a specification of the text as a whole. It is these stable bonds (within each level and between levels) which give the text the quality of an invariant. Functioning in its social environment, a text has a tendency to break up into variants. This phenomenon has been thoroughly studied in folklore and medieval literature. It is usually supposed that printing, by imposing its graphic language on a new culture, was responsible for the disappearance of variant texts. This is not altogether true. We need only record various people reading the same poem to be convinced that the

---

2 For a more detailed discussion of the concept of "text" see: A. M. Pjatigorskij, "Nekotorye obʼʼsčie zamečanija. . ." op. cit.; Ju. Lotman, A. M. Pjatigorskij, "Tekst i funkcija," *3-ja letnjaja škola po vtoričnym modelirujuščim sistemam. Tezisy. Doklady.* (Tartu, 1968).

printed text is only a certain type of invariant text (on the level of intonation, for example), and the recordings are its variants. If we study contemporary literature, not from the customary perspective of the author, but from the perspective of the reader, it is obvious that texts still retain their variance. And finally, the problem of the text and its variants continues to exist for the textologist.

The fact that a text is an invariant system of relations becomes absolutely clear when we consider the reconstruction of defective or lost works. Though folklorists[3] deal successfully with this problem and though it is the traditional concern of medievalists,[4] nevertheless the problem regularly arises to some extent in the study of more modern literature. We could point, for example, to the attempts by Puškin specialists to reconstruct the plans and creative designs of the poet, and to interesting efforts to reconstruct lost texts. If the text were not a structure constant within its own limits, it would be inadmissible even to consider such tasks.

It is clear, however, that given this approach to the question, we can take a group of texts (Russian eighteenth century comedy, for example) and view it as one text, describing the system of invariant rules which govern it and treating all differences as variants engendered in the process of its social functioning. Such an abstraction could be constructed on a very high level. It would probably be entirely possible to examine the literature of the twentieth century as a describable text with complex variant and invariant, extra-systemic and systemic bonds.

It follows that if we take a group of texts which are in some respect isomorphic and describe them as one text, such a description will, in its relation to the described texts, contain only systemic elements, and the texts themselves, in relation to the description will emerge as a complex combination of organized (systemic, relevant) and unorganized (non-systemic, irrelevant) elements. Consequently, a text of a higher level, in its relation to texts of a lower level, will be the language of description. And the language used to describe artistic texts in turn will be in some sense isomorphic to these texts. Another consequence is that a description of the highest level (for example, "an artistic text") which contains only systemic relations will serve as the language used to describe other texts, but will not itself be a text (in accordance with the rule that a text, being a materialized system, contains extra-systemic elements).

3 I refer to the attempt to reconstruct Protoslavic texts which proved most instructive. See: V. V. Ivanov, V. M. Toporov, "K rekonstrukcii praslavjanskogo teksta," *Slavjanskoe jazykoznanie. V Meždunarodnyj s"ezd slavistov* (Moscow, 1963).

4 A. A. Šaxmatov's superb reconstructions of chronicle texts still await thorough analysis in the light of contemporary scholarly methods (for a critique of methods of reconstruction see D. S. Lixačev, *Russkie letopisi* [Moscow—Leningrad, 1947]). I. P. Eremin also criticizes the premises of Šaxmatov's methods of reconstruction (*Povest' vremennyx let* [Leningrad, 1947] as did N. S. Trubetzkoy (in an early work on this problem that has been lost). Regardless of how Šaxmatov's work is evaluated in the future, it remains a shining example of an early attempt to apply spontaneously structural methods to the reconstruction of texts.

On the basis of these statements we can formulate some useful rules. First, the language used to describe a text is a hierarchy. The mixing of descriptions of various levels is inadmissible. We must stipulate exactly on what level or levels the description is carried out. Second, within the confines of a given level the description must be structural and complete. Third, the metalanguages of the various levels of description can be different.

We should stress, however, that the reality of the researcher's description does not completely coincide with the reality of the reader's perception. For the one doing the describing, the hierarchy of the texts is real, almost as though one text were inserted into the other; for the reader, only one text is real—the one created by the author. We can treat a genre as a single text, but it is impossible to make it an object of artistic perception. In perceiving the text created by the author as the sole text, the receiver of information views everything superimposed on it as a hierarchy of codes which reveal the hidden semantics of one actually given work of art.

It is obvious that the definition of an artistic text cannot be complete without additional classification that takes the addresser and addressee into consideration. Thus various interpretations of a dramatic role, a piece of music, a subject in painting ("Madonna and Child," for example), and so on, can be perceived from one point of view as repetitions of a single text (differences go unnoticed—the unprepared audience claims that "everything in the Hermitage is the same," that "all icons are identical," that "it is impossible to distinguish one poet of the eighteenth century from another,"), as variants of one invariant text, or, from another point of view, as different, even mutually opposing texts.

The Representational Verbal Sign (Image)

It is the nature of artistic texts to be transformed into codes, into modeling systems; this entails that certain features which are specific for the text as such be carried over into the sphere of coding systems in the process of artistic communication. For example, demarcation becomes not only a feature of the text, but an essential property of artistic language.

We will not dwell here on the meaning of demarcation as a structural principle of composition, but rather on the consequences it has for the language of art.

Verbal art begins with an attempt to overcome the fundamental property of a word as a linguistic sign—the arbitrariness of the connection between the planes of expression and content; it constructs a verbal artistic model according to the iconic principle, as in the fine arts. This is not accidental, but organically linked to the use of signs in human culture.

The signs of a natural language, conventional with regard to signifier and signified, and intelligible only within a particular code, can easily become unintelligible, and where the coding semantic system is enmeshed in the life of society, the signs can easily prove false. The sign as a source of information can just as easily become a source of social misinformation. The tendency to battle with the word, the recognition that it can deceive, is rooted in its very essence. It is as constant a factor in human culture as is the tendency to bow before the power of the word. No wonder that for many cultures the highest form of understanding is something beyond words and is associated with nonverbal forms of communication: music, love, the emotional language of paralinguistics.

Representational signs have the advantage of suggesting an external graphic similarity between signifier and signified, between the structure of a sign and its content, and thus they do not require complex codes to be understood (to the naive addressee of this sort of message it seems that he is using no code whatsoever in this case). Consider a road sign which combines two elements: a circle with a horizontal stripe [indicating "no entry"] and the image of a horse's head. The first element is a convention; in order to understand its meaning, one must master the specific code of road signs. The second is iconic and is coded only in terms of previous experience (a man who has never seen a horse would not understand). Now let us perform another mental experiment: let us couple the horizontal stripe with a number or a word. Both elements will now be conventions, but to a different degree. Against the background of the road sign, which can be deciphered by using a special code known only to an exclusive circle, the word or number will stand out as generally intelligible and will be functionally equivalent to the horse's head and to any other iconic element. The fact that a conventional sign can be functionally equated with a representational sign has fascinating implications for literature. From the material of natural language, a system of signs that are conventional but so comprehensible to an entire collective that their conventionality ceases to be felt against the background of other, more specialized languages, there arises a secondary representational sign (which could very well correspond to the "image" of traditional literary theory). This secondary representational sign has the properties of iconic signs: it bears a direct resemblance to the object; it is graphic; it gives the impression of being less dependent on a code and therefore would seem to insure greater truthfulness and greater intelligibility than conventional signs.

This sign has two inseparable aspects: its similarity to the object designated and its dissimilarity to the same object. One feature is always accompanied by the other.

4. TEXT AND SYSTEM

Systemic and Extra-systemic Aspects of the Artistic Text

In both the reader's and the scholar's approach to a work of art, two points of view have long battled for primacy. Some readers believe that the most important thing is understanding a work, others that experiencing aesthetic pleasure is most important; some scholars regard the structuring of concepts as the primary purpose of their work (the more general, abstract the concept, they would claim, the more valuable it is); others insist that any concept "murders" the essence of a work of art by subjecting it to logic and thereby impoverishing and distorting it.

The irreconcilability of these premises has led to charges and counter-charges: one scholar accuses the other of using abstract logic, the other faults the first for his agnostic denial of the very foundations of scientific cognition—the right to formulate abstract theories.

Paradoxically, each side can bring very weighty arguments to bear in its favor. Indeed, scarcely anyone would deny that the perception of a work of art is an act of cognition, or that the perception of a work of art affords sensuous pleasure. The issue is complex, however, because these assertions are not only contrary, but essentially incompatible.

The process of cognition can be viewed as the deciphering of some message. From this perspective it can be broken up into the following stages: the reception of a message, the choice (or manufacture) of a code, and the comparison of text and code. In the process systemic elements, which are the carriers of meaning, are distinguished in the message. Non-systemic elements are not perceived as carriers of information and are discarded.

Thus the process of cognition inevitably implies the elevation of a text to the level of abstract language.

After the message is deciphered and the text understood, there is nothing left to be done. But so long as the external stimuli continue to act on our organs of sense, we continue to see, hear, feel and experience joy or suffering, regardless of whether we understand what these things mean or not. A given textual element may be systemic or extra-systemic from the perspective of the given code, but in either case, by virtue of its physical materiality it can act on our organs of sense and afford us joy or suffering. Thus the impression is created that the difference between the pleasure of intellectual understanding and the pleasure of physical perception is not only very great, but does not in principle permit the concurrence of these two essential aspects of art. This in turn condemns the art critic to duality in approaching the object of study.

But if we look at the problem from a slightly different angle, we cannot help but recognize that any process of sense perception can also be viewed as the reception of information. Roughly speaking we can define sensuous pleasure as the reception of information from non-systemic material (as opposed to intellectual pleasure—the reception of information from systemic material).

To speak of the reception of information from non-systematic material is a contradiction in terms, since by definition information can be found only in a definite system and a definite type of structural relation. The point here is that any process of sense perception involves the prolonged, multiple application of diverse and often unrelated codes to the text, the goal being to introduce a maximum range of extra-systemic elements into the system. Man does not receive information only from signs and sign systems. Any sort of contact with one's environment, any type of biological assimilation represents the reception of information and can be described in terms of information theory. A system of sense receptors or a bio-chemical mechanism may be represented as orgainizations of codes which decode information. This does not contradict the assertion (see page 8) that languages serve to implement communication among individuals. Information theory is broader than semiotics. It studies not only individual cases of communication such as the use of social signs in a collective, but all cases involving the transmission and storage of information, understanding the latter to mean the degree of orgainization—the opposite of entropy. Let us take as a text, for example, a piece of food we are eating. The whole process of digestion can be divided into stages of interaction between nerve receptors, acids and enzymes. On every level some portion of what was not assimilated on the previous level, that is, which did not carry information, which was extra-systemic and neutral, joins in the active process of meta-bolism, becomes systemic and yields the information contained within itself.

Thus intellectual pleasure occurs as a result of the application of a code or a small number of logically connected codes to the message (this is itself the source of pleasure—a mass of variegated material is reduced to one system[1]). In considering the speed with which the human brain works, we should note that the time span of intellectual pleasure or understanding (assuming that we do not include the preceding moments of "non-under-standing") is infinitesimally small. It is instantaneous.

Sensuous pleasure entails the multiple application of diverse codes. It is protracted and may continue to be felt as long as there is a certain reality which can be perceived by the senses, as long as there is extra-systemic material which can be introduced into various systems.

All of the above implies not only a distinction between intellectual

1 If we define information in the broad sense of the word as any structure—the opposite of entropy—then we can define pleasure as an emotional upsurge, as tension and the resolution of tension in connection with the reception of necessary information that is difficult to acquire.

and sensual pleasure, but also their theoretical unity from the perspective of antinomy: information vs. entropy.

For intellectual pleasure the utilization of the material aspect of the sign is instantaneous: an expression, like a nutshell, is cracked open only to be thrown away. Physical pleasure strives for protraction since it deals with non-semiotic information in which expression itself (the impact on the senses) possesses content. Art, on the one hand, transforms non-semiotic material into signs which afford intellectual joy; on the other hand, it constructs an imaginary physical reality of the second order out of sign material, transforming the semiotic text into a quasi-material fabric capable of affording physical pleasure.

In this fashion those seemingly irreconcilable points of view discussed at the beginning of this section can in essence be reduced to the correlation of the information load of systemic and non-systemic material in an artistic text.

Here one can easily perceive two approaches: "in a work of art everything is system (nothing is accidental, everything has a purpose)" and "everything in a work of art is a violation of the system."

In order to understand this antinomy, we must make a few preliminary comments of a more general nature.

The Multiplanar Character of the Artistic Text

It follows from the arguments above that an artistic text can be viewed as a multiply encoded text. This is the property we have in mind when we speak of the polysemy of the artistic word, the impossibility of paraphrasing poetry in prose or a work of art in non-artistic language. On the basis of this wholly justified claim critics often conclude that literary scholarship, in constructing general models of a text, cannot grasp the unique essence of a work of art. It we are to show the invalidity of this conclusion, we must bring forward some additional arguments.

That which is individual and concrete in art differs from the individual and concrete realities that art models.

I regard as individual in nature that which from my point of view is extra-systemic and not inherent to the given structure as such. Literature imitates reality; it creates a model of the extra-systemic out of its own inherently systemic material. In order to appear "accidental," an element in a work of art must belong to at least two systems and must be located at their intersection. That aspect of the element which is systemic from the point of view of one structure will appear "accidental" when viewed from the vantage of the other.

Thus the accidental, individual, concrete facts of life do not for me enter into any system; abstract, logical facts all belong to one system; and the secondary, concrete facts found in art belong to at least two systems. The capacity of a textual element to enter into several contextual structures

and to take on different meaning in each context is one of the most profound properties of the artistic text.

It is this feature of works of art which makes us aware of their specificity
among other analogues of reality (that is, models) which man employs in
the process of cognition.

Suppose that a man engaging in an activity has to resort to a model of
that activity in order to make sense of it. In laying out an itinerary, for
example, a tourist stops his progress while he traces his movements on a
map; then he resumes his actual journey. Without defining the essence of
these two forms of behavior, let us simply note their clear-cut delimitations. In one instance practical behavior is realized, in the other abstract
behavior. The purpose of the one is to achieve practical results; that of the
second is to acquire the knowledge necessary in order to achieve those
results. In the first case a man finds himself in a practical situation, in the
second case in a theoretical one.

The distinguishing feature of behavior realized through the use of
scientific cognitive models is its demarcation, setting it apart from ordinary
practical behavior. No one using a map imagines that he is, by virtue of
that fact, making a real journey.

Between these two planes there exists a relation of semantic correlation
without which the investigation of signs and models could not serve as a
means of cognition. But simultaneously there is a tendency to draw a
clear line between the two types of behavior and, in correlating their
results, to refrain from carrying out the operation of semantic interpretation
each separate detail. In his cycle of essays, *Living Numbers,* Gleb Uspenskij
sheds light on the semantics of statistical data (cf. his essays, "A Quarter of
a Horse" or "Zero Point. . . ," which show what kind of reality is concealed
in a statistical index of the type 0.25). But this is not the customary way
of treating statistical economic data. As a rule, something completely
different occurs: the person using a statistical reference work makes no
attempt to look for the reality behind each number. He studies a statistical
model of certain economic processes and semantically interprets only
the results of his study.

No one would shudder in terror as he examined a battle plan plotted
on a map, though he would undoubtedly be aware that the map he was
looking at corresponded in reality to a field strewn with corpses. When
Tvardovskij says that Vasilij Terkin

> . . . was partially routed
> and partially destroyed

and Terkin himself declares that he "partially" has lice, the humor arises
because the relative independence of a conventional sign image of the world
(in this case of an army communiqué) is violated because unexpected
comparisons are made with the world of realia.

Thus in the sphere of behavior, practical activity and employing a model are sharply divided, although they are interrelated.

There is, however, a type of modeling activity where this sort of delimitation does not apply. That activity is play.

The opposition of play to cognition has no foundation in fact. Play is extremely important not only in man's life, but also in the lives of animals.[2] Play is indisputably one of the serious, organic needs of the human psyche. Various forms of play accompany each man—and mankind as a whole—at all stages of his development. Science can hardly benefit from a careless dismissal of this fact. And what is especially important, play is never opposed to cognition; on the contrary, it is one of the most important means for mastering life situations and teaching types of behavior. The higher mammals teach their young all aspects of behavior which are not automatically regulated by the genetic code only by means of play. Play is of enormous significance in teaching behavior since it allows the teacher to model situations which in real life could mortally threaten the unprepared individual, or situations whose creation is not dependent on the teacher's will. An unconventional (real) situation is replaced by a conventional one (the play situation). This has great advantages. First, the trainee can halt the situation in time (correcting his course, retaking his move). Second, he learns to model this situation in his consciousness, since he enacts a certain amorphous system of reality in the form of a game whose rules can and must be formulated. This brings us to yet another important aspect of play: it allows man to achieve an imaginary victory over the invincible (death, for example) or over a very strong adversary (the re-enacted hunt in a primitive society, for example). Hence the magical significance of play and its crucial psychological, educational property: it helps one to overcome the terror one would feel in similar real-life situations and cultivates a structure of emotions which is indispensable in practical activity. Suvorov's *skvoznaja ataka,* an exercise which converts a battle situation into a conventional game situation and consists in the swift convergence of two battle lines (sometimes cavalry and infantry) passing through the gaps in their opponents' ranks , was designed to overcome the terror a soldier would feel in an analogous situation in reality, and constructed an emotional model of victory. Sports are of tremendous significance in a man's upbringing; in their relation to workaday reality, they are also play.

A game is a particular type of model of reality. It reproduces certain aspects of reality and translates them into the language of its own rules. This is related to the instructional importance of play and its capacity to train, which psychology and pedagogy have long acknowledged. Many aestheticians are afraid to deal with the problem of play (to avoid charges Kantianism) and firmly believe that any comparison of art and play leads

2 See Karl Gross, *Die Spiele der Thiere* (Jena, 1896).

to the promulgation of "pure art" and a denial of the ties between creative and social activity; this only reveals their profound ignorance of the related disciplines of psychology and pedagogy.

Play entails the realization of "playlike" behavior distinct from both practical behavior and from the kind that involves the use of scientific models. Play implies the *simultaneous* (not consecutive!) realization of practical and abstract behavior. The player must remember that he is participating in a conventional (not a real) situation (the child remembers that it is a toy tiger and is not afraid) but must simultaneously *not* remember that fact (in the game the child thinks of the tiger as alive). A child experiences only fear before a real tiger; he experiences no fear at all before a stuffed tiger; but he is a *little bit* afraid of the pair of striped overalls thrown over a chair which, in the course of play, *looks like* a tiger. The child is afraid and not afraid *simultaneously*.

The art of play consists in the mastery of biplanar behavior. Any withdrawal into uniplanar behavior of either a serious or conventional type destroys its specific character. This sort of confusion of play and reality is common among children who cannot distinguish the biplanar emotions of play from the uniplanar emotions of everyday life, and thus a game often turns into a fight. We might cite by way of illustration an episode described by Krylov, as recorded by Puškin. Shortly after the suppression of the Pugačev rebellion children started playing "Pugačev;" they "split up into sides, the soldiers and the rebels, and the fights that ensued were in earnest." Play reverted to genuine hostility. "A certain Ančapov (who is still alive) almost became a casualty. Mertvago caught him on one expedition and hung him from a tree with his sash. A passing soldier freed him."[3]

This example is paralleled in the familiar plots where a man's mask becomes his very essence. This plot (the kind we find, for example, in Musset's *Lorenzaccio*), so popular in the nineteenth century, was used quite recently by Rossellini as the basis for his film *Generale della Rovere*. A bum and petty thief, who is basically a good man with a profoundly artistic temperament, falls into the hands of the Gestapo. He is ordered, under threat of execution, to play in prison the role of Generale della Rovere, an aristocrat and hero of the Resistance; the purpose is to trick the imprisoned members of an underground organization into revealing their identity. In the course of the film the hero, who begins with a nonchalant but brilliant play imitation, turns into the man he is impersonating. Before the eyes of the spectators and the dumbfounded Gestapo chief he becomes an aristocrat and patriot; the mask of Generale della Rovere becomes his real face, and he goes voluntarily to his death, lifting the spirits of those who believe him to be a heroic Resistance leader.

In this case the problem of how play is transformed into reality, a mask into actuality, is followed by another. The spectator remains convinced

3 A. S. Puškin, *Polnoe sobranie sočinenij*, vol. IX, bk. 2, p. 492.

that the hero discovers himself, the true essence of his character, only at the end of the film after he has become Generale della Rovere, that his true character would have come to light in his life as a bribe-taker and swindler, the role which reality thrust upon him. Without touching on the film's artistic complexities, let us merely point out how the film relates to a real psychological problem. Play, with its biplanar behavior, makes it possible for a man to enter into situations that are beyond his reach in real life, and thus it is play which permits a man to discover his true essence. Running a little ahead of ourselves, we might note that art performs this essential function to an even greater degree.

By making it conventionally possible for man to converse with himself in various languages, by recoding his "I" in various ways, art helps man to resolve one of his most pressing psychological problems: defining his own essence.

The converse way of violating the biplanar nature of play is to refuse to take it seriously, to uniliniarly underscore its conventional, unreal character. Such is the purely utilitarian attitude of the Gestapo chief toward the imaginary general's playacting; such is the attitude toward games that others are playing—the attitude of adults toward children's games, for example. For the person who does not accept its rules, a game is something incongruous which bears no relation to serious reality. We might cite by way of example the following episode from Lev Tolstoj's *Childhood:*

> Volodja's condescension afforded us very little pleasure; on the contrary, his lazy, bored look destroyed all the charm of play. When we sat on the ground, pretending we were fishing, and began to row with all our might, Volodja sat idly by, assuming a stance that had nothing in common with that of a fisherman. I made some remark to him about it, but he answered that no matter how much or little we might wave our hands, we would neither gain nor lose anything, and wouldn't get anywhere. I reluctantly agreed with him. When I pretended I was out hunting and set out for the forest shouldering a stick, Volodja lay on his back, his hands folded behind his head, and told me that he'd already gone hunting. Such words and deeds which dampened our interest in playing games were extremely unpleasant, all the more so because we could not help but agree in our hearts that Volodja was acting sensibly. I myself know that it is quite impossible to shoot with a stick, let alone kill a bird. It is a game. By the same token, it is also impossible to ride on chairs. . . . If we were to judge things in the right way, there would be no play. But if there were no play, what would remain?[4]

While employing an ordinary cognitive model a man engages in only

4 L. N. Tolstoj, *Sobranie sočinenij v 14-ti tomax,* vol. 1, (Moscow, 1951) pp. 27-28.

one form of behavior per unit of time, whereas a game model in each unit of time engages man simultaneously in two types of behavior: practical and conventional.

There is profound significance in the fact that one stimulus simultaneously evokes more than one conditioned reaction, that one element evokes two different structures of behavior, that it acquires a different meaning within each structure and consequently becomes unequal to itself; to a considerable degree it reveals the social significance of game models. In a game model each element and the model as a whole are themselves, but not only themselves. A game models the randomness, the incomplete determinacy, the probability of processes and phenomena. Therefore a logical cognitive model is better suited for reproducing the *language* of a cognizable phenomenon, its abstract essence, while a game model is better suited for reproducing its *speech,* its incarnation in material that is random with respect to language.

For example, the verbal text of a play vis-a-vis its performance is the language of the system. In its embodiment that which is monosemous becomes polysemous due to the introduction of features which are "random" with respect to the verbal text. The meanings of the verbal text are not cancelled out, but cease to be the only meanings. A performance is the verbal text as it is played out.

A game is a particular reproduction of the conjunction of regular and random processes. Because the repetition (regularity) of situations (the rules of the game) is stressed, deviation becomes particularly meaningful. At the same time the initial rules do not allow one to predict all the moves which are random with respect to the initial repetitions. Thus each element (move) takes on dual meaning, representing on one level the affirmation of a rule, and on another, a deviation from that rule.

The dual (or multiple) significance of elements forces us to perceive game models, in contrast to their corresponding logical scientific models, as semantically rich and meaningful.

> How much courage is needed
> To play on the centuries
> As ravines play,
> As a river plays,
>
> As diamonds play,
> As wine plays,
> As it is sometimes fated
> To play without ceasing,
>
> As a young girl played
> Among the simple people,
> In a white striped dress
> And with a thick braided tress.
>
> (Boris Pasternak)

A game model and its logical, homomorphic counterpart are perceived, not in terms of the antithesis "true vs. false," but as respectively richer and poorer reflections of life, both equally true. (A determinate ethical model of human behavior is felt to be something too correct and is opposed to a game (artistic) model which allows for multiple resolutions. Both models are regarded as true and opposed to a model of immoral behavior).

In *A Living Corpse,* for example, Tolstoj contrasts the ethical standards of Liza and Karenin, on the one hand, and Fedya Protasov, on the other, to the ethical standards of state regulations. The antithesis is morality vs. immorality. But Liza's morality is too proper, too narrowly defined: "The main thing that tormented me was that I felt I loved two men. And that meant I was an immoral woman." (This agitated monologue is both logically and grammatically correct.) Fedya Protasov's words embody another type of resolution:

> My wife was an ideal woman. She is still alive. But what can I say? There wasn't any spice—you know, spice?—no play in our lives. And I needed to forget myself. But without play you can't forget yourself.[5]

The context of Tolstoj's play shows that to forget oneself here means to find a symbolic gamelike resolution for conflicts which cannot be resolved in practical behavior or within the confines of a given social system.

Art has a number of traits which link it to game models. The perception (and creation) of a work of art demands a special artistic form of behavior which has a number of traits in common with play behavior.

An important property of artistic behavior is that a person simultaneously realizes two forms of behavior: he experiences all the emotions which an analogous practical situation would evoke, and at the same time he clearly realizes that he should not carry out those actions (such as helping the hero) connected with this situation. Artistic behavior entails a synthesis of the practical and conventional.

Consider Puškin's line "I shall melt into tears over a flight of fancy." Here is a brilliant description of the dual nature of a work of art. The recognition that we are dealing with a flight of fancy would seem to exclude the possibility of tears. Or just the reverse—an emotion that calls forth tears should make one forget that it is a flight of fancy. But in fact both of these opposing types of behavior exist simultaneously and the one increases the impact of the other.

In art this property acquires special significance: the artistic model as a whole, and each of its elements, enter simultaneously into more than one system of behavior, in each of which they take on their own specail meaning. Meanings A and A' (of each element, each level and the structure as a whole) do not cancel each other out, but are correlated with each other. The game principle becomes the basis for semantic organization.

5 Ibid., vol. XI, pp. 255, 261-262.

Let us examine three types of texts: a scientific exposition, a parable from a religious text and a fable. The scientific text is unambiguous, and therein lies its value. It interprets a general law and in this sense is a model of an abstract idea.

Religious texts are often constructed on the principle of multi-level semantics. In this case the same signs serve to express different content on different structural-semantic levels. Meanings which are accessible to a given reader in accordance with his degree of sanctity, initiation, "book-learning" and the like are not accessible to another who has not reached that degree. When a new semantic level is "opened up" for the reader, the old level is tossed aside because it no longer contains the truth for him. This is the principle behind Masonic symbolism, and, via Masonic literature, the early political writings of the Decembrists. The same text may contain a secret (conspiratorial) meaning for the initiate and plain meaning for the "layman." The truth is revealed to each in proportion to his ability to accommodate it. For the layman, the text contains truth which has ceased to be truth for the initiate. For any *given* reader it conveys only one meaning.

An artistic text is structured differently; each detail, and the text as a whole, enter into various systems of relations, and as a result they simultaneously take on more than one meaning. When laid bare in metaphor this property has a more general character. Let us analyze an example of medieval Russian oratory, the *Sermon on Law and Grace,* as an ecclesiastical, political work and as an artistic text.

Metropolitan Illarion's work is marked by distinct levels. On the first level, freedom and slavery are opposed to each other as positive and negative phenomena:

Freedom	Sarah	Isaac
Slavery	Hagar	Ishmael

This entails new signs and a new reading of the old signs:

Christianity	Christ	The Crucifixion	Christendom
Paganism	Isaac	Abraham's Feast (the eating of the calf)	Judea

The third level presents the opposition between the new and the old:

New	New Christianity	Rus'
Old	Old Christianity	Byzantium

And all these oppositions are brought together in the antithesis "Grace vs. Law."

Thus the reader who regarded parables as short stories and nothing more could have found one here too—the story of Sarah's and Hagar's rivalry. In this case each word would have been a sign whose content was that dictated by the natural language. However the opposition "Law vs. Grace" which runs through the whole text would have induced the reader

Grace" which runs through the whole text would have induced the reader to search for a secret text, an allegory, which according to Svjatoslav's *Collection* of 1073* "is to say something but to show another meaning." In this instance, with the reader's perception of the text concentrated on the first semantic level, Law found its synonyms in Hagar, Ishmael (as opposed to Isaac), Isaac (as opposed to Christ), Sarah (as opposed to the Virgin Mary), Judea (as opposed to Christendom), the Old Testament (as opposed to the New) and Byzantium (as opposed to Rus'). All these signs, as well as others, connoted "slavery," a concept of great social significance in eleventh century Rus' and associated with the semiotics of rejection, humiliation and low standing. The synonyms for Grace were Sarah (as opposed to Hagar), Isaac (as opposed to Ishmael), the Virgin Mary, Christ, Christianity, the New Testament, and Rus'. All these signs connoted freedom, equal social standing, the right to social activity, and spiritual significance ("The image for Law and Grace is Hagar and Sarah, the bond-woman Hagar and the freewoman Sarah. . . and Grace was born, and truth, not the Law; a son, not a slave").

On the second level the socio-semiotic opposition between man and bondsman acquired a new turn—it was equated with the opposition "Christianity vs. paganism." Christianity was perceived as spiritual liberation, imparting to each true believer that moral significance which only the free man had in the social hierarchy.

Finally, the reader initiated into the complex relations of the courts of Jaroslav and Byzantium grasped the antithesis between the new man and the old man ("first a bondwoman, *and then free*"—italics mine) and interpreted Grace and all its synonyms as a symbol of Rus', and Law as a symbol of Byzantium.

The *Sermon on Law and Grace,* however, is a work of art and this is reflected in the fact that these meanings do not cancel out each other, reproducing a *sequence* of steps leading the uninitiated to the secret meaning, but rather are all present *simultaneously,* producing a game effect. The author permits us, as it were, to delight in the abundance of meanings and possible interpretations of the text.

The mechanism of the game effect does not consist in the static, simultaneous coexistence of different meanings, but in the constant recognition that there may be other meanings besides those perceived at the moment. The game effect means that different meanings of one element do not statically coexist, but "flicker." Each interpretation forms a separate synchronic slice, but it preserves the memory of previous meanings and recognizes the possibility of future meanings.

Consequently a strictly monosemous definition of the meaning of an

* Svjatoslav's *Izbornik* of 1073 is an encyclopedic collection of excerpts translated primarily from the works of such church fathers as SS John Chrysostom, Basil the Great and Gregory the Great; it also includes an essay on tropes and figures referred to here—Tr.

artistic model is possible only when it is recoded into the language of non-artistic modeling systems. An artistic model is always broader and has greater vitality than any interpretation attributed to it, and an interpretation will always be an approximation, and nothing more. This accounts for a familiar phenomenon: when we recode an artistic system into a non-artistic language, we are always left with an "untranslated" remainder, that "supra-information" which is possible only in an artistic text.

Though it is necessarily accompanied by certain losses and has often provoked protests (sometimes totally justified), the recoding of specifically artistic information into the language of an non-artistic modeling system has been done innumerable times in the history of culture, since the endeavor to correlate aesthetic models with ethical, philosophical, political and religious models procedes organically from the very role that art plays in society. Therefore it would be fitting here to point out a possible way for making such comparisons with the least loss.

Semantic interpretation always involves the establishment of a correspondence between two structural series. If both these series are of equal length, they will be correlated on a one-to-one basis. If they have a different number of dimensions, then a one-to-one relation will not be established, and a point in one series will correspond, not to a point, but to a group of points, a certain section, in the other.

As we have seen, artistic and non-artistic models have a different number of dimensions. The recoding of artistic texts with two or more planes into any monoplanar non-artistic language will not give us a one-to-one correspondence.

Therefore we should not speak of one exclusive (moral or philosophical) interpretation of *Hamlet,* but of the *sum of permissible interpretations.* Probably all past interpretations of *Evgenij Onegin* together with those that will arise before the work ceases to interest the reader, will constitute the novel's range of meanings when translated into non-artistic language. This view forces us to pay far greater attention to the history of the way texts have been received in the reader's consciousness. Each new code of consciousness brings out new semantic layers in the text.

The greater the number of such interpretations, the more profound the specifically artistic meaning of the text and the longer its lifespan. A text which lends itself to only a limited number of interpretations comes close to being a non-artistic text and loses its specific artistic longevity (which of course does not foreshorten its ethical, philosophical, or political longevity—but these are determined by different factors).

While noting those traits which link aesthetic and game models, we should also stress the profound, fundamental difference between them.

Art is not play.

The genetic tie between art and play, which has been established in ethnographic studies, as well as the fact that the disemy or polysemy produced in play is one of the basic structural features of art, does not mean that art and play are the same thing.

Play means acquiring a skill and training oneself in a conventional situation; art means acquiring a universe (modeling a universe) in a conventional situation. Play is "pretending work;" art is "pretending life." It follows that in play, observing the rules is the goal. The goal of art is truth expressed in the language of conventional rules. Therefore play cannot serve as a means for storing information and producing new knowledge (it is only a way of refining skills that have already been acquired), whereas this is precisely what constitutes the essence of art.

Play in essence is very different from art. And while we can discover certain aspects of artistic models by comparing the two, setting them in opposition produces no less significant results.

Scientific models are a means of cognition—they organize man's intellect in a certain manner. Game models are a school of activity—they organize man's behavior. (So obviously the thesis that there is an element of play in art does not contradict the idea of art's social function—in fact the opposite is true. Play is one way of transforming an abstract idea into behavior, into activity.)

An artistic model is a unique combination of scientific and game models, organizing the intellect and behavior simultaneously. Play in comparison to art is *without content;* science in comparison to art is *inert.* It does not follow that there is *only art* in a work of art. A work of art can also fulfil numerous non-artistic functions which at times may be so vital that for contemporaries they push the narrow aesthetic perception of the text into the background. At certain historical moments a text must have not only an aesthetic, but also, say, a political or religious function in order to be perceived aesthetically. This aspect is obvious, but it is not the subject of investigation in this book. We are not examining the way texts function in a collective, but the system of their internal organization. We cannot claim that the question, "How are artistic texts organized?" can replace the broader question, "What is art?" or "What is art's role in society?" But this does not mean that the question we are dealing with is unworthy of consideration.

Elements of scientific modeling in artistic texts, the non-artistic function of art, interesting cases where non-artistic texts function artistically, the regularities observed in interpreting artistic texts on more abstract (social, politicial or philosophical) levels—all these are fully independent areas of scientific research and deserve individual attention.

The Principle of Structural Transposition
In the Construction of an Artistic Text

The above observations are of a more general nature: the principle whereby several planes are formed when the same elements enter into many structural contexts has historically become one of the central attributes of poetic semantics.

This is where one of the most profound distinctions between the structure of art and that of all modeling systems would appear to lie.

We have already mentioned that in all modeling systems extra-systemic material is "eliminated." In art both systemic and non-systemic material convey meaning. But let us look at the question from another point of view: in non-artistic communication systems the "grammar" of any structural level entails that certain achronic rules be formulated for the entire text, and that the violation of these rules can be attributed only to error. Error is noise in the communication channel, and a text resists accidental distortions not only through the redundancy of its structure, but also the systemic nature of its construction. The subordination of the same text simultaneously to two grammars is almost impossible in non-artistic systems; as soon as those transmitting and receiving information master the grammar of the communication system, it ceases to be information for them and becomes, not the content of information, but the means for its transmission.

An artistic text's relation to "errors" that violate the rules is different in principle. Even if we ignore the struggle waged against established norms in the history of art (a question which, despite its complexity, has undergone considerable study and in many respects is well understood) and speak only of one text examined from the perspective of its synchronic construction, we cannot help but notice that no matter how precisely we formulate some structural rule, we are immediatlely obliged to point out deviations. The number of deviations noted in describing any given level is so great that it commands our attention. But quantity, of course, is not at all the real issue.

One could object and point out that deviations from the rule are not the exclusive property of artistic structures. On the level of its material embodiment any structure is only a variant of an ideal construct abstracted from the random deviations of each concrete sign or text. In this sense it might appear that there is, in principle, no difference between a phoneme which arises as an ideal construct on the basis of a large number of individual variants, and poetic meter, which arises as an ideal generalization of the rhythmic deviations actually present in the text. The difference here, however, is of profound and vital significance. A phoneme is presented in concrete texts through a large number of variants, united at times only by their common relation to an ideal phonological construct; physical differences in the individual structure of speech organs and a number of other extra-structural factors account for this. If we agreed on some acoustic standard as the sound correlate of a given phoneme, if everyone had a recording of this standard and always used it in place of a given phoneme in pronunciation; if we artificially removed variation from the sphere of pronunuciation as we remove polysemy from terminology,[6] language as a system of communication would not suffer.

But if we forbade the use of rhythmic variants (which would be much easier than in the case of the phoneme), the structure of verse would immediately lose its vitality. Here is one more example. In the Doric and Tuscan orders of classical architecture the line of a column shaft, as we know, is not straight from capital to base. Already in ancient times it would have been technically possible to build a column with a geometrically faultless shaft (at least approximately). But a column hewn in this fashion would have seemed repellent and lifeless. In fact, about a third of the way down from the capital there is a slight swelling which, though indiscernible to the eye, is unmistakably felt. This is what gives the body of the column a lively elasticity.

Thus anomalies in art take on a structural meaning, and by virtue of that fact they differ radically from anomalies in other modeling systems.

People often cite this particular attribute of art to support a conclusion, with which we cannot concur, namely, that scientific analytical methods cannot be applied in the sphere of art and literary criticism because of the infinite individualization of objects being studied. To deal with this question we must understand the function and origin of extra-systemic elements in an artistic text, those near misses which Tolstoj wrote about.

We have already noted that in non-artistic communication systems the grammar for participants in the transmission-reception process is given in advance and therefore is not informative. Structures of this type are a powerful modeling apparatus of the normative type, forming a collective consciousness of an entire social group. They are carriers of the given system, and therefore they do not create *ad hoc* models.

Since the structure of artistic models would appear to stand out in much greater relief (it is no accident that the language of verbal art is often described as a natural language with additional limitations superimposed on it), predictability must increase with each succeeding element, and consequently, the structure itself must carry even less information than in a natural language. But experiments have shown[7] that an artistic text is less predictable than coherent non-artistic texts, a paradox that seems inexplicable at first glance. It is curious—and we will return to this point again— that different indices of predictability generate genuine poetic values and epigonic imitations. Here another vital point emerges: the predictability of a non-artistic text increases in proportion to the reader's perception so that at the end of a sentence a considerable part of its structural means becomes redundant. In an artistic text this is not the case: the degree of "unexpectedness" in the sequence of elements either remains approximately

6 Increasing the role of sound communication between man and computer may impose a similar requirement.

7 See Ivan Fonagy, "Informationsgehalt von Wort und Laut in der Dichtung," *Poetics, Poetyka, Poètika*, I (Warsaw, 1961).

the same, or may even increase toward the end (again in non-epigonic works). All this is because of the integral sturcture of the artistic text.

In order for the general structure of the text to retain its informativeness, it must constantly free itself from a state of automatism which is inherent to non-artistic structures. But an opposing tendency is simultaneously at work: only those elements which are set in definite predictable sequences can perform the role of communication systems. Thus two opposing mechanisms are simultaneously at work in the structure of an artistic text. One of them strives to subordinate all elements of the text to the system, to transform them into an automatized grammar, without which the act of communication is impossible, while the other strives to destroy this automatization and make the structure itself convey information[8]

In this connection the mechanism for violating the systemic arrangement acquires a special form in an artistic text. A fact that opposes a given artistic system by virtue of being "individual" or "extra-systemic" is in reality completely systemic, but belongs to *another* structure.

From the point of view of a given structure an extra-systemic fact simply goes unnoticed, just as occasional radio interference, misprints or slips of the tongue go unnoticed (assuming that they are not of such magnitude that they drown out the information) until we apprehend them as a system.

Any "individual" fact, any thing that is "a near miss" in an artistic text comes into being when the basic structure is complicated by additional structures. It arises as the intersection of at least two systems and takes on a special meaning within the context of each one. The greater the number of regular features intersecting at a structural point, the greater the number of meanings this element will acquire, the more individual and extra-systemic it will seem. What is extra-systemic in life is represented as poly-systemic in art. Let us return to the bulge in the column shaft: it is a chance deviation with respect to the straight line running from capital to base (we immediately perceive the straight line as a structural law automatically organizing its form, and the slight bulge as an extra-systemic "near miss") but simultaneously it is an absolutely regular feature. It is subject to precise computation and in all cases is uniformly situated. We perceive the intersection of these two regular features as extra-systemic individualization. It is important to stress that a new structural subsystem can perform a deautomatizing role only if it does not replace (destroy, reject) the old, but functions simultaneously with it in such a way that each serves as a backdrop for the other. It follows that although an artistic structure is syntagmatic in relation to reality and to non-artistic modeling systems, internally it is constructed in such a way that each level, each individual

8 The problem of deautomatizing the structural laws of an artistic text was treated in the 1920's by Viktor Šklovskij and Jurij Tynjanov, who anticipated many essential premises of information theory.

structure, except for the immanent syntagmatic construction, bears some relation to other levels and substructures. The effect of the action of a given level cannot be understood in isolation; one must take into account what may be called the internal semantics, the recoding of the elements of one structural level by means of another.

Here we can distinguish two possible types of recoding: 1) internal recoding (from the viewpoint of a given level), which can be viewed as an individual case of structuring on the syntagmatic axis; 2) external recoding (from the viewpoint of a given level), an indvidual case of structuring on the paradigmatic axis (the axis of equivalence).

The first instance, like all instances of structuring on the syntagmatic axis is, from the point of view of the addressee, subject to a temporal sequence. The initial elements of the text perceived by the addressee, besides having their own intrinsic meaning, are signals of certain codes or groups of codes (schools, genres, plot types, categorization as verse or prose, and so on) which already exist in the consciousness of the receiver.

But as soon as the recipient of information is confirmed in his choice of decoding systems,[9] he immediatiely begins to receive structural signs which clearly cannot be decoded in the chosen key. He may want to brush them aside as nonessential, but their repetition and obvious internal systemic arrangement do not allow him to do so. And so he constructs a second system which from that moment on is superimposed on the first.

The relation between rhythm and meter is a case in point. So too are all abrupt changes in style, such as the ironical, colloquial, satirical shifts in tone which occur when the reader has apprehended the author's lyrical intonations:

> *Kogda, strojna i svetlooka,*
> *Peredo mnoj stoit ona. . .*
> Ja myslju: "V den' Il'ji-proroka
> Ona byla razvedena!"

> [*When she stands before me,*
> *Slender and bright-eyed. . .*
> I think, "She was divorced
> On the feast of Elijah!"]
>
> (Puškin)

The first two lines are the bared signal of the code—a quote taken word for word from Podolinskij's poem "Portrait." Puškin refers the reader to a

---

9 Any culture contains a set of codes, and a choice made among them already carries information; for a person speaking only Russian, however, the choice of the Russian language has no informational meaning since it is not a choice. But while two persons who know only one natural language represent a model of any linguistic communication, the scheme of cultural communication will be as follows: two polyglots—one chooses the best language for speaking on a chosen subject, while the other begins the act of reception by establishing in which language, of those known to him, he is being addressed.

certain style, a type of lyric, a set of clichés. But the second two lines obviously do not correspond to this demonstratively indicated but misleading source. A complex collision is effected between the code system of the lyrics of popularized Romanticism in the 1820's, and ironical poetry on themes of everyday life. Each of these codes is taken, not by itself, but in relation to the other, not in its immanent syntagmatics, but within the semantic relations of mutual recoding.

In light of this complex code system the semantics of the message becomes markedly more complicated: Anna Kern, the object of appraisal, is "slender and bright-eyed," the Romantic "she,"[10] but at the same time she is "a divorced wife," a figure who in Puškin's time fell in a class far removed from lyrical Romantic cultural conceptions. Both these codes and both interpretations of the text function simultaneously in a state of mutual superimposition (though they are perceived sequentially by the audience).

A second instance of recoding occurs when the deautomatizing system is situated on another structural level, but in such a way that when the constructional nature of one of the basic structural levels becomes absolutely clear to the audience, it loses its dominance and some hitherto secondary textual level comes to the forefront. A classic example is the correlation between rhythmical and phonological levels in verse. It is no coincidence that in virtually all cases the rhythmical statement is given at the beginning of the line, whereas the center of phonological organization—the rhyme—is placed at the end. Because of this multidirectional quality of structural levels, predictability, as we have seen, does not increase, but may even decrease despite the large number of additional limitations which an artistic structure imposes on a natural language text. In determining the overall predictability of the next element in an artistic text we should, in some cases, subtract rather than add up the givens of separate levels, since the automatism of one level cancels out the automatism of another.

Also in this connection, between separate structural levels a compensatory relation may arise. For example, it has long been noted that within the confines of certain poetical structures when fewer limitations are imposed on the rhythm, greater demands are put on rhyme; the freedom to improvise in the general structure of a commedia dell'arte text is accompanied by the rigid standardization of masks, style of behavior,

10 Contemporaries were conscious of an intonation characteristic of the Romantic lyric that began with the construction *Kogda ja—ty* ["When I—you"]; the extension *to tolpa. . . .* ["then the crowd. . ."] was optional. Cf. *Kogda v ob"jatija moi. . .* ["When into my arms. . ."]; *Kogda tvoi mladye leta. . .* ["When your youth. . ."]; *Kogda tak nezno,tak serdecno. . .* ["When so tenderly, so warmly. . ."]; and *Kogda ljuboviju i negoj upoennyj. . .* ["When drunk with love and languor. . ."] (all poems by Puškin). This differed from the solemn intonations of the type one finds in Puškin's *Kogda vladyka Assirijskij. . .* ["When the Assyrian lord. . ."], which influenced the intonational structure of Axmatova's poem *Kogda v toske samoubijstva. . .* ["When in a suicidal yearning. . ."].

situations, and so on.

"Noise" and Artistic Information

Information theory defines noise as the intrusion of disorder, entropy or disorganization into the sphere of structure and information. Noise drowns out information. All forms of destruction—the muffling of a voice due to acoustic interference, the destruction of books due to mechanical causes, the distortion of a text's structure due to the censor's interference— all these are noise in the communication channel. According to the well-known law any communication channel (anything from a telephone wire to the centuries that lie between us and Shakespeare) contains noise which consumes information. If the level of noise is equal to the level of information the message will be zero. Man constantly senses the destructive workings of entropy. One of the basic functions of culture is to resist the onset of entropy.

Here art is assigned a special role. From the point of view of non-artistic information there is no difference between an extra-systemic fact and a fact belonging to another system. For a Russian who does not understand French a conversation in the latter will be just as much a disturbance as mechanical noise.

Art—and here it manifests its structural kinship to life—is capable of transforming noise into information. It complicates its own structure owing to its correlation with its environment (in all other systems the clash with the environment can only lead to the fade-out of information).

This peculiarity of art, as we have seen, is related to the structural principle which determines the polysemy of artistic elements; new structures which enter into a text or the extra-textual background of a work of art do not cancel out the old meanings, but enter into semantic relations with them. A structure that enriches the informational content of a text differs from a destructive heterogeneous structure in that everything heterogeneous which can be correlated in some way with the structure of the authorial text ceases to be noise.

A statue tossed in the grass can create a new artistic effect if a *relation* arises between the grass and the marble. A statue tossed in a rubbish heap does not create such an effect for the contemporary observer: his consciousness cannot work out a structure which would bring these two essences together in a unity of mutual correlation and projection. But this still does not mean that such a union is in principle impossible. Consequently the question of whether "noise" is transformed into artistic communication always presupposes a description of the type of culture which we take as the observer.

Up to this point we have been saying that a heterogeneous system (an "extra-systemic" system from the perspective of a given text) manifests itself through a certain repetition of its elements, which the listener also perceives as another regularity and not as something random. But in an artistic text the matter is more complicated: we can point to a number of instances where elements known to be individual and random that encroach on the text, though leading to the partial destruction of its semantics, themselves give rise to a number of new meanings. Venus de Milo's broken arms, like all cases involving the decay of historical monuments or the darkening of canvases with time, are, from the point of view of artistic information, a trivial case of noise, the onset of entropy in a structure. In art, however, the matter is more complicated: resolute immoderate "restoration" carried out without the necessary caution and tact, powerless to restore the unknown appearance of a work as seen through the eyes of the creator and his contemporaries, scrapes away all the succeeding cultural contexts and often occasions a far greater degree of entropy than the on-slaughts of time (that, of course, cannot be said of necessary preservation or thoughtful, tactful, scholarly restoration).

We are interested, however, in another aspect of the problem. Here are two more examples. The first is the artist Mixailov in *Anna Karenina* who cannot find the required pose for the figure he is drawing until a chance spot of stearin comes to his assistance: "Suddenly he smiled and joyfully flung his hands in the air. 'That's it, that's it!' he said, and immediately took up his pencil and began to sketch quickly. The spot of stearin gave the figure a new pose."

The second example is Axmatova's *Poem Without a Hero:*

> . . . a tak kak mne bumagi ne xvatilo,
> Ja na tvoem pišu černovike.
> I vot čužoe slovo prostupaet. . .

> [. . . but since I did not have enough paper
> I am writing on your rough draft.
> And suddenly another's word appears. . .]

The stearin spot and the extraneous word illustrate isolated cases of extra-systemic interference which does not provide us with a series of repetitions. Nonetheless the structure is made more complex because we compare this fact with others in our consciousness, we make it part of an extra-textual series which comes into conflict with the text only once (as applied to Venus de Milo's arms, such a series might be "antiquity," "genuineness," "the unspoken," etc.). And once again an isolated fact, a part of the material or substance of the text, proves to be an artistic reality because it arises at the intersection of two regular series.

So we are obliged to conclude that a relational structure is not a sum of material details, but a set of relations which is primary in a work of art and constitutes its base, its reality. But this set is constructed not like a multi-storied hierarchy without internal intersections, but like a complex structure of mutually intersecting substructures with the same element frequently entering into various constructional contexts. It is these inter-sections which constitute the "thingness" of an artistic text, its material diversity, which reflects the fantastical non-systemic order of the surrounding world with such verisimilitude that the unattentive reader begins to believe that this randomness, the unique individuality of an artistic text, and the properties of reality it reflects, are all identical.

An artistic text obeys the following law: the greater the number of regular series which intersect at a given structural point, the more individual the text seems. For this very reason the study of the unique in a work of art can be carried out only after we have discovered what features regularly occur, while at the same time recognizing the inexhaustibility of these regular features.

Here we have an answer to the question, "Does precise knowledge destroy a work of art?" The path leading to knowledge—always an approx-imate knowledge—of the diversity of an artistic text does not proceed by way of lyrical conversations on the meaning of uniqueness, but by studying uniqueness as a function of certain repetitions, by studying what is individual as a function of what occurs regularly.

As is always the case in genuine science, we can only proceed along this path. It is impossible to reach the end. But this is a shortcoming only in the eyes of those who do not understand what knowledge is.

5. STRUCTURAL PRINCIPLES OF THE TEXT

Earlier we spoke of the poetic text's potential ability to transfer any word from the reserve of semantic capacity (h_1) to the subset that determines the flexibility of the language (h_2) and vice versa. The structuring of a text on the syntagmatic and paradigmatic axes is organically related to this phenomenon.[1] The essence of this division manifests itself in the fact that when a speaker generates a grammatical phrase in any natural language, he performs two distinct acts: a) he combines words to form chains that are semantically and grammatically correct (marked); b) from a certain set of elements he selects the one used in the given sentence.

The conjunction of textual segments, the consequent formation of additional meanings according to the principle of internal recoding, and the equation of segments of a text, which transforms them into structural synonyms and forms additional meanings according to the principle of external recoding, together compose the basis of the mechanics of an artistic text. Two points should be made here: 1) equalization here has a different meaning than in natural languages—as a result of the contrast and opposition* of textual units, similarity is revealed in diversity, and diversity in similarity of meaning; 2) conjunction and selection are possible in an artistic text where they would be totally impermissible in a non-artistic text.

Thus an artistic text is constructed on the basis of two types of relations: the contrast and opposition of repeated equivalent elements and the contrast and opposition of adjacent (non-equivalent) elements.

All the structural diversity of a text can be reduced to these two principles. The first principle corresponds to the $h_1 \rightarrow h'_2$ transition. All elements of the text become equivalent. This is the principle of repetition, of rhythm. It equates elements which in natural language are not equivalent. The second principle corresponds to the $h_2 \rightarrow h'_2$ transition, the principle of metaphor. It conjoins that which cannot be conjoined in natural language. If in the first instance we interpret the concept of rhythm broadly enough to include all cases of equivalence in a text (phonological equivalence, for example), in the second instance we can interpret metaphor just as broadly

---

* The word *so-protivopostavlenie* is the author's own creation, a combination of *sopostavlenie* (contrast, comparison) and *protivopostavlenie* (opposition). For clarity's sake we prefer to render it as "contrast and opposition" here.—Tr.

1 The significance of this division was first established by the Polish Linguist Kruszewski. Roman Jakobson noted the vital role played by the mutual projection of these two axes in the structure of a poem: "In poetic language, and only in poetic language, we witness the projection of the axis of similarity onto the axis of contiguity." He continues, "Since the principle of identification is projected from the sphere of selection to the sphere of combination. . . the question of equivalence inevitably arises with regard to any linguistic unit, any plane of speech" (*IV Meždunarodnyj s"ezd slavistov. Materialy i diskusii,* vol. I Moscow, 1962, p. 620). Cf. Roman Jakobson, "Linguistics and Poetics," *Style in Language* (Cambridge, 1960).

to include the possibility of removing any restrictions on the conjunction of textual elements (including grammatical restrictions: in this sense such words as *smrad', rugliv, priparadjas'*, or *Zevs-oproveržec* ["stinkage," "quarrelly," "dressed-to-killing," "Zeus the Blunderer"] which we find in Majakovskij's verse are also metaphors).

The tendency toward repetition can be treated as a principle of verse construction, and the tendency toward conjunction as a principle of prose construction. This may seem paradoxical. Since the triumph of prose (in most modern European literatures and particularly in Russian literature) coincided with the period of struggle against Romanticism, the rejection of highly metaphorical language came to be taken as one of the basic features of prose structure. We should emphasize, however, that we are examining the phenomenon of metaphor on a broader scale. The ordinary treatment of the metaphor–trope is only one part of our discussion, which also includes other types of conjunction between elements which cannot be conjoined outside of the given construction of the text.

When the question is put in this way we grasp what the ordinary treatment of metaphor has in common with the typical structural principles of prose–with "prosaism" on the level of style, with plot design on the level of compostion, and so on. In light of the injunction against combining words with different stylistic marking, texts written by Puškin in the 1830's appear prosaic for this very reason–they remove this restriction.

> On pisan vo ves' rost. Čelo, kak čerep golyj
> Vysoko losnitsja, i, mnitsja, zalegla
> Tam grust' velikaja. . .
>
> [He is portrayed full length. His brow, like a bald skull,
> Has a high gloss, and, it seems,
> A great sadness has taken root there. . .]

The conjoining of *čelo* ["brow"], *vysoko* ["high"], *velikij* ["great"], and *mnitsja* ["it seems"], with *čerep golyj* ["bald skull"] (in reference to the head of a live man, that is, to a bald spot), the word *losnitsja* ["has a gloss"], the very combination of the "poetic" image of the hero and the "anti-poetic" image of a man with a shiny bald spot is perceived as the interjection of prose into poetry. If we reject the view that a prosaic text is "unstructured" it will become obvious that the lifting of injunctions agaisnt the conjoining of elements on the syntagmatic axis is a fundamental structural principle in prose. It is no coincidence that metaphor (in a restricted sense), which permits the conjunction of semantically unconjoinable elements, served as the foundation for the tremendous work carried out by Majakovskij and Pasternak in "prosifying" Russian verse. The metaphoric nature of these poets' style is as readily apparent as their orientation toward prose. The description of Rilke's poetry which Pasternak gives in his autobiography can be applied to his own verse:

For Blok prose remains the spring from which the poem flows.
It is not included among the means of expression which he
employs. For Rilke, the devices of painting and psychology
used by contemporary novelists (Tolstoj, Flaubert, Proust,
the Scandinavians) are inseparable from the language and style
of his poetry.[2]

The idea expressed here is very profound and deserves careful scrutiny by
those who wish to reflect on the structure of prose and poetic "prosaism."

The Paradigmatic Axis of Meanings

Repetition is synonymous with that equivalence which arises on the
basis of a relation of incomplete equality; it occurs where there is a level
(or levels) on which elements are equal and a level (or levels) on which
they are not equal.

Equivalence is not static uniformity and for that very reason it also
entails dissimilarity. Similar levels organize dissimilar levels, establishing a
relation of likeness in them as well. Simultaneously dissimilar levels perform
the opposite task, revealing differences in the similar. Since the ultimate
goal of this complex self-adjusting system is the formation of a new
semantics not existing on the level of natural language, the role of elements
which in natural language are responsible for semantic and formal ties will
be different. Phonological-grammatical elements will organize semantically
heterogeneous units into equivalent classes, injecting the element of identity
into the semantics of distinction. When semantic elements coincide, formal
categories will activate a relation of distinction, revealing semantic differentiation on the level of artistic structure in elements which are semantically
similar on the level of the natural language. We could say that in a relation
of equivalence, the formal and semantic elements of natural language
which enter into a poetic structure constitute complementary sets: the
coincidence of some elements entails the non-coincidence of others.

Here is an example:

> Mogla by—vzjala by
> V utrobu peščery:
> V peščeru drakona,
> V truščobu pantery.
>
> [If I could—I would take
> Into the womb of the cave:
> Into the cave of the dragon,
> Into the covert of the panther.]
>   (Marina Cvetaeva)

On the level of natural language the lexico-semantic units of this text are
different (except for the twice repeated *peščera* ["cave"]). On other levels,

2 Boris Pasternak, "Ljudi i položenija," *Novy mir* No. 1 (1967) p. 216.

however, complex relations of equivalence are established.

On the metrical level, the text falls into isometric line units (two-foot amphibrachs) with a caesura after the first foot. This establishes a certain equivalence among the lines and between each pair of hemistiches.

Syntactically, however, the first line is not parallel to the remaining three; it is divided into two hemistiches in which unequal syntactical relations (the syntactic construction *esli mogla by–to vzjala by* is expressed elliptically*) are expressed by means of strictly repeating grammatical elements. But the following three lines (taken independently) are strictly parallel. Their positional difference relative to each other, expressed in the author's punctuation, is activated against the background of their parallelism.

On the *grammatical* level the two hemistiches of the first line are strictly parallel, as are the opening hemistiches of the following three lines and the closing hemistiches of the same lines (2-4). Anaphora arises on the basis of the grammatical parallelism, and two out of three rhymes are grammatical (as is the compound internal rhyme in the first line). The internal rhymes connecting the opening hemistiches of lines 2-4 are also grammatical.

On the *phonological* level the text is clearly divided into two unequal parts. The one consists of the first line, where the phonology is completely organized by the grammatical level; the other is constructed along structural principles which constitute a wholly independent level. For the sake of brevity, let us examine only the second part, excluding the vertical, anaphoric series of prepositions (*v* ["into"]) which on the phonological level comprise a totally independent subset—in all three lines the phoneme *v* is not encountered in other positions. So let us examine the phonological text set off in italics:

> Mogla by–vzjala by
> V *utrobu peščery:*
> V *peščeru drakona,*
> V *truščobu pantery.*

We will regard each word as a segment of the phonological text. We are justified in doing this because the words here are segments not only on the semantic, grammatical-syntactic, and rhythmic levels, but on the phonological level since they can be grouped—the phenomenon is striking—according to the number of letters (phonemes) in each word: 6,6,6,7,7,7. Although in the "six or seven" group distribution some additional ordering is evident, we will disregard it (from the perspective of our initial approximation this is permissible), and consider that the boundaries of the words form quantitatively identical groups of phonemes. This simplifies the task of comparison. We must expose the phonological ordering of the text. To

---

* The ellipsis is untranslatable in English. In Russian the sense of the "if. . . then" construction is conveyed by both the juxtaposition and the intonation, making it possible to omit the words *esli* ("if") and *to* ("then")–Tr.

do this, let us consider all the segments as equivalent sets and determine the set power of their intersection.

Sets where the intersecting part is greater than the nonintersecting part we will call equivalent sets with a high power. In examining the phonological level, we will disregard the sequence of phonemes and consider only their presence (in order to simplify the problem). The phonemes common to the equivalent segments constitute their set power (disregarding the order in which they appear).

The phoneme *r* is the smallest intersecting group: it occurs in all segments. For four pairs of segments, the set power will be exhausted by this one phoneme.

The group with the set power consisting of one phoneme (*r*) includes:

> ut*r*obu—pešče*r*y
> pešče*r*u—d*r*akona
> pešče*r*y—d*r*akona

Note that in two out of three cases the word *drakon* reflects the least degree of phonological organization in the text (similarly it is not bound by rhyme or grammatical categories to other segments: *peščera* and *pantera* are feminine substantives, whereas *drakon* is masculine, a fact which will prove to be of great semantic importance). This word is the least "bound" in the text.

The group with a set power consisting of two phonemes (*r* + vowel in two cases, *r* + consonant in the other) includes:

> *tr*
> *tr*uščobu—pan*ter*a
> *ur*
> u*tr*obu—pešče*ru*
> *ro*
> d*r*akona—t*r*uščobu

In this group, too, *drakon* has the lowest set power.

The group with a set power consisting of three phonemes includes:

> *ran*
> d*r*akona—*pan*te*r*y
> *ščru*
> pešče*ru*—t*r*uščobu
> *per*
> *per*ru—*pan*te*r*y

The group with a set power of four phonemes is:

> *pery*
> pešče*ry*—*pan*te*ry*

The group with a set power of five phonemes is:

> *pešč*er

peščery—peščeru

The group with a set power of six phonemes is:

truobu[3]
truščobu—utrobu

Let us examine which pairs of segments form sets with a high power by composing a table in which the outer columns will indicate the number of non-coincident phonemes, and the central column—the number of coincident phonemes in a segment.[4] We will arrange them in order of increasing power (the left column pertains to the word on the left, the right to the word on the right).

utrobu—peščery	5–1–5
peščery—drakona	5–1–6
peščeru—drakona	5–1–6
utrobu—peščeru	4–2–4
utrobu—drakona	4–2–5
utrobu—pantery	4–2–5
peščery—truščobu	4–2–5
drakona—truščobu	5–2–5
truščobu—pantery	5–2–5
drakona—pantery	4–3–4
panteru—truščobu	4–3–4
peščeru—pantery	3–3–4
peščery—pantery	2–4–3
peščery—peščeru	1–5–1
truščobu—utrobu	1–6–0

In the last line, the entire second segment consists of phonemes found in the first segment. The last lines form sets with intersections of highest power. However, one intuitively feels that the sound of the second to the last pair differs from the sound of the last pair.[5] In order to explain why, we should compose analogous tables of intersections for the grammatical and lexico—semantic levels (for other texts it would be necessary to include intonational, syntactic, and other tables; however, here we observe total identity on these levels).

The relations among these data could be incorporated into a general

---

3 When the same phoneme occurs in one segment once and in another segment twice, we consider it as one phoneme intersection; when it occurs twice in two segments, we count it as two phonemes.

4 A phonological frequency chart of this text shows the following indices. There are thirteen phonemes in this text which, arranged in descending order, appear as follows: r–6 times: e–5; u–4; $t, o, p, šč, a,$–3; y, n–2; k–1. To lend these microdata greater clarity, they must be considered against the background of a phonological frequency list of Russian. Two y's and two m's, of course, yield different degrees of intended phonological organization in the text.

5 Quantitatively these two cases coincide, but the combination of the phoneme r common to all the words, with t results in a greater degree of textual organization than ro because the former combination occurs less freqently in the language.

table for the next level. We would thereby obtain the most objective picture of the connection of elements in the text. Apparently conditions for the emergence of secondary meanings are most advantageous when the highest degree of linkage is located on some levels and the lowest degree on other levels. In the first place this provides us with criteria for determining the degree of organization of the text (which could be very useful in gauging the equivalence of a translation, since the degree of power of the inter-secting subsets in the translated text will inevitably diverge from that of the original, though the former could achieve the same degree of linkage between semantic segments that exists in the original by regulating the construction of other levels). In the second place, by investigating those semantic bonds formed when equivalent elements are united in semantic groups, we can distinguish those of the greatest importance.

The semantic group *V utrobu – V peščeru – V truščobu,* and the group *V utrobu peščery – V truščobu pantery* takes the meaning of movement into a closed, inaccessible, dark area and singles it out as the common semantic kernel, the basis for comparison. Introducing the spatio-sematic positions "closed vs. open," "near vs. far," "in vs. out," and "accessible vs. inaccessible," as well as the secondary positions "protected vs. unprotected," "dark vs. light," "warm vs. cold," and "secret vs. obvious," this construction situates the group at the intersection of the given semantic poles. The left-hand components of the above oppositions become synonyms as do the ones on the right. They can be reduced to the principal opposition "subject vs. object" (for example, in the variant "one's own vs. another's") and to the opposition "I vs. you."

All this reveals the basic semantics of the desire to surmount the opposition "I vs. you," and the invariant scheme: *Vzjala by tvoe ty v moe ja* ["I would take your *you* into my *I*"]. In this sense, the low power of equivalence of the groups which contain *drakona* is no accident – the fact that its gender is masculine evidently prevents it from entering as a variant into the invariant groups of the semantic subject of the text. However, the singling out of the semantic kernel activates the significance of differential elements.

> V utrobu peščery:
> V peščeru drakona. . .

The double bond – the coincidence of the root of the word *peščera,* leading to a clear-cut formal semantization (difference in likeness), and the singling out of the formal element as an essential distinctive feature heightens the semantic significance of grammatical category to a maximum degree (in this case it heightens the semantic role of the spatial relations it expresses) and prepares us for one of the last lines (lying outside the fragment we are considering):

> ... V peščeru–utrobu.
> Mogla by–vzjala by.
>
> [... Into the cave–the womb.
> If I could–I would.]

Further study of the semantic role of equivalent segments could be focused on two areas:

First, to reveal the semantic role of variant elements of the invariant arrived at (to explain why the given semantic invariant is expressed through the given variants). The differences between them, which arise as a result of the equivalence structurally assigned to them, allow us to examine each one as an element selected from some set of mutually equivalent elements, as a result of which the choice of one element rather than another makes the differences meaningful.

Second, to discover how a given semantic invariant is related to the semantic invariants in other parts of the text and in other texts by the same author. Here the semantic invariants will be variants of a second-degree invariant, once again forming an equivalent set from which the author makes a choice. In the case at hand, this will be the relation of the text under investigation to other texts by Cvetaeva which deal with the poet's attempt to close in the gap between her "I" (in all its manifestations) and "not I" (likewise in all its manifestations).

The Syntagmatic Axis in the Structure of an Artistic Text

The conjoining of elements is another operation in the construction of any text (message). Here it would be helpful to distinguish two types of conjunction: that of identical or structurally equivalent elements, and that of diverse structural elements.

In the first case we do not get a phrase type construction: the repetition of identical elements combined in a whole results in a construction similar to a geometrical design. The essential difference between constructions with an internally specialized chain (a phrase) and an internally non-specialized chain (the geometrical design) consists in the presence or absence of a structurally marked end and beginning. Correspondingly, if in the first case the length of a phrase defines its construction to a considerable degree, in the second case the text is open.

The conjunction of identical elements in a chain is governed by laws other than those governing the conjunction of heterogeneous elements—it is constructed according to the principle of addition, and in this sense reproduces the basic trait of supra-phrasal construction characteristic of a spoken text. The following point is essentail: the repetition of the same element mutes its semantic significance (cf. the psychological effect produced when a word is repeated several times, with the result that it begins to sound like nonsense).[6] At the same time, the means for conjoining these elemets which have lost their meaning is brought to the forefront. Thus elements themselves are formalized and simultaneously their formal bonds are semanticized. This is corroborated in numerous cases where designs are formalized, where meaningful patterns are transformed into geometric patterns. Simultaneously the geometrical design becomes a model of any conjunctive bond—the scheme of a narrative text, for example. The tendency of narrative genres to divide the text into equivalent segments (strophes for the poetic text, chapters for prose) would seem to be a related phenomenon. In the first approximation we could say that within a segment (a line, strophe, or chapter) the text is constructed on the principle of the phrase (the conjunction of diverse but non-equivalent elements), and that between segments a conjunctive bond of the sort that exists between paragraphs, chapters and the line holds sway.[7]

The pronounced structural markedness of segment borders (in the absence of the structurally marked categories of the beginning and end of a text) creates the illusion of a structure that seems to reproduce a text of speech (infinite) activity (for example, a text of actual speech activity) and therefore can be broken off or continued at any point, like a design or an endless story. Such texts as *Evgenij Onegin, Vasilij Terkin, A Singer in the Russian Soldiers' Camp* and all sorts of couplets, noëls, and other songs of this type are constructed in principle as open texts. Puškin repeatedly stressed the fact that his work on *Evgenij Onegin* ("a collection of motley chapters") consisted of "accumulating" new stanzas.

If we take a closer look, however, we find it difficult to pose any absolute opposition between the phrasal and supra-phrasal conjunction of elements on the syntagmatic axis of an artistic text's construction. By introducing the concept of the beginning and end of a text as structural elements whose presence is obligatory, we permit the whole text to be examined as one phrase. But its constituent elements, which have their own beginning and end and are constructed along syntagmatic lines, are also phrasal in nature. Thus any meaningful segment of an artistic text can be interpreted both as a phrase and as a sequence of phrases. Moreover, as a result of what Jurij Tynjanov calls the "compactness" of the verbal series in a line, and Roman Jakobson—the projection of the axis of selection onto the axis of combination—the words set together in an artistic text form a semantically indissoluble whole, a "phraseologism," within a given segment. In this sense any meaningful segment (including the universal

6 The artistic effect of persistent repetitions in a literary text is constructed on this principle.

7 See E. V. Padučeva, "O strukture abzaca," *Trudy po znakovym sistemam,* II (Tartu, 1965); I. P. Sevbo, "Ob izučenii struktury svjaznogo teksta," *Lingvističeskie issledovanija po obščej i slavjanskoj tipologii* (Moscow, 1966); V. M. Gasparov, "O nekotoryx lingvističeskix aspektax izučenija struktury teksta," *3-ja letnjaja škola. . .* op. cit.

segment—the entire text of a work) is correlated not only with a chain of meanings, but also with one indivisible meaning. In other words, any meaningful segment is a word. The possibility of viewing a text and any one of its meaningful parts as a particular occasional word was noted by Boris Pasternak (and before him, by Potebnja):

> Čto emu počet i slava,
> Mesto v mire i molva
> V mig, kogda dyxan'em splava
> *V slovo sploĉeny slova?*

> [What are honor and glory to him,
> High standing in the world and fame
> At that moment, when with the breath of a fusion
> *Words are joined together in a word?*]

The situation, however, is complicated by the fact that although intra- and supra-phrasal bonds can be clearly distinguished from the point of view of any one level, we must remember that any text can be regarded from the perspective of several levels; interphrasal bonds inevitably become intra-phrasal, and vice versa.

The opposition between metaphor (the semantic bond which arises on the syntagmatic axis) and rhythm (the semantic bond which arises on the axis of equivalence) is not absolute, if for no other reason than that comparison of two segments on the axis of contiguity inevitably entails their prominence. The division of the text into segments that are in any way equivalent (otherwise they could not be compared) by the same token introduces rhythm into the structure of the syntagmatic axis, as well. A complex interweaving of relations takes place. A certain isomorphism among the elements makes it possible to divide the text into equivalent segments (individual and comparable). Subsequently their meanings form equivalent sets of a particular power and set their differential semantic elements in relief.

However, the same text could be "read" in the light of other bonds. Each segment can be examined as a part of some sentence. In this case it enters into certain fixed relations (depending on the type of sentence) with the syntagmatic whole and its parts. Due to these bonds, each segment predicts the next segment in a certain way. "Very often," C. V. Padučeva remarks, "the laws governing the combinability of units can be reduced to the necessity of repeating some constituents of these units. Thus the formal structure of a line is based (particularly) on the repetition of like-sounding syllables; the agreement of a substantive with an adjective is based on the identical meaning of gender, number and case markers; the combinability of phonemes can often be reduced to the rule that in adjacent phonemes, one and the same value of some distinctive feature must be repeated. The connectedness of the text of a paragraph is based, to a considerable degree, on the repetition of identical semantic elements in adjacent phrases."[8] By removing prohibitions on certain levels (grammatical, semantic, stylistic, intonational, and so forth) concerning the ordering of textual segments, the artistic text activates the structural function of those elements whose coincidence is a necessary condition for the combinability of those same segments in a non-artistic text.

Thus poetry violates the principle of observing rules which prohibit the combining of certain elements in a text. This is by no means the exclusive property of twentieth century poetry. Besides "linking disparate ideas," which Lomonosov regarded as an essential rhetorical device, the conjunction of large plot sections of text (episodes, "motifs," images, chapters) is based to a considerable degree on this particular property.

Let us examine a text by Tjutčev:

> Večer mglistyj i nenastnyj. . .
> Cu, ne žavaronka l' glas?
> Ty, li, utra gost' prekrasnyj,
> V ètot pozdnij, mertvyj čas?. . .
> Gibkij, rezvyj, zvučno-jasnyj,
> V ètot mertvyj pozdnij čas,
> Kak bezum' ja smex užasnyj,
> On vsju dušu mne potrjas!. . .

> [An evening, misty and overcast. . .
> Hark! Is that the voice of the lark?. . .
> Is that you, beautiful morning guest,
> At this late, dead hour?. . .
> Supple, playful, sonorously clear,
> At this dead, late hour,
> Like the terrible laughter of madness
> It has shaken me to the depths of my soul!]

The poem is clearly constructed so as to combine two semantically uncombinable groups: a rainy, overcast evening and the song of the lark. At the same time, on all linguistc levels its structure implements certain bonds in accordance with the rules prohibiting or permitting these bonds. The combination of the uncombinable here occurs on another level, that of extra-linguistic reality. The injunction against combinability is removed, not on a linguistic level (including the semantic level—there is no metaphor here in the narrow sense of the word), but rather in the construction of the message. "An evening, misty and overcast" presents a real situation. The interjection *Cu* ["Hark"] makes us expect that something will be said about sounds in the words that follow. The presence of these two messages forces us to construct a set of possibilities from which the author must choose what follows (e.g. "the screech of an owl," "the creaking of dry wood," "a moan," "the rattle of bones," "the sound of a bell"). The choice

8 E. V. Padučeva, op. cit., p. 285.

of any of these elements (or others equivalent to them) in turn allows us to construct a field of that which is possible and impossible in the messages that follow. Tjutčev makes his choice from the set of improbable rather than probable continuations. In doing so he deceives our expectation, as always, only on one level. *Čú* foretells some sound, and subsequently the author indeed describes a sound. If we transform the line, "Hark! Is that the voice of the lark?" into "Hark! Is that the cry of a bird?", none of the restrictions placed on the message are violated, although obviously the "voice of the lark" and the "cry of a bird" could be easily interchanged in certain contexts. Thus of all the semantic features of the lark, the one activated is "*morning* bird" (cf. "beautiful morning guest"), which is uncombinable with the picture painted at the beginning. Further on the whole poem is constructed on this combining of uncombinables: "beautiful morning guest" and "late, dead hour;" "supple, playful, sonorously clear" and "dead, late hour" (note the transposition of words in the repetitions of the fourth and sixth lines—the syntagmatic axis dissimilates them, thus lowering their predictability). All this is crowned by "the terrible laughter of madness." This is the way the author constructs the message he wishes to convey: unpredictability, the chaos of nature itself, disorder as a cosmic law.

Here a question arises: is the poetic lifting of restrictions on the combination of units of some level on the syntagmatic axis itself restricted in some way? One can answer only in the affirmative. A series in which there are no restrictions on combinability (after each element the appearance of any possible succeeding element is equally probable) is not a structure. Conjunction would appear to be possible only when a set of distinctive features for each conjunction forms an intersection through at least one element. This, in fact, is the basis for Aristotle's classic definition of metaphor: "Metaphor is the transference of a word whose meaning has been altered from genus to species, or from species to genus, or from species to species, or by analogy."

Two centruies ago Lomonosov formulated a law which noted the connection between the poetic value of a metaphor and the minimalness of intersection ("the linking of disparate ideas").[9] Moreover we ourselves have spoken of the *continuous* process of removing restrictions and historical material would seem to provide evidence of the same. In medieval literature the range of permissible metaphors is severly limited—they could be set down in a finite list—whereas for Pasternak or Voznesenskij, any two words standing side by side should in effect be considered a metaphor.

But the fact that a poetic metaphor by its very nature strives for a minimal intersection of distinctive features of its constituent members,

9 Today specialists in the physiology of the brain are studying the relation between the irritation of topographically distant psychic centers in the brain and emotional excitability.

and the fact that it tends to diminish that intersection, is only an apparent contradiction: the very concept of "minimal" intersection has real meaning only in connection with the entire specific sum of restrictions and allowances inherent to a given structure as a whole.

The destroyed syntagmatic link takes on a particular significance—it emerges as the differential feature of a given type of combination. Uncombinable combinations could be classified in the following manner:

1. The lifting of restrictions, on the level of natural language, on the conjunction of elements within one semantic unit (a word or phraseological combination). This category includes the majority of lexical neologisms in poetry and also the reinterpretation of combinable units as uncombinable (a common word becomes a neologism):

> Čto v mae, kogda poezdov raspisan'e
> Kamyšinskoj vetkoj čitaeš' v puti,
> Ono grandioznej svjatogo pisan'ja,
> Xotja ego syznova vse perečti.

> [That in May, when you read the train schedule
> While traveling on the branch line to Kamyšin,
> It is more majestic than Holy Scripture
> Even if you read it again.]
>
> (Boris Pasternak)

In the word *raspisan'e* ["schedule"] the prefix *raz* is taken to mean an action in the superlative degree (by analogy to the verbs *rasxvalit'* and *raspisat'* ["to praise extensively," "to write all over some surface"]). It is quite natural, then, that a *raspisan'e* should seem more majestic than mere *pisan'e* ["writing, Scripture"].10

> Kto iz vas
>   iz sel,
>   iz koži von,
>   iz štolen
> ne šagnet vpered?!

> [Which of you
>   out of your villages
>   out of your skins*
>   out of your mines
> will not jump forward?!]
>
> (Majakovskij)

* The phraseological unit *iz koži von* is de-automatized because of its syntactic equivalence with the phrases in the environment. Normally it is used in the phrase *Lezt' iz koži von* meaning "to go all out," "to break your back doing something."—Tr.

10 Naturally the words *Pisanie* ["Scripture"] and *raspisanie* ["schedule"] retain the everyday meaning they have in the natural language; on this level there arises a stylistic opposition, creating a proscription on the combination which is surmounted by the text. The secondary meaning is set against this basic background.

Skorej so sna, čem s kryš; skorej
Zabyvčivyj, čem robkij,
Toptalsja doždik u dverej
I paxlo vinnoj probkoj.

[Rather from sleep than from roofs; rather
Absentminded than timid,
The rain shower stamped at the doors
And the air smelled like a wine cork.j
(Pasternak)

The phraseologisms are set in a position syntactically equivalent to the analogously constructed free word-combinations. An unusual type of bond gives the component parts of the phraseologisms a syntactic independence and concrete object meaning not characteristic of them (already lost in the language). But the conjunction of words with this concrete meaning is impossible in the natural language. The above examples are, in fact, already on the verge of overcoming syntagmatic restrictions.

2. The lifting of restrictions on the rules governing the conjunction of meaningful units in a natural language (morphological and syntactic restrictions).

Bylo mračno i temno.
Bylo strašno i okno.

[It was gloomy and dark.
It was terrible and window.j
(A. Vvedenskij)

Here *okno* ["window"] functions as a stative. Syntactical parallelism and the phonological homonymy of morphemes is the minimal common characteristic allowing for such a reinterpretation.

3. The lifting of restrictions on the semantic markedness of a sentence. All traditional tropes are constructed on this basis. We should remember that the rules of semantic markedness are inversely related to syntactic rules. Where there are no formally expressed bonds, semantic conjoinability becomes the only criterion of correct construction. Consequently the poetic principle of contiguity as a semantic bond represents the transference of interphrasal syntagmatics into the phrase.

It should be noted that although the bonds—obligatory in language—between segments of a text are reduced to a minimum, the introduction of additional orderings compensates for this fact. In the seventeenth century proverb *Komu smex, a u mas v laptjax sneg* ["Others may laugh, but we've got snow in our bast shoes"] (*sneg* is pronounced *snex*), additional phonetic and rhythmic ordering must be introduced in order to establish equivalence between *smex* ["laughter"] and *sneg* ["snow"] (the pattern is *komu xorošo, a nam ploxo* ["Others have it good, but we have it bad"]), and conjoin them in a semantically parallel pair.

Thus two orderings are at work on the syntagmatic axis. One corresponds to general linguistic rules governing the conjunction of segments. On this level the tendency to "loosen" bonds and reduce restrictions to a minimum is constantly at work; since the poetic text in this respect is projected on the general linguistic text, as speech is projected on language, the lifting of restrictions becomes a highly significant semantic element.

But the intensified disordering of a series is simultaneously the intensified ordering of another—poetic—structure. Both series complement each other. This apparently explains the curious fact that the most significant elements of a poetic structure come at the end of segments (lines, strophes, chapters, works). The text as a general linguistic structure becomes more and more redundant toward the end. Structural predictability increases sharply as one moves from the beginning to the end of a segment in a general linguistic text. A poetic construction, taken by itself, is also constructed in this fashion. But when both come together in a real text a number of bonds which are obligatory in the general linguistic text can be done away with. The poetic construction suppresses the redundancy of the general linguistic text. Since poetic ordering appears to be disordering from the general linguistic point of view, a tendency arises (in defining a text as an artistic text) to view any disordering of the text as ordering of a particular type. Hence the tendency to interpret the message of the text as language, and hence the special informational saturation of poetry.

The Mechanism of Intra-textual Semantic Analysis

It follows from the above that for intra-textural (abstracted from all extra-textual bonds) semantic analysis, the following operations must be carried out:

1. Breaking up the text into levels and groups according to the levels of syntagmatic segments (the phoneme, morpheme, line, strophe and chapter for a poetic text: the word, sentence, paragraph and chapter for a prose text).

2. Breaking up the text into levels and groups according to the levels of semantic segments (types of characters, for example). This operation is particularly important in the analysis of prose.

3. Singling out all pairs of repetitions (equivalences).

4. Singling out all pairs of contiguities.

5. Singling out repetitions with the highest power of equivalence.

6. Superimposing equivalent semantic pairs on each other in order to single out the distinctive semantic features of the text and the basic semantic oppositions on all basic levels. The examination of the semantization of grammatical constructions.

7. Assessing the structure of the syntagmatic construction and significant divergences from it in pairs formed by contiguity. Examining the semantization of syntactic constructions.

The operations recounted above give only a general and deliberately rough semantic skeleton, since a description of all connections arising in the text and of all extra-textual relations which could be ascertained would be an unrealistic task in terms of sheer volume. Thus the very crudeness of the results of such an analysis may not only be a fault, but also a virtue. The first thing we must do is formulate the problem: how complete a description is required and what levels will be viewed as dominant; what will not be examined and why; in what cases dominant elements will be selected on the basis of precisely formulated criteria, and in what instances these concepts are to be regarded as intuitively given.

6. ELEMENTS AND LEVELS OF THE PARADIGMATICS OF THE ARTISTIC TEXT

Poetry and Prose

In literary theory critics generally accept the assertion that ordinary human speech and prose speech are one and the same, and consequently, that prose in relation to poetry is the primary, initial phenomenon. The distinguished expert on the theory of verse, B. V. Tomaševskij, summarizing years of research in that field wrote, "A prerequisite to any judgment on language is the axiom that the natural form of organized human speech is prose."[1] This has given rise to a second assertion just as widely accepted, that poetic speech is something secondary whose structure is more complex than that of prose. Zigmunt Czerny, for example, suggests the following degrees of transition from structural simplicity to complexity: "Utilitarian prose (the prose of science, administration, the military, jurisprudence, commerce, journalism, etc.)—ordinary prose—literary prose—poetry in prose —rhythmic prose—vers libre—strophes of unequal length—metrical verse of irregular line length—strictly regulated classical verse."[2]

Another arrangement would be more accurate. In the hierarchy of movement from the simple to the complex, the arrangement of genres is different: conversational speech—the song (text and motif)—classical poetry —artistic prose. Of course this scheme is only a crude approximation (provisions will be made for vers libre separately). It is hardly correct to maintain that artistic prose is historically the initial form, coinciding with conversational, non-artisitc speech.

History testifies that poetic speech (as well as singing or chanting) was initially the only possible speech of verbal *art*. [3] First came the "dissimilation" of the language, its separation from ordinary speech; only later came the "assimilation". Out of "dissimilated," already radically different material, a picture of reality was created.

Descriptive prosodic studies and descriptive poetics proceed from the notion that an artistic construction is the mechanical sum of a number of independently existing "devices;" artistic analysis is understood to mean

---

1 B. V. Tomaševskij, "Stix i jazyk," *IV Meždunarodnyj s"ezd slavistov. Doklady* (Moscow, 1958) p. 4. Reprinted in his book *Stix i Jazyk* (Moscow–Leningrad, 1959). The same point of view is maintained by M. Janakiev in his interesting book *B"lgarsko stixoznanie* (Sophia, 1960) p. 11.

2 Zygmunt Czerny, "Le vers libre français et son art structural," *Poetics, Poetyka, Poetika,* I, p. 255.

3 It is significant that the first form of verbal art for a child is always poetry, that is, speech which is not like ordinary speech. Mature art eventually strives to imitate non-artistic speech, to approach it, but the first stage is always rejection. Art realizes its specificity in striving to differ as much as possible from non-art (poetic diction, fantastic plots, "noble" characters).

an enumeration of the poetic elements which the researcher discovers in the text and an assessment of the style and ideas expressed. This method of analysis has become firmly established in the schools. Procedural handbooks and textbooks abound in such expressions as "pick out the epithets," "find the metaphors," "what did the artist intend to say in such-and-such an episode?" and so on.

A structural approach to a literary work assumes that the "device" is examined not as a separate material fact, but as a function with two or, more often, many generatrices. The artistic effect of a "device" is always a relation (for example, the relation of a text to a reader's expectations, the aesthetic norms of an epoch, the customary plot or clichés of other types, rules of genres, and so on). Apart from these connections there simply cannot be an artistic effect. Any enumeration of devices (or, for that matter the examination of "devices" in general outside the organic unity of the text) gives us nothing, since the same material element of a text inevitably takes on a different, sometimes opposite meaning when it enters into different structures of the whole. This manifests itself most clearly in the use of negative devices—"minus-devices." Take Puškin's *Vnov' ja posetil. . .* ["Once again I visited. . ."] , for example. From the perspective of descriptive poetics this poem scarcely yields to analysis. While such a method can still be applied to a Romantic poem—selecting copious metaphors, epithets and other elements of what is called "figurative speech" and on that basis evaluating the system of ideas and style—it is decidedly inapplicable to works like Puškin's lyrics of the 1830's. Here there are no epithets, no metaphors, no rhyme, no strongly stressed rhythm, or any other "artistic devices."

From the viewpoint of structural analysis, the catalogue approach to a text is always ineffectual since an artistic device is not a material element, but a *relation.* For example, there is a difference in principle between the absence of rhyme in verse which has *not yet* assumed the possiblility of its existence (for example, ancient poetry, Russian epic verse, and so on) or verse which has *already* decisively rejected it, where the absence of rhyme is expected, is an aesthetic norm (for example, contemporary vers libre),— and verse in which rhyme is one of the most characteristic features of the poetic text. In the first case, the absence of rhyme is not an artistically meaningful element, whereas in the second case the absence of rhyme may be considered as the presence of non-rhyme—"minus-rhyme." In an epoch when readers raised on the poetry of Žukovskij, Batjuškov and the young Puškin identified Romantic poetics with the very concept of poetry, the artistic system of "Once again I visited. . ." gave the impression not of the absence of "devices," but a maximum saturation of devices. But these were "minus-devices," a system of consistent conscious rejections sensed by the reader. In this sense, there is nothing paradoxical about the assertion that in 1830 a poetic text written according to the accepted norms of

Romantic poetics would have produced a more "naked" impression, would in reality have possessed fewer elements of artistic structure than "Once again I visited..."

That resemblance to non-artistic reality is a merit or even a condition of art, an idea canonized by the tastes and aesthetic theories of the nineteenth century, is quite a recent phenomenon in the history of art. In the initial stages it was precisely non-resemblance, the difference between the sphere of the ordinary and the artistic, which made people perceive a text aesthetically. To become the material of art, language was first deprived of its resemblance to everyday speech. Only much later did it return to prose— not to the original "unconstructedness" of speech, but only to its imitation. This is what occasioned the advent of "prosaisms" and of "poetic license" in poetry, prose and literature as a whole. This secondary simplicity, however, is artistically active only against the background of an extensive poetic culture constantly present in the reader's consciousness. It is hardly coincidental that periods in which poetry and prose dominate alternate regularly. Thus the development of a powerful poetic tradition at the beginning of the nineteenth century, leading, after Puškin's works in the 1820's, to the identification of poetry with literature as a whole, served as a point of departure for the energetic development of artistic prose in the second half of the century. But when the Puškinian tradition was transformed, as it appeared in those years, into a historical tradition no longer felt as a living literary fact, *when prose triumphed over poetry to such an extent that it was no longer perceived in relation to poetry,* a turnabout occurred and poetry once again emerged. The beginning of the twentieth century, like the beginning of the nineteenth, saw Russian literature under the sign of poetry. And poetry in turn was the background against which the growth of artistic prose in the 1920's was perceived.

This shift in the dominant type of poetic speech was not only a causative, but also an intrinsic factor in the history and development of artistic forms in those years. There was a reserve of information from which the complex and multifarious processes of literature's historical development could draw what corresponded to their internal needs.

The complex interweaving of prose and poetry in a single functioning system of artistic consciousness is closely bound up with more general problems concerning the construction of a work of art. An artistic text never belongs to one system or one tendency: regularity and its violation, formalization and, in the end, the automatization and de-automatization of the structure of a text are all engaged in a constant struggle. Each of these tendencies enters into conflict with its structural antipode, but exists only in relation to it. Therefore the victory of one tendency over another does not mean the cessation of conflict, but the transference of conflict to another plane. The tendency that wins out becomes artistically unviable.

Thus the opposition of poetry and prose in nineteenth century Russian literature is perceived against the background of a general antinomy between the well-constructed, artificial and false, on the one hand, and the natural, ingenuous and true, on the other. The requirement of the period that art be close to life did not imply, however, that the one should *replace* the other. The artistic text strives for a maximum approximation of life precisely because, in accordance with its initial premise, it is not life. So at first a certain degree of conventionality is established, an initial dissimilarity, and then the fight begins, and similarity is stressed. Two paths of struggle are theoretically possible: movement toward similarity within a given system of conventionality, attempting to reconstruct it from within, and discarding the whole system, demanding that it be replaced by another. When the existing system is accepted as the initial, negative background, the new system of artistic language is activated in relation to the old as its negation.

Applied to the example that concerns us, this means that there are two ways of surmounting that poetic tradition which at the close of the first third of the nineteenth century was regarded as "Puškinian." On the one hand, there may be a tendency to prosify verse (rhythmically, intonationally, thematically, and so on); on the other hand, poetry might be rejected in principle and replaced by prose, regarded as the negation of poetry against the background of verse culture.

In this way the opposition "poetry vs. prose" partially expresses the opposition "art vs. non-art." It is no accident that parallel with the shift of a work within the semantic field "poetry—prose," "non-art" is continually attracted into the sphere of artistic texts, and works of art and entire genres are thrust into categories of non-artistic texts. Thus the rejection of poetry as the fundamental means of literary expression in the 1830's was accompanied by the exclusion of traditional eighteenth and early nineteenth century prose genres (the picaresque, family and other forms of the novel) from the sphere of art. They were replaced by the literary sketch, valued for its documentary quality and ranked as an artistic genre precisely because it did not pretend to be artful. The uncontrived quality of the sketch is manifested above all in its absence of plot construction, testifying to its veracity; it penetrated poetry (the poetic feuilleton, the poetic sketch), drama (the appearance of a particular genre—"scenes") and painting (the triumph of genre painting over historical painting, the popularity of travel sketches, and the like). And in succeeding periods the broad movement toward the prosification of artistic culture, on the one hand, confirmed the authority of "non-art" (reality, everyday life, the document), and on the other hand made a norm of *the reproduction of life* by means of art. Even immediate raw reality as a document spliced into artistic prose[4] or a cinematic narrative, while remaining materially unchanged, functionally

4 This device is most often used by twentieth century writers, but it was known earlier: Puškin used it in his *Dubrovskij*, incorporating actual legal documents in the text of the novel.

alters its nature in a fundamental way: while infecting other sections of
the text with the feeling of authenticity which it provokes, it takes on the
"artificaility" of its context and becomes a reproduction of itself. Narrative
speech in art shows an analogous fact: artistic speech is not identical to
non-artistic prose, but is related to it the way a reproduction is related to
the object reproduced. There are numerous and profound differences
between the two which escape our attention only because we are insuf-
ficiently attentive. The most essential difference can be reduced to the
following: oral speech differs radically from written speech. On all levels—
from phonemes to supra-phrasal syntactic units—oral speech is constructed
as a system of reductions, omissions and ellipses. But the *reproduction* of
oral speech in literature is constructed according to the laws of written
speech. Elements of the reduced oral structure are introduced only in certain
places, where they perform the role of signals: through them we discover
that the denotatum of the normalized text is the verbal fabric of oral speech,
which is considerably more abridged and dependent on the extra-verbal
situation and on intonation. Oral speech can penetrate deeply into the
fabric of a narrative, particularly in twentieth century art. But it can never
fully dislodge the written structures because even in the most extreme cases
the artistic text is not oral speech, but rather the reflection of oral speech
in written speech. We should note that even when we are not dealing with
written forms of verbal art, oral artistic speech—from the improvisations of
the folk singer to dramatic speech—is constructed on the basis of full,
normalized speech, not an abridged variant. Even on the stage this difference
does not surprise us if the whole system of conventions accepted in the art
form satisfies our artistic sense. The eighteenth century reader was not
struck by the improbability of the following simulation of oral speech:

> "What has become of your fomer serenity, in which your heart
> rejoiced? Oh dear Kamber!" cried Arisena in a pitiable voice.
> "Now I understand, to my most bitter agony, that one should
> not believe in the false glitter of fortune."[5]

This text was as believable as the various forms of *skaz** or stream-of-
consciousness are to the contemporary reader, although we need only
compare the latter with a recording of real colloquial speech to discern a
radical difference: any contemporary *skaz*, any simulation of an ordinary
fragmented dialogue, is constructed in such a way as to reproduce all forms
of contact, including non-verbal contacts, with the help of words. Therefore
it creates an integral model of communication and is comprehensible in
and of itself. Oral speech recorded on a tape and transcribed loses its

---

* *Skaz*—"A principle of narration based on the stylization, in mundane form, of
the style of a substitute narrator—as a rule, a representation of some social, historical
or ethnographic milieu." (*Dictionary of Literary Terms,* Moscow:Prosveščenie, 1974,
p. 354)—Tr.

5 F. Emin, *Ljubovnyj vertograd, ili Nepreoborimoe postojanstvo Kambera i
Ariseny* (St. Petersburg, 1763) p. 40.

connection with paralinguistics and intonation, remains a *part* of communication and, taken by itself, could be simply incomprehensible. Any "approximation of colloquialism," whether it be the deliberate alogisms and violations of syntax which Rousseau used to imitate the "chaos of passion," Tolstoj's labored periods reproducing the flow of inner thought, or the stream of consciousness structures so popular in twentieth century prose–all of these things signal the dissatisfaction of writers with the conventionality of the preceding literary tradition. Only to a much lesser extent do they represent a naturalistic reproduction of "raw" speech. The process of transition from poetic structures to an imitation of everyday speech by means of artistic prose is in many ways analogous to the transition from direct written forms of language to the imitation of colloquialism. In both cases a consciously conventional system is first set up which by nature is separated from the texture of the world that is reproduced, and then the two begin to converge.

This explains why certain original artistic types[6] in a given culture always constitute systems with a maximally expressed number of restrictions. In the course of evolution, as a rule, certain restrictions are lifted or transferred to the category of the optional. Subjectively, therefore, such evolution is thought to involve a *simplification* of the original type. All rebellions in art against the original type have rallied around the banner of "naturalness" and 'simplicity", against the oppressive and "artificial" limits of the preceding period. From a structural point of view, however, the construction of the text grows more complicated, although basic elements of construction are removed beyond the text and are realized in the form of "minus-devices." From this viewpoint prose as an artistic phenomenon is a more complex structure than poetry.

But this does not exhaust the matter. In the period when prototypes of artistic construction are being created, the most active tendency on

6 The concept of an "initial type" can be explained as follows: each type of culture can be conceived of as a set of certain stable forms. In the process of historical evolution, initial types can be radically deformed, but they continue their homeostatic efforts to attain unity: all subsequent forms are perceived as variants of the initial form. Thus to this day the metrical structure which was formulated in the epoch of Trediakovskij and Lomonosov remains an "initial type" for all subsequent rhythmic systems. The norm for the Russian *vita,* which was established in the Kievan epoch, remained an "initial type" for all future modifications of that genre up to the works of Archpriest Avvakum, whose text is perceived as innovative in light of that norm, that is in relation to it. One might suggest that for all the theatrical revolutions that shook the French stage, from the Romantics to the Avant-gardists, the theatre of Racine still remains the "initial type" for all French drama. It is the stability of the norm forming the basis for a given culture that makes far-reaching artistic deformations possible. In place of the usual ("everyday") notion that the farther it is from tradition, the bolder the innovation, the structural approach suggests another principle: the farther removed an innovation is from tradition in the confines of a given cultural type, the closer it is to tradition. In culture a break with tradition means the resurrection of tradition under different conditions. Naturally we are not speaking of a mechanical break, which is not a cultural fact at all. A genuine break with an "initial type" begins when its violation ceases to be artistically meaningful.

different levels is to assign a hierarchy of different types of artistic languages
to separate areas of the content. Thus a certain style and meter is assigned
to one genre (in the Classical period, for example); fixed genres are assigned
to certain types of plots; certain personae are assigned a particular language,
and so on. Further "shake-ups" of original types might lead to the appearance of significant delimitations within a previously unified type of artistic
structure,[7] as well as the possibility of violating the boundaries of the
original codification. Where the prototype allowed for one structural possibility, *a choice now arises.*

Prose and poetry are correlated in one way when any plot, theme,
image or genre unambiguously defines whether a work is poetic or prosaic;
they are correlated differently when an artistic choice between two solutions
is possible. Karamzin, who wrote "Alina," a story in verse, and at the same
time "Poor Liza," and Puškin, who called *Evgenij Onegin* a novel in verse
and the *Bronze Horseman* a "Petersburg story," who chose themes characteristic of prose tales for his narrative poems *Count Nulin* and *A Little
House in Kolomna,* both consciously proceed on the assuption that verse
and prose could be viewed in some respect as structures of equal value.
The appearance of Nekrasov's *Saša* and Turgenev's *Rudin* in the same issue
of the periodical *The Contemporary* is no less significant in this sense.
However, the novels of Tolstoj and Dostoevskij, the satires of Saltykov-
Ščedrin, and the sketches of Gleb Uspenskij unambiguously defined the
choice of prose as the structural foundation of the text. The position that
existed in the eighteenth century was rehabilitated: prose and poetry were
divided (on completely different grounds, of course) into two non-intersecting artistic spheres. The reader knew exactly what group of artistic
phenomena was assigned to prose and what to poetry. The possibility of
a choice, of a conflict between expectation and realization, was removed.

Processes which made their way into prose beginning with Garšin and
Čexov, and into poetry beginning with the Symbolists, again led to the
"Puškinian" equation of poetry and prose which, for example, is charact-
istic of Pasternak. Thus in the prose fragment *Povest'* ("A Tale") published
in 1929, Pasternak wrote:

> For ten years now the odds and ends of this story have been
> floating about before my eyes, and at the beginning of the
> revolution some of them wound up in print. The reader should
> forget those versions lest he become confused about what lot
> fell to which characters in the final drawing. Some of them I
> renamed; as far as their lots are concerned they remain now as I
> found them in those years in the snow under trees, and between
> the novel in verse called *Spektorskij* which I began later, and
> the prose offered here, there will be no contradiction—it is one
> life.[8]

7 Thus for Lomonosov all phenomena that can be defined as "iambic tetrameter"
are one and contain no gradations in content among themselves. Subsequently on this
basis a complex system arises where rhythmic figures and word boundaries allow for
many semantic oppositions.

8 Boris Pasternak, *"Povest',"* Novy mir, No. 7 (1929) p. 5.

As we see, the difference between verse and prose lies not only in the material expression of a structural edifice of some text, but also in the function of the text defined by the whole type of culture; by no means can this function be unambiguously extracted from its graphically fixed part.[9]

Thus artistic prose arose against the background of a poetic system as the negation of that system.

This permits us to look dialectically at the problem of the borders of poetry and prose and the aesthetic nature of such marginal forms as vers libre. In this connection we cannot help but notice the following paradox. The view that poetry and prose are independent, isolated constructions which can be described without mutual correlation ("Poetry is rhythmically organized speech, prose is ordinary speech"), unexpectedly leads the scholar to a position in which he cannot delimit these phenomena. After encountering a mass of intermediate forms, he is obliged to conclude that one cannot draw a definite line between poetry and prose. This was Tomaševskij's conclusion: "It is more natural and more productive to examine verse and prose, not as two areas with strict borders, but as two poles, two centers of gravity around which real facts are historically situated. . . . One may legitimately speak of more or less prosaic and more or less poetic phenomena." Further on, he writes:

> But since different people are in different degrees receptive to individual features of poetry and prose, their claims ("This is verse;" "No, this is rhymed prose") do not contradict each other, as it seems to the parties involved in the argument. From this we may conclude the following: in order to resolve the basic issue of the distinction between poetry and prose, it would be more productive not to study border phenomena, to define poetry and prose not by establishing borders which may, perhaps, be imaginary; rather we should first turn our attention to the most typical, most pronounced forms of verse and prose.[10]

A similar point of view was expressed by Boris Unbegaun in his study on the theory of Russian verse.[11] Beginning with the premise that verse is ordered, organized, that is "non-free" speech, he declares that the very concept of vers libre is a logical antinomy. He sympathetically quotes G. K. Chesterton: "Free verse, like free love, is a contradiction in terms." This view is shared by M. Janakiev:

> Free verse (vers libre) cannot be the subject of prosodic studies since it in no way differs from common speech. On the other hand, prosody should concern itself with even the most

9 We will not discuss the correlation of a text and its functions, which is a completely independent problem. On this question see the article by Ju. Lotman and A. Pjatigorskij referred to above.

10 B. V. Tomaševskij, *Stix i jazyk*, pp. 7-8.

11 B. Unbegaun, *La versification russe* (Paris, 1958).

incompetent "non-free" verse since it may reveal "clumsy, perhaps, but tangible material poetic organization."[12]

Citing Elizaveta Bagrjanaja's "The Clown Speaks," the author concludes, "The general impression is one of artistic prose. . . . The rhymed assonance of *mestata* and *zemljata* is insufficient to transform the text into verse. Similar types of assonance occur from time to time in ordinary prose as well."[13]

However such a treatment of a tangible, material, poetic organization is fairly narrow. As already indicated, it examines only the text which is understood to mean "all that is written." The absence of some element of the text where its presence would be inconceivable and unanticipated in a given structure is equated to the removal of an anticipated element; the rejection of well-defined rhythm in the period preceding the rise of a verse system is equated with the rejection of this element afterwards. An element is isolated from its structure and function; a sign is taken without its background. If this is the approach taken, then vers libre can, in fact, be equated with prose.

We get another answer to the question of the nature of vers libre if we examine verse and prose in their historical and typological correlation. J. Hrabák comes close to such a dialectical approach, for example, in his essay "Observations on the Correlation of Poetry and Prose, Particularly in So-called Transitional Forms." The author proceeds on the assumption that prose and poetry form an oppositional structural binomial (we should stipulate that the opositional correlation does not always exist here; in addition one must differentiate between the structure of ordinary speech and artistic prose). Although Hrabák seems to approve of the traditional formula, writing that prose is speech "bound only by grammatical norms," he later expands his point of view, proceeding from the fact that for the contemporary reader prose and poetry are projected on each other. Consequently, he believes it is impossible not to consider the extra-textual elements of an aesthetic construction. On this basis Hrabák determines where the border between poetry and prose lies. Believing that in the consciousness of author and reader there is a clear-cut division between the structures of poetry and prose, he writes, "In cases where the author stresses typical elements of poetry in prose, this border not only fails to disappear, but on the contrary takes on the greatest significance."[14] Accordingly, "The fewer elements in a poetic form that distinguish verse from prose, the more clearly one must distinguish between prose and poetry, and stress that one is dealing with the latter. On the other hand, in works written in free verse certain individual lines, isolated and taken out of context, could be perceived as

12 M. Janakiev, *B"lgarsko stixoznanie*, p. 10.
13 Ibid., p. 214.
14 Josef Hrabák, "Remarques sur les correlations entre le vers et la prose, surtout les soi-disant formes de transition," *Poetics, Poetyka, Poètika*, I, pp. 241, 245.

prose."[15] For this very reason the border between free verse and prose must be clearly discernible; that is why free verse requires a special graphic construction to be apprehended as a form of poetic speech.

Thus the metaphysical concept of "device" is replaced here by a dialectical concept—"the structural element and its function." The idea of a border between poetry and prose begins to be bound not only to the realization of structural elements in a text, but also to their meaningful absence.

In contemporary molecular physics the concept of a "hole" by no means refers to the simple absence of matter, but rather the absence of matter in a structural position which implies its presence. Under these conditions, a "hole" behaves so much like "matter" that its weight can be measured—in negative terms, of course. And physicists naturally speak of "heavy" and "light" holes. The student of prosody has to deal with analogous phenomena.

It follows that the concept of a "text" for the literary scholar is considerably more complex than for the linguist. If we equate it with the real givenness of a work of art, then we must also consider the "minus-devices," the heavy and light holes of an artistic structure. In order not to stray too far from customary terminology, we will define the text in more familiar terms as the sum of the structural relations which are given linguistic expression (the formula "graphic expression" is not suitable as it does not cover the concept of a text in folklore). In taking such an approach, however, we must distinguish not only *intra-textual* but also *extra-textual* constructions and relations as a special object of investigation. The extra-textual part of an artistic structure is a very real (and often very significant) component of the artistic whole. Of course it is more unstable, more mobile, than the textual part. It is clear, for example, that for those who have studied Majakovskij in school and accept his poetry as the aesthetic norm, the extra-textual part of his work takes on a completely different form than it did for the author himself, and his immediate audience. For the contemporary reader too, the text (in a narrow sense) is thrust into complex general structures—the extra-textual part of the work exists for the contemporary reader as well. But for him it is already quite different. Extra-textual bonds are quite subjective, possessing many individual personal traits which are scarcely subject to analysis by means presently available to literary criticism. But they also have their own regular historically and socially determined content and as a structural whole they can be examined even now.

Further on we will examine extra-textual bonds in their relation to the text and to each other. We are assured success in scientific terms if we strictly demarcate the levels we are dealing with and search for precise criteria in determining the perimeters of the area accessible to contemporary scientific analysis.

15 See J. Hrabák, *Úvod do teorie verše* (Prague, 1958) p. 7 ff.

The difficulty of constructing generating models is one argument in favor of the proposition that prose is comparatively more complex than verse. Here it is perfectly clear that a verse model is distinguished by greater complexity than a general linguistic model (the second enters into the first), but it is no less clear that modeling an artistic prose text is incomparably more difficult than modeling a verse text.

Hrabák is incontestably right when, along with other prosodists (Tomaševskij, for example) he stresses the significance of graphic signs in distinguishing verse from prose. Graphic indicators here are not a technical means of fixing the text but a signal of a structural nature, in compliance with which or consciousness "pushes" the text at hand into an extra-textual structure. We also have no choice but to agree with Hrabák's position when he writes:

> Some may object, for example, pointing out that Paul Fort or Maxim Gorkij wrote a number of their poems without breaking them up into lines (*in continuo*), but in these two cases it was a matter of verse with a traditional and standard form and pronounced rhythmic elements, which excluded the possibility of confusion with prose.[16]

The Principle of Repetition

In natural language, besides orderings on the level of language which have a differentiating character, certain orderings sporadically arise on the level of speech. We do not notice them because they carry no structural load in the act of linguistic communication.

When we deal with an artistic text the situation is radically altered. On the basis of the text, the receiver of the message also has to reconstruct that specific language in which the act of artistic communication is realized. As we noted earlier, the properties of the message become properties of the code and any ordering of the text begins to be interpreted as a structural ordering, as a carrier of meaning. And if, in a text of his own construction, the poet finds additional orderings with respect to natural language, then the reader in turn has the right to proceed in a similar fashion and discover additional orderings of the second degree in the poet's creation. Earlier we showed that these orderings can be divided into two classes: 1) orderings based on equivalence, and 2) orderings based on sequence. All forms of repetiton in an artistic text belong to the first class.

In distinguishing orderings based on equivalence and orderings based on sequence, we ascribe relations between identical elements without regard to the syntagmatics of a text to the first class, and relations between different elements on the syntagmatic axis to the second. It should be emphasized that we can define which aspects of structure we are dealing with only when we specify the particular level we have in mind.

16 Ibid., p. 245.

I *v* *b*ereg *b*'et *v*olnoj *b*ezumnoj.

[And beats against the shore like a mad wave]
(Baratynskij)

On the phonemic level, the alternation of *v* and *b* creates repetitions which allow us to regard certain segments of the text as equivalent. But simultaneously, on the grammatical level *v* *bereg* *b*'et ["beats against the shore"] may be viewed as a word chain divided into groups whose ordering is based on sequence. Here the features of this kind of ordering include both verbal government and the presence of the anaphoric phoneme element *b* (on the model of grammatical agreement). Simultaneously between the groups *I* *v* *bereg* *b*'et and *volnoj* *bezumnoj* ["like a mad wave"] , a parallelism is established based on rhythmic equivalence and the presence of the anaphoric phonemes *v–b* in each group (the initial *i* ["and"] does not correlate with the internal organization of the line, but binds it anaphorically to other lines). If the *v–b* of the first hemistich relative to the *v–b* of the second represents an ordering of the phonemes based on equivalence, among themselves they form a relation based on sequence.

Since any text is formed through the positional combination of a limited number of elements, the presence of repetition is inevitable. But in a non-artistic text these repetitions might not be realized as a form of ordering with respect to the semantic level of the text.

Consider the following lines by Griboedov:

> Organ moi sozdali ruki,
> Psaltyr ustroili persty.

[My hands created the organ,
My fingers tuned the psaltery.]

In relation to its general linguistic, phonological or grammatical structure, this text is distinguished by a certain degree of ordering, but in relation to the semantic structure of the text, these orderings manifest themselves in only one respect: it is sufficient for us to know that the structure of the text is capable of transmitting a certain content, that it is grammatically correct. As soon as we establish that the text is constructed grammatically, its formal ordering ceases to interest us. From the perspective of general linguistic content, the repetition of certain phonemes is absolutely accidental. In the first line:

Or*ga*n–*so*zd*a*li (o-a–o-a)

In the second line:

*Psalty*r'–*persty* (p-s-t-y-r–p-r-s-t-y)

Between the first and second lines:

Or*ga*n *so*zd*a*li r*u*ki
*Psalty*r' *u*stro*i*li *persty*

The same might be said for the parallelism of grammatical forms between paired memebers of the first and second lines. Moreover, if we regard the text as an extra-artistic message, then we must either suppose that the words "organ" and "psaltery" stand for different objects, or we must consider the message of the second line completely redundant. That particular kind of ordering which in Biblical poetry is usually created by repetition ("I was the least among my brethren and the youngest in the house of my father. . . . My hands made the organ, my fingers tuned the psaltery"*) and which D. S. Lixačev defines as "stylistic symmetry"—pointing out the fact that "stylistic symmetry can be regarded as an instance of synonymy"[17] —also is purely redundant from the perspective of a general lingusitic message.

But if we define the text as artistic, the presumption that all the orderings in it are meaningful comes into force. Then, not one of the repetitions will emerge as accidental in relation to the structure. On these grounds, the classification of repetitions becomes a definitive element in the description of the structure of a text.

Repetition on the Phonological Level

Phonological repetition is the lowest structural level of a poetic text. For the time being, we will not examine those instances where phonological repetition represents the inevitable consequence of repetitions on higher levels (grammatical repetition, rhymes, and so on).

Phonological repetition was first noted by Osip Brik, and since that time has frequently attracted scholarly attention. Its place in poetic structure is considerable—no one doubts this now. The real question is this: what is its relation to the content structure of a text?

Obviously no sound in poetic speech has independent meaning when taken in isolation. The meaningfulness of a sound in poetry does not arise from its particular nature, but is presumed deductively. The apparatus of repetition singles out some sound in poetry (and in general in any artistic text) and does not single out the sound in everyday linguistic communication. As soon as the concept of a completely regulated text arises, the opposition between regulated and non-regulated texts[18] takes shape, and the poetic text begins to be perceived in the light of this antithesis as something fully

*The quotation is from the last (and unnumbered) psalm in the Orthodox Book of Psalms. It is not included in the Authorized King James version or other Protestant translations of the Bible.—Tr.

17 D. S. Lixačev, *Poètika drevnerusskoj literatury* (Leningrad, 1967) p. 173.

18 A text which is regulated only by the rules of the given natural language is perceived as non-regulated, while the concept of "full regulation" is always realized on a particular level. Regulation on the phonological, grammatical, rhythmical and other levels may not be maximally realized with respect to the ideal, whose norms are formed under the influence of the general cultural context and are broader than any single artistic text. In this case a given form of regulation is not noticed by the poet or the reader and no meaning is ascribed to it. Consequently the concept of total regulation, though logically confined to a certain maximum of linguistic elements, in reality is always correlated with some conventional aesthetic norm.

regulated. The possibility of finding additional meaning arises. The reader begins to notice orderings that he earlier regarded as spontaneous. But the writer is also a reader, and armed with the primal idea that sound organization has meaning, he begins to organize it according to his particular structural plan. The reader continues this work and further organizes the text in accordance with his own ideas.

When sound repetitions become an object of the poet's attention, he seeks to assign some objective meaning to them. Obviously all arguments concerning the meaning which phonemes are alleged to possess independent of words are not in the least compelling and rest upon subjective associations. However, the persistence of such attempts, from Lomonosov to Andrej Belyj, is significant and assertions regarding the emotional, chromatic or any other meaning of phonemes cannot simply be dismissed. Two processes seem to be at work here. First, a phoneme is presumed to have an independent meaning; it is elevated to the rank of a sign and, moving up in the linguistic hierarchy assumes the rank of an individual word. Second, it becomes, as it were, an "empty word," a unit whose meaningfulness is a presumption[19]—but whose actual meaning has yet to be established. Subsequently these phonemes are filled in by those meanings which the given textual or extra-textual structure creates and they become special "occasional words." The presence of such "empty words" is an intrinsic feature of the artistic text. It is precisely because phonemes lack their own meaning (lexical and grammatical) in language that they are the basic reserve in the construction of empty words, a reserve for the further semantic regulation of the text.[20]

Sound repetitions, however, possess another semantic sense which is considerably more amenable to objective analysis. Sound repetitions may establish additional bonds between words, introducing contrasts and oppositions into the semantic organization of the text which are less clearly expressed or completely absent on the level of natural language.

Let us compare two texts taken from Lermontov's poems.* They are

* In the exposition that follows some of the author's claims will seem confusing for the reader who does not know Russian. The following remarks should clear up some apparent inconsistencies. 1) *Nebo* is the ordinary word for sky; the plural form marks an elevation in style and is best rendered as "heavens." 2) The primary meaning of *tajat'* is "to melt;" there are at least two secondary meanings—"to fade away" and "to languish." Obviously "melt" will not fit all the contexts when the word is used in the Russian text. 3) The subject and verb are inverted in the last two lines of the first excerpt below; this is quite natural in Russian but would be offensive in English (Like a kiss sounds and fades/ Your youthful voice"). Nonetheless the reader must keep this inversion in mind in order to make sense of the opposition formulated in the description that follows.—Tr.

19 For a discussion of the "presumption of meaningfulness" in language see: I. I. Revzin, *Modeli jazyka* (Moscow, 1962) p. 17; and "Otmečennye frazy, algebra fragmentov, stilistika," *Lingvističeskie issledovanija po obščej i slavjanskoj tipologii*, op. cit., pp. 2-4.

20 The way a reader completes the regulation of a text is examined at length in V. A. Zareckij's Candidate dissertation "Semantika i struktura slovesnogo xudožestvennogo obraza," (1966).

convenient, not because the sound organization stands out—in that respect we could find more graphic examples—but for different reasons of interest to us here. If we understand content to mean the concrete message on the level of natural language, then in both these texts the content is identical. At the same time it is clear that they convey different artistic information. Since the construction of tropes in these texts is of a single type, the basic part of the supra-linguistic semantics arises out of phonological ordering of a poetic type.

> Kak nebesa tvoj vzor blistaet
>   Emal' ju goluboj,
> Kak poceluj zvučit i taet
>   Tvoj golos molodoj.

> [Like the heavens, your glance shines
>   Like blue enamel,
> Like a kiss your youthful voice
>   Sounds and fades away.]

> Ona poet—i zvuki tajut,
> Kak pocelui na ustax,
> Gljadit—i nebesa igrajut
> V ee božestvennyx glazax.

> [She sings—and the sounds fade away
> Like kisses on the lips,
> She gazes and the heavens play
> In her divine eyes.]

If these were not artistic texts they could be reduced to a common semantic parallel:

> Your her voice—fades like kisses,
> Your her eyes—like the sky

However the spontaneous reaction of the reader does not permit him to see a simple tautological repetition of the same message in these texts. Let us examine the sound construction of the text, disregarding all other levels of analysis (although absolute isolation of the phonological level from the prosodic or grammatical levels is sometimes difficult). The lines:

> Kak nebesa/ tvoj vzor/ blistaet
> Kak poceluj/ zvučit/ i taet

> [Like the heavens/ your glance/ shines
> Like a kiss/ sounds/ and fades away]

are clearly divided into three mutually isometric groups. If we ignore the syntactic-grammatical parallelism, the isometric parts of the lines form phonologically correlated pairs:

Kak nebesa–kak poceluj

The group *kak* ("like") forms a single anaphoric phonological segment–the basis for comparison, while *nebesa* ("heavens") and *poceluj* ("kiss") are the differentiating elements of the phonological group. In the second rhythmic group we find reverse sound repetition:

Tvoj vzor–zvučit
tvz–zvt

The third rhythmeme is phonologically opposed to the first as rhyme is to anaphora; it is opposed to the second by virtue of the fact that its repetitions are built both on vowels and consonants:

blistaet–i taet
iae–iae; tt–tt

As a result of this complex system of phonological orderings, which are absolutely random in a non-artistic text (where they would be destroyed by any semantically accurate translation, since from the viewpoint of general linguistic norms they belong to the plane of expression), semantic oppositions arise which are specific to the text at hand. *Nebesa* and *poceluj*, words from different semantic fields, become antonyms. This necessitates the creation of a special semantic construction. The concepts are described in the oppositions: "close vs. far," "warm vs. cold," "attainable vs. unattainable," "inner (intimate) vs. outer (alien)," "human vs. non-human." The semantics of the word *poceluj* ["kiss"] (in its supplementary occasional meaning) is seen to lie at the intersection of meanings of the left-hand members of the opposition, while *nebo* ("sky") lies at the intersection of the right-hand members of the opposition (therefore "enamel" besides having a particular color also takes on another feature: it is cold). On this level of semantic construction, the opposition between *vzor* ("glance") and *golos* ("voice") takes form–an utterly typical opposition in the Romantic portrait of the enigmatic man.[21]

The relation of the first rhythmemes confirms this antithesis, but the second two remove it. In an artistic construction, as opposed to a logical construction, stating and then withdrawing a proposition is not the same as not stating the proposition in the first place. *Tvoj vzor–zvučit* share a clearly designated consonantal group. The group of vowels forms an opposition: *o-o–u-i*. However the antithetical relation of the vowels (they become a basic feature of the differentiation between the lexical semantic groups of sight and hearing), while accentuating their independence, sets new bonds in relief:

goluboj–poceluj–zvučit[22] [blue–kiss–sounds]
ouo⟨j⟩–oeu⟨j⟩–ui

21 Cf. *Liš' oči pečal'no gljadeli, a golos tak divno zvučal.* . . ["Only your gaze was sad, but your voice had a wondrous ring. . ."] (A. K. Tolstoj).

22 In the above examples it would be advisable to consider the Russian *j* in the

tvoj vzor–golos–molodoj   [your glance–voice–young]
o⟨j⟩o–oo–ooo⟨j⟩

In all these bonds, one thing stands out: the group "sky" and the group "kiss" are equated. To this end they are transformed into two different but comparable spheres of one semantic field, that of sensory perception: sight (sky, glance) and sound (kiss, voice). Roughly speaking, sound parallelism equates the segments *tvoj vzor* ["your glance"] and *zvučit* ["sounds"] (actually, the reverse repetition *tvz–zvt* creates a somewhat more complex semantic relation between the meanings of these groups). The differences between sound and sight prove to be less essential than what they have in common semantically. It is no accident that the construction brings *tvoj vzor* ["your glance"] close to the group *golos-molodoj* ["voice–young"]. But in the series *goluboj–pocelui–zvučit* ["blue–kiss–sounds"], the differentiation of attributes of sound and color is removed as something extra-systemic. As a result of the rhymed endings *blistaet–i taet*, the group *nebo–poceluj* ["sky–kiss"] whose elements are differential in the first rhythmeme are now equated in their synonymic replacement *sijaet* [sic] *–taet* ["shines–fades away"], and thereby the group becomes the common semantic kernel of both lines.

The second and fourth lines supplement this structure:

Emal' ju goluboj
Tvoj golos molodoj

On the consonantal level we find the repetitions:

m–l–g–l
g–l–m–l

On the vocalic level:

o–o⟨j⟩
o⟨j⟩–o–o–o–o–o⟨j⟩

The equating of *èmal' golubaja* ["blue enamel"] and *golos molodoj* ["young voice"] in a semantic unity is combined with the cross phonetic assimilation *èmal' ju–molodoj* and *golos–goluboj* ["enamel–young" and "blue–voice"]. We shold note that all these additional orderings also activate additional differentiations which are superimposed on them. Such is the postposition of the adjective in the first and second case. The example in question allows us to underscore yet another point: any ordering is artistically active if it is not carried to its conclusion, but leaves a reserve of non-ordered

same organizational series as the vowel phonemes. We are all the more justified in doing this since the poet's phonetic consciousness was strongly influenced by graphics. Cf., for example, the influence of graphics on the phonological consciousness of Lermontov in the lines: *Ja bez uma ot trojstvennyx sozvučij i vlažnyx rifm, kak, naprimer, na "ju."* ["I'm crazy about treble assonances and moist rhymes, like those based on *ju* . ."]. *Ju* and *u* do not blend together for Lermontov.

elements. Thus in the vocalism of the two analyzed lines the following phonemes (in brackets) are unorganized from the perspective of sound repetition:

$$[e\text{-}a\text{-}ju] -o-[u] -o\langle j\rangle$$
$$o\langle j\rangle -o-o-o-o-o-\langle j\rangle$$

Only the unconditional dominance of the phoneme *o* in the second line makes the first ordered in relation to it.

Thus the phonological structure which is part of the plane of expression in natural language passes into the structure of content in poetry, forming semantic positions inseparable from the given text.

The phrases *zvučit i taet* and *zvuki tajut* ["sounds and fades away" and "sounds melt away"] are semantically and phonologically so similar that it would seem difficult to detect any perceptible semantic difference between them. If we were not dealing with verse, this would indeed be the case. But in a poetic text seemingly insignificant sound distinctions alter the fabric of semantic linking. The vocalic group in the words *zvučit* and *taet* consists of *ui* and *ae*. These groups of sounds are unique. On the one hand, what we have here are *different* phonemes. Not one phoneme of the first vocalic group is repeated in the second. On the other hand a sort of parallelism is established. We can formulate the combination: "back or central vowel + front vowel." It is the distinctive features of position [front/central/back] which are activated, not only because this regularity is established, but also because a sort of deautomatizing variance may be observed within its framework. In the first case, the extreme vowels are taken (front and back) but in the second case intermediate vowels. This also establishes the independence of the words *zvučit* and *taet*, their semantic "separation" and the parallelism of their meanings which outside the context of the poem belong to a series different in principle. The syntactical equation (the conjunction "and") of these opposing meanings (sounds and fades away) creates a new montage-like meaning.

Zvuki tajut (taj ut) gives us another construction: *u-i-a-u*. A phonological ring is created—not the equation of two independent systems, but a single structure. (The grammatical forms are also constructed in a parallel fashion: in the first case we have two homogeneous verb forms, while the second example is a unified construction based on grammatical agreement.)

Let us construct a scheme of the vocalism of this quatrain (singling out the stressed phonemes):

```
a o u a
- u - a
i - a a
- e - a
```

The first two lines have a common, distinctly binary organization— they are built around two phoneme centers: *a* and *u*. Each of these is lexically colored, borrowing its semantics from the words *ona* ["she"] and *zvuki* ["sounds"]. Moreover there is a group of words which synthesize both sound themes: *tajut (ta j ut)* ["melt away"], *na ustax* ["on the lips"]; the coincidence of *u* transforms *zvuki* and *pocelui* ["sounds" and "kisses"] into occasional synonyms.

The *a-u* group creates a chain of meanings connecting *eë* ("her") with the chain of words whose common semantic feature is passion: *poët, pocelui, ustax* ["sings," "kisses," "lips"]. Under the impact of this series *taet* ["melts away"] also undergoes a certain semantic shift.

Compare Puškin's lines:

> I, polnyj strastnym ožidan'em,
> On taet serdcem i gorit.
> Vostorgi bystrye vostorgami smenjalis',
> Zelan' ja gasli vdrug i snova razgoralis';
> Ja tajal...
>
> [And filled with ardent expectation,
> His heart languishes, he is on fire.
> Raptures were quickly succeeded by raptures,
> Desires were extinguished suddenly and flared up anew;
> I languished...]

The second half of the quatrain is built on the combination *ai/ae*. It forms a chain of words with another meaning: *nebesa, božestvennyj* ["heavens," "divine"]. *Gljadit* ["she gazes"] in combination with *nebesa* comes to signify an upward movement, merging with a higher world, and begins to be perceived as an occasional antonym for the word "sings" with its passionate connotations. Antonymic relations arise between "lips" and "eyes" (the archaic coloring of the first and the oppositional neutral coloring of the second would appear not to be meaningful in Lermontov's text due to the absence of any systematic use of Slavonicisms). So a sort of dual image is created consisting of earthly and heavenly charm.

There can be no doubt that such features as the abundance of hiatuses in the poem, which create a parallel sound effect, and the fact that the ordering of consonants is less significant than the ordering of vowels, have an indisputable impact on the semantic structure of the text.

We saw from the start that the juxtaposed texts were very close semantically—an inevitable consequence of their common lexical composition. But even if we ignore the differences in their rhythmic systems, the various convergences which arise on the phonemic level in each poem create a unique fabric of meanings.

Rhythmic Repetitions

Modern studies of rhythm and meter date back to the work of Andrej Belyj; since his time these phenomena have undergone considerable study.

In these drafts from the first chapter of *Evgenyj Onegin* the segments *kak glupo, pritvorstvom* and *smirjat' i* ["how stupid," "by pretense," "humble and"] can be substituted for each other. In the given instance, of course, we are speaking of a semantic constant within whose boundaries the selected elements vary, although we should note that it would be difficult to imagine these segments as in any way equivalent outside the given rhythmic construction.

When we compare the rough drafts of a poet and a prose writer we find comfirmation of the profound difference in their respective ways or choosing the required material. The prosaist has two options: he can either clarify an idea by making a choice within the limits of general linguistic synonymity or he can change the thought. The poet finds himself in another situation: first, the clear articulation of a textual segment makes it more independent in relation to the whole. Fundamentally altering the meaning of a segment as a whole can be seen as identical to the process of expressing a thought more precisely in a non-poetic text by replacing a word with its synonym:

> Ljubvi nas ne priroda učit,
> A pervyj pakostnyj roman. . .

> Ljubvi nas ne priroda učit,
> A Stal' ili Šatobrian. . .

> [It isn't nature that teaches us love,
> But the first dirty novel. . .]

> [It isn't nature that teaches us love,
> But de Staël or Chateaubriand. . .]

Taken separately, the second pair of lines produces a distinct change in content, but within the structure of the ninth stanza of the first chapter of *Evgenij Onegin,* this is perceived only as a more precise expression. The *flexibility of language* (h_2) to use Academician Kolmogorov's terminology *grows markedly when the text is broken up into rhythmically equivalent segments.* Apparently this is one of the reserves which compensates for the information expended on the limitations of a poetic text.

The rhythmic division of a text into isometric segments creates an entire hierarchy of supra-linguistic equivalences. One line is correlated with another line, one strophe with another strophe, one chapter with another chapter of a text. This repetition of rhythmic segments creates that presumption of mutual equivalence among *all* segments of the text on their respective levels which constitutes the basis for perceiving the text as poetic.

Equivalence, however, is not identity. The fact that segments which are semantically different in a non-poetic text are equivalent in a poetic text, on the one hand, compels us to construct common (neutral) archesemes for them, and, on the other hand, it transforms their differences into a system of relevant oppositions.

Thus in the first approximation the impression is created that the semantics of a word in a line recedes in the background: acoustical, rhythmic and other repetitions come to the fore. We can cite clear examples of how the poet changes words while maintaining the phonological or rhythmic construction. I will limit myself to one.

In the rough drafts of Puškin's poem "Two feelings are wonderfully close to us..." we find the following line in the second stanza: *Samostojan'e čeloveka* ["Man's independence"]. It is built around an unusual metrical variety of the Russian iambic tetrameter:⏑⏑ ⏑⏑⏑⏑. This variety (sixth) is comparatively rare. According to Kiril Taranovskij, in the lyrics of the 1828–1829 period, it comprises 9.1% of all four foot iambs, and in the period from 1830 to 1833–8.1%[28] The poem we are dealing with was written in 1830. The entire second stanza was discarded, including the line *samostojan'e čeloveka*. But in the new variant of the stanza we find: *Život-vorjaščaja svjatynja* ["Life-giving sacred relic"] with the same rhythmic scheme.

This cannot be a chance occurrence: two lines absolutely different from a lexico-semantic point of view proved to be equivalent in Puškin's consciousness due to the common metric figure.

But we need only go beyond the limits of this one line to see that we are dealing, not with another idea, but with a variant of the same idea—the result of the increased flexibility of the language. We will quote the first stanza and two variants of the second to demonstrate this more clearly:

Stanza I

Dva čuvstva divno blizki nam—
V nix obretaet serdce pišču—
Ljubov' k rodnomu pepelišču,
Ljubov' k otečeskim grobam.

[Two feelings are wonderfully close to us—
In them the heart finds nourishment—
Love for our hearth and home,
Love for our father's graves.]

First Variant of Stanza II

Na nix osnovano ot veka
Načalo   vsego
Samostojan'e čeloveka
I sčast'e.

[On them is founded from the past
The beginning   of all
Man's independence
And happiness.]

28 Kirill Taranovsky, *Ruski dvodelni ritmovi*, I, II (Beograd, 1953), appendix.

Second	Životvorjaščaja svjatynja!
Variant	Zemlja byla(b) bez nix mertva
of	Kak pustynja
Stanza II	I kak altar' bez božestva.

> [Life-giving sacred relic!
> Without them, the earth would be dead
> Like   a wasteland
> And like an altar without a deity.]

Thus it only seems that semantics is relegated to the background. The meaning of the separate word retreats before the construction. But the construction creates a secondary meaning, bringing out at times unexpected relevant elements of secondary meaning in that separate word.

Repetition and Meaning

On the lowest level one may distinguish positional (rhythmic) and euphonic (sound) equivalences in a line. The intersection of these two classes of equivalences is defined as rhyme. But we have already said that all types of secondary equivalences lead to the formation of supplementary semantic units in a text. The phenomenon of structure in a line always, in the final analysis, turns out to be the phenomenon of meaning. This is particularly clear with regard to rhyme.

The school of phonetic verse study (*Ohrphilologie*) defined rhyme as sound repetition: rhyme is the coincidence of the stressed vowel and the posttonic part of the word. Later there were attempts to broaden the definition of rhyme, taking into consideration twentieth century poetry, the possible coincidence of pretonic sounds, consonantism, and so on. In his book *Rhyme, Its History and Theory,* V. M. Žirmunskij first pointed out rhyme's role in the rhythmic design of poetry: "Any sound repetition which has an organizing function in the metrical composition of a poem should be included in the concept of rhyme."[29] Žirmunskij's observations were clearly correct and his definition has been generally accepted. Thus Tomaševskij characterizes rhyme in the following way:

> Rhyme is the consonance of two words in a given place in the rhythmic construction of a poem. In Russian verse (and not only in Russian) rhyme must occur at the end of a line. It is this end-line consonance creating a bond between two lines that we call rhyme. Consequently rhyme has two properties: the first is rhythmic organization, because rhyme marks the ends of lines, the second is consonance.[30]

Similar definitions are given by G. Šengeli, L. I. Timofeev, And V. E.

29 V. Žirmunskij, *Rifma, ee istorija i teorija* (Petrograd, 1923) p. 9.
30 B. V. Tomaševskij, *Stilistika i stixosloženie* (Leningrad, 1959) p. 406.

Xolševnikov [31] who disputes Tomaševskij's claims that rhymes must be positioned at the end of a line, but otherwise essentially concurs with his definition.

Thus rhyme is described as phonetic repetition which plays a rhythmic role. This makes rhyme of particular interest in making general observations on the nature of rhythmic repetitions in a poetic text. We are well aware that poetic speech has a different sound than prosaic or colloquial speech. It is melodious and lends itself to declamation. The presence of special intonational systems exclusive to poetry permits us to speak of the melodics of poetic speech. As a result, people very often get the impression that there are two *independent* elements of poetry: semantic and melodic. The first is often identified with the rational, the second with the emotional principle. And while some authors maintain that the semantic and melodic aspects of poetry are correlated, many are convinced that these are separate or even opposed to each other.

Even today one can find critics reproaching certain poets for their preoccupation with thoughtless melodiousness, intricate sound play that has no meaning and the like. Their misgivings, however, are hardly justified.

No matter how we attempt to separate sound from content, whether to exalt or denounce the author suspected of isolating the sound of poetry from its meaning—we are faced with a hopeless task. In an art form which uses language as its material (verbal art), sound cannot be separated from meaning. The musical sound of poetic speech is *also a means of transmitting information,* that is, transmitting content, and in this sense it cannot be set in opposition to the other means of transmitting information which are characteristic of language as a semiotic system. This means—"musicality"— arises only when there is a high degree of correlation in a verbal structure, that is to say in poetry, and should not be confused with elements of musicality in the system of natural language, such as intonation. Below, we will attempt to show the degree to which the sonority, the "musicality," of rhyme depends on the amount of information it contains, on its semantic load. This will also shed some light on the functional nature of rhyme in general.

Along with other principles of classification in prosody, we find a distinction being made between rich and poor rhymes. Rich rhymes have a large number of repeating sounds and poor rhymes few repeating sounds: it is assumed that rich rhymes are sonorous, while poor rhymes sound worse as the number of coinciding sounds decreases, until they approach the status of non-rhymes. If we interpret the concepts in this way, the musicality or sonority of a rhyme is made to depend on phonetic rather than semantic features of poetic speech. This conclusion seems so obvious that it is usually

31 See G. Šengeli, *Texnika stixa* (Moscow, 1960) pp. 241-242; L. I. Timofeev, *Osnovy teorii literatury* (Moscow, 1959) p. 250; V. E. Xolševnikov, *Osnovy stixovedenija. Russkoe stixosloženie,* (Leningrad, 1962) p. 125.

taken for granted. But one has only to examine the problem more closely to become convinced of the falseness of such a conclusion.

Let us take two pairs of phonetically identical rhymes; one homonymic and the other tautological. It will be readily apparent that the sonority or musicality of the rhyme will be completely different in each case. The first example has been devised to graphically demonstrate this principle; the second is taken from Valerij Brjusov's *Experiments:*

1
Ty belyx lebedej kormila,
A posle ty gusej kormila.

[You fed white swans,
But afterwards you *fed* geese.j

2
Ty belyx lebedej kormila. . .
. . . Ja rjadom plyl—sošlis' kormila.

[You fed white swans. . .
. . . I sailed alongside—our *helms* met.]

In both cases the rhyme is phonetically and rhythmically identical, but it sounds different. The tautological rhyme which repeats both the sound and the meaning of the rhyming word has a poor sound. Phonic coincidence combined with semantic difference produced a rich sound. If we try a few more experiments, transforming homonymic rhymes into tautological rhymes, we will be convinced that this operation, which does not affect either the phonetic or rhythmic boundaries of the line, consistently deadens the sound of the rhyme:

More ždet napast'—
Sžeč' grozit sinica,
A na Rus napast'
Londonskaja ptica.

[The sea awaits *disaster*—
The tomtit threatens to set it on fire*
And the London bird
To *attack* Rus'.]
(Vjazemskij)

Vse ozirajas' sleva, sprava,
Na cypkax vystupaet trus,
Kak budto pod nogami lava
Il' zemlju vzbudoražil trus.

* The phrase comes from a Russian proverb: *Poxvaljalas' sinica more spalit'* (literally, "The tomtit boasted that he would burn up the sea"). The expression "The mouse that roared" conveys the general idea.—Tr.

> [Looking to the left and right
> The *coward* tiptoes forward,
> As though there were lava beneath his feet
> Or a *quake* shook the earth.]
>   (Vjazemskij)

> Lyseet ximik Kablukov—
> Proxodit v topot kablukov.

> [The chemist *Kablukov* is balding—
> He passes by to the patter of *heels.*]
>   (Andrej Belyj)

In any of these examples (*napast* ["disaster—attack"], *trus* ["coward—earth-quake"], *Kablukov* ["a proper name—heels"]) one has only to replace the homonyms with tautological repetitions, and the sonority of the rhyme vanishes. The sonority of rhyming words and the physical sound inherent to words in the language are completely different things. The same complex of physical sounds in speech, realizing the same phonemes of the language, can sound very rich or extremely poor in rhyme:
The following example is telling in this respect:

> Bog pomošč' vam, grafu von Bulju!
> Knjaz' sejal: prišlos' vam požat'!
> Byt' možet, i drugu Džon Bulju
> Pridetsja plečami požat'.

> [God help you, Count von Bülow!
> The prince sowed: you had to reap!
> Perhaps friend John Bull
> Will also have to shrug his shoulders.]
>   (Vjazemskij)

Let us conduct two experiments. First, we will change the word "von" in the first line to "John." The rhyme *Bulju–Bulju* undergoes neither phonetic nor rhythmic changes. But the degree of sonority undergoes a decisive change. Our second experiment is even more interesting. We will not change a word of the text, but will only suppose that it is read to two listeners. One knows that von Bülow is an Austrian diplomat of the nineteenth century, that the prince is Bismarck and John Bull—a common noun denoting Englishmen. The second is not aware of this and imagines that the first and third lines refer to a person unknown to him, say, a Count John von Bülow. The sonority of the text for each listener will be different. All this shows that the very concept of sonority is not absolute and is not only physical (or physical—rhythmic), but also relative and functional in nature. It is determined by the information contained in the rhyme, by its meaning. The first listener perceives the rhyme *Bulju–Bulju* as homonymic, the second as tautological. For the first it is rich, for the second poor.

In all the above examples, the rhymes are phonetically absolutely identical and occur in the same rhythmic position. But some seem sonorous, resonant and musical, while others do not produce this impression. What is different in these apparently coinciding rhymes? Semantics. When the rhyme sounds rich, we are dealing with homonyms; words whose sound composition coincides but whose *meaning differs*. In poor sounding tautological rhymes not only the phonic form, but also the semantic content is repeated.

From the above we can draw the following two conclusions: first, the musicality of rhyme is produced not only by phonetics, but also by the semantics of words; second, we can formulate a very approximate definition of rhyme as the phonic coincidence of words or their parts in a position that is marked relative to the rhythmic unit whose meanings do not coincide. This definition also embraces tautological rhyme since poetic speech, as opposed to colloquial speech, knows no absolute semantic repetition; the same lexical or semantic unit occupies a new structural position when it is repeated and consequently acquires new meaning. As we will see, the fact that we were obliged to use artificial examples to demonstrate full semantic repetition is no accident: full semantic repetition in an artistic text is impossible.

We have seen that phonic coincidence only accentuates semantic difference. The coinciding part of similar but different semantic units in a given instance becomes "sufficient grounds" for comparison: the common denominator is singled out thus stressing the differences of phenomena designated by rhyming words.

The mechanism by which rhyme works can be divided into the following processes. First, rhyme is repetition. Scholars have repeatedly noted that rhyme returns the reader to the preceding text. It shold be emphasized that this "return" animates not only the consonance, but also the meaning of the first of the rhymed words in the reader's consciousness. Something profoundly different from the usual linguistic process of information transmission occurs here: instead of a temporally consecutive chain of signals serving to convey certain information, we find a complex signal, spatial in nature, a return to that which has already been perceived. Series of verbal signals and individual words (in this case rhymes) which have already been perceived according to the general laws of linguistic meaning take on new meaning when they are perceived a second time (here the perception is not linear, as in speech, but structural and artistic).

The second elment of the semantic perception of rhyme is the comparison of word and its rhyming word, the emergence of a correlating pair. Two words which, as linguistic phenomena, have no connections (grammatical or semantic) are joined within poetry into a single constructive pair.

Tvoj očerk strastnyj, očerk dymnyj
Skvoz' sumrak loži plyl ko mne,
I tenor pel na scene gimny
Bezumnym skripkam i vesne. . .

[Your passionate features, misty features
Floated toward me through the twilight of the Loge,
And the tenor on the stage sang hymns
To mad violins and spring. . .]

(Aleksandr Blok)

If we take the text as ordinary information, ignoring its poetic structure, the concepts "misty" and "hymns" [*dymnyj–gimny*] are so different that they cannot be correlated. The grammatical and syntactic structure of the text, similarly, provides no basis for their comparison. But when we look at the text as a poem, we discover that *dymnyj* and *gimny* are related by the double concept "rhyme." This duality is such that it includes both the identification and opposition of the concepts that comprise it. Identification becomes the condition of opposition. Rhyme fits into a formula that is extraoridinarily important to art in general: "x, and simultaneously not x."

In this case the comparison is primarily formal, and the opposition primarily semantic. The identification belongs to the plane of expression (on the phonetic level), and opposition to the plane of content. When it is placed in a rhyming position, *dymnyj* requires consonance, just as a syntactic relation (agreement, for example) requires a certain inflectional ending. Here sound coincidence becomes a point of departure for semantic opposition.

But it would be an oversimplification to say that rhyme is merely phonic coincidence with semantic non-coincidence. Even with respect to sound, rhyme, as a rule, represents only a partial coincidence. We identify words which sound different, but have common phonological elements, ignoring the difference in order to establish likeness. Then we use the established likeness as a basis for opposition.

But the semantic aspect of rhyming words is a more complex issue, since all of our experience in aesthetic communication teaches us that certain forms of expression reveal certain elements of content. The presence of a bond between rhyming words on the plane of expression obliges us to assume the presence of certain bonds on the plane of content which bring the semantics of the two words together. In addition, as we will atempt to show further on, while in the language a word is an indivisible unit of lexical content, in poetry a phoneme becomes not only an element of semantic distinction, but also a carrier of lexical meaning. Sounds have meaning. For this very reason phonic (phonological) convergence becomes the convergence of concepts.

Thus one might say that the process of comparison and opposition, whose various aspects are manifested with varying degrees of clarity in the phonic and semantic facets of rhyme, constitutes the essence of rhyme as such. It is in the nature of rhyme to bring differences together and to reveal the differences in likeness. Rhyme is dialectic by nature.

In this sense it is by no means coincidental that a culture of rhyme arose precisely at the moment when a sense of the complex interweaving of concepts as an expression of the complexity of life and the consciousness of men ripened within the framework of the medieval awareness of scholastic dialectics. Žirmunskij made the interesting observation that early Anglo-Saxon rhyme is related to the effort to compare and contrast concepts earlier seen as simply different: "Above all, rhyme appears in certain consistent stylistic formulas of the alliterative epos. This applies to so-called 'paired formulas,' which unite two similar concepts (synonymous or contrasting) in a parallel grammatical form by means of the conjuction 'and'."32

It is no accident that rhyme became an element of artistic structure in Russia during the period of "word-weaving," in the intensive style of Muscovite literature in the fifteenth century that bore the imprint of medieval scholastic dialectics.

At the same time we should note that the principle of rhyme construction differs considerably in medieval and contemporary art. This is explained by the specifics in form of medieval and persent-day artistic consciousness. While contemporary art begins with the premise that originality, uniqueness and individuality are virtues in a work of art, medieval aesthetics considered everything individual as sinful and a manifestation of pride, and demanded that the artist be faithful to age-old "God-inspired" models. Skillful repetition of the intricate conventions of artistic ritual, rather than inventivenss, was required of the artist. This aesthetic had its own social and ideological foundation, but we are concerned with only one aspect of the question here.

The aesthetic thought of certain epochs (which had special meaning in each epoch, each philosophical and artistic system) allowed for an aesthetics of identity, where the precise reproduction of a work already created, rather than the creation of something new, was considered "beautiful." This kind of aesthetic thought was based on the following epistomological idea (with respect to the art of the Middle Ages): we cannot perceive the truth by analyzing separate individual phenomena—individual phenomena stem from certain true, general categories which are given beforehand. Cognition proceeds throught equating these individual phenomena with general categories which are conceived of as primary. The act of cognition does not consist in the revelation of the individual or the specific, but in the process of abstraction from the particular, raising it to the general, and in the end, to the universal.

32 Žirmunskij, *Rifma*. . . op. cit., p. 228.

This frame of thought determined the specific nature of rhyme as well. The abundance of inflectional "grammatical" rhymes is striking. From the viewpoint of poetic notions current in modern art this is bad rhyme. The lazy reader attributes the plethora of grammatical rhymes in the Middle Ages to poor poetic technique. But our attention should probably be concentrated elsewhere. The choice of a series of words with identical inflections was perceived as the inclusion of each word in a general category (a participle of a certain class, a substantive denoting an "agent" and so on), that is, it activated both lexical and grammatical meaning. The lexical meaning conveyed semantic variety, while the suffixes placed the rhyming words in a single semantic series. Meaning was generalized. The word was saturated with supplementary meanings and the rhyme was perceived as rich.

The contemporary perception of rhyme is constructed differently. First the common features of the elements classed as "rhyming words" are established, and then the meanings are differentiated. Common elements become the basis for comparison, and difference becomes a "differential" distinctive feature. In those cases where both the phonological and morphological aspects of the coinciding parts of rhyming words are identical, the semantic load shifts to the root of the word, and repetition is excluded from the process of semantic differentiation. The general semantic load decreases, and as a result, the rhyme sounds impoverished (cf. *krasoj–dušoj* ["beauty–soul"] in A. K. Tolstoj's ballad *Vasilij Šibanov*). Particularly curious is the fact that the same structure which, in the light of certain epistemological principles and a certain aesthetic model, guarantees the rich sonority of rhyme, turns out to be impoverished in another system of artistic cognition. Once again this confirms the falseness of the notion that the history of rhyme is a long process of technically perfecting some "artistic device," with the same poetic content given once and for all.

At the same time the common function of rhyme in the art of different epochs is also readily apparent: rhyme reveals many aspects of words that are semantically neutral in general linguistic usage and makes them semantically distinctive features, loading them with information, with meanings. This explains the high semantic concentration of rhyming words, a phenomenon long ago noted in prosodic studies.

As seen from the preceding discussion, the more general aesthetic propensity for everything that is structurally meaningful in a text to be semanticized is most clearly evidenced in repetitions. Here we can distinguish two types: the repetition of elements which are semantically heterogeneous on the level of natural language (elements which belong to the plane of expression are repeated), and the repetition of semantically homogeneous elements (synonyms; an extreme case would be the repetition of the same word). We have already spoken in detail of the first type. The second also warrants our attention.

Strictly speaking, total, unconditional repetition is impossible in poetry.

The repetition of a word in a text, as a rule, does not mean the mechanical repetition of a concept. Most often it points to a more complex, albeit unified, semantic content.

The reader accustomed to the graphic perception of a text sees the repeated outlines of a word on paper and assumes that he is looking at the mere duplication of a concept. In fact he is usually dealing with another, more complex concept, that is related to the given word, but whose complication is by no means quantitative.

> Vy slyšite: groxočet baraban
> Soldat, proščajsja s nej, proščajsja s nej,
> Uxodit vzvod v tuman, tuman, tuman,
> A prošloe jasnej, jasnej, jasnej. . .

> [You hear the drumbeat rolling,
> Soldier, bid her farewell, bid her farewell,
> The platoon is leaving in the mist, the mist, the mist,
> And the past grows clearer, clearer, clearer.]
>   (Bulat Okudžava)

The second line is not an invitation to bid farewell twice.[33] Depending on the intonation, it may mean "Soldier, hurry to bid farewell, the platoon is already leaving." Or: "Soldier, bid her farewell, farewell for ever, for you'll never see her again." Or: "Soldier, bid her farewell, your one and only." But it could never mean, "Soldier, bid her farewell, bid her farewell again." Thus the duplication of the word does not imply the automatic duplication of the concept, but rather another new, complication of its content. "The platoon is leaving in the mist, the mist, the mist" can be deciphered as: "The platoon is leaving in the mist, going farther and farther, it is disappearing from view." It can also be deciphered in other ways, but can never have a purely quantitative meaning: "the platoon is leaving in one mist, then in another, then in a third." In the same way the last line can be interpreted to mean: "And the past is becoming more and more understandable, and now it is blindingly clear," and so on. But the poet did not choose any one of our interpretations precisely because his means of expression includes all of these nuances. It attains them since the more exact the repetition, the greater the role of intonation in semantic differentiation, until it becomes the only distinctive feature in a chain of repeating words.

But the repetition of words has yet another structural function. Let us recall a line from the poem by Blok cited earlier:

> Tvoj očerk strastnyj, očerk dymnyj. . .

> [Your passionate features, misty features. . .]

---

33 We will not discuss the degree of variety which the movement of the melody imparts to these lines. Here we are concerned with the informational essence of repetition in poetry.

"Passionate features" and "misty features" are two independent phraseological combinations, one based on direct, the other on figurative usage.
The word combinations "passionate features" and "misty features" create
two semantic wholes which are more complex than the mechanical sum of
the concepts "features" + "passionate" and "features" + "misty." But the
repetition of the word destroys the independence of these two word combinations, binding them into one, even more complex semantic whole. The
word "features," repeated twice, becomes a common member of these two
word combinations, and such disparate, unconjoinable words as "misty"
and "passionate" prove to be a single contrasting pair, forming a higher
semantic unity which cannot be broken down into the semantic meanings
of its verbal components.

Let us examine Leonid Martynov's poem "O, My Land!" from the
viewpoint of the function of repetition:

> O zemlja moja!
> S odnoj storony,
> Spjat polja moej rodnoj storony,
> A prismotriš'sja s drugoj storony—
> Tol'ko dremljut, bespokojstva polny.
>
> Bespokojstvo—
> Èto svojstvo vesny.
> Bespokoit'sja vsegda my dolžny,
> Ibo spesi my smešnoj lišeny
> Čto zadači do odnoj rešeny.
>
> I toržestvenny,
> S odnoj storony,
> Očertanija sedoj stariny,
> I, estestvenno, s drugoj storony,
> Byt' ne sleduet slugoj stariny.
>
> No ved' skoro
> I ustrojstvo luny
> My rassmotrim i s drugoj storony.
> Videt' žizn' s ee ljuboj storony
> Ne zazorno ni s kakoj storony.
>
> [O, my land!
> On the one *hand*
> The fields of my native *land* sleep,
> But if you look closely, from another *vantage point*,
> They only dream, full of restlessness.
>
> Restlessness
> Is a property of spring.
> We must always be restless,
> For we are not so foolishly arrogant
> To believe that every last one of our problems is solved.

And the outlines of hoary antiquity
On the one *hand*
Are sacred,
And naturally, on the other *hand*
One should not be a slave to the past.

Only timid
Minds are distressed
By the other *side* of calm,
They prefer a property of the moon—
To be accessible from only one *side*.

But soon, after all,
We'll also look at the layout of the moon
From the other *side*.
To see life from any of its *angles*
Is not shameful from any point of *view.*]

The whole rhyme scheme of this poem is built on the frequent repetition of the word *storona* [denoted in italics in the English text—Tr.]. The repetition is tautological (although individual semantic "bundles" of meanings here are so far removed from one another that the words expressing them are perceived as homonyms).

In the first stanza alone, the word *storona* occurs three times, in the same case, but each time it is repeated, the word in essence carries a different syntactic and semantic load. This is particularly evident if we compare the first and third occurrences (*s odnoj storony* and *s drugoj storony* ["on the one hand" and "on the other hand, from the other vantage point"]) with the second where *storona* (with the epithet "native") is synonymous to the concept of "motherland." Closer examination reveals, however, that the semantics of this word is not identical in the first and third instances either: the introductory word group "on the one hand" is not equivalent in meaning to the verbial modifier of the place of action *prismotriš'sja s drugoj storony* ["if you look closely from another vantage point"]. In the latter instance *storona* is a concrete concept (a point from which one should look closely); in the former case we are dealing with a connecting phrase characteristic of bureaucratic speech, implying that only to an unattentive, unimaginative bureaucrat would his native fields appear to be sleeping, whereas an observant person sees the full latent force of the land, despite its quiescence.

The second stanza introduces the theme of restlessness as the most vital feature of a living, developing world and the most active, dialectical perspective which corresponds to it; it is built on other repetitions (*bespokojstvo—bespokoitsja* ["restlessness, uneasiness—to worry, be uneasy"]). Only by allusion does this stanza return the reader to the semantic group *storona* already discussed, singling out the word *odna* ["one"] from the phrase "on the one hand," etc., which we have already encountered and which will continue to recur. Here we find it in the phrase "that every last one of our problems is resolved." The function of this device is to keep the reader intuitively aware of the theme we are concerned with.34

In the third stanza "on the one hand" and "on the other hand" are syntactically synonymous, but they do not evoke the same meaning. The latter has a touch of irony and sounds like a parody, a paraphrase of the first. The contrast between the two phrases is also determined by the fact that both are part of an antithesis: "sacred, on the one hand" vs. "naturally, on the other hand." By virtue of their position in the natural language "sacred" and "naturally" are not antithetic since they occupy syntactically incomparable positions. The contextual meaning of the adverb *estestvenno* is simply "of course."

But poetic opposition knows another logic: "on the one hand—on the other hand" is perceived as a neutralized archeseme which emphasizes the contrasting, differential semantic pair *toržestvenny—estestvenno*. In this case a new meaning is disclosed in the adverb *estestvenno*—simplicity, as the antithesis of sacredness or solemnity, which in turn divides the entire stanza into two antithetical halves. This, in the final analysis, singles out the difference in the previously equated "on the one hand—on the other hand." Here the difference is intonational: it is readily apparent that each of the two halves will be read in a different declamatory key. One must convey information about bureaucratic, deadly pomposity, the other about natural life.

In the fourth stanza the same phrase takes on a clearly new meaning. The bureaucratic *s odnoj storony—s drugoj storony* is set in opposition to *oborotnaja storona tišiny* ["the other side of calm"]—the life forces that are still slumbering, but already beginning to awaken and trouble timid minds. They oppose the affirmation of the revolutionary dynamics of the life "of the fields of our native land," preferring the idea of onesidedness and immobility as laws of nature:

> Prijatnee im svojstvo luny—
> Byt' dostupnym liš' s odnoj storony.
>
> [They prefer a property of the moon—
> To be accessible from only one side.]

Because of the intense development of the theme under discussion, "the other side" and "from one side" are not randomly chosen words with little meaning of their own. They are the basis of the antithesis between the dynamics of society and the immobility of "eternal" nature, the many-sidedness of life and the dogmatism of timid minds.

But the next and final structure removes this antithesis as well. The fifth stanza affirms a new idea. There is no immobility in nature: nature

34 Simultaneously a new repeating semantic field, "one (the only one)," is created. It is opposed to the concept "many," "any," and clearly tinged with irony; the author reduces all indisputable dogma to the viewpoint of "one" person.

too submits to the revolutionary dynamics of human life. Parallelism is established between the conviction that even the moon will be examined "from the other side" (at the time it had not been!) and the appeal to "see life from any of its angles." As a result the concluding bureaucratic phrase "from any point of view" sounds like a merciless gibe—the antithesis of the solemn bureaucratic "on the one hand" at the poem's beginning. Thus the basic artistic idea of the poem is revealed: the image of life with all its facets, requiring that an artist take a multifaceted approach.

The absence of total, absolute semantic repetition in art is particularly noticeable when we examine homonymic rhymes. Such rhymes occur frequently in poetry which strives to reveal the inner diversity of externally indistinguishable phenomena. A graphic example is the *ghazal,* a medieval poetic genre of the Middle East, with its *redif* (words repeated in the rhymes). Although the role of the *redif* differs in the poetry of Hafiz and the fifteenth century scholastic poets, it always has a similar aesthetic function: it reveals the diverse aspects of one concept. The fifteenth century Central Asian poet Katibi wrote his moralistic narrative poem *Dah bab* using exclusively *tedžnisy*—homonymic—rhymes. Concerning the homonymic rhymes of Maulana Muhammad Ali of Shiraz (fifteenth centry), E. E. Bertel's writes, "The homonyms are extraordinary subtle: *humor* (a hangover)— *hummor* (bring the jug); *sharob* (wine)—*shar r'ob* (evil-water)." The same author testifies that the poet Atai "frequently uses homonymic rhymes, which make his verse particularly witty."[35]

In essence the same is true of the form of repetition favored by the folk song—the refrain. Coming after different couplets, and thereby entering into different contexts, it continually takes on new semantic and emotional connotations. The repetition of the words only serves to emphasize them. True, this sort of treatment is comparatively recent. In ancient songs, which are not rhymed, we find a truly unconditional repetition of the refrain, but this is engendered by a specific aesthetics, the aesthetics of identity. Contemporary songs, whether folk, classical or literary, invariably lend the refrain an endless number of nuances. In Robert Burns' ballad "Findlay," for example, the constantly repeated " 'Indeed will I,' quo' Findlay" sounds different each time. The same is true of the refrain "Ha, ha, the wooing o't" in the ballad "Duncan Grey" (translated by S. Ja. Maršak); it invariably takes on new semantic shadings.

It would be just as simple to prove the same point using examples of anaphora,[36] the repetition of a word or words at the beginning of the line, or the various types of intonational unity inherent to poetic and rhetorical texts. Intonational parallelism of lines and periods here becomes that "grounds for comparison" which discloses semantic opposition or

35 E. E. Bertel's, *Navoi. Opyt tvorčeskoj biografii* (Moscow—Leningrad, 1948) pp. 37, 58.
36 For a discussion of anaphora see M. Dluska, "Anafora," *Poetics, Poetyka, Poètika,* II.

distinction. Thus we see it is the correlation and organic connection between parts and not their mechanical repetition that constitutes a sufficiently general law for the structure of a poetic text. Therefore no one part of a poetic text can be understood without defining its function. By itself it does not exist: all of its properties and specific features emerge in its correlation (comparison and opposition) with other parts and with the text as a whole. This act of correlation is dialectically complex: one and the same process of juxtaposing parts of an artistic text, as a rule, both bring meanings together (comparison) and sets them apart (opposition). Bringing concepts together singles out their differences; setting them apart reveals their similarity. Therefore by picking out some repetition, we are still saying nothing about the text. Identical (repeating) elements are functionally not identical if they occupy different structural positions. Furthermore, since it is identical elements which reveal the structural difference between parts of a poetic text, making that difference more conspicuous, it is all the more certain that an increased number of repetitions leads to greater diversity, not uniformity. Ther greater the likeness, the greater the difference. The repetition of identical parts reveals the structure.

Thus repetitions of various types represent a semantic fabric of great complexity which is superimposed on the fabric of language, thereby creating a special concentration of thought that is found only in poetry. There can accordingly be no greater mistake than to assume, as is so often the case, that while verse has a special extra-semantic musicality, it is semantically much poorer than prose. We have already been able to ascertain that the high degree of structural organization of verse, which creates a feeling of musicality, also implies a high degree of semantic complexity quite inaccessible for an amorphous text.

The same is true of the aesthetic nature of repetitions of large textual units—lines, stanzas, and compositional elements ("situations," motifs, etc.). And here we can distinguish two different though similarly based types of repetitions. The first is this: when units are repeated there is partial coincidence and, accordingly, partial non-coincidence of the text:

Dár naprásnyj, dár slučájnyj

[Useless gift, fortuitous gift. . .]

The line falls into two distinct hemistiches whose syntactic constructions and intonational structure are identical. The first members of these parallel units (the word *dar* ["gift"]) coincide in full, as do the grammatical forms of the second members. The lexico-semantic content and sound form (with the exception of the stressed vowel and ending *nyj*) of the second members differ. As we have already remarked several times, coincidence singles out and structurally activates the non-coincident part. The semantics of the words "useless" and "fortuitous" form a contrasting pair, and these words themselves become the semantic center of the poem; the semantic load depends on the extent of non-coincidence and this, in turn, is directly proportional to the significance of the coincidence in the remaining part of the line. The greater the number of coinciding elements and aspects in the partially repeated sections of text, the greater the semantic activity of the differential element. Therefore, to reduce the degree of coincidence in the hemistich, for example, revising the line to read *Dar naprasnyj i slučajnyj* (where the repetition of "gift" as well as the syntagmatic-intonational parallelism of the parts is eliminated) would diminish the prominence of the words "useless" and "fortuitous." The same thing would happen if the parallelism of the grammatical form of the second members were destroyed, or in any other instance where repetition was weakened. We should bear in mind that the degree to which a text's meaning depends on its structure in the given case is considerably higher than in cases where semantically contrasted sections rely on antonym units known to be contrastive, regardless of their position in the line (*I nenavidim my i ljubim my slučajno* ["We hate and we love by chance"]). In the last example the contrast between "we hate" and "we love" is taken for granted outside any artistic construction as well. It necessarily enters into the general linguistic semantics of these words, which gain little or nothing from being placed in a given structural position. The contrasted pair "useless–fortuitous" is generated by the *given* construction. The semantics of these elements is altogether individual and disappears when the given structure is destroyed. The semantics of the words is occasional and wholly engendered, not only by the meanings of the words in the context, but also by their interrelation in a certain structural position.

The second possible type of parallelism in a text occurs when repeated elements textually coincide. It may seem that we are dealing here with total coincidence, but that is not the case. *Textual* coincidence reveals *positional* variance. When textually identical elements are positioned differently in a structure, they correlate in different ways with the whole. And accordingly they must be treated differently. When everything but the structural position coincides, positionality is activated as a structural distinctive feature. Thus "total" repetition turns out to be parital both on the plane of expression (positional difference) and, accordingly, on the plane of content (cf. what was said earlier about the refrain).[37]

The problem of the repetition of large compositional elements naturally leads us to the problem of the repetition of the entire text. Quite obviously an artistic structure is designed to transmit the information it contains more than once. A person who has read and understood a newspaper item will not read it again. But it is quite natural to reread a literary work, listen again to a musical piece, or view a film a second time if we find that these works of art are executed with sufficient mastery. How can we explain the

---

37 Truly total repetition in works related to the "aesthetic of identity" (see below) will have another meaning.

recurring aesthetic effect here?[38]

First, we should dwell on the individual interpretation, a factor which is always applicable to works where creation and performance are two separate arts. Repeated listening to a work, assuming a professional level of performance (the art of the orator, the musician or actor) presents a fascinating picture of the correlation between repetition and non-repetition. It was long ago observed that the peculiarities of a performer's individual interpretation are set in particularly strong relief when we compare different performances of a given work, play or role. When the element of likeness is heightened to such an extent that the textual parts absolutely coincide, the difference of the non-coinciding part—in this case the individual interpretation—is also heightened.

Second, we should examine a second case, a case where there is apparently total repetition. We frequently encounter this sort of repetition when a work which does not require the mediation of an interpreter—a work belonging to the fine arts, a film, recorded music, a work of literature held in one's hands—is perceived for the second time, or several times. To under-

_____

38 The repeated reading of a non-artistic text has a special nature. If the information contained in a non-artistic text has already reached the user (redundancy significantly exceeds noise), repeated readings are of a special type: the text no longer conveys information, but acts as an emotional stimulant. Thus Grinev's father always went into a rage upon reading the court calendar. The nature of the rage or of any other emotion experienced by the reader of an artistic text is different. The author conveys his model of the world to the reader, correspondingly organizing the personality of the reader himself. Consequently, emotions in an artistic text are conveyed through meanings. This can be ascertained in the following way: in ordinary speech interjections are the most loaded with emotion, whereas in artistic speech they are perceived as lacking in emotion since they are least capable of conveying information about the structure of the individual—the carrier of emotion. Cf. V. Kamenskij's narrative poem *Stepan Razin:*

> Po carevym mednym lbam
> Bam!
> Bam!
> Bam!
> Back!
> Buck!...
>
> [On the czar's bronze heads
> Bam!
> Bam!
> Bam!
> Bang!
> Bong!...]

and in the same text:

> Bam!
> Vam!
> Dam!
>
> [Bam!
> /I'll/give
> You/ what for!/]

The second excerpt conveys greater emotion than the first because it is richer in meaning.

stand this instance of repetition, we should remember that a work of art is not exhausted by the text (or its "material" part in the fine arts). It is a *relation* between textual and extra-textual systems. As we have seen, without considering a text's correlation with its extra-textual part, we cannot determine what is a structurally active element (device) and what is not. Correspondingly, as a result of change in the extra-textual system—a process which is constantly taking place in our consciousness, a process in which traits of individual subjective development and objective historical development are present—the degree of structural activeness of certain elements in the intricate complex of the artistic whole is constantly changing for the reader. Not everything objectively present in a work of art is revealed to each reader at every moment of his life. Just as the repeated performance of one and the same play by various actors accentuates the specific nature of each performance, the differences in each performance, so too the repeated perception of the same text lays bare the evolution of the perceiver's consciousness, the differences in its structure, which would easily escape our notice if different texts were being read. Here too, therefore, we are speaking of relative rather than absolute repetition.

Thus the differentiating, i.e. the semantics—distinguishing function of repetition—results from the difference in the construction or position of repeating elements and structures.

While this is an essential aspect of the problem, it does not exhaust it. Identity, the process of assimilation rather than opposition, also plays an important role in repetition as an element of artistic structure. We will examine this question more specifically further on.

We can draw one essential conclusion from what has been said: partial equivalence is a fundamental element of artistic synonymy.

The division of the text into structurally equatable segments orders the text in a certain way. But it is absolutely essential that this ordering should not be carried to its extreme, or it will be automatized and become structurally redundant. The ordering of the text always acts as an organizing tendency structuring heterogeneous material into equivalent series without simultaneously canceling out the element of heterogeneity. Setting aside artistic systems constructed according to the principles of the aesthetics of identity, we can observe a fairly common property of the language of art in the partial equivalence of rhythmic series, as well as in other types of artistic synonymy. The structure of natural language is an ordered set and for those who speak correctly, information about its construction is redundant. The structure is fully automatized. The speaker's attention is concentrated exclusively on the message: the perception of the language (code) is wholly automatized. In modern artistic systems the very structure of the artistic language is informative for those who take part in the act of communication. Therefore it cannot remain in a state of automatism. Some type of ordering given in a text or group of texts must always be in conflict with material that is non-ordered in relation to it. This explains the difference between the metrical scheme:

$$\cup' \; \cup' \; \cup' \; \cup'$$

and Lermontov's line: *Kakój-to zvér' odním pryžkóm.* . . ["some animal in one leap. . ."]. The first is a totally ordered series (the alternation of identical elements). The second represents a struggle between order and diversity (a necessary condition of informativeness). It can be transformed into non-verse (Kakój-to zvér' odním pryžkóm výprygnul iz cášči. . . ["some animal in one leap sprang from a thicket. . ."] with a total loss of metrical order, or transformed into an abstract metrical scheme (where it would lose its element of non-order). But the actual line exists only as the mutual tension between these two elements. Once again we confront an essential principle: the artistic function of a structural level (here, rhythmic) cannot be understood merely by syntactic analysis of its inner structure; it must be semantically correlated with other levels.

Principles Governing the Segmentation Of the Poetic Line

In analyzing the line as a rhythmic unit, we proceed on the assumption that a poem is a particularly complex semantic structure, which is necessary if one is to express a particularly complex content. Therefore the transmission of the content of a line by means of prose is descriptively possible only to the extent that we could take a shattered crystal and convey its properties through words by describing its form, color, transparency, strength, and the structure of the molecule.

We have already said that repetition is the basic structure of the line. This is not only correct, it is common knowledge. Numerous literary theories confirm that a line is built on the most varying types of repetition: the repetition of certain prosodic units at regular intervals (rhythm), the repetition of identical sounds at the end of a rhythmic unit (rhyme), the repetition of sounds in a text (euphony).

Closer examination, however, convinces us that this seemingly elementary truth is not so simple.

Above all, are the repeating elements that identical? We have already seen that rhyme is not simply the phonetic phenomenon of sound repetition, but a semantic phenomenon that combines sound repetition and the non-coincidence of concepts. Rhythm is even more complex a phenomenon.

Ja pámjatnik sebé vozdvíg nerukotvórnyj

[I raised a monument to myself not made by human hands]

We generally assume that a regular repetition of stresses occurs here. But it is quite clear that stressed and unstressed syllables, and sounds abstracted from the quality of those sounds, in the "pure state," exist only in the schemes drawn up by prosodists. If we do not bring in acoustics, but speak simply of language, there exist only real sounds which occur in stressed and unstressed positions.

Real stressed and unstressed sounds, rather than "pure" stressed and unstressed syllables, are not only an acoustical given, but also a structural, phonological given. After Roman Jakobson established the connection between a line's structure and phonological elements,[39] it became evident that on this level elements of the phonological structure, and not abstracted features of these elements, emerge as elements of rhythmic structure.

In the example given above we find a sequence of stressed vowels: $a-e-i-o$. Where is there full repetition here? In a concrete line there are totally different sounds, different distinctive elements. Where is the "systematic, measured repetition of speech units similar to each other," which the Concise Dictionary of Literary Terms[40] gives as the definition of rhythm? To the listener, it is precisely the difference of these sounds that is noticeable. Their one common property, stress, creates the basis for their opposition.

In the case we are discussing, stress is the "grounds for comparison" that permits us to single out the distinctive features of these phonemes. The difference between poetic speech and ordinary speech in this case is that in the latter the phonemes $a,e,i,$ and o do not have this property, and consequently cannot be contrasted. Thus in place of a mechanical "repetition of identical elements," we find a complex, dialectically contradictory process: the singling out of variance through likeness, on the one hand, and the discovery of common elements in apparently profound difference, on the other. The result of the rhythmic structuring of the text is the ability of sounds to be set in opposition to each other, thus forming correlating series with a distinctive feature—a common position with regard to stress (tonic, pretonic, pre-pretonic, posttonic and post-posttonic position). This involves words comprising lines in supplementary, supra-grammatical relations.

The significance of this circumstance increases sharply in connection with the difference in the semantic load of sounds in ordinary as opposed to poetic speech. The word is the final, indivisible unit of the lexical system of language. Since the transmitter and receiver of information must use the limited number of sounds which speech has at its disposal for the transmission of a considerable number of concepts, it became necessary to combine sounds; as we know, phonemes in the natural language are distinctive elements and carriers of content; if we change only one of them, the receiver may not understand the meaning of the transmitted information

39 See Roman Jakobson, "O češskom stixe, preimuščestvenno v sopostavlenii s russkim," Sbornik po teorii poetičeskogo jazyka, vol. V (RSFSR, 1923) p. 37 ff. De Groot's most recent objection was countered by V. V. Ivanov in his article "Lingvističeskie voprosy stixotvornogo perevoda," Mašinnyj Perevod, Issue 2 (Moscow, 1961) pp. 378-379.

40 L. Timofeev and N. Vengrov, Kratkij slovar' literaturovedčeskix terminov (Moscow, 1955) p. 117.

or his understanding may be distorted. But the carrier of lexical meaning is the word as a whole, a combination of given phonemes in a given sequence. This implies that pause, the sign of word boundary, can be placed only before or after this combination of phonemes in connected speech. If we put a pause in the middle of a word ("carton" and "car ton") we change its lexical meaning.

The situation is different in poetic speech. In order to elucidate one of the most crucial aspects of the nature of rhythm, let us focus on one particular problem—that of scansion. Acknowledged authorities on Russian verse have expressed highly contradictory opinions on this matter. Tomaševskij defines scansion as, "something absolutely natural, presenting no difficulties whatsoever. For a properly constructed line scansion is a natural operation, for it is merely the underscoring and clarification of meter." He continues, "Scansion is analogous to counting aloud while practicing a musical piece, or to the movement of a conductor's baton."[41]

As respected an authority on Russian verse as Andrej Belyj held another point of view:

> Scansion is something that does not exist in real life; the poet does not scan lines in their internal intonation; nor does a performer, whether poet or artist, even read the lines *Dux otrican'ja, dux somnen'ja* as *duxot rican'ja, duxso mnen'ja** —these *duxots, rican'ja*'s and *mnen'ja*'s make me run away in horror.[42]

Who is correct, Belyj or Tomaševskij? We note in passing that they emphasize different but closely related sides of the question. Tomaševskij emphasizes the appearance of additional stresses in the process of scanning, while Belyj emphasizes the appearance of pauses that violate the integrity of the word as a unit. If we look more closely, we will see that both scholars are right in a certain sense, which implies that regarding the problem as a whole, both are wrong.

Scansion does in fact reveal rhythmic patterns actually present in a line (as we will see, the missing stresses which we replace with real ones in the process of scanning are very real elements of rhythm). The rhythmic scheme really does divide the text of a line into segments which do not coincide with semantic segments. Whether we pronounce the line *Dux otrican'ja, dux somnen'ja*, or *Duxot rican'ja duxso mnen'ja* or more accurately still, *Duxot rican' jadux somnen'ja*, we are in all cases dealing with poetic reality. In the first case the pauses elucidate the structure of

---

* *Dux otrican'ja, dux somnen'ja*—"Spirit of negation, spirit of doubt." When Belyj canges the natural word boundaries to reflect the meter, new words and comical associations arise. The vague equivalent of the new line would be, "of stuffiness speeching, two hundred opinion." A comparable effect in English would be achieved by breaking up a line by Shakespeare to conform to the meter: Tolin gerout apur posedo verthrow (Sonnet X)'–Tr.

41 B. V. Tomaševskij, *Stilistika.* . . , op. cit. p. 354-355.

42 Andrej Belyj, *Ritm kak dialektika i "Mednyj vsadnik"* (Moscow, 1929) p. 55. Belyj polemicizes with Kručenyx over the latter's *Sdvigologija*, which caused quite a stir at the time.

the lexical units, in the second and third—of the rhythmic units. In modern poetic perception the line is meant to be pronounced as it is in case one. Rhythmic pauses are negatively realized through non-pronunciation. But the absence of pause where we anticipate it (the rhythmic pause in a line) and the absence of such anticipation are two very different things. While descriptive poetics views each element as something separate and only mechanically joined to another element, and thus only deals with realized "devices," the structural study of verse regards artistic elements as relations and clearly recognizes that a negative quantity is just as real as a positive quantity; that an unrealized element is not a zero quantity and is felt just as distinctly as a realized element. If we mark real pauses with a **V**, and "minus-pauses," places for pauses that are felt but not realized, with a **Λ**, the actual pronunciation of the line will look like this:

Dux **V** otΛrican' **Λ** ja **V** duxVΛ[43] somnen' **Λ** ja.

But in fact the text is broken up into even smaller units. The comparison and opposition of sounds with regard to stress (the question of whether the stress is realized—whether we have plus-stress, or not realized—a minus-stress, is not important here; this is confirmed by the fact that in relation to a syllable in an unstressed position, a stressed syllable in a stressed position and an unstressed syllable in stressed position act in precisely the same way) permeates the verse with pauses after each syllable. These, as a rule, are minus-pauses, but they are quite real all the same. We should note that any minus-pause can easily be turned into a real pause in the act of declamation. Realized and unrealized pauses are freely interchangeable. If the reader, wishing to strengthen the intonation says, *Dux otrica* **V***n'ja, dux somnen'ja*—there can be no doubt that it does not sound absurd to his audience. The pattern of rhythmic pauses is superimposed on the pattern of lexical pauses. So if speaking of iambs we designate an unstressed syllable as "0" and a stressed syllable as "1," the iambic (tetrameter with masculine endings) skeleton of the rhythm is expressed:

$$0, \pm 1, 0 \pm 1, 0 \pm 1, 0 + 1, [0]$$

This scheme covers all combinations of iambs and pyrrhics; this is the scheme which reflects the rhythmic reality.[44]

But the breakdown of the line does not stop on the level of syllables. As we will see further on, the sound organization of a line breaks verbal units down into individual phonemes. Thus it may seem that the sum of structural boundaries of a line breaks up the constituent words into phonological units and transforms the line into a sound sequence. But the whole point is that this is only one aspect of the process, which exists only in combination with its opposite.

43 The rhythmical and lexical pauses coincided.

44 If we take into account the possibility of spondees, which should be regarded as unrealized, unstressed syllables, then we must introduce the sign ± 0.

The specific nature of verse structure consists, in particular, in the following: a flow of speech signals, broken down into phonologically elementary particles, does not lose its ties with lexical meaning; words are annihilated and not annihilated at the same time.

The segmenting of a line does not lead to the destruction of its constituent words. Various rhythmic boundaries are imposed on the word, splitting it up without fragmenting it. The word is broken up into units and recomposed of these same units. In Puškin's line, *Ja útrom dólžen být' uvéren*—["In the morning, I must be certain"], the pause after the first *u* is greater than the pause before it. Actually, it is pronounced *Jaú trom*. Yet no one ever makes a mistake in dividing this text into lexical units. Kručenyx's fear that "shifts" would obscure meaning was clearly without foundation. He looked for *ikanie i za-ik-an'e* ["hiccuping and stut-ter-ing"] in *Evgenij Onegin:*

> I k šutke s želč' ju popolam. . .
> I kučera vokrug ognej. . .
>
> [And to jokes, half spiteful. . .*
> And coachmen around fires. . .]

(cf. Lermontov's *i kušči roz* [literally "and bowers of roses" or in Kručenyx's thinking, "and of roses hiccuping"] where *ikušši* is formed on the model of the present active pariticiple *iduščij* ["going"]. Or in the title *Ikra á la Onegin* ["Caviar á la Onegin"]:

> Parter i kresla, vse kipit. . .
> I kraj otcov i zatočen'ja. . .
> I kryl'jami treščet i mašet. . .
> I krug tovariščej prezrennyx. . .[45]
>
> [Parterre and stalls, everything buzzes. . .
> And the land of our fathers and incarceration. . .
> And cracks and flaps its wings. . .
> And the circle of despised friends. . .]

But these examples in fact most convincingly demonstrate the stability of lexical boundaries within the line.

No pause, realized or unrealized, which the line structure interposes within a lexical unit, destroys the unit in our consciousness. In fact the very concept of word-boundary is by no means determined primarily by pauses. Its basic feature lies elsewhere: we master the vocabulary of a given language and in our consciousness the whole vocabulary exists in potential,

---

* In each line, Kručenyx picks out various forms of the verb *ikat'* ("to hiccup"): *ik* ("hic"), *ikušči* (improperly formed present active participle, "hiccuping"). These are invariably found when the conjunction *i* ("and") precedes a word beginning with a *k*.—Tr.

45 A. Kručenyx (comp.), *500 novyx ostrot i kalamburov Puškina* (Moscow, 1924) pp. 30-31.

unspoken form; we identify some series of uttered sounds with this vocabulary, thus giving them lexical meaning. Trubetzkoy observes with some justification that:

> The possibility of misunderstanding is, as a rule, quite insignificant, mainly because in the perception of any linguistic expression we usually tune ourselves in beforehand to a defined, limited sphere of concepts and pay attention only to those lexical elements which belong to that sphere. While each language nonetheless has special phonological means which, at a given point in the uninterrupted flow of sound, signal the presence or absence of the boundaries of a sentence, word or morpheme, these means play only an auxiliary role. They could be likened to traffic signals. Not so long ago such signals did not exist even in major cities, and even now they have not been introduced everywhere. We could get along without them after all; we would just have to be more careful and more attentive![46]

The active mastery of a vocabulary does not permit any "shiftology,"* Even in the most exaggerated forms of scanning, the sense of the unity of lexical units is not lost, while in cases when the listener is dealing with an unknown vocabulary "shifts" can easily arise and a rhythmic pause begins to be perceived as the end of a word. It is revealing that something takes place analogous to folk etymology. A "shift" occurs because an unfamiliar, imcomprehensible vocabulary interspersed with pauses is interpreted against the background of the familiar comprehensible vocabulary that is potentially present in the speaker's consciousness. In this way we get such classic misunderstandings as: *Šumi, šumi volna Mirona* ["Roar, roar, wave of Miron"] instead of: *Šumi, šumi, volnami Rona* ["Roar, roar with your waves, O Rhone"]. The unfamiliar "Rhone" is apprehended as the name "Miron." Another somewhat different instance is described by Feliks Kon in his memoirs. He relates how students of Russianized schools in pre-revolutionary Poland, mistook the expression *dar Valdaja* ["gift of Valdaj"] for the gerund of a verb *darvaldat*.[47] Here lexical unitelligibility made it impossible to recognize a grammatical form, and a series of sounds was projected onto the gerundial form potentially present in the listener's consciousness. The rarity or near singularity of lexical units in a text being improperly articulated

---

* Kručenyx's term for the "art" of discovering new meanings by altering word boundaries. Cf. A. Kručenyx, *Sdvigologija russkogo stixa* (*Shiftology of Russian Verse*) Moscow, 1923, and *500 novyx ostrot i kalamburov Puškina* (*500 New Witticisms and Puns of Puškin*), Moscow, 1924.—Tr.

46 N. S. Trubetzkoy, *Osnovy fonologii* (Moscow, 1960) p. 300.

47 Andrej Belyj mentions this in his poem *First Meeting:*

> Tak zvuki slova "dar Valdaja"
> Baldy nad partoju boltaja,—
> Pereboltajut v "darvaldaja"...

> [So blockheads babbling behind their school desks
> Will take the sounds of "gift of Valdaj,"
> Reshuffling them into "darvaldaj-ing"...]

during scanning and our analysis of the causes and nature of such mistakes show us that words in a poetic text divided by rhythmic pauses, no matter how prolonged these pauses may be, still remain *words*. They retain tangible juncture features—morphological, lexical and syntactic. The word in poetry recalls Gogol's "red caftan"*—it is cut up by rhythmic pauses (and other rhythmic means), but knits itself together again, never losing its lexical integrity.

Thus a line is at once a sequence of phonological units perceived as separate, and a sequence of words perceived as coherent units of phoneme combinations. Both sentences are united, as two hypostases of one reality—the line. They constitute a correlating structural pair.

The relation of word and sound in verse differs substantially from their correlation in non-artistic language where the bond between a word and the phonemes that comprise it is, as we know, historical and conventional. Words in verse are divided into sounds which, due to pauses and other rhythmic means, assume a certain autonomy on the plane of expression; this creates the precondition for the semantization of sounds. But since this division does not destroy the words which exist alongside the chain of sounds and from the perspective of natural language are the basic semantic medium, lexical meaning is transferred to individual sounds. The phonemes comprising a word take on the semantics of that word. Experience confirms the futility of the many attempts that have been made to establish the "objective" meaning of sounds independent of words (if we exclude onomatopoeia, of course). But the transfer of meaning from a word to the sounds that comprise it is just as obvious. For example:

> Tam voevodskaja mètressa
> Ravna svoeju stepen'ju
> S žirnoju gadkojy *kry*soj.

> [There a governor's mistress
> Is equal in her rank
> To a fat, digusting *rat*.]
> (Sumarokov)

> Ne slyšim li v boju časov
> Glas smerti, dveri *skry*p podzemnoj. . .

> [Do we not hear in the striking of the clock
> The voice of death, the *creak* of a subterranean door.]
> (Deržavin)

---

* The caftan (svilka, in Ukranian) belonged to a devil who had been kicked out of Hell. To forget his sorrows, he went on a binge and was finally reduced to pawning the caftan. He warned the pawnbroker not to sell it, but it was so lovely that the latter could not resist. When the devil came to recover it, it had vanished. Since that time, various owners have attempted to sell it, burn it, cut it up—all to no avail. The full tale is told in the story "The Fair at Soročincy" in the collection *Evenings on a Farm Near Dikan'ka*.—Tr.

Iskusstvo vos*kres*alo
Iz kaznej i pytok
I bilo, kak *kres*alo,
O kamni Moabitov.

[Art *rose*
From executions and torture
And struck like a *flint*
Against the stones of the Moabites.]
(Voznesenskij)

The phonetic combinations *krys, skry, kres,* all of the same type, sound completely different in each of these three passages where each is semantized according to the lexical unit it enters into.

Each sound which takes on lexical meaning acquires independence, which is by no means akin to "self-sufficiency,"* for its independence is totally determined by its ties with the samantics of the word. These semantically charged phonemes become the bricks from which this same word is reconstructed. Thus the mere inclusion of a word in a poetic text effects a decisive change in its character; it is no longer a word in the language, but a reproduction of the word in the language and is related to it just as an image of reality in art is related to the real thing it reproduces. It becomes *a sign model of a sign model.* In its semantic saturation it differs radically from words in non-artistic language.

Once again we see that the special musicality and sonority of a poetic text derives from the intricacy of its structure, from a special semantic concentration that is utterly foreign to a structurally unorganized text. A simple experiment could demonstrate this fact: no line consisting of meaning-less sounds (sounds outside the framework of lexical units), no matter how artfully composed, could be as musical as an ordinary poetic line. Here we should bear in mind that "trans-rational" words** are not the least devoid of lexical meaning in the strict sense of the word.[48] Trans-rational words in poetry are not equivalent to a meaningless selection of sounds in ordinary speech. In so far as we perceive the sounds produced by the speech organs as language, we attribute meaning to them. A unit of speech apprehended as a word by analogy with others, but which has no meaning in itself, will

* "Self-sufficiency"—in Russian *samovitost'*, an occasionalism invented by the Futurists to describe the "new word" that made (or was to make) its appearance in Futurist verse. Cf. the collective manifesto *Poščečina obščestvennomu vkusu* (*A Slap in the Face of Public Taste*), Moscow, 1912, that speaks of the "New-coming Beauty of the Self-sufficient [*samovitoe*] Word."—Tr.

** "Trans-rational language"—in Russian *zaumnyj jazyk* is a Futurist formula designating the new medium of the new poetry. See Vladimir Markov's *Russian Futurism: A History*, Berkeley, 1968, pp. 127-132, 344-354, et.al. for a discussion of the term and the phenomena.—Tr.

48 See M. Janakiev, op. cit., pp. 13-16; I. I. Revzin, *Modeli jazyka*, op. cit., p.21; B. V. Tomaševskij, *Stilistika. . .*, op. cit., pp. 181-183.

represent an absurd case of expression without content, *signifiant* without *signifié*. The word in poetry in general, and the trans-rational word in particular, is composed of phonemes which in turn were derived by breaking down lexical units and which have not lost their connections with these units. While in the ordinary poetic word the relation connecting a sound with a given lexical content is obvious and meaningful for everyone, in trans-rational language, in accordance with the overall subjectivism of the author's position, this bond remains unknown to the reader. The trans-rational word in poetry is not devoid of content, but endowed with so personal and subjective a meaning that it cannot convey generally meaningful information, which is not the author's goal in any case. We must bear in mind, however, that on the level of morphology the trans-rational word does not, as a rule, differ from the marked words of a language.

If we wish to compare an experimental nonsensical text with a meaninful text to determine their respective musicality, the sounds of human speech will not do: we inevitably ascribe some meaning to them. We must know that a flow of sounds we are perceiving is *not* speech. For this purpose mechanical sounds are more convenient. But even mechanical sounds can be carriers of information (musical information) if they are structurally organized (structure is potential information). Accumulations of sounds which are unstructured and absolutely random for both sender and receiver cannot convey information, nor will they be musical in any sense. *Beauty is information.* The difference between "musicality" or "beauty of sound" in poetry and in music is this: in poetry the ordering of elements conveys information, not about pure relations of units (which *in isolation* mean nothing, but in a structure form a model of the emotions of the personality) but about the relations of meaningful units, each of which constitutes a sign or is apprehended as a sign on the linguistic level. We may not know the meaning of *aonidy* or *of Bajja* in Batjuškov's line *Ty probuždaeš'sja, o Bajja, iz grobnicy.* . . ["You wake, o Baiae, from your tomb. . ."].[49] But we cannot help but realize that Baiae and *aonidy* ["muses"—Tr.] are *words*, signs of content, and we must perceive them in this way. A word devoid of content (in general, or for me in particular, say, due to my ignorance) is not the same as a meaningless group of sounds. The latter has zero meaning on the lexical level, whereas a *word* that is not understood has minus-meaning.

But the rhythmic units which form a system of correlations that is exclusive to poetic speech do not divide lines (and the lexemes that comprise them) into phonemes, but rather into syllables. That sort of division which leads to the segmentation of a word on the phonemic level occurs as a result of sound repetitions.

49 Cf. in the memoirs of N. A. Pavlovič: "His eyes half closed, Mandelštam descends, muttering: "The yawning of *aonidas*, the yawning of *aonidas*. .." He collides with me: "Nadežda Aleksandrovna, what are *aonidas?*" (*Blokovskij sbornik* [Tartu, 1964] p. 492).

The phenomenon of sound repetitions as such in verse has been well studied. Its relation to the semantic structure of verse is a far more complicated issue. Rhythmic structure leads to the contrast and opposition of elements which convey lexical meaning and to the formation of semantic oppositions. In ordinary speech these oppositions would be impossible; they form a system of relations independent of syntactic relations, but in like fashion they organize lexemes into a structure on a higher level. Sound repetitions form their own, analogously functioning system. The imposition of these systems on each other results in the breakdown of words into phonemes.

In the lines:

> Ja utrom dolžen byt' uveren,
> Čto s Vami dnem uvižus' ja—

> [In the morning I must be certain
> The we will meet in the afternoon—]

the words *utrom, uveren* and *uvižus'* ["morning," "certain," "meet"] are related to each other independent of ordinary syntactic or other purely linguistic bonds. The sound *u* (despite Viktor Šklovskij's claims in one of his early works) has no meaning in itself, of course. But when it is repeated in a series of words it is singled out in the speaker's consciousness as an independent unit. The phoneme *u* is apprehended as both independent and dependent in relation to the word *utrom* ["morning"]. Being separate and non-separate, it derives its semantics from the word *utrom,* but then is repeated in other words in the series, thus acquiring new lexical meanings. As a result, the words *utrom, uveren* and *uvižus',* which in a non-poetic text would be independent, incomparable units, begin to be perceived as semantically superimposed on each other. The comparison of words which occurs during this process makes it necessary to find a common element in their variance. In view of such semantic superimposition, an enormous part of the conceptual content of each word is pared off, just as the context pares off polysemy. On the other hand, meanings arise which would be impossible if there were not such comparison, meanings which alone express the complexity of the author's thought. Here such a unit of content emerges as a result of the neutralization of the words *utro, uveren, uvižus',* forming an archiseme which includes the intersection of their semantic fields.

The complexity of the phenomenon, however, lies in the retention of the whole non-poetic structure of language, all the syntactic relations and all the meaning of the words determined by the context of the phrase when perceived as a non-poetic phenomenon. But simultaneously other relations and meanings arise which do not cancel out the original ones, but correlate with them in a complex way.

In a concrete poetic text, however, we are dealing not only with the sporadic repetition of any one sound, but with the entire sound system of verse, which we find to be a field of complex correlations.

Phonemes endowed with lexical meaning enter into oppositions with other phonemes 1) on the basis of their identical relation to stress or non-stress; 2) on the basis of the repetition of identical phonemes; 3) on the basis of the semantization of linguistic phonological oppositions, since the very fact that a text is poetic means that all its elements are semanticized.

At the same time, the comparison and opposition of phonemes takes place 1) in one line; 2) in various lines. In reality this does not signify the comparison and opposition of phonemes, but the formation of an extremely complex system of semantic comparisons and oppositions; the singling out of mutual and different features in concepts which cannot be compared outside verse; the formation of "archesemes" which in turn enter into oppositions with each other. Thus arises the enormously complex conceptual structure which we call verse or poetry.

The term "archeseme" is formed by analogy with Trubetzkoy's archiphoneme to designate units of meaning which include all the common elements in a lexico-semantic opposition. An archeseme has two aspects: it indicates common features in the semantics of opposition members and at the same time singles out differential elements in each. An archeseme is not given directly in a text. It is a construct based on word-concepts which form bundles of semantic oppositions; the latter are invariants of the archeseme. Here we must bear in mind one particular feature of archesemes.

Linguistic archesemes such as:

North ⎱ opposite points of the compass
South ⎰ ("not East–West")

are absolute in the framework of a given culture; they are derived from the very system of accepted meanings. In poetry we encounter a different situation: a structural poetic opposition is *perceived* as semantic. Its elements are words which simply cannot be correlated outside the given structure, which reveals in these very words common features (or differences), an occasional content which could not be brought to light outside the given opposition. The archesemes that arise in the process are specific to this given poetic structure. Subsequently a semantic structure is built on the level of the archesemes, which enter into oppositions and reveal the comparisons and oppositions of their content, forming archesemes on a second and higher levels; in the final analysis, this allows us to comprehend one aspect of the structure of a work. We can illustrate this with a concrete example–Andrej Voznesenskij's poem "Goya."

GOJJA

Ja–Gojja!
 Glaznicy voronok mne vykleval vorog,
  Sletaja na pole nagoe.

Ja—Gore.
Ja—golos
Vojny, gorodov golovni
          na snegu sorok pervogo goda.
Ja—golod.
Ja gorlo
Povešennoj baby, č'e telo, kak kolokol,
          bilo nad ploščad'ju goloj. . .
Ja Gojja!
O grozdi
Vozmezd'ja! Vzvil zalpom na Zapad—
          ja pepel nezvannogo gostja!
I v memorial'noe nebo vbil krepkie zvezdy—
Kak gvozdi.
Ja—Gojja.

[I am Goya!
     My crater-like eyes were plucked out by the raven
     Swooping down on the naked field.

I am Grief.
I am the voice
Of war, of the charred wood of cities
     in the snow of 'forty one.

I am hunger.
I am the throat
Of a hanged woman whose body, like a bell
     tolled above the naked square. . .

I am Goya!
O Grapes
Of wrath! In a salvo aimed at the West—
          I fired off the ashes of the univited guest!
And into the memorial sky I drove strong stars

Like nails.
I am Goya.]

Repeptitions in this poem are constucted on the principle of rhyme and
convincingly corroborate the idea that rhythmic and euphonic aspects are
inevitably correlated in verse.
     A chain of short, anaphoral lines with parallel syntactic constructions
runs through the entire poem. The pronoun "I" beginning each line—the
same in all of them—is their common member, the "grounds for comparison."
In this connection, the second members of the binomials (*Gojja, Gore,
golod* ["Goya," "Grief," "hunger"] and so on) are opposed to each other:
their non-identity and their specificity are stressed. The difference between
the first line and the third, fourth, and other lines is concentrated on the
second member of the binomial, and this difference is primarily semantic.
But the words comprising the second member are perceived not only in

their relation to the first member, but in their relation to each other. Their common rhythmic and syntactical positions and the sound repetitions in the words *Gojja, Gore,* and *golod* serve as the basis for these correlations. But within this mutually correlated series there are forces of attraction and repulsion which also apply to the semantic plane and not only to the plane of sound. On the one hand, semantic variance is revealed (we touched on this in our discussion of rhyme). The coincidence of individual phonemes in non-coincident words only stresses the difference between the words, above all in content, for, as we have already seen, when a total phonic coincidence is accompanied by coincidence of meaning, rhyme loses its musicality.

But another process takes place: the words *Gojja, Gore, golos golod* and *gorlo* set a common group *go* in relief and a comparison of *golos* and *golod,* say, singles out other phonemes as well. A system is created where the same sounds in identical or consciously different combinations are repeated in various words. And here we see a manifestation of the fundamental difference in the nature of words in ordinary langauge and in an artistic (in particular, a poetic) text. In the language a word clearly breaks up into the plane of content and the plane of expression, and it is impossible to establish a direct connection between the two. The closeness of the plane of content of two words may not be reflected on the plane of expression, and the closeness of the plane of expression (sound repetitions, homonyms, and so on) may have no relation to the plane of content. It is also impossible to establish the relations of word elements (for example, on the phonemic level) to the plane of content in ordinary speech.[50]

I am Goya. . .

The opening line establishes the identity of two members—"I" and "Goya." The specific meaning of these words in the text is still unknown. "I" is "I" in general, the dictionary "I." The semantics of the name Goya do not go beyond its generally known meaning. At the same time even this first line adds something to the dictionary definition, the extra-contextual meaning of the two words. Even taken by itself, and not in relation to other lines, the construction "I am Goya" is not of the same sort as, for example, "I am Voznesenskij." The latter construction would confirm the unity of concepts that are identical from the perspective of author and reader and outside the given text. One of them ("I") would simply be a pronominal designation of the second. The line "I am Goya!" is built on the identification of two concepts known to be nonequivalent ("I ⟨the poet⟩ = Goya," "I ⟨not Goya⟩ = Goya"). In itself the line already shows that "I" and

50 Cf. "The sign and the signifié have an arbitrary relation. Any sign may be connected with any signifié, and any signifié with any sign," (N. I. Žinkin, "Znaki i sistemy jazyka," *Zeichen und system der Sprache,* Vol. 1 of the series *Schriften zur Phonetik, Sprachwissenschaft und Kommunikationsforschung,* No. 3 [Berlin, 1961] p. 139).

"Goya" have a special meaning here, that each must be a special conceptual structure in order for the two to be equated. This specific structure of concepts is revealed through a system of semantic oppositions, a system of special, complexly constructed meanings which arise as a result of the structure of the poetic text.

The very first line singles out the combination of phonemes *go* as the basic carrier of meaning in the name "Goya."

If we pronounce the line *ja—go—ja,* the phonetic identity of the first and last elements is perceived as a semantic tautology (ja—ja ["I–I"]) because in poetry the planes of expression and content cannot be separated. The element *go* conveys the basic semantic meaning. Of course the semantic meaning of the phonological organization of the first line is realized only in relation to other lines, and the prominence of the group *go* within the confines of the isolated line *Ja—Gojja* exists only potentially. But its prominence is clearly realized when the first line is compared with those that follow:

> Ja—Gore
> Ja—golod.

> [I am Grief.
> I am hunger.]

A state of analogy is established between the words "Goya," "Grief," and "hunger." Each in its own way is equated with the common element "I." It is extremely significant that all three lines have the same syntactic construction, in which the roles of the second members are equivalent. Not only the syntactic position, but also the phonological parallelism (the repetition of the *go* group) forces us to perceive these words as semantically correlated. From this mass of meanings, a common semantic nucleus—the archeseme—is singled out. Its meaning is complicated by its parallelism with the lines:

> Ja—golos
> Vojny, gorodov golovni
>   na snegu sorok pervogo goda. . .

> Ja—gorlo
> Povešennoj baby, č'e telo, kak kolokol,
>   bilo nad ploščad'ju goloj. . .

> [I am the voice
> Of war, of the charred wood of cities
>   in the snow of 'forty one.

> I am the throat
> Of a hanged woman whose body, like a bell
>   tolled over the naked square. . .]

The second half of each line is equated to *gore* and *golod* from the lines quoted above by virtue of its predicative function. The sound repetition:

golos, gorodov, golovni, goda, gorlo, golaja is interesting. In addition the word combination *golos vojny*, supported by the prominence which the phoneme *v* acquires as a result of its repetition in the lines:

> Glaznicy *v*oronok mne *v*ykleval *v*orog,
> sletaja na pole nagoe. . .

> [My crater-like eye sockets were plucked out by the enemy
> Swooping down on the naked field. . .]

establishes a relation of semantic correlation between the words modulating *v* and *g*. We should note that *g* in the word *vorog* ["enemy"] receives particular structural emphasis since the entire semantics of the words and phraseologisms *vykleval glaznicy* and *sletaja* ["plucked out my eye sockets" and "swooping"] point to the word *voron* ["raven"] (phonetically anticipated by the word *voronok* ["craters"]). The unnamed *voron* and the actual *vorog* form a correlated pair in which the phonemes *n–g* single out semantic difference, while the coincidence of the group *voro* establishes the meaning held in common. Hence the formation of a complex content structure: *Gore, golod, golos vojny, gorodov golovni, glaznicy voronok, gorlo povešennoj baby* and *pole nagoe* ["Grief," "hunger," "voice of war," "charred wood of cities," "crater-like eye sockets," "throat of a hanged woman" and "naked field"] form a mutually correlated structure, On the one hand, this structure is traced back to the archeseme level, the semantic kernel arising at the intersection of fields of meanings of each basic semantic unit. On the other hand, those features are activated which isolate each singled-out group from the archeseme meaning which they all have in common. The fact that each semantic unit is perceived in relation to the semantic kernel dictates, in a number of cases, an absolutely different perception of its meaning than would be true if it were isolated from the series.

One additional correlation must be pointed out. Two groups of lines stand out in clear relief in the passage we are dealing with, first:

> I am Grief.
> I am hunger.

and second:

> I am the voice
> Of war, of the charred wood of cities
> in the snow of 'forty one.

> I am the throat
> Of a hanged woman whose body, like a bell,
> tolled over the naked square.

The following line adjoins this group:

> My crater-like eye sockets were plucked out by the enemy
> Swooping sown on the naked field.

Both groups of lines are equated, as we noted earlier, by their parallel syntactic construction (the extended predicates in the second group only emphasize the kinship of their syntactic structures). We have also established the correlation of sound organization in the elementary lexical units of both groups.

But on the other hand, common elements only stress the difference between the two groups of lines. The short lines require a completely different sort of breathing, and, consequently, a different tempo and intonation, than the long ones do. But that is not the only difference: "grief" and "hunger" are abstract nouns. The subject, "I," equated with them is far more concrete and individual. In this respect the long lines are more complex. Here the predicate is not only concrete, it designates a part, a part of a man, his body (cf. throat, voice, eye sockets). In correlation with it the subject "I" is something more general and abstract. But simultaneously the predicate is part of a metaphoric series—"the voice of war" (cf. "crater-like eye sockets;" the accompanying "throat of a hanged woman" is taken as a symbolic sign of a more general content). An anthropomorphic metaphoric image is created (voice, eye sockets, throat) which is simultaneously composed of details taken from a war landscape (craters, naked field, the charred wood of cities in the snow of 'forty one). These two series are synthesized in the image of a "naked square" and the woman hanged there. All of these figurative semantic series converge at one center: they are equated to "I," the authorial subject. But this equivalence is parallelism and not identity. Just as the predicates in each group of lines, and in each separate line, are not identical but only parallel, including both common and different elements, so too the "I"s which follow one after the other are also not equal; each time this "I" is equated with a new semantic structure, that is, it *receives new content*. A revelation of the complex dialectical process involved in filling out this "I" is one of the fundamental aspects of the poem. Here the predicate is a model of the subject, and the comparison and opposition of predicates which form an extremely complex system of meanings, an image of the tragedy of war, at the same time models an image of the author's personality. And when Andrej Voznesenskij sums up the first part of the poem with the line "I am Goya!" the subject absorbs all the "I"s of the preceding lines with all their differences and intersections, while the predicate sums up all the preceding predicates. The line "I am Goya!" in mid-text is by no means a mere repetition of the first line, but rather its antithesis. For it is in contrast with the first line, where both "I" and "Goya" have only general linguistic meaning, that we discover the specific semantics of these words as imparted to them in Voznesenskij's poem, and only in this poem.

We could also analyze the second half of the poem in a similar fashion, showing how the fianl line "I am Goya" acquires its meaning. We could observe, in particular, that all the elements of difference which show up when the words are repeated (for example, the fact that the first two lines "I am Goya!" have an exclamatory intonation, while the last does not) become carriers of meaning.

Here it will suffice to underscore a more restricted idea: sound in verse does not remain within the confines of the plane of expression, but enters as one element into the comparison and opposition of words in poetry according to laws of the figurative rather than the linguistic sign, that is, into the structuring of content.

The formation of archesemes is not an antilogical process. It can be analyzed with scientific accuracy. But as we study it we must constantly bear in mind that in a poetic text, because of the marked fragmentation of words into phonemes and their simultaneous non-fragmentability, the relation of expression to content is established quite differently than in a non-artistic text. In the latter, one can establish only historical and conventional connections. In the former (the poetic text), a relation is established and as a result the expression itself begins to be perceived as the representation of content. In this case the sign, while remaining verbal, acquires features of a figurative (iconographic) signal.

It should be particularly stressed that the fragmentation of words into phonemes, as well as the formation of occasional word meanings as a result of the contrast and comparison of phonemes and prosodic units, is not limited to those cases where the text is deliberately orchestrated. The very nature of rhythmic structure divides the text into units that do not coincide with semantic units, but which acquire semantic significance in the line. Scansion, either as a reality or as a possibility which serves as a background for the perception of poetic reality, is constantly present in the reader's consciousness. No wonder children begin to read (and perceive) verse by scanning it. In that form verses seem more sonorous to them. The history of poetry is also revealing in this respect.

Reading "by syllables" was typical for Russian syllabic verse. All syllables were read as thought they were stressed, and when the reader took a breath it had to correspond with one of the pauses between syllables. Boris Tomaševskij analyzed the rhyme schemes of Russian syllabic verse and concluded.

> The only thing that can account for such phenomena is the extreme weakness of the opposition between stressed and unstressed syllables, that is, when "reading by syllables." Later, without a doubt, the manner of reading must have changed, hence the idea of tonic verse, which opposes stressed syllables to unstressed.[51]

Thus, in syllabic verse, stress could not become a distinctive feature precisely because all syllables were stressed. This called for inevitable pauses between syllables, but simultaneously it practically abolished word-boundary

51 B. V. Tomaševskij, *Stix i jazyk*, op. cit. p. 101.

pauses. Simeon Polockij's verses were read in the following manner (ıı = pause and breath): *fi-lo-sof-vxu-dyx-ri-zax* ıı *o-byč-no-xo-žda-še* ıı *E-mu-že-vo-dvor-car-skij* ıı *nuž-da-ne-ka-bja-še.*

> (Filosof v xudyx rizax obyčno xoždaše,
> Emu že vo dvor carskij nužna neka bjaše)

> [The philosopher usually walked about in torn clothes;
> At the czar's court they had no need of him]

The same tendency, on a different basis, also appears among several twentieth century poets (Majakovskij, Cvetaeva). In Cvetaeva's poetry the urge to stress the syllable-boundary at times finds graphic expression:

> ... Boj za su-šče-stvo-van'e ...

> ... Bez vytja–givanija žil! ...

> ... Pravo–na–žitel'stvennyj svoj list
> No-gami topču!

> [... The battle for existence ...]

> [... Without pulling out the tendons ...] *

> [... I trample on my right to a residence permit!]

The question, however, is not whether the rhythmic nature of a line is revealed through scansion. When we scan lines the boundaries between lexical units not revealed in pronunciation are distinctly maintained in the reader's consciousness and correlate with the real pauses that break up the sound series. When we read lines and observe the lexico-semantic pauses, in our consciousness we retain the rhythmic pauses which remain real as "minus-devices."

Finally we should stipulate that when we took the repetition of the same sound or certain groups of sounds as an example of the correlation of phonemes we chose a case (Voznesenskij's "Goya") that would best lend itself to graphic demonstration. All phonemes in language are perceived in their mutual correlation, in a system which, in poetry, becomes the structure of content, an idioethnic structure, just like the plane of expression in language. Since the idioethnic phonological structure of a text becomes, in poetry, the basic structure of concepts, the non-translatable idioethnic nature of consciousness is expressed with considerably greater force in poetry than in a non-artistic text, or even prose.

In literature the sign remains verbal. It is not perceived by someone who has not mastered the given linguistic structure. Nevertheless in accordance with the principle of the correlation of content and expression, it approximates a figurative sign. The words of a nautral language as a communicative structure are compsed of elements of lower levels which are

---

* The idiomatic meaning of *vytjagivat' žily* is "to torment" in the sense: 1) to "slave-drive," "break someone's back," and 2) "to make things rough on someone."–Tr.

bereft of lexical meaning of their own. By virtue of the lexico-semantic significance of phonemes (and morphemes) in a poetic text, as we have already demonstrated, the structure of expression becomes the structure of content. The inclusion of elements of the lower levels in the process of concept-formation gives rise to occasional semantic oppositions, occasional archesemes which are impossible outside the given textual structure of expression. (That, incidentally, is why the most exact translation of a poetic text reproduces the structure of the content only in that part of the structure which is common to both poetic and non-poetic speech. Those semantic relations and oppositions which arise as a result of the semantization of the structure of expression are replaced by others. They are untranslatable, just as idioms in the structure of content are untranslatable. In view of what has been said, in speaking of a poetic text it would be more correct to speak of the endeavor to achieve functional adequacy rather than exact translation.)

We must take note of yet another circumstance. When a lexical meaning is "transmitted" by the phonemes which make up the word, and as a consequence, when a complex system of intra-textual oppositions is formed, not all the phonological elements which make up a given vocabulary behave identically.

We know that the question of a word's sound composition is, in principle, resolved differently in "language" than in "speech." In the first case we are dealing with a structure which is indifferent to the physical nature of a real signal, and therefore such phenomena as reduction are of interest only to those who study the speech aspect. This gives rise to questions concerning the nature of a text's predictability and the distribution of information in a word. It becomes clear that the distribution of information in a word is not equal in contextual written and oral speech. Experimental data for Russian speech (the informational load of the word *xorošo* ["good"] in context was analyzed) show that in written speech "information is wholly concentrated in the first half of the word, while its second half proves to be redundant." In oral speech "the end of the word carries the information load, relying on the stressed syllable. The beginning of the word [xʌr] proves to be redundant here."[53] Thus when the flow of speech is segmented into words, the semantic load is very unequally distributed.

The specific nature of a poetic text consists particularly in the fact that non-structural elements, peculiar to speech but not to language, acquire a structural character. As a result not all the phonic elements of verse carry an identical semantic load. Some are semantically reduced, others are emphasized as they enter into various oppositional relations. However, a poetic structure does not simply elevate speech to the class of language, lending non-structural elements a structural character. It radically changes

53 R. G. Piotrovskij, "O teoretiko-informacionnyx parametrax ustnoj i pis'mennoj form jazyka," *Problemy strukturnoj lingvistiki* (Moscow, 1962) p. 57.

the correlation of the degree of information borne by elements within speech: those which are redundant in non-artistic communication may become semantically loaded in poetry. Semantically poor elements of speech (for example, the end of a word in a written text) take on an uncharacteristic informational load in a particular structural position (for example, in the appearance of rhyme, which is a phenomenon of written poetry and is unknown in ancient folklore). This leads to another important feature of poetry. Poetic speech is not written, as the advocates of graphemic philology suggest. Neither is it oral speech, as the proponents of the phonetic method believed. The poetic structure of contemporary poetry, as opposed to folklore, is the *relation* of the oral text to the written, an oral text *against the background* of the written. Thus, the graphic nature of a text is by no means irrelevant for its comprehension.

The Problem of the Metrical Level of Verse Structure

The rhythmic and metrical aspect of verse is traditionally considered to be its most important feature; to this day it is the basic province of prosodic studies and has received greater elaboration than any other.

Earlier we attempted to show that a certain, highly significant, part of the artistic effect of poetic speech derives from the fact that it is attributable to rhythm, but does not belong to it. Rhythm and meter are to a significant degree only a means of segmenting the text into units smaller than words.

It does not follow, of course, that the metrical structure of verse is without its own significance. But its significance remains quite obscure.

In speaking of the significance of rhythm, we should delineate two aspects of the problem.

The first is this: meter can be treated as a way of structuring a given text in connection with a certain verbal-semantic fabric. In this case, meter is not a sign, but a means for structuring a sign. It "cuts" the text and participates in the formation of semantic oppositions (which we dealt with earlier), that is, it is a means of forming that specific semantic structure which constitutes the essence of verse.

The second aspect of the question consists in the creation of abstract rhythmic schemes which could be derived by abstracting the system of stresses and pauses. This aspect is the one which usually attracts the prosodist. Such a system is also real—it exists in the consciousness of the poet and his audience. Its nature, however, is different than what is usually supposed. And once again in our discussion we encounter extra-textual relations.

In order for a proffered text to be perceived as poetry, that is, in order for the listener to perceive everything that is redundant in ordinary speech as semantically distinctive and to comprehend the complex fabric of recurrences, comparisons and oppositions specific to poetry (or rather to any artistic text in varying degrees), he must *know* that he is confronting artistic poetic speech not ordinary speech. He must receive, therefore, a specific signal which will result in the proper perception.

A system of such signals has many ramifications. In the early stages of verbal art, this system included specific conditions of performance (cf. the tabu against telling stories during the daylight hours), ritualized poetic openings, fantastic subjects, a particular style of poetic speech and "unusual" pronunciation (declamation). All these things signaled to the reader that the proffered text was to be perceived as artistically constructed, that is, "pushed" into a fixed idealized structure and existing only in relation to it.

But rhythm is not only a signal that the text being perceived appertains to "poetry as such." It does not merely illuminate those facets of poetic speech which are revealed through the oppositions "poetry vs. prose" and "poetry vs. non-artistic text."

The semantic associations evoked by concrete meters also appertain exclusively to extra-textual relations. For various reasons a particular meter is associated with a genre, a fixed range of themes and vocabulary. A given poetic tradition gives rise to a characteristic "expressive aureole" (V. V. Vinogradov's term; Kolmogorov's term "the image of rhythm" expresses a similar idea). In his essay "On the Interrelation of Poetic Rhythm and Thematics," Kiril Taranovski concludes, "We should note that although poetic rhythm is devoid of autonomous meaning, it nonetheless carries certain information perceived outside the cognitive plane."[54] Taranovski's work splendidly corroborates the notion that the semantic interpretation of rhythm appertains to extra-textual relations. In tracing the history of the Russian five-foot trochee, the author shows how its intonational, semantic characteristics take shape (basically under the influence of Lermontov's use of this type of verse).

As an intra-textual structure meter performs a basic function—it divides the text into segments—lines, sub-linear and supra-linear sections. The division of the text into segments that are rhythmically equal creates a relation of equivalence betweeen them (the line is equivalent to a line, a foot to a foot). The non-repeated elements of equivalent parts of a text (semantic parts, for example) become semantic differentiators.

But in those cases where the possibility of rhythmic "figures" arises, against the background of a metrical constant, rhythmic division may fulfil a dual function: the assimilation of semantically dissimilar segments of the text (division into equivalent parts), and the dissimilation of these segments (division ito rhythmic variants). The possibility of resorting to various rhythmical subsystems within the limits of one metrical system and the varying probability that any one of them will be used, create the possibility of supplementary orderings which in concrete textual constructions are semantized in one way or another.

54 Kirill Taranovsky, "O vzaimootnošenii stixotvornogo razmera i tematiki," *American Contributions to the Fifth International Congress of Slavists* (Sofia, 1963).

As a result of the multiplicity and mutual intersection of these orderings, that which is regular and predictable on one level represents the violation of regularity and the lowering of predictability on another level. So on the rhythmic level too, a kind of "play" of orderings arises, thus creating the possibility of high semantic saturation.

Let us look at an example taken from Kolmogorov's notes on the margin of the manuscript of V. V. Ivanov's essay "The Rhythmic Structure O Mežirov's 'Ballad of the Circus'." Kolmogorov cites examples of the rare "fifth form" (in Taranovsky's terminology, the "seventh figure") of iambic tetrameter and concludes, "In modern Russian poetry the fifth form apparently came to be used more freely beginning with Pasternak in 'A Lofty Malady:'

> I po vodoprovodnoj seti. . .
>
> Za železnodorožnyj korpus,
> Pod železnodorožnyj most. . .
>
> [And through the plumbing system. . .]
> [Behind the railroad building,
> Under the railroad bridge. . .]

"Here in all three lines the secondary stress is on the third and not the second or fourth syllable:* there are many examples of forms with unstressed first and second feet in the iambic pentameters of Pasternak's *Spektorskij*."[55]

One cannot help but note that here the choice of a rarely used rhythmic figure (Taranovsky notes that in eighteenth and nineteenth century Russian poetry this form is virtually nonexistent)[56] compensates for the accentuated ordinariness of the speech. But at the same time the lexical ordinariness, the "anti-poetic" phraseologisms "plumbing system" and "railroad building" is not ordinary in poetry, but exotic, and the rare (and therefore unexpected) rhythmic figure also becomes anti-poetic under the influence of the vocabulary with the prosaic structure of speech being transmitted by means of verse.

However, in the poet's consciousness the rhythmic variants of verses might have certain independent emotional connotations which do not depend on the lexical "filling" of the line and which create additional semantic possibilities. This is confirmed by the fact that in their rough drafts poets sometimes change all the words in a line while maintaining a particular rhythmic figure (at times a very rare one).

---

* When consulted on this matter, native informants objected that despite the stress pattern dictated by the dictionary, one could quite naturally read the lines with the secondary stress on the second syllable of the line under the influence of the prevailing iambic tetrameter.—Tr.

55 V. V. Ivanov, "Ritmičeskoe stroenie 'Ballady o cirke'. . ." op. cit., p. 280.
56 Kirill Taranovsky, *Ruski dvodelni ritmove*, op. cit., p. 86.

Grammatical Repetition in the Poetic Text

The grammatical structure of a text, like phonological and other orderings which we examined earlier, has additional functions in a poetic work which are definitely not characteristic of it outside of literature. The poet, as a rule, cannot change the norms of a text's grammmatical organization. It does not follow, however, that the grammatical structure is neutral in its artistic function.[57]

From the viewpoint of the listener, on the one hand, a presumption of the total artistic significance of the text is operative here. The listener is inclined to consider all elements of a work of art the result of deliberate action on the part of the poet, since he knows of the presence of some design but does not yet know what that design consists of.

From the viewpoint of the author, on the other hand, linguistic redundancy provides for the constant possibility of choice between certain forms of grammatical expression for achieving semantic content.

The significance of grammatical repetitions is two-fold. First, there arises appreciable supplementary organization of the text, which proves to be permeated with equivalent or antithetical grammatical positions. As Roman Jakobson clearly demonstrated, the study of the artistic function of grammatical categories is equivalent in certain respects to the play of geometric structure in spatial forms of art. While the notion that the aesthetic aspect of a text is the exclusive domain of "images" forces one to suppose that only an insignificant stratum of a work is artistically organized, the revelation of the aesthetic function of grammatical sturcture allows one to see the entire text as aesthetically active. Grammatical repetitions, like phonological repetitions, take lexical units which are heterogeneous in an unorganized artistic text and bring them together into groups that are compared and contrasted, arranging them in columns of synonyms and antonyms.

Second, grammatical repetitions draw certain grammatical elements of the text out of a state of linguistic automatization. They begin to attract attention. But since everything noticeable in an artistic text is inevitably perceived as meaningful, as something carrying a certain semantic load, the grammatical elements which stand out are inevitably semanticized. The semantics ascribed to them may convey information regarding certain relations which closely resemble the relational bonds of grammar. Thus the system of verb tenses often organizes the temporal aspect of an artist's view of the world; categories of number enter into oppositions like "singular, unique vs. plural," and so on. In this case a system of unconditional connections of an iconic type is formed between the grammatical structure of the text and its semantic interpretation. But another case is often encountered: the relation between textual segments is given by the grammatical structure,

---

57 For the most detailed account of a text's grammatical structure see Roman Jakobson's "Grammatika poèzii i poèzija grammatiki," op. cit. Cf. "Linguistics and Poetics," *Style and Language* (New York, 1960).

but the interpretation of these relationships is determined by its correlation with other subclasses of the general artistic system and its organization as a whole.

Let us illustrate this proposition by examining the verb forms we encounter in Žukovskij's poem on the death of Puškin:

A. S. Puškin*

1. On ležal bez dvižen'ja, kak budto po tjažkoj rabote
2. Ruki svoi opustiv; golovu tixo sklonja,
3. Dolgo stojal ja nad nim, odin smotrja so vniman'em
4. Mertvomu prjamo v glaza; byli zakryty glaza,
5. Bylo lico ego mne tak znakomo, i bylo zametno,
6. Čto vyražalos' na nem—v žizni takogo
7. My ne vidali na ètom lice. Ne gorel vdoxnoven'ja
8. Plamen' na nem; ne sijal ostryj um;
9. Net! no kakoju-to mysl'ju, glubokoj, vysokoju mysl'ju
10. Bylo ob"jato ono: mnilosja mne, čto emu
11. V ètot mig predstojalo kak budto kakoe viden'e,
12. Čto-to sbyvalos' nad nim; i sprosit' mne xotelos': čto vidiš'?

[1. He lay motionless, as though after difficult work
2. He has dropped his hands; quietly bowing my head
3. I stood over him for a long time, alone, attentively looking
4. The dead man in the eye; the eyes were closed,
5. His face was so familiar and one could see
6. That it expressed something that in life
7. We had not seen on that face. The fire of inspiration
8. Did not burn there; the keen wit did not shine.
9. No! But some thought, a deep, lofty thought
10. Had enveloped it: it seemed to me
11. At that moment that some sort of vision appeared before him,
12. Things were happening to him; and I felt like asking, what do you see?

The sequential construction of verb forms is so distinct in this text that it cannot be considered as accidental. The verbal contrasts proceed along two lines: "personal forms vs. impersonal forms" and "active vs. passive." The text begins with two distinctly parallel constructions that are personal and active:

He lay—(having) dropped his hands
I stood—bowing my head

These introduce the two subject-object centers of the text (he—I), compared and opposed (the parallelism of grammatical forms accentuates the semantic

* The translation attempts to render the basic meaning of the Russian text, but here it is impossible to repeat all of the grammatical forms (e.g. active, or passive) as they are in the original. When phrases are quoted in the subsequent discussion, the original grammatical forms are maintained where possible.—Tr.

difference between "lay" and "stood"). In lines three and four there is an opposition: the antithesis "I vs. he" finds its parallel in the opposition "active vs. passive."

> I
> Stood, looking in the eye
> He
> Eyes were closed.

Lines five and six, as opposed to the first three lines, are passive at both semantic centers.

"We had not seen" in line seven begins a new group of verbal forms (7-10). The active form of the verb is accompanied by the negative particle "not", while the substitution of the plural "we" for "I" lends the category of person a feeling of generality, serving in the given context as an intermediate stage between the personal and impersonal constructions. Lines 7-10 present the antithesis:

> Did not burn
> Did not shine   —was enveloped

The opposition is realized along the lines "active voice vs. passive voice." But this opposition differs from the one at the beginning of the poem since the action designated in the left-hand member of the opposition is negated as something unreal. The quality of non-realization is assigned to the active voice and realization to the passive voice. Lines 10-12 begin a new segment built on the concentration of impersonal verb forms.

> It seemed to me—appeared before him

In the pair: "Things were happening to him—I felt like asking," the first member is not, formally speaking, impersonal. But Žukovskij perceived the passive form (in combination with the indefinite pronoun čto-to) as identical to an impersonal form. This is obvious from the entire construction of this part of the text.

The concluding "what do you see?" brings us back to the active and personal verbal forms of the beginning, but with a change in oppositions: "I vs. he" is replaced by "I vs. you [ty]," and the declarative intonation by an interrogative intonation.

Thus the text is indisputably broken up into segments which are organized differently in relation to verbal groups. What type of grammatical semantics is activated by such a division? At first the subject and object of the poetic world (I-he) are personal and active, then personal and passive, and finally impersonal.

Of course in common linguistic usage, where verbal categories are ordered grammatically but do not have to be ordered semantically (the same system of meanings can be conveyed within the confines of one or several languages by various means), the same verbal categories might be considered entirely formal. In the sentence *bylo prinjato rešenie dejstvovat' energično* ["the decision was made to act with vigor"] the passive construction does not signify passivity. This is not the case in a poetic text. But here too we deal with a secondary phenomenon—the semantization of a formal structure. This semantization (cf. analogous phenomena in folk etomology) can proceed along paths that are more general and "natural" for an entire speech community. Such is the case when grammatical gender is given sexual meaning or when the active and passive voices are interpreted in terms of activity and passivity. But in this type of secondary semantization an occasional element, created in the given text, will also be present at all times.

The ordering of grammatical categories creates the presumtion of their meaningfulness. We know they have meaning. But we can discover the nature of that meaning only from the construction of the given text. There always remains a certain structural leeway for purely individual interpretation as well.

Here too, in the text we are examining, the grammatical ordering is semanticized in two ways: through the "natural" interpretation of the "active-passive" and "personal-impersonal" categories, and in connection with other structural levels of the text.

The vocabulary is of great significance in interpreting the semantics of grammatical forms:

1. He lay motionless, as though after difficult work
2. He had dropped his hands; quietly bowing my head
3. I stood over him for a long time. . .

The grammatical construction semanticizes these lines in terms of their opposition to passive and impersonal constructions. "I" and "he" represent two subjects in two parallel sentences. Their predicates are identical in terms of gammatical form (both are personal and active). The category of tense is not significant in the poem, since the entire text is in the past with the exception of the last line, to which we will devote individual attention. But by shifting our analysis to the lexical level we can clarify a number of points.

"He" and "I" are not only equated but opposed. The first thing we should note is a kind of syntactic palindrome:

1	2	3	4
Subject	Predicate	Adverbial of Manner	Adverbial Participial construction
he	lay	motionless	having dropped his hands
4	3	2	1
quietly bowing my head	long	stood	I

The constructions which include "I" and "he" are not simply similar; they are also opposed as mirror images of each other. The opposition on the semantic level is even sharper.

The verbs "lay" and "stood" which are united in their grammatical antithesis to the second and their parts of the poem, are semantically antonymous. But this antonymy is of a particular type: it does not permit us to determine with certainty whether we are dealing with an opposition involving only the position and actions of "I" and "he" ("He lay" and "I stood"–the same type of opposition we find in the line "Some polished their beat-up shakos, others sharpened their bayonets, murmuring angrily"*) or whether "stood" and "lay" are metonymic substitutions for another antithesis: "I was alive–he was dead." The opposition is constructed in such a way that there is room for both these disparate interpretations. "He" and "I" are equally valid. The fact that there are two subjects forces us to assume an equal degree of animation in both cases (the combination *nas bylo dvoe–ja i trup* ["there were two of us–the corpse and I"] is semantically impossible). The condition "lay motionless" is amplified by the words "as though after difficult work/ He had dropped his hands." All this stresses the semantics of life in the verb "lay," although the reader knows the true meaning of the opposition, not only from the comparitive conjunction "as though" with a connotation of conditionality, but also because the poem is dedicated to the deceased poet. Beginning with the third line, however, the ambiguity is swiftly resolved:

> 3. I stood over him for a long time, *alone* attentively looking
> 4. The *dead man* in the eye; the eyes were closed. . .

The second subject "he", an equal of "I", is transformed into an object expressed by a pronoun in an oblique case: *Ja stojal nad nim* ["I stood over him"]. It is no accident that precisely at this point "alone" makes its appearance and that "he" is transformed from a "second" subject into a dead man. This unidirectional movement is expressed in two ways: 1) grammatically, through antithesis "active movement vs. passive movement;" "I looked him in the eye–the eyes were closed;" and 2) lexically: the mutual relation of "I" and "he" in lines one and two becomes onesided: "I looked him in the eye, but his eyes did not look at me;" "the eyes were closed."

Further on "I" and "he" are equated in a new way, but no longer as equivalent-active, but as equivalent-passive:

> Bylo lico ego mne tak znakomo. . .
>
> Bylo zametno, čto vyražalos' na nem. . .
>
> [His face was so familiar, . .]
>
> [One could see that it expressed something. . .]

* This line is from Lermontov's ballad "Borodino."–Tr.

While in the personal, active grammatical construction "I" was the center of action, in the impersonal passive construction, "I" becomes only a passive observer involved in the basic action of "he." Lines seven, eight, nine, and ten present a grammatical antithesis: the actions expressed by verbs in the active voice are rejected (given in negative form), and what is really occurring is expressed in passive form:

> The fire of inspiration did not burn. . .

> The keen wit did not shine. . .

"Burned" and "shone" are synonyms on a certain level accentuating the common semantic features of fire and light, which are metaphorically ascribed to "inspiration" and "wit," the latter being regarded as synonyms. We will not explore all the facets of the semantic shift engendered by this secondary synonymy; let us simply note that "wit" and "inspiration" are perceived under the influence of this grammatical antithesis as personal, active characteristics, as the luster and brightness of the active individual. "Thought" is opposed to these qualities. Its grammatical structure and the semantics of the passive construction "was enveloped" convey a sense of the supra-personal, which is expressed in man, but not created by man.

There then follows a group of impersonal verbs (or their structural equivalents) which take in both centers of the text:

I	He
Seemed to me	Appeared before him
(I) felt like asking	Were happening to him

"He" is a participant in some impersonal and supra-personal action, although he takes part in this passively. The semantics of the verbs oblige us to interpret these grammatical constructions as the expression of an act of initiation.

The concluding "What do you see?" returns us grammatically and semantically to lines three and four. There "I" looks "attentively" while "he" is dead; his eyes are closed. "He" does not see. Here, "he" (thou, the familiar form) sees something that is invisible to "I."

The concluding line, however, takes on special meaning, and not only because of semantic antithesis (the closed eyes of the dead man see things which are hidden from the eyes of the living) not only because as a result of grammatical opposition, a passive construction is interpreted as participation in real acts, while an active condition is interpreted as participation in imaginary acts. The opposition of grammatical tenses is no less meaningful: the entire poem is written in the past, but the concluding hemistich is in the present tense. In the poem's context this organization is semanticized as the antithesis of real time (both "I" and "he" are included in the past) to some "non-time" (the present tense includes only "he—you" as a participant in this "non-time").

Thus the complex picture of the relationship of life and death, of "I" and "not I," is to a considerable degree revealed through the verbal structure of Žukovskij's poem.

Grammatical categories, as Roman Jakobson indicated, express relational meanings in poetry. It is these categories which to a significant degree create a model of the poet's vision of the world, a structure of subject-object relations. Clearly it is a mistake to reduce the specificity of poetry to its imagery, rejecting the *material* which the poet uses to construct his model of the universe.

All grammatical classes express relational fuctions. Conjunctions, for example, are extremely important:

> V trevoge pestroj i besplodnoj
> Bol'šogo sveta i dvora. . .

> [In the restlessness, motley and barren
> Of the *beau monde* and the court. . .]

The two conjuctions "and" are placed close to each other in a markedly parallel arrangement as two ostensibly identical grammatical constructions. However they are not identical, but parallel, and their juxtaposition only stresses their difference. In the second line "and" conjoins two members which are so alike that it loses its character as a means of conjuction. The expression *"beau monde* and court" blends into a phraseological whole whose separate components lose their autonomy. In the first line the conjunction "and" links concepts that are not only heterogeneous, but belong to different planes as well. It helps to single out a common semantic core, an archeseme, by stressing their parallelism, and because the difference between the archeseme and each of these concepts in isolation is keenly felt, the concepts in turn lend as adversative meaning to the conjunction. This meaning assigned to the relation between the concepts "motley" and "barren" might pass unnoticed if the first "and" were not parallel to the second, which totally lacks this shade of meaning and accordingly is marked in the act of comparison.

One could cite examples for all grammatical classes which would demonstrate that grammatical elements acquire special meaning in poetry. Thus the system of grammatical relationships constitutes an important level of poetic structure. It is, in addition, organically related to the entire construction of the text and cannot be understood outside it.

Structural Properties of Verse on the Lexico-Sematic Level

Although each of the levels singled out in an artistic text is important for the construction of the work's integral structure, the basic unit of the verbal artistic construction remains the word. All structural layers below the word (organization on the level of word components) and above the word (organization on the level of word chains) acquire meaning only in relation to the level formed by the words of a natural language. The violation of this principle in "trans-rational" texts, as well as the necessity of "empty words"—units semantically filled *ad hoc*—does not negate this basic proposition, but rather supports it, just as the phenomenon of aphasia confirms rather than disproves the structural quality of language.

Linguists, as we know, find it very difficult to define what a word is. This, however, cannot force us to forego a working definition of the elements of this basic textual level, the level which represents the upper limit of all units on the paradigmatic axis, and the lower limit on the syntagmatic axis.

We need not be discouraged by the fact that linguistic scholarship finds it difficult to define the word, since there is a parallel situation to be considered: every person using a language is convinced that he knows what a word is. If we define a word according to those of its features which manifest themselves on the structural level pertaining to it, then it appears as the most elementary unit on the syntagmatic (compositional) level. If we take its relation to other levels as a basis for our definition, then its semantic integrality comes into the foreground.

In order to understand this, let us compare a verbal text to a nonverbal text—a painting, or ballet—and attempt to find some common structural invariant which would be manifested in the literary text as a word, and in the non-literary text as its perceptible correlates. It is clear that we can speak of composition in a scene from a ballet, meaning the correlation of steps and positions (we easily distinguish "nouns," their actions and predicates). But the relation between the size of a dancer's hand and the size of his foot will not be an element of composition (syntagmatically) because the human body is an integral unit. Similar observations could apply to painting: until the dismemberment of the object into aspects and planes became an artistic possibility, composition included the *arrangements* of the objects represented as integral entities.

However the singling out of this elementary level of compositional structure only begins the elucidation of the concept of the word in art. As we have seen, because of the constant play of levels in art, no one level in an artistic work has an absolute, previously specified, isolated existence; while remaining itself, it is constantly recoded into units of the other levels. As a result a word, while remaining a word, tends to be equal to smaller units, to be a part of itself (each part of the word strives to become autoomous, to become an integral unit of the compositional whole). At the same time, the word strives to expand its boundaries, to transform the entire text into one, integral whole—one word.

The simultaneous functioning of all these structural types of textual delimitation (basic semantic units are sometimes transferred into a word and sometimes transferred to the outer limits of the text) creates that wealth of semantic play which is inherent to works of art.

Poetic form was born of the effort to place words with different meanings into a position of maximal equivalence. The poetic structure employs every form of equivalence—rhythmic, phonological, grammatical, syntactic—so that the text will be perceived as a construct governed by the law of mutual equivalence of parts, even when this is not clearly expressed in the explicit structure (when the minus-structure is dominant).

In the poetic text, therefore, it is in essence impossible to isolate the word as a separate semantic unit. Each semantic unit existing separately in non-artistic language acts only as a functive of a complex semantic fuction when it occurs in poetic language.

The "connectedness" of a word in a poetic text finds its expression in the fact that a word is correlated with other words situated in a parallel position. While the contextual connections in natural language are determined by the mechansim of grammatical assembling of words into syntactic units, the basic mechanism of poetic language is parallelism.[58] Different words are found to be in a position of equivalency which gives rise to complex semantic correlation, the singling out of a common semantic kernel (unexpressed in ordinary language) and a contrastive pair of distinctive semantic features.

> Gljažu na buduščnost' s bojazn'ju,
> Gljažu na prošloe s toskoj,
> I kak prestupnik pered kazn'ju
> Išču krugom duši rodnoj. . .
>
> [I gaze on the future with fear,
> I gaze on the past with anguish,
> And like a criminal before his execution
> I search about for a kindred soul. . .]
>   (Lermontov)

In this example we easily detect that the words composing these four lines in many respects form parallel pairs. The overall parallelism of the first two lines, based on the anaphoric repetition of an identical element of the rhythmic and syntactic construction ("I gaze on") singles out two lexical pairs: "future—past," and "with fear—with anguish." The nature of these oppositions differs. "Future" and "past" are antonyms, and their intra-textual meanings are close to their general linguistic meanings. "Fear" and "anguish" do not form a lexical pair in non-artistic language—they are more similar than dissimilar in their extra-textual semantics. Thus the act of parallelism has different meanings here. In the pair "future—past," it basically singles out what is common in what is opposed. ("Future" and "past" are opposites, but since they give rise to the same attitude—"fear" and "anguish", they appear to be identical.) In the pair "fear—anguish," separate meanings reveal opposition in their correlation, with diversity revealed in likeness.

In the first line, additional groupings may be distinguished:

58 Naturally, this does not cancel out the significance of principles operating in the ordinary language, which govern the establishment of contextual relations.

Gljaž*u* na bu*duščnost'* na *buduščnost'* s *b*ojazn'ju

Similar relations are also established between words of the second line and are perceived by the listener as semantic. But here sound repetition is not sufficiently stressed and consequently the semantic relations between these words are not so clearly expressed as they are, for example, in Majakovskij's phrase: *Stisnul tors tolp* ["The torso of crowds pressed..."], where two pairs are set in sharp relief: s*tisnul tors* and to*rs tolp*. At the same time phonetic non-coincidence is also stressed (*tis—tors*), showing that we are dealing here with semantic convergence, not identity. It is interesting that phonic difference stands out more clearly in the pairs *stisnul tors* and *tors tolp* than in *gljažu na buduščnost'* which would seem to be far less convergent. So we must not only establish the presence of connections, but also introduce the concept of their *intensity* which characterizes to what degree an element is connected in a structure. We suggest that the degree of intensity of poetically bonded words is relatively measurable. For this one must compose a matrix of the features of parallelism and calculate the number of realized connections. (To simplify matters we will not initially consider the problem of extra-textual connections.)

Returning to the excerpt from Lermontov's text we notice that while the anaphoric symmetry of the first two lines suggests the idea of their parallelism, their obvious rhythmic non-equivalence and, conversely, the equivalence of the first and third lines becomes an oppositional feature.*

Rhythmic equivalence suggests the semantic parallelism of the first and third lines. This is strengthened by the presence of the rhyming pairs *bojazn'ju—kazn'ju* ["fear—execution"], where the basis for the comparison is the grammatical element (the inflectional ending *'ju*), although the roots, the principal carriers of semantics, are not wholly opposed. The repetition of the phonemes of the stem (*a,z,n*) and their clear semantic proximity provide the grounds for the emergence of the intra-textual semantic interdependence of the rhyming words.

In the third line we can discover still another complex semantical construction. Logically, this line is constructed as a simile: 'I, like a criminal.'' The image of the poet, however, which is the ideological center of the poem, is not named in the text. Even the personal pronoun "I" is missing. The only grammatical carrier of the idea of the subject is the inflectional ending of the first person singular—*u* (*gljažu* ["I look"]). The semantic load of the phoneme *u,* its role in the quatrain, is determined by its grammatical function as the carrier of the idea of the subject. It is curious that when the personal pronoun "I" appears later in the poem, the phoneme *u* almost disappears from the text. In the identifying phrase "and like a criminal" in the third line, the subject is not named, but the emphatically stressed *u* in the word *prestupnik* ["criminal"] is perceived as merging with

* The Russian text reads, "the rhythmic equivalence of the first and *second* lines becomes an oppositional feature;" this would appear to be an error.—Tr.

the subject. The correlations in the fourth line in the pair *išču–duši* ["seek–soul"] are of a different nature (*duši* is phraseologically connected with *rodnoj* ["kindred"], which in turn forms the pair *rodnoj–s toskoj* ["kindred–with anguish"]). *Išču–duši* manifests reverse parallelism–it is a phonological palindrome (like Cvetaeva's *Ad?–Da.* ["Hell? Yes."]). Subject-object relations are syntactically established betwee *išču* and *duši*, and seem to divide them, but the phonological parallelism reveals that system of inter-relations which is elucidated by the epithet *rodnaja* ["like, kindred"]. This epithet unites the two syntactic centers of the phrase (the subject and object are "kindred"). This parallelism, which differs both from identity and from a state of disparity, reveals the complex dialectics of relations between the poetic "I" and "kindred soul." By analyzing the rest of the text we could show the complex correlation of its structuro-semantic planes–that of the poetic subject, the hostile world of God, whom he reproaches, and his readiness for a "different life," expressing the note of social Utopianism so important for Lermontov.

Of course this sort of "connectedness" of words in an artistic text is not absolute. The presumption of connectedness which characteristically arises when a text is perceived as poetic also makes minus-connectedness (non-connectedness) a structurally active element. At the same time a text exists against the background of numerous extra-textual connections (the aesthetic task, for example). Therefore structural simplicity (a low degree of connectedness) may be set against the background of a complex structure of extra-textual relations, and thus acquire semantic saturation (the poetry of the mature Puškin, Nekrasov, and Tvardovskij is typologically of this sort). Only in the absence of complex extra-textual bonds does the weakness of structural relations within the text become a sign of primitiveness and not simplicity.

Thus the establishment of universal correlations for words in a poetic text deprives them of that autonomy inherent to them in a text in ordinary language. The entire work becomes a *sign of a single content*. Potebnja was acutely aware of this fact; he expressed the opinion (which appeared para-doxical in his time, but in fact was extraordinarily penetrating) that the entire text of a work of art is essentially one word.

But despite the validity of all that has been said, the lexical level is the ground on which the entire edifice of semantics is constructed in the integral structure of the artisitic text. The transformation of a word in a poetic text from a unit of structure into an element thereof cannot destroy the general linguistic perception of the word as the fundamental unit of cor-relation between designator and designatum. What is more, the numerous relations of parallelism between words in a poetic text not only emphasize what they have in common, but also underscore the specificity of each word. It follows that the connectedness of words in a poetic text entails the accentuation of their semantic "separateness" rather than its obliteration.

Earlier we said that the rhythmic segmentation of verse heightens rather than obliterates the feeling of word-boundary. All the grammatical aspects of a word which would be obliterated in the speaker's consciousness due to the automatism of speech, also acquire meaning. This separateness of the word, much more pronounced in poetry than in non-artistic speech, is particularly evident in auxiliary words, which would have only grammatical meaning in natural language. Pronouns, prepositions, conjunctions or particles need only be placed in a poetic text in positions where, due to metrical pauses, they acquire the "separateness" characteristic of notional words in the natural language, and immediately such words take on an additional and now *lexical* meaning which they would not possess in a different text:

> . . . . il' *ešče*
> Moskvič v Garol'dovom plašče.
>
> [. . . . . or *else*
> A muscovite in Childe Harold's cloak.]
>   (Puškin, *Evgenyj Onegin* 7:24)

> *Vot*
> xotite,
> iz pravogo glaza
> vynu
> celuju cvetuščuju rošču?!
>
> [*Here*,
> if you wish,
> from my right eye
> I'll pluck
> A whole flowering grove?!]
>   (Majakovskij)

> Loži, v slezy! V nabat, jarus!
> Srok, ispoln'sja! Geroj, bud'!
> Xodit zanaves—*kak*—parus,
> Xodit zanaves—*kak*—grud'.
>
> [Loges, weep! Tiers sound the alarm!
> Time, be fulfilled! Hero, be!
> The curtain rises—*like*—a sail,
> The curtain rises—*like*—a breast.]
>   (Cvetaeva)

It is revealing that if we simply change the rhythmic structure of the last text (the last two lines) from:

to the more usual structure (which can be done in these last two lines):

Xodit zanaves kak parus,
Xodit zanaves kak grud'.

Thus removing the stress on *kak* and the pause that follows it, the unusual plurality of meanings disappears. The great semantic capacity of *kak* ["like"] is explained in particular by the fact that both metric schemes on which the text can be superimposed are correlated and form a sort of opposition.

Thus the semantics of words in natural language are only raw material for the language of the artistic text. Drawn into supra-linguistic structures, lexical units are like pronouns which derive meaning from their *correlation* with the entire secondary system of semantic meanings. Words which are mutually isolated in the system of natural language prove to be functionally synonymous or antonymous when they occur in structurally equivalent positions. This reveals semantic differentiators in them which are not manifested in their semantic structure in the system of natural language. But the capacity of transforming different words into synonyms, and of making the same word semantically unequal to itself in different structural positions, does not change the fact that the artistic text remains a text in a natural language. This dual existence, the tension between these two semantic systems, accounts for the richness of poetic meanings.

Let us examine a poem by Marina Cvetaeva in order to discover the way in which structural repetitions divide a text into mutually equivalent semantic segments which enter into complex secondary relations with each other. Our choice of a poem written by Cvetaeva is not accidental. Like Lermontov, she is one of those poets whose texts are clearly and explicitly segmented into equivalent sections.

Her verse is just as apt for demonstrating the semantic paradigmatics of the poetic text as that of Majakovskij or Pasternak would be for demonstrating semantic syntactics:

O slezy na glazax!
Plač gneva i ljubvi!
O Čexija v slezax!
Ispanija v krovi!

O černaja gora,
Zatmivšaja—ves' svet!
Pora—pora—pora
Tvorcu vernut' bilet.

Otkazyvajus'—byt'.
V Bedlame neljudej
Otkazyvajus'—žit'.
S volkami ploščadej

Otkazyvajus'–vyt'.
S akulami dolin
Otkazyvajus' plyt'–
Vniz po tečen'ju spin.

Ne nado mne ni dyr
Ušnyx, ni veščix glaz.
Na tvoj bezumnyj mir
Otvet odin–otkaz.

[Oh, tears in the eyes!
The weeping of rage and love!
Oh, Bohemia in tears!
Spain covered with blood!

Oh, black mountain
That has eclipsed–the whole world!
Time–time–time
To return the Creator his ticket.

I refuse–to be.
In the Bedlam of non-people
I refuse–to live.
With the wolves of the squares

I refuse–to howl.
With the sharks of the valleys
I refuse–to swim
Down the stream of backs.

I do not need the holes
Of ears, or prophetic eyes.
To your insane world
There is only one answer–refusal.]
                        15 March–11 May, 1939

All four lines of the first stanza are clearly equated by their identical intonation and syntactical and semantic parallelism. In the first line, "Oh, tears in the eyes," "tears" have only a general dictionary meaning for the reader. But in the text of the poem, this dictionary definition is only a pronoun, a substitute, an indication of the specific secondary meaning created by the semantic structure of the text.

In the dictionary "rage" and "love" are antonyms, but here they are structurally equated (syntactically and intonationally).[59] The simultaneous functioning of antithesis on the level of general linguistic semantics and of synonymy on the level of the poetic structure, activate both those features

59 Cf. another type of synonymic equation in Tjutčev's poem:

No kto v izbytke oščuščenij,
Kogda kipit i stynet drov',
Ne vedal vašix iskušenij–
Samoubijstvo i Ljubov'!

which unite these two words in an archeseme and those which set them in polar opposition. The opposition of these concepts makes us perceive "rage" as "anti-love" and "love" as "anti-rage," while equating them reveals their common content: "strong passion."

Archeseme

Semantic units

```
        strong passion
         /        \
      rage        love
```

In combination with this semantic group, "weeping" is not perceived as the expression of passive emotion, like grief or impotence. It is not opposed to activity. In this sense a semantic tension inevitably arises between the first line, where the word "tears" still has a dictionary meaning, and the second; this tension is complicated by correlations with the last two lines.

Bohemia and Spain are synonymous as two heroic symbols of the struggle against Fascism (the similarity and difference between the fate of Spain and Czechoslovakia in 1939 were so topical an issue that the mere mention of them together revealed a whole system of semantic comparisons and oppositions; at the same time a chain of antithesis arose—from the bloody stamping-out of freedom to the "bloodless surrender," as well as geographical oppositions).

The role of geographic names in the poetic text is a special subject for investigation. Hemingway expressed an interesting point of view about the attitude toward geographical terms during World War I:

> There were many words that you couldn't stand to hear and finally only the names of places had dignity. Certain numbers were the same way and certain dates and those with the names of places were all you could say and have them mean anything. Abstract words such as glory, honor, courage or hallow were obscene beside the concrete names of villages, the numbers of roads, the names of rivers, the numbers of regiments and the dates.[60]

The function of such geographical terms as "Hill 101" or "Nameless Hill" in wartime is contiguous not only to that of scientific terms, but also to that of occasionalisms in poetry. These words receive their meaning from the given situation and make no sense out of context. They may become the key word in a situation and then instantly lose all meaning.

> [But who, overcome with sensations,
> When the blood boils and freezes,
> Has not known your temptations,
> Suicide and Love!]

"Boils and freezes" and "Suicide and Love" are paired equivalents, which only activates their differences, transforming difference into opposition. If we compare Tjutčev's and Cvetaeva's constructions, we see that one word ("love") is filled with different meanings depending on the synonymic series that is asigned to it.

60 Ernest Hemingway, *Izbrannye proizvedenija v 2-x tomax,* vol. 1 (Moscow 1959) p. 311.

On the other hand, the juxtaposition of the names of geographically distant places in a text produces the same effect as the "conjunction of disparate ideas;"

Ot potrjasennogo Kremlja
Do sten nedvižnogo Kitaja. . .

[From the shaken Kremlin
To the walls of immutable China. . .]
(Puškin)

In this passage we find not only the antinomy "shaken vs. immutable," but also spatial opposition "very close, one's own vs. very far, alien." The effect of equating distant points in space is identical to the rhetorical equating of distant ideas. Thus in poetry, geographical terms (particularly the juxtaposition of distant points) are primarily a feature of high style. It is revealing that Vjazemskij described the style of Puškin's poem "Slanderers of Russia" as a "geographical fanfaronade," and viewed it not only as a political, but also as a poetic anachronism, an example of the eighteenth century odic style.

The opposition of Spain and Bohemia in Cvetaeva's poem also brings together the names of geographically distant points in an original metaphor. Simultaneously, the following oppositions arise:

krov'–slëzy	[blood–tears] (both opposed and
Čexija–slëzy	[Bohemia–tears] equated)
Ispanija–krov'	[Spain–blood]

The first two lines and the third and fourth are contrasted and opposed (this is underscored by the parallelsim of the anaphoral *o*). The first two speak of the poet, the latter of the world around her. The poet is bound to this world, the world of victims, by the identity of her feelings.

The second stanza is parallel to the first in accordance with the structural scheme "poet–world."[61] But here the resolution is quite different. While in the equation of Spain and Bohemia the political and symbolic rather than the concrete, geographical content is stressed, in the antithesis:

Bohemia ⎫
　　　　⎬　　the whole world
Spain 　⎭

the left-hand member is geographical and concrete, while the right-hand member is extremely generalized, and the generalization is spatial (the world). But in the opposition:

black 　　　　　⎫
　　　　　　　　⎬　　world [*svet*]
that has eclipsed ⎭

___

[61]The incipient automatism of this division is corrected by a transposition: the first two lines are about the world, the last two about the poet.

we discover that "light" is included in the semantics of the right-hand member.62* The antithesis:

gora zatmivšaja—svet

[Mountain which has eclipsed—light]

gives *svet* a new semantic feature, including it within certain spatial confines beyond which there is "no light," as in the line *ne ves' v okoške belyj svet* ["you can't see the whole world through the window"] (Tvardovskij). In addition this line introduces another aspect of the poetic subject, its spatial perspective: a *black* mountain lies between the poet and the light, and a black *mountain* lies between the poet and the *whole* world (in one case light is the relevant feature, in the other case the spatial feature dominates).

The phonological convergence of *gora* and *pora* ["mountain" and "time"] incorporates the semantics of mountain into a series of temporal phenomena that are utterly alien to it and (in conjunction with the semantization of the prefix *za*) lends the *zatmivsaja gora* ["the mountain which has eclipsed"] the feature of an action unfolding in time and space—*a crawling movement.*

The triple repetition of "time" with total coincidence of the lexico-semantic dictionary meaning reveals a single differentiator: intonation. And the intonation, established in this way, permits us to include the modal feature of decisiveness, the energy of confirmation, which is not part of the word's natural linguistic meaning; this feature is not only introduced, but forms a quantitatively rising scale.

The line "To return the Creator His ticket" is a double quotation, and its semantics are revealed through extra-textual relations. First, Cvetaeva is of course referring to the words of Ivan Karamazov: "They set too high a value on harmony, you know; we can't afford to pay the entrance fee. So I hasten to return my ticket for admission. . . . It's not God I don't accept, Aleša, only I am respectfully returning the ticket to Him."63

* *Svet* can mean both "world" and "light" in Russian. In the line by Tvardovskij quoted below, the wordplay is based on this ambiguity. *Belyj svet* taken by itself simply means "the world," but when the word "window" is introduced the "world" becomes "light."—Tr.

62 Cf. the revitalizing of the semantic opposition *sevt* vs. *t'ma* ["light, world" vs. "darkness"] in Pasternak's use of the phraseologism *belyj svet* [literally "white light," figuratively, "the wide world"]:

Ja bol'še vsex udač i bed
Za to tebja ljubil,
Čto poželtelyj belyj svet
S toboj—belej belil.

[I loved you more
Than all successes and misfortunes
Because the yellowed white light/wide world
Is whiter than white with you.]

63 F. M. Dostoevskij, *Sobranie sočinenij v 10-ti tomax*, vol. IX (Moscow, 1958) p. 308.

But Ivan Karamazov's words are a free rendering of a famous passage from a letter Belinskij wrote to Botkin on March 1, 1841: "I humbly thank you Egor Fedorovič,–I bow to your philosopher's cap; but with all due respect to your philosophical philistinism, I have the honor to inform you that if I were able to climb to the top rung of the evolutionary ladder, I would ask you there, too, to give me an account of all the victims of the conditions of life and history, all the victims of chance, superstition, the inquisition, Phillip II and so on and so forth. Otherwise I would throw myself down from the top rung."[64]

Comparing Cvetaeva's poem with its sources confirms not only this coincidence but also a significant divergence in thought.

The following two stanzas are connected by their common meaning, by the anaphoral beginning "I refuse" and the parallelism of their syntactic structures; they are constructed like transformations of the first and central line:

Otkazyvajus'–byt'   [I refuse–to be]

Both the lexical and grammatical meaning of the word *byt'* (the infinitive ["to be"]) stress the feature of universality. In its semantic universality and generaltity, "to be" almost becomes a pronoun; it replaces *all* verbs of being and action verbs. The antithesis of the first person singular "I refuse" and the infinitive "to be" gives the most general formula of the relation "I and the world."[65]

But this is not simply a rejection of the world, but a rejection of a world where Fascism triumphs. Therefore "to be," while remaining general and philosophical, unravels a chain of meaings that grows broader and increasingly concrete.

> *otkazyvajus'–byt':*
> V Bedlame neljudej–*žit'*
> S volkami ploščadej–*vyt'*
> S akulami dolin–*plyt'*
> Vniz–po tečen'ju spin.

> [*I refuse–to be:*
> In the Bedlam of non-people–*to live*
> With the wolves of the squares–*to howl*
> With the sharks of the valleys–*to swim*
> Down the stream of backs.]

64 V. G. Belinskij, *Polnoe sobranie sočinenij,* vol. XII (Moscow, 1956) pp. 22-23. Marina Cvetaeva's long acquaintance in Prague with E. Ljackij, the publisher and commentator on Belinskij's letters (G. G. Superfin was gracious enough to call my attention to this) means it is quite probable that she was familiar with this quote. Superfin referred me to the remarks, "The poem paraphrases the famous Schiller-Dostoevskij formula," (S. Karlinsky, *Marina Cvetaeva. Her Life and Art* [Los Angeles, 1966] p. 98).

65 The nontextual relation of the phrase to Hamlet's question, "To be or not to be" is undoubtedly significant here.

This entire chain of synonyms (the vertical column) reveals the common elements and specific features of the semantic degrees. Bedlam is the mad inhuman world and the refusal to "live" means that it is impossible to exist in this world.

The next synonymic series gives a much more socially concrete description of the scene of action. The combination of the lexical elements "wolves" and "squares" activates features of predation and the street. But the verbal infinitive relates differently to this group (cf. the extra-textual "You live among wolves, you howl like a wolf");* this is not merely co-presence, but complicity. Now "to be" means *to act like* a wolf. "To be" is consecutively equated with "live in the Bedlam of non-people" (the feature of passive coexistence is specified); "to howl with the wolves of the squares" (the feature of joint action is specified); and "*to swim* with the sharks of the valleys" "*down* the stream of backs" (the feature of obedience is specified). There is a sequential extension of the description of place and circumstances of action. In the first case it is expressed by an empty square—"to be" has no words that relate to it; it is followed by adverbial groups of two words (not counting prepositions) and finally a group of four words.

Not only are the verbs "to be—to live—to howl— to float" equivalent, but also the adverbial groups: "Bedlam of non-people—wolves of the squares—sharks of the valleys. . . down the stream of backs." The equivalence, however, not only stresses the semantic equality ("non-people—wolves—sharks" is perceived as a synonymic series), but also singles out variance. "Bedlam of non-people," when compared to "wolves of the square," brings out a series of semantic differentiations:

> a mad world—a predatory world
>
> non-people—anti-people

It is no coincidence that in the first case we are dealing with a *locative adverbial and in the second—a manner* adverbial. The second group specifies the semantics of an evil activity. The synonymic repetition "wolves of the squares—sharks of the valleys" singles out a new archeseme, "plunderers of cities and villages," and on the visual plane of the metaphor singles out the common feature of sharks and wolves—*teeth* (in a survey of seminar students at Tartu University, in response to the question, "How do you picture this image?" eighty percent affirmed that they associated the image with teeth).

Further on, a differential group is singled out: together with "sharks" the phrase "a stream of backs" appears; the author refuses to swim down this stream. While the earlier refusal expressed a reluctance to be a wolf among wolves, here it is a refusal to be the stream down which sharks swim, to be the *facelessness* (a stream of *backs*) that encourages predation. But

* One rough English equivalent of the Russian proverb would be "When in Rome, do as the Romans do."–Tr.

since all of these descriptions are equated with the universal "to be," a model of the world is created which permits no other possible existence. As a result, the four repetitions "I refuse—I refuse—I refuse—I refuse" are not equal. They differ in the quantity and quality of the rejection expressed: the first is similar to a generalizing word in an enumeration, the rest to the enumeration itself (as in the construction ". . .everything—this, that, and the other thing").

The text is divided into larger segments as well, which must be discussed if we are to understand the semantics of the last word in the poem: "refusal."

In the first two stanzas, we find the opposition "poet vs. world." But this opposition is posed from some third, objective point of view which observes both semantic centers from without. The persistent avoidance of personal verb forms and the presence of verbless one-member syntactic structures are no accident.

In the two following stanzas there appears a structurally expressed "I" which functions as the semantic center of the text. True, it is given not in the form of a personal pronoun, but as a first person verb. In this way a gradational reserve is maintained which allows for an even more emphatic expression of the first person. But if we are to understand the "I" of this text, we must find out what is opposed to it.

In the first segment, "tears in the eyes (subject)—world—Creator" form one series from the narrative point of view. The second two are constructed on the opposition "I vs. the world." The Creator is not mentioned.

The concluding stanza reduces everything to the basic antithesis "I vs. Creator." The latter is totally identified with the world. The introduction of the dialogue form "I—thou" is characteristic. But when we construct a paradigm of the concept "I," the "thou" opposed to it and also the structure of their relations, we can make several interesting observations on the semantics of these compositional centers of the text. Previously we have observed the growing prominence of "I" and its opposition to the world, but now we witness its disintegration. One side of the "I," the side connected with the senses and materiality, is singled out. The fact that hearing and sight are only metonymic here is a result of the equation of opposing styles: the vulgar "ear holes" and the literary "prophetic eyes." This is not meant to imply that hearing belongs to a lower sphere than sight. Rather, the point is that "from the lofty to the vulgar, from hearing to sight—*anything* that serves as my window to the world is unnecessary." The fact that something within *me* may be unneeded by *me* illustrates the splitting up of the "I." One part of it is identified with the paradigm which includes the Creator, His mad world, my sight and hearing, and me as part of that world, as its manifest forms. The other part constitutes a second paradigm that is negatively defined, through refusals, as an opposition to the properties of the first part.

But while the material nature of "I" brings the image of this "I" into the world of the Creator, the refusal—self-destruction—takes on not only theomachic, but theocidal connotations. This is what makes the text one of the most scathing condemnations of God by man in Russian poetry, and lends a special semantic weight to the concluding line: "There is only one answer—refusal." Alliteration and isometry equate all three words, transforming them, as it were, into one word with a complex meaning which includes objection to the world and God, the possibility of only one response (the presence of any other possibilities being precluded) and total negation. That which is individual finds its fullest manifestation in non-existence.

As we have demonstrated, the full complexity of Cvetaeva's antifascistic and theomachic views is realized only through the structure of the text, and primarily (in this case) through a system of lexico-semantic equivalences which form supra-linguistic lexico-semantic paradigms.

The Line as a Melodic Unity

Prosodic studies have repeatedly demonstrated that the line is the basic elementary unit of poetic speech. It was noted long ago that a precise definition of the features of this unit is difficult to formulate. Describing it as a rhythmic constant contradicts the well-known facts regarding the history of metrical and non-metrical free verse. Free iambic meters, common in the Russian fable, comedy and sometimes in narrative poems (Bogdanovič's *Dušenka,* for example) of the eighteenth and early nineteenth century, deviate markedly from the parctice of dividing the text into rhythmically constant units (with equal number of feet):

> I sám
> Letít trubít' svojú pobédu po lesám.

> [And he himself
> Flies off to trumpet his victory throughout the woods.]
> (Krylov)

We could cite similar examples from twentieth century free verse or other forms of poetry as well. The presence or absence of rhyme is not relevant in this case either, since we can cite numerous examples of blank verse texts which cannot be divided into isometric units on the level of the line (Heine's cycle *Nordsee,* for example). The familiar phenomenon of enjambment does not permit the line to be associated with a syntactic or intonational constant. Thus isorhythmicality, isotonalism and syntactic commensurability are better regarded as a widespread practice rather than a law whose violation deprives a line of its rights to that name.

After sorting through all the possibilities, the scholar discovers to his amazement that almost the only absolute feature of a line is its graphic form. But still it is difficult to accept this conclusion without some reservations, not only because there is such a phenomenon (atypical, in general, for contemporary poetic culture) as the auditory perception of poetry unconnected with the graphic text, but also because of the superficial, formal nature of such a feature.

The essence of the phenomenon lies elsewhere. A line is a unit of the rhythmic-syntactic and intonational segmentation of the poetic text. This seemingly trivial, unoriginal definition implies that the perception of an individual segment of a text as a line is *a priori*, that is must *precede* the singling out of the concrete "features" of the line. In the consciousness of the author and his audience there must exist, in the first place, a concept of poetry, and, in the second place, an agreed-upon system of signals compelling the transmitter and receiver to attune themselves to the form of communication which is called poetry. The signals may include the graphic form of the text, declamatory intonation, and a number of other features, down to the speaker's posture, the name of the work or even a certain nonverbal situation (we come to a poetry reading and know that the man ascending the platform is a poet, for example).

Thus the notion that the text perceived by us is poetry and that consequently it falls into lines is primary; its division into concrete poetic lines is secondary. For it is due to the *presumption* that a poetic text is divided into lines that we begin to seek linear symmetry in that text, experiencing the absence of any of its features as a "minus–presence" which does not disturb the system itself. In particular, if segments of a text are felt to be lines, the absence of syntactic isometry (enjambment) is seen as a deviation from a principle, that is, as a confirmation of that principle (obviously without some notion of the syntactic isometry of lines, we cannot speak of the artistic significance of enjambment).

Therefore the features of a line in a given artistic system that are obligatory are a more individual and secondary phenomenon than the presumption of the division of the poetic text into lines. Of course, we should at the same time distinguish between the features of a line as a structural phenomenon and signals which inform the audience of the poetic nature of the text (for example its graphic arrangement). True, a feature of a line can also be a signal of this type. One example is the special poetic intonation of recitation, which is both an essential feature of the line for certain poetic systems (when intonation marks the borders of lines) and also a signal that the text should be perceived as poetry.

B. M. Ejxenbaum and V. M. Žirmunskij were the first Soviet prosodists to study the role of intonation in works on the melodics of Russian verse. Ejxenbaum did not investigate intonation and melodics arising from the rhythmic construction of the text, concentrating instead on the intonational aspect of syntactic figures. While in his essay "The Melodics of Verse" (1921) Ejxembaum claims that "melodization," "a special lyrical melody," arises "on the basis of the rhythmic-syntactic system,"[66] in his book on

66 B. Ejxenbaum, "Melodika stixa," *Skvoz' literaturu* (Leningrad, 1924) p. 214.

this subject he does not discuss rhythmics and, correspondingly, formulates his basic thesis in the following manner: "By melodics I mean only the intonational system, that is, the combination of certain intonational figures that is realized in syntax."[67]

L. I. Timofeev resolves this problem differently. He devotes particular attention to intonation and is inclined to see intonation as one of the principal elements of verse structure. He sees melodics as an emphatic, emotional principle, and is convinced that it distinguishes poetry from prose.[68]

B. V. Tomaševskij's *Toward a History of Russian Rhyme* handles this question in a very productive way. We find here an attempt to relate melodics to the norms of declamation, and declamation in turn to the general historical development of literature. All these viewpoints must be considered in order to determine the role of intonation in verse.

First of all we must distinguish two aspects of the problem of intonation: 1) the intonational structure inherent to *poetry in general* and, more specifically, to its separate classes (all verse written in iambic tetrameter, for example, has a characteristic intonation) and genres; 2) the role of intonations in poetry that are inherent to given syntactic structures (a question discussed by Ejxenbaum, and by Zirmunskij in *The Composition of the Lyric* somewhat earlier and in a different vein).

Let us deal first with the first case in both of its varieties. As Tomaševskij in his time perceptively observed, the "intonation of verse" (a term whose complement will be the "intonation of non-verse") is not constantly present throughout the history of Russian poetry. It is historical, that is it enters into different oppositional pairs and takes on different meanings in connection with changes in historical and social conditions and philosophical structures.

The first stage of Russian poetry was related to the syncretism of words and music. Here we are referring not only to oral folk poetry, but also psalms, which the cultured Russian in the Middle Ages undoubtedly perceived as poetry. The psalms lived on in the artistic consciousness of the medieval Russian audience, not in combination with the special rhetorcal intonation characteristic of religious oratorical prose or the specific, deliberately monotonous intonations so distinct from those of ordinary speech in which vitae, epistles and other genres of religious prose were read,[69] but in uninterrupted syncretism with recitative chanting; this chanting intonation made the psalms be perceived as "non-prose."

67 B. Ejxenbaum, *Melodika russkogo liričeskogo stixa* (Petrograd, 1922) p. 16. See the objections of V. M. Žirmunskij in "Melodika stixa," *Mysl'* No. 3 (1922), and also in the book *Voprosy teorii literatury* (Leningrad, 1928).

68 See L. I. Timofeev, *Očerki teorii i istorii russkogo stixa* (Moscow, 1958) pp. 109-116 ff.

69 There is sufficient evidence to demonstrate that in medieval Russian literature, which was intended to be read aloud, each genre had its own inherent manner of intonation.

Thus when Russian syllabic verse emerged it was perceived as something that complemented two other concepts. It was, on the one hand, not prose, and, on the other hand, it was not the poetry of the psalter.

This unusual structural mode also gave birth to a special type of declamation which was supposed to differ from the intonational system of "readings," the system of Russian medieval prose, and from the recitative chanting of the psalms (it goes without saying that both these systems were part of one general intonational category opposed to the intonations of "ordinary" Russian speech, which corresponded to the antithesis between verbal art and verbal non-art). Thus a special, emphatically declamatory method of reading verse arose, a method which, as Tomaševskij noted, was inherent to Russian syllabic poetry. Above all it achieved the division, characteristic of verse as such, of the indivisible, the division of the word into parts semantically equivalent to the whole. This occurred because the pause between syllables within the word was of the same duration as the pause between words. Another effect was the rise of a specific intonation incorporating a lofty solemnity, since it was oversaturated with stresses (every syllable was stressed), and extra-grammatical stress in Russian is usually perceived as logical stress, a marker of semantic significance. At the same time this type of declamation had a melodiousness not usually found in other styles of recitative speech since the fact that all syllables had to be stressed forced the reader to lengthen each one. This gave rise to pronunciational melodics, with obvious semiotic import: it signaled that the text belonged to a certain structural category.

If we view declamation or singing(a musical motif or recitative + words) and the intonations of ordinary non-artistic speech as two poles, then the transition to the expiratory, melodic declamation of syllabic verse can be regarded as a step from the first toward the second. We should not forget, therefore, that this declamation which to us seems the quintessence of artificiality was felt to be a stylistic "simplification." The fact that a manner of declamation more prosaic than religious chanting was a sign of a text's artistic nature reflected a new conception of art as a phenomenon opposed to reality to a lesser degree. This was related to the separation of "high" culture from the church.

A new stage in the history and melodics of Russian verse came with the transition to Trediakovskij's and Lomonosov's syllabo-tonic verse system. The artifical stressing of all syllables was eliminated. Words in verse now received their natural grammatical stress.[70] This moved verse intonation still further away from the musical, recitative pole and, when set against the familiar background of the syllabic manner of declamation, was again seen as a simplification.

But melodics not only had to approach the pole of conversational

---

70 Characteristically Lomonosov's occasional violations of natural stresses (in the rhyme *ximīja–Rossīja*, for example) were ridiculed by his literary opponents.

intonation, it had to remain distinct from it. This function was implemented in two ways.

First, poetry (not poetry as a whole, strictly speaking, but the ode, which was the leading genre and in many respects determined the shape of poetry) was composed according to the rules of the oratorical genre.[71] This determined both the specific features of syntax ("figures") and, consequently, the appearance of special rhetorical intonations, which began to be perceived as specifically poetic. Naturally non-rhetorical intonations were also present in the poetry of the time (the intonation of the elegy, for example) but it was considered "low style" *in relation* to the odic intonation which was taken as the *norm*. Recall the description of eighteenth century poetic intonation by a man of another epoch, Turgenev, whose character Punin "did not read [verse], he shouted out lines, majestically, lustily, with gusto, with a nasal twang, as though he were intoxicated, frenzied like Pythia!" Turgenev continues, "Punin pronounced these verses in a measured melodious voice with every *o** pronounced, as verse was intended to be read."[72] *Okan'e,* as we recall, was introduced in the eighteenth century as the pronunciational norm for high style.

Second, an extremely constant type of intonation was established for each meter, supported by the strict coincidence of the rhythmic unit—the line—and the syntagm: eighteenth century poetry avoided enjambment. Therefore the rhthmic isometry of the line was reinforced by intonational isometry. The intonation of different forms of rhythmic speech (iambic tetrameter, for example, or trochaic pentameter) gave the impresssion of total autonomy with regard to the words that composed the line, that is, with regard to the semantics of the line. Naive attempts to attribute meaning to the intonation of iambs or trochees (as for example in the dispute between Lomonosov and Trediakovskij) are more likely to convince one of the opposite. And in fact many people believe that the semantics of the line and the intonations of the rhythmic structure are non-intersecting, unrelated spheres. Objections, however, can be raised with regard to either point of view.

Our point of departure in examining the relation between the rhythmic intonation and semantics of verse should be the conviction that this rhythmic-intonational system is not an autonomous structure, but an element that extends into a number of individual substructures which interact to form the one system of the text we call a poem, a sign with

---

* In standard Russian *o* in unstressed position is reduced. *Dorogój* (dear; expensive), for example, is pronounced [dər ʌ 'goi]. Punin in reading verse would have pronounced it [doro 'goi]. The latter phenomenon is called *okan'e*, the former (and standard Russian) *akan'e.* —Tr.

71 See Ju. N. Tynjanov, "Oda kak oratorskij žanr," *Arxaisty i novatory* (Leningrad, 1929).

72 I. S. Turgenev, *Sobranie sočinenij v 12-ti tomax*, vol. VIII (Moscow, 1956) pp. 198, 219.

particular content that models a particular reality.

The intonational constant of verse, in the first place, together with the rhythmic constant, lends further credence to the notion that lines are correlated; in art this means that we inevitably begin to perceive their content to be correlated as well:

> Vam ot duši želaju ja,
> Druz'ja, vsego xorošego.
> A vse xorošee, druz'ja,
> Daetsja nam nedeševo!

> [With all may heart, I wish you,
> Friends, all the best.
> But all the best, my friends,
> Is not there for the asking.]
> (Samuil Maršak)

If we disregard the relations created by the rhymes, we observe that it is the rhythmic and intonational isometry of the second and fourth lines which make us perceive their conceptional centers—*vsego xorošego* ["all the best"] and *nedeševo* ["not cheaply, not there for the asking"]—as semantically parallel.

In the second place, the constant intonation of verse is inevitably correlated with the logical intonation of the text. In its monotony it serves as a background against which syntactic and intonational differences between sentences are singled out more clearly as "grounds for comparison," the common element of different semantic intonations. For example, in the passage from Maršak quoted above, the adversative semantics of the last two lines, conveyed directly by the conjunction a ["but"] underscores the rhythmic-intonational kinship of these lines, and also the lexical palindrome of sorts that we find in the second and third lines. At the same time if the words in these two lines did not coincide and were not transposed, but simply different, the adversative intonation would not be so meaningful.

The notion that the non-realization of a structural element is its negative realization entails that the two possible readings of the lines are, in essence, functionally the same. We can stress the semantic intonation and read "with expression." In this case the intonational curve of the "expressive" (logical) reading and the rhythmic constant will be correlated as a contrasting pair. There is, however, another possible reading, insistently monotonous, which accentuates the melodics of the rhythm itself. Poets themselves often read verse in this way. This was observed by Ejxenbaum, who writes, 'Most accounts of the way poets recite characteristically emphasize their monotonous, melodious form of reading."[73] Aleksandr Blok, for example, is known to have read in a special manner, with intonations and a deliberately muted voice. Naturally this sort of reading is inherent to verse without

73 B. Ejxenbaum, *Melodika russkogo liričeskogo stixa*, op. cit., p. 19.

enjambments, where the autonomy of rhythmic intonation is expressed with particular clarity. But the common assumption that these are instances of "pure musicality" divorced from meaning is highly erroneous. The point is that in this sort of reading semantic intonation is present as an unrealized, but structurally perceptible element, a "minus-device." When the reader grasps the meaning of the verse, he also senses the presence of possible, but unrealized semantic intonations. In this respect verse is also different from ordinary speech, where there is only one intonation psosible—semantic intonation—with no other alternatives. In verse, however, semantic intonation can always be replaced by the rhythmic intonation which is its paired correlative; thereby setting the former in even greater relief. In poetry "monotonous reading" consequently only emphasizes the semantics. Against the background of rhythmic intonation, semantic intonation violates our expectations, and vice versa. Both these forms of intonation form a correlated opposition.

There is one other point that should be made. Rhythmic intonation itself results from the neutralization of the opposition between the intonations of meter and rhythm. Here too a semantic load complementary to that of ordinary speech arises. In a letter written by E. P. Ivanov, a close friend of Blok, we find remarkable evidence that the reciter is aware of the correlation between two possible "motifs" in verse—semantic and rhythmic intonation. "It seems," he writes, "that I have not entirely forgotten how to read verse. I *bury the chant deep* in the verse and it turns out better. The motif is concealed by pauses. This comes close to the way Blok himself used to read."[74]

We are all aware that the historical development of the intonational structure of Russian poetry was not limited to the transition to syllabo-tonic verse. The picture grew more complicated when poets could substitute pyrrhic feet for iambs and trochees. Now alternative pairs could appear: real rhythmic intonation with a pyrrhic in a given foot, and the standard metrical intonation functioning as a foot.[75] But since the presence *or absence* of stress where it is expected on account of inertia is seen as logical stress, as semantic accentuation—the varieties of Russian iambs and trochees open up a wealth of semantic accents. We should remember that this is possible only because pyrrhic and standard intonations are correlated.

Various concrete problems relating to the variations in the standard rhythmic and intinational systems of the Russian iamb and trochee have been thoroughly studied by Belij, Brjusov, Šengeli, Bondi, Timofeev, Vinokur, Štokmar, and currently by Taranovsky, Kolmogorov and Kondratov. We only want to stress that any attempt to study these systems without considering the alternatives actually opposed to them in the poetic structure,

74 *Blokovskij sbornik* (Tartu, 1964) p. 464. Italics mine.
75 Accordingly if we take into account the appearance of spondees, alternative pairs of a different type will arise: a real rhythmic intonation with a spondee, and a standard metrical intonation.

the problem of their background, and actual and potential intonations and stresses, prevents us from examining the whole problem in relation to the content of poetic texts and its interpretation, which makes such attempts considerably less interesting from a scientific point of view.

The intonational system of Russian verse underwent a radical change in connection with the overall "prosifying" of verse beginning in the 1830's when realism was starting to take shape. This period marked the formation of a "conversational" [*govornoj*] system, to use Ejxenbaum's term. Various sorts of "rejections" went into the creation of that intonational system: the rejection of special, measured "poetic" syntax permeated with interrogatory and exclamatory constructions, the rejection of a special "poetic" vocabulary (the new prosaic vocabulary called for a new kind of declamation as well) and a change in melodic intonation as a result of the legitimatization of enjambment—the violation of the correspondence between rhythmic and syntactic units. As a result the very concept of verse changed. The fact that we have repeated the word "rejection" so many times in our attempt to define the elements of "conversational" intonation, is itself evidence that this intonation is not an isolated phenomenon but rises against the background of melodious intonation as a correlative but contrasting system.

Developing this thought, we should point out that the next step in the history of Russian verse—the transition to the intonations of Majakovskij's tonic verse, which represented a violation of the norms of nineteenth century Russian rhythmics—could only exist as an artistic fact against the background of the view that these norms were obligatory. Without an awareness of the syllabo-tonic background, it would also be impossible to sense the semantic saturation of the tonic system.

The Line as a Semantic Unity

While we have already said that a work as a whole is a sign, a "word," this does not invalidate the fact that the separated elements are more or less independent. The following general proposition might be formulated: the larger an element of structure, the higher its level, the greater its relative autonomy in that structure.

In a specifically poetic structure, the line is on a level where the semantic independence of separate elements begins to be perceptible. A line is not only a rhythmic—intonational, but also a semantic, unity. Because of the special iconic nature of a sign in art, the spatial correlation of structural elements is meaningful and directly related to content. As a result, words in a line are much more tightly connected than they would be in a syntactic unit of the same length outside verse. In a certain sense (we are speaking metaphorically, of course, not giving a precise definition) a line is like a word in the general language. The words that comprise it lose their independence and become components of a complex semantic whole, where they act as "roots" (the semantic dominant of a line) or "ornamental" elements which could metaphorically be likened to suffixes, prefixes and infixes. Two or more semantic centers are possible (as in the case of compound words).

But the parallelism between line and word stops here. The integration of semantic elements of a line into a whole proceeds according to complex rules which are very different from the principles whereby parts of a word are combined into words.

First we should point out that a word is a sign, constant for a given language, with a strictly fixed designator and a specific semantic content. At the same time the word is also composed of constant elements with a fixed grammatical and lexical meaning; they can be enumerated in a relatively short list. Ordinary dictionaries and grammars give them. In comparing the line with the word, we should remember that this "word" is always occasional.

We can liken a line in the language of poetry to a word in the natural language because in poetry the linguistic division of units into those that are meaningful (lexical) and those that express relations (syntagmatic) is by no means absolute. As mentioned earlier, purely relational units of language may acquire lexical meaning in poetry. Here is an elementary example:

> Udelu svoe*m*u i *m*y pokorny bude*m*,
> *M*jatežnye *m*ečty s*m*iri*m* il' pozabude*m*.

> [We too will submit to our lot,
> We will subdue or forget dreams of rebellion.]
> (Baratynskij)

The second line falls into semantically contrastive hemistiches: "dreams of rebellion" and "subdue or forget." The words *mjatež* ["rebellion"[and *smirenie* ["submission"] whose dictionary definitions also set them in opposition to each other are all the more contrastive here because one phoneme *m* serves as the basis for their contrast and opposition. In natural language the verb endings *smir*im and *pozabud*em have a purely relational function; in verse they carry lexical meaning equal to that of the radical *m* in the first of these two words (*smirim*).[76] Due to their repetition on the phonemeic level, the inflectional endings acquire the semantics of the root, spreading it out over the second hemistich and at the same time contrasting with the first half of the line.

> U nix ne kisti,
> A kisteni.
> Sem' gorodov, antixristy,
> Zadumali oni.

---

76 Simultaneously there arises a "play" of elements of lower levels since the radical combination "M + vowel"– My, Mja*tež*nye, Me*č*ty, s*mir*im ["We, "rebellious," "dreams," "subdure"] corresponds to the "reversed" affixal-inflectional combination "vowel + M"–*bud*em, si*mir*im, poza*bud*em ["we will," "subdue," "forget"] the exception is *svoemu* ["our"]).

[It's not a brush they have,
But bludgeons.
They set their eye on
Seven cities, the antichrists.]

(Voznesenskij)

The first two lines are pronounced *ni kisti/ a kistini*. The relational element—
the case ending *kisti* becomes a radical element in *kistini*; the negative
particle (*ni*) is transformed into a case ending. The *sound coincidence* of
relational and material elements becomes a *semantic correlation*.

In lines, as we see, auxiliary words (those that are relational and have
grammatical-syntactical functions) and parts of words are semanticized.

The rules for combining semantic elements into a whole differ for a
linguistic word and a line. In the first case we are dealing with elements of
common usage whose meanings are given beforehand, in the second—with
occasional elements whose meanings derive from a given text. Therefore in
the first case a mechanical summary of concepts will be a frequent occurrence
and in the second—the complex construction of a semantic model formed
by the relation between conjunction of semantic fields of elements and
their intersection.

This, of course, does not mean that the line ceases to be perceived, in
the sense it has in ordinary language, as a sentence or part of a sentence;
the presence of a supra-linguistic structure always assumes rather than
countermands the perception of poetry as ordinary speech as well. The
aesthetic effect is achieved through the presence of both systems of
perception, through their correlation. Naturally if we cease to perceive
poetry as an elementary speech act (that is if we simply cannot understand
poetry in the general linguistic sense) we cannot perceive its poetic structure.[77]
Therefore the line, which most often contains a distinct syntagm, retains
all differences which distinguish a syntactic unit from a word. The integration
of meanings and the emergence of new meanings occurs not on the linguistic
level, but on the level of the supra-linguistic line structure.

The semantic center of a line is also determined differently than the
root of a word. One can speak of the rhythmic center of a line, which
most often gravitates toward the rhyme. It is correlated with the semantic
center of the phrase, which is given in the speech material of the line.
When these centers do not coincide, a phenomenon occurs similar to
enjambment, and this is an additional source of "semantic play" in poetry.

Finally, the line differs essentially from the word because the latter
can exist independently, outside the sentence. The line, in our contemporary
conception of poetry, cannot exist outside its relation with other lines.

77 The fact that we are dealing here with correlated but different systems is
confirmed by observations of the aesthetic perception of a poem in a conprehensible,
but foreign language. If experiments were set up to work with different degrees of
linguistic knowledge, this interesting problem could give results similar to those
achieved in modern linguistic studies of various types of speech defects.

When we do deal with one line, it is in its relation to the zero member of a couplet: it is perceived as consciously unfinished or cut off.[78] As an obligatory form of the realization of a verse text, as a part of the text, the line is secondary in relation to the text. The linguistic text is made of words, the poetic text is divided into lines.

Supra-Linear Repetitions

Repetitions of supra-linear elements of the text are constructed on a higher level according to the same constructive principles that apply to the repetition of lower units. Revealing identity in opposition and variance in likeness, supra-linear repetitons form a semantic paradigm which gives each section of text a meaning that is entirely different from that which emerges from isolated examination' For example, in Tuwim's poem "The Lesson," two themes, two types of vocabulary and two semantic fields—the world of the child at school and horrors of war, occupation and violence—which seem quite removed from each other, are compared and opposed and it is the unexpectedness of this convergence which generates new semantic possibilities:

> Learn to speak Polish. . .
> There are the graves not far along,
> There are the crosses standing in the churchyard,
> You see, little boy, it's not so hard. . .

A similar semantic effect can be seen in Tjutčev's poem, "Send, O Lord, Thy Consolation:"

> Pošli Gospod', Svoju otradu
> Tomu, kto v letnyj žar i znoj
> Kak bednyj niščij mimo sadu
> Bredet po žarkoj mostovoj;
>
> Kto smotrit vskol'z' čerez ogradu
> Na ten' derev'ev, zlak dolin,
> Na nedostupnuju proxladu
> Roskošnyx, svetlyx lugovin.
>
> Ne dlja nego gostepriimnoj
> Derev'ja sen'ju razroslis',
> Ne dlja nego, kak oblak dymnyj,
> Fontan na vozduxe povis.
>
> Lazurnyj grot, kak iz tumana,
> Naprasno vzor ego manit,
> I pyl' rosistaja fontan
> Glavy ego ne osvežit.

---

78 The monostich is not simply identical to a text—it is a part which is *equal to the whole,* a subset which is equal to the universal set, its own complementary "empty set" being zero.

Pošli, Gospod', Svoju otradu
Tomu, kto žiznennoj tropoj
Kak bednyj niščij mimo sadu
Bredet po znojnoj mostovoj.

[Send, O Lord, Thy consolation
To him who in summer's burning heat
Wanders like a poor beggar past the garden
Along the hot pavement.

Who looks, in passing, through the fence
At the shade of trees and the grain of valleys,
At the unattainable coolness
Of lush bright meadows.

Not for him did the hospitable
Trees grow to spread their canopy,
Not for him did the fountain
Hang in the air like a smoky cloud.

The azure grotto, as through a mist,
Vainly attracts his gaze,
And the dewy fountain spray
Will not cool his head.

Send, O Lord, Thy consolation
To him who along life's path
Wanders like a poor beggar past a garden
Along the burning pavement.]

The composition of the poem is organized by the parallelism of the first
and last stanzas. The full coincidence of the first, third and fourth lines,
and partial coincidence of the second only singles out the distinctive
semantic group "hot midday—life." The compositional function of the
three stanzas that make up the central part of the poem and are framed by
parallel stanzas is of considerable interest. The deliberate disproportion of
this part would seem to be as follows.

1. The parallel between a difficult road and life's path is fairly trivial
and taken by itself this comparison could hardly be the source of a profound
poetic thought. But Tjutčev's construction activates not only the totality
of *common* semantic features (difficulty, extended in time, and so on) but
also the *difference* between the pedestrian and the traveller on life's path.

The basic semantic difference between the second lines of the first
and last stanzas consists in the opposition of the direct and figurative use
of meanings. In and of itself, the first stanza could easily be opposed to a
metaphorical image of a traveller on life's path. But the abundance of
material details and the description of visual minutiae ("the fountain hung
in the air like a *smoky* cloud")—the sort which cannot be simplistically
deciphered in light of the metaphorical interpretation of the image of a

road—should convince the reader that in fact the poet is speaking of an actual hot day and a real traveller. Then the comparison, which would otherwise be rather trivial (had Tjutčev confined himself to the first and last stanzas), impresses one as unexpected and meaningful. The possibility of *such* a last stanza is apparent after the first stanza and then becomes improbable after the fourth. For that very reason it has meanings which would not be present if it were the second stanza.

2. The second, third, and fourth stanzas are an extension of the first. They describe the garden and the poor beggar passing by. After reading the poem we discover that the image was a metaphor. This forces us to reinterpret the central stanzas as metaphorical. This dual perception of the text as unequal to itself is complicated by the fact that the central part of the poem, as we already mentioned, cannot be deciphered allegorically. A semantically complex collision takes place: after reading the text we understand that it must be understood metaphorically, but the structure itself resists this interpretation. In this way a semantic tension is created which is far richer in meaning than it would be in a text consisting only of the first or last stanza.

But the repetition in the "coincident" parts of the first and last stanza is also not so absolute. Disregarding the substitution of "burning pavement" for "hot pavement," there is an obvious intonational difference: the sententiousness of the last stanza, which sums up the poem, is clearly opposed to the first because, on the one hand, we are dealing with a closed, syntactic whole, and on the other, with a part which will be continued. Thus even on the supra-linear level repetition does not present us with lifeless identity, but with a complex play of similarities and differences that account for the richness of semantic structure.

The Energy of Verse

The energy of an artistic structure, which is always perceived by the reader and frequently figures in criticism, is not mentioned in theories of literature. In our understanding this concept, as will be apparent in the discussion that follows, is akin to the concept of "function" in the theories of Tynjanov, and of the Czech scholar Mukařovský and his students.

In the organization of verse we can trace a constant tendency toward collision and conflict, a struggle between different constructive principles. Each principle has an organizing function within the system it creates, and functions as a disorganizer outside of that system. Thus word boundaries interfere with the rhythmic ordering of verse; syntactic intonations conflict with rhythmic intonations, and so on. When opposing tendencies coincide, we are not dealing with an absence of conflict but with a particular instance of conflict; the zero expression of structural tension.

Taken individually, structural regularities generate closed synchronic systems devoid of inner dynamics. In isolation these systems readily yield to structural description. Such partial descriptions may give a complete picture of a construction, but often entirely overlook the problem of correlation. Two functionally opposing constructions may seem unrelated when each is deciphered in isolation. But taken together they may turn out to be functionally opposed: things proscribed by one system may be prescribed by another.

Two constructions may also prove to be coordinated in some way, in which case optional variants emerge within the confines of the dominant structure as a result of their correlation. Thus the correlation of rhythmic schemes and word stress, on the one hand, or word boundaries, on the other, create variation within a given rhythm. The possibility of choice among several variants of a structural scheme creates conditions for the additional semantization of the text. The tension between various textual substructures first increases the possibility of choice and the number of structural alternatives in a text, and second, eliminated automatism, forcing regular features to be realized through numerous violations. One need not have a profound knowledge of the laws of transmission of information to understand how greatly this increases the informational possibilities of the artistic text in relation to the non-artistic text. Herein lies the value of structures built according to the principle of "play" from the perspective of the volume of information that can be contained in them.

In looking at verse from this point of view, it seems, we must conclude, on the one hand, that any structural phenomenon in an artistic text's structure is meaningful, for an artistic construction always has content; and on the other hand, we avoid the superfluous approach to this question which, for example, gives rise to discussions about the *absolute* meaning of the phoneme *u* or of iambic tetrameter.

When we say that the structure of the artistic text is always constructed on the conflict of the paricular substructures which comprise it, we must distinguish one of the basic aspects of this situation.

We have observed several times that because of the intersection of various structural parallelisms, any word in a poetic text, in principle, can be the synonym or antonym of any other. With this in mind, let us look at Anna Axmatova's poem "Couplet:"

> Ot drugix mne xvala—čto zola,
> Ot tebja i xula—poxvala.

> [Coming from others, praise for me is ashes,
> Coming from you, even abuse is praise.]

We can easily single out pairs of words in comparison and opposition:

ot—ot	[from—from
drugix—tebja	others—you
xvala—xula	praise—abuse

xvala–poxvala	praise–praise
xvala–zola	praise–ashes
xula–zola	abuse–ashes
xula–poxvala	abuse–praise
zola–poxvala	ashes–praise]

It is immediately apparent that the bases for the emergence of semantic oppositions differ in each case, just as there are differences in the relation of the occasional poetic semantics to the normal meanings of the corresponding words in the system of natural language. The primary opposition "others–you" is based on the relation between the words that coincides with the structure of their meaning in the natural language. True, here too both words do not designate complementary concepts, that is are not fixed, exclusive antonyms of each other. So when "others" acquires the meaning in the text of "not you" and "you" comes to mean "not others," there is a sort of shift in the meaning of these words, and their oppositional meanings are activated: "multiplicity (repetition) vs. uniqueness (non-repetition)," "distance vs. closeness" (the feature of intimacy opposes the pronouns "I" and "you" to all the others; in this respect, "others" is set in the greatest opposition to "I" and "you"). Thus this opposition: 1) lies within the general structure of meanings of the natural language; 2) is related to a semantic shift; and 3) is based entirely on the *semantics* of these words.

"From–from" can be viewed as a relation of identity, as an anaphoral beginning that serves as the basis for the opposition of the following pronouns. But it also can be perceived as a lexically unexpressed opposition. Then we face a rather interesting situation: identity of expression where the content is not the opposition of two concepts, but a model of opposition in its pure form.

The opposition *xvala–xula* ["praise vs. abuse"] is built on the combination of the relation of antonimy provided by the semantic structure of the natural language, and the relation established by the phonological parallelism *x-la–x-la*. Meaning and sound are oriented differently: the one affirms opposition, the other coincidence. The resultant tension is similar to that which we observed in rhyme. In the pair *xvala–zola* ["praise–ashes"] we find an analogous situation: syntactic construction and phonological parallelism confirm the closeness, the semantic unity of the two words, while their semantics in the ordinary language confirms their opposition. Once again two regularities clash. The same is true of the pair *zola–poxvala* ["ashes–praise"]. The pair *xvala–poxvala* ["praise–praise"] would be tautological but for the fact that: 1) the words are in syntactically opposed positions; 2) *poxvala* in this construction of the given text is not approval, but "abuse," which only seems to be *xvala* ["praise"]. Thus the identity of the dictionary meanings of words and the abundance of sound repetitions conflict with their positional oppostion and directly opposite contextual, occasional meaning. The pair *xula–zola* ["abuse–ashes"] manifests an analogous semantic tension.

The essential conclusion is this: a poetic construction creates a special world of semantic convergences, analogies, contrasts and oppostions which does not coincide with the semantic network of relations of the natural language, but enters into conflict with them and struggles with them. This struggle itself creates an artistic effect. The total victory of one or the other tendency, the immutability of meanings present in a system before the creation of the given text, or their total annulment, allowing for the unopposed creation of any textual combinations without any resistance— both are contraindicated for art. In the first case we would be dealing with that zero flexibility of language which, according to Kolmogorov, does not permit the creation of art. In the second case certain structural rules would be implemented, but without creating a work of art. Let us take an example:

> To kak Jakobija ostavit'
> Kotorogo ves' mir tesnit?
> Kak Longinova dat' opravit',
> Kotoryj zolotom gremit?
>
> [Then how can we abandon Jakobij
> Whom the whole world persecutes?
> Can we let Longinov be vindicated
> Who jingles his gold?]
> (Deržavin)

The names Jakobij and Longinov function as antonyms in Deržavin's poem. But for the modern reader who knows nothing about the Irkutsk governor-general I. V. Jakobi, accused of attempting to provoke armed conflict with China, and has never heard of the Petersburg merchant I. B. Longinov, or of the passions and intrigues that surrounded their controversial trials—these names have no meaning outside the text of the poem. Deržavin's identification of Jakobi with a "persecuted upright man" and Longinov with "evil triumphant" does not coincide with or stand in opposition to anything in the reader's consciousness (we should recall that coincidence is a particular instance of conflict). The poetic tension that existed in this passage has been lost.

If we describe the system of poetic equivalences created by Andrej Voznesenskij in *Mosaics* and *Antiworlds,* and compare them to texts written later by the same author, we come to an interesting conclusion: the same system (in an isolated synchronic description) which for a given period of time sounded new and original is now perceived as imitative (mostly imitative in relation to itself). What is the point? *The system has triumphed.* What seemed extraordinary has become the ordinary; the "anti-system" has ceased to offer resistance.

Thus a synchronic, internally stable description of a text's structure, above all its paradigmatic structure, which is a necessary condition if we want to get an exact idea of the nature of artistic activity is, in itself, insufficient.

If, in addition, we describe internal or external structures struggling against the system, we are beginning to focus our attention of the *aspect of energy*. A text functions in relation to a given system of prohibitions which precede it and lie outside it. But these prohibitions are not equal in force. Some are absolute for a given system and cannot be overcome. Consequently there is no possibility of achieving a semantic effect by overcoming them. (The violation of these prohibitions does not create new meanings, but leads to the disintegration of art.) At certain stages the demand that genres not be mixed, that limitations be placed on the use of a given vocabulary, and that grammatical norms be strictly observed can function as absolute prohibitions.

At the other end of the spectrum we find optional restrictions which are so commonly violated that they cannot have an active effect on the plane of content. Very often these optional limitations were far more obligatory in preceding systems, where they functioned as fundamental content-forming boundaries.

A hierarchy of prohibitions inherent to a given artistic language, a given epoch and national culture (and to the natural language as its fundamental element) is situated between these two poles. The violation of these strong (for a given system) semantic oppositions is possible, but it is strange and unusual. Depending on the structural markedness of these prohibitions, how strong or weak they are, their violation will be structurally active in varying degrees, will demand a varying intensity of thought, and correspondingly the entire system will assume a different energy specification.

In a critical sketch written in 1827, Puškin observed:

> There are vaying degrees of boldness: Deržavin wrote, *"orel na vysote parja"* ["an eagle soaring on high"] when happiness *"tebe xrebet svoj s groznym smexom povernulo, ty vidiš', kak mečty sijan'e vkrug tebja zasnulo"* ["... turned her back on you with a terrible laugh, you saw, saw how the radiance of a dream around you fell asleep"].

Description of a waterfall:

> Almazna sypletsja gora
> S vysot i proč....
>
> [A diamond-like mountain pours
> From the heights, etc. ...]

Žukovskij says of God:

> On v dym Moskvy sebja oblek.
>
> [He cloaked himself in Moscow's smoke.]

Krylov tells of the brave ant who,

daže xažival odin na pauka.

[even used to take on the spider by himself]

Calderon calls lightning "the fiery tongue of the heavens speaking to the earth." Milton says that hellfire only helped him to discover the eternal darkness of the nether regions. All of these expressions seem very bold to us, for they convey a clear idea and a poetic image in a powerful, unusual way. The French still marvel at Racine's boldness in using the word *pavé*, dais

Et baise avec respect le pavé de tes temples.

And De Lisle was proud of having used the word *vache*. How contemptible the literature that listened to such petty and capricious criticism.[79]

Puškin's opinion is of extraordinary interest for defining the nature of poetic supra-meanings. Semantic connections are established between words; in one system—the new system which the text creates—these connections are the only true connections and the most precise ones, that is, they convey a "clear idea." In another system that is also active, however, these connections are strictly prohibited. For this very reason the surmounting of the restriction is felt as energetically "powerful" (the evaluation of textual connections as "extraordinary" points to a preceding tradition of texts which observed these prohibitions) What Puškin called "poetic boldness" is required to overcome highly meaningful prohibitions. When a poet utilizes his energy to smash insignificant barriers, prohibitions of little importance, the literature is "contemptible." "How pitiable the fate of poets," writes Puškin, "if they are compelled to glory in such triumphs."[80]

Puškin's reasoning graphically illustrates our idea of artistic effect as a kind of exertion, and permits us to discuss its relative measurability. At the very least we can already easily distinguish the following degrees: the total impossibility of overcoming the initial prohibitions: total observance of the initial prohibitions; the overcoming of strong prohibitions and the overcoming of weak prohibitions. But Puškin's reasoning also leads to another conclusion concerning the historical relativity of the concepts of powerful and weak prohibitions. This opposition is only valid in relation to some historically and nationally stipulated structure. For example, the very prohibitions that Puškin cites as being insignificant and easily surmouted do not appear so in all artistic structures. If we consider the existence of a type of culture where the major opposition organizing the entire system of meanings is the oppostion between the lofty and the base, the abstract and

79 A. S. Puškin, op. cit., vol. IX, pp. 60-61.
80 Ibid.

concrete, the noble and the vulgar, we realize that the use of direct words or the mention of mundane phenomena in a tragic or touchingly poetic text is "insignificant" only for a consciousness that has discarded all of these notions. We too are no longer aware of Deržavin's boldness in using the phrase *na vysote* in place of *v vyšine**; we cannot appreciate Krylov's daring use of the expression *xažival odin**, which has a swaggering air and is used colloquially in hunting circles, to characterize an ant.

The prohibitions against whose background the text functions are, in the broad sense of the word, the entire system of construction of an artistic work. But in the narrow, most immediate sense we mean that the final result of any artistic construction is the formation of equivalent or opposing series of significant elements. In verbal art, these elements almost always prove to be words. Therefore an important consequence of poetic organization is the appearance of new, previously nonexistent series of semantic identifications and oppositions. These series of occasional poetic synonyms and antonyms are perceived in relation to semantic fields that are active in the extra-textual systems of communication. In the reader's consciousness, common associations exist which are confirmed by the authority of the natural language and its inherent semantic structure, the authority of everyday consciousness and the conceptual structure of the reader's cultural period and type, and finally by the authority of the structure of artistic constructions to which he is accustomed.

Systems of conceptual relations, we should recall, are the most real expression of a model of the universe in a person's consciousness. Thus an artistic text is perceived against the background of, and in conflict with, the entire set of models of the universe that are active for the reader and the author. In describing a particular model of this type (for example, the model of the ordinary consciousness of a certain epoch and culture), we can fairly accurately determine the basic semantic oppositions and distinguish them from derivative and optional oppositions. Naturally a text that does not observe the former will be perceived as more "powerful."

Furthermore we can fairly objectively show which of these general modeling systems most sharply conflicts with the text. Here both artistic and extra-artistic systems may be activated. In *Boris Godunov*, for example, the major conflict involves the norms of construction of a dramatic text; Majakovskij's bright yellow shirt conflicted with the norms of the bourgeois notion of how a poet ought to look.*

* Both phrases mean "on high;" the latter is more bookish than the former.—Tr.

* *Xažival odin*—"took on by himself." The phrase is usually *xažival' v odinočku* and almost invariably refers to a situation when a wild, dangerous beast is being hunted.—Tr.

* In the heyday of Futurism Majakovskij, the brothers Burljuk, Vasilij Kamenskij and others would stroll about the capital (and occasionally the provinces) in outrageous dress. Davyd Burljuk favored a flower painted on the cheek. Majakovskij's trademark was a yellow shirt with a wooden spoon in the buttonhole. Xlebnikov eschewed this sort of publicity.—Tr.

But all models of the universe in the general system of culture are not equally meaningful. By taking into account the qualitative index (the relative importance in the general conception of the world of those semantic structures which conflict with poetry) and the quantitative index (any one familiar model of the world or a significant part of the aggregate of models is considered) we get an idea of the objective laws of poetic power and artistic impotence and can hope to distinguish the energy of the innovator from the futile pseudo-innovative attempts of the epigone.

Here too we come to the conclusion that there can be no serious discussion about the individual features of a work of art without describing typical structures: the power and activeness of an innovative text is determined to a considerable degree by the significance and force of the obstacles in its path. The great victory of the epigone over the reader's consciousness as it was in the past, is like Falstaff's heroic feat when he killed the corpse of Henry Hotspur.

7. THE SYNTAGMATIC AXIS OF STRUCTURE

Repetitions on various levels play a leading role in the organization of a text and have long attracted the attention of scholars. But it would be a mistake to reduce the entire artistic construction to repetition alone. The point here is not only that repetitions, particularly in prose, often comprise an insignificant part of the text, with the rest remaining outside the scholar's field of vision as ostensibly lacking in aesthetic organization and artistically passive as a result. The essential point is that the repetitions themselves are artistically active precisely because there are certain violations of repetition (and vice versa). Only an account of both these opposing tendencies will permit us to discover the essence of their aesthetic functioning.

The conjuction of repeating elements and the conjuction of non-repeating elements of a structure are based on different linguistic mechanisms. The first is based on those connections which arise between speech segments that are larger than a sentence; the second—on segments within a sentence. In the first case, a relation of formal independence and structural equality exists between the conjoined parts. The connection between them is only a semantic one, and it is expressed through simple contiguity. In extreme cases, even the semantic bond may be absent:

> Na uglu stoit apteka,
> Ljubov' sušit čeloveka.

> [On the corner is a drugstore,
> How love drys out a man.]

> Kak po našemu po sadu vse letaet belyj pux—
> Xuže netu toj dosady, kogda milyj ljubit dvux.

> [White fluff floats all about our garden
> Nothing is more vexing than when your sweetheart
> loves two girls.]*

Textual segments which are perceived as being equivalent in any way are combined by means of contiguity or combination. Ornament can serve as a model of such a construction.

Another type of conjunction is associated with the sphere of traditional syntax. It entails the conjunction of various elements imposing additional conditions. 1) All elements must form a structural whole—a sentence, in which they acquire a kind of constructional specialization. Thus a text

---

* Both of the couplets cited above are called in Russian *častuskas*—a form of folk lyric which goes back to Medieval Russian verse. Such verses are generally topical and humorous; they are usually sung, but may be read as well and their influence can be seen in such poems as Aleksandr Bolk's "The Twelve."—Tr.

viewed as a sentence must be finite and divided into functionally unequal elements. 2) The bonds between elements must have a formal expression, which entails, in particular, that certain identical structural features must be assigned to bonded members (for instance, agreement and other forms of grammatical connection between elements of a sentence).

It is essential to stress that bonds between uniform elements create a repeating structure that is in principle unbounded, whereas bonds between heterogeneous elements create a finite structure, which we will discuss in greater detail below.

Phonological Sequences in Verse

Let us examine the phonological structure of a passage from Batjuškov's poem "To a Friend," the lines which caused Puškin to exclaim, "Italian sounds! What a wonder-worker that Batjuškov is!"

> Nrav tixij angela, dar slova, tonkij vkus,
> Ljubvi i oči i lanity,
> Čelo otkrytoe odnoj iz važnyx muz
> I prelest' devstvennoj Xarity. . . .

> [An angel's quiet ways, the gift of words, exquisite taste,
> The eyes and cheeks of love,
> The high brow of an important muse
> The charms of virginal Grace. . .]

> a i i a e a a o a o i u
> u i i o i i a i y
> e o o y o e o o i a y u
> i e e e e o a i y

Obviously the principle governing phonological construction changes radically at the end of each line.* If we count three or four phonemes from the end and divide the line at that point, the left half will clearly show a tendency toward phonological unification, the right half toward phonological variation.

The vowels which occur only once in the left half are isolated cases and their appearance is clearly random, the inevitable result of constructing the lines from meaningful material. The endings (three of four phonemes from the end) consist entirely of different phonemes (if they repeat any of the vowels contained in the first half, it will be a vowel unrepeated in that half).

The first conclusion we can draw is that around the line endings, phonological ordering conflicts with deliberate "disorder."

***

* The reader who does not know Russian should be made aware of the fact that here and in the discussion that follows the author is dealing with "ideal" vocalic schemata which represent the letters that make up the words. In some cases actual pronunciation corresponds fairly closely to a given schema. In others the difference is rather considerable.–Tr.

In several cases, however, the opposite is true: the line moves from "disorder" to the ordering of identical phonemes at the end of the line. This shows that above all it is essential to *change* the constructive principle at the end of a structural unit (a verse or stanza) at the moment when the possibility of prediction increases radically. Here is one example:

> Unylo junoša gljadel
> Na opusteluju ravninu
> I grusti tajnuju pričinu
> Istolkovat' sebe ne smel.

> [Despondently the youth stared
> Across the deserted plain,
> And he did not dare to explain to himself
> The secret source of his sorrow.]
> (Puškin)

The last line of this fragment is a finished, syntactical—intonational whole which, from the viewpoint of the phonology of the vowels, looks like this:

> i o o a e e e e

The transition from the conjuction of different vowels to the repetition of one is obvious here.

But it would be a mistake to say that the conjuction of different elements is significant only because it contrasts with the principle of repetition. It also has totally independent meaning:

> Okna zapoteli
> Na dvore luna.
> I stoiš' bez celi
> U okna.

> [The windows misted over,
> The moon is out.
> And you stand aimlessly
> By the window.]
> (Andrej Belyj)

The last line forms a chain of vowels: $u-o-a$. Qualitatively these vowels differ, and at the same time they are linked in a certain structural sequence. The result is something that could not occur in the repetition of identical structural elements, namely, the fragmentation of each element into distinctive features on a lower level where we can distinguish common and contrastive features in the structural series.

The chain $u-o-a$ contains a set of distinctive features common to all its constituent elments: the oppositions "vocalic—nonvocalic" and "front—non-front" reveal their common features. But with regard to the features "closed—open" we see a sequentially gradational increment. The phonological structure of the vowels in this line activates the feature "closed—

open," elevating it to the rank of a meaningful structural element.

On k Iovu iz tuči rek.   [He spoke to Job from a cloud.」
                    (Lomonosov)
o–i–o–u–i–u–i–e

With the exception of *e* (for we have already accounted for the appearance of an extra-systemic phoneme at the end of a series), we can discover a regular sequence in the progression of elements which initially seem unordered.

First, the entire line is organized in terms of shift of front and back vowels (here *o* and *u* constitute one element, as do *i* and *e*). If we mark the front vowels "+" and the back vowels "-" we get the following scheme:

- + - - + - + +

Against the background of the expected ideal scheme:

- + - - + - - + (-)

The occasional disordering we observe only activates the feature of transition from front to back vowel and vice versa, preventing it from becoming automatic and unnoticed.

But if we break up the sequence of vowels into combinations of three, we get the following groups of environments for vowels:

oio–iou–oui–uiu–iui

Here the sequential realization of all possibilities is of interest. The sounds occur in homogeneous and non-homogeneous environements. At times the same element is a central member, at times a frame. But each combination activates new distinctive features. The phoneme *i* in the environment *o i o* has a different content than in the environment *u i u;* different distinctive features come to the forefront, and the "group of common features" and the "group of different features" are redistributed differently in each case. If we return to the lines from Puškin's narrative poem *The Gypsies* cited earlier, we will observe a rather interesting phenomenon.

Breaking up the vowels into groups of three (all the more justified in this text, where such divisions almost always coincide with word-boundaries), we get the following:

uyo uoa ae
aou eu   aiu
iui auu iiu

Recall that in the fourth line *u* does not occur. But here *u* occurs in the most varied combinations (in terms of quality and order). Let us look upon *u* as an element that is everywhere identical, an element equal to itself. Then it will become a repeating element in certain non-repeating units, the condition of their agreement. There is no need to break down the phoneme *u* into distinctive features. Moreover this phoneme will itself be reduced to the status of a distinctive feature in a structure built of elements on a higher level. If we take note that the combination $o-u$ activates the feature open–closed, $i-u$ the labial–non-labial feature, and $e-u$ the front–back feature it becomes obvious that different aspects are actualized in each of these u's; the unity itself does not consist of some physical reality (as was the case in the first instance), but as a construct, the combination of different phonological oppositions given in the text. Thus the combination of identical elements points to structures on higher levels, while the combination of non-identical elements points to lower levels. But since an element in an artistic structure is not equal to itself, any level of that structure, in the words of Tjutčev, lies "between two abysses." It is translated into the language of higher and lower levels in the structure.

We should note that most instances of this sort of secondary semantization, which are dependent on the attribution of direct significance to sounds in poetic language, and in particular all cases of onomatopoeia, are not connected with phonemes but with distinctive features, since they express the acoustical character of onomatopoeia more directly. The well-known phrase *tjaželozvonkoeskakan'e* ["heavy-ringing galloping"]* conjures up many associations with the world of real sounds, not because of repetitions of certain phonemes, but to the degree that the opposition $z-s$ reveals the feature of voicedness. The oppositions $v-k$, $s-k$, and $n-k$ activate various distinctive features of the phoneme k. the features of voice, plosiveness, and obstruence are bared in the same way, and are then easily semanticized as imitations of real sounds.

It is the distinctive features of phonemes which are the carriers of different types of articulation and in this connection are easily associated with certain facial expressions, which entails secondary semantization.

Even when it is difficult to grasp the principle of phonological organization, it manifests itself at the end of a line in the shifting of the system of phonemes. The tendency to alter the vocalic structure of a line around the clausula is best documented in texts that abound in exotic names or trans-rational words (also in "nonsense" texts). The greater freedom of semantic combinations here allows the laws of phonological organization to reveal themselves more clearly. It is telling that the presence or absence of rhyme makes this law more or less explicit but never cancels it out. Here are two examples.

In Bunin's translation of Longfellow's *Song of Hiawatha* the absence of rhyme makes the phonological break at the end of each line especially obvious:

> I opjat' oni besedu
> Prodolžali: govorili
> I o Vebone prekrasnom,
> I o tučnom Savondazi,
> I o zlom Kabibonokke;
> Govorili o Venone. . .

* From Puškin's narrative poem *The Bronze Horseman.* –Tr.

[Then they talked of other matters;
[First of Hiawatha's brothers,]
First of Wabun, of the East-Wind,
Of the South-Wind, Shawondasee,
Of the North, Kabibonokka;
[Then of Hiawatha's mother,]
Of the beautiful Wenonah. . .]

i o a o i *e e u*
o o a i o o *i i*
i o e o e e *a o*
i o u o a o *a i*
i o o a i o o *e*
o o i i o *e o e*

And Xlebnikov's "The Prževal'skij Horse:"*

Čtob, cenoj raboty dobyty,
Zelenee stali čoboty,
Černoglazye, ee
Šepot, ropot, negi ston,
Kraska temnaja styda,
Okna, izby s trex storon,
Vojut sytye stada. . .

[That the *čoboty* obtained
At the cost of labor
Might become more green,
Blackeyed, and her own.
Whispers, murmurs, moans of languor,
The darkling hue of shame,
Windows, cabins, from three sides,
Sated cattle low. . .]

o e o e o *y o y y*
e e e e a *u o o y*
e o a y *e e o*
o o o o *e i o*
a a e a *a y a*
o a i y *e o o*
o u y y *e a a*

---

* The examples that Lotman uses to illustrate his point require some commentary. The passage from the *Song of Hiawatha* is from Canto IV, "Hiawatha and Mudjekeewis." Bunin left out the lines "First of Hiawatha's brothers" and "Then of Hiawatha's mother," and also the words "East-Wind," "South-Wind," and "North." Still, the exotic names would be quite comprehensible to a Russian reader if the passage were read in the context of the canto, where the necessary associations (between Wabun and the East-Wind, for example) are clearly established.

The fragment from Xlebnikov's poem requires considerably more commentary, lest the reader be convinced that the text is "trans-rational" or "nonsensical." First the passage quoted here begins in mid-sentence, which of course does not facilitate

The Syntagmatics of Lexico-Semantic Units

Elements of ordinary language become artistically meaningful if one can discern premeditation in their use: if a norm obligatory for a non-artistic text is violated; if the frequency or rarity of a given form perceptibly differs from general linguistic indices; if there are two or more equivalent mechanisms for expressing the same linguistic function and one is chosen, and so on. Due to the grammatical, semantic and stylistic bonds present in language certain requirements arise for the "correct" construction of word-chains. The violation of any of these rules (or prohibitions) makes the broken bond (transferred from the obligatory to the facultative category) a carrier of certain meanings (as an obligatory feature it was semantically neutral).

comprehension. The curious reader should consult the full text in Xlebnikov's *Sobranie proizvedenij,* vol. II, Leningrad, 1929, pp. 111-113. Second, the last word in line 3 should read *eja,* not *eë,* and should be followed by a full-stop. Ordinarily this sort of change would be irrelevant (*eja* is simply the old orthographic form of *eë*), but here the word rhymes in its old form with *zmeja* ("snake") and *struja* ("stream"), which occur a few lines earlier. This change naturally reflects on the vowel scheme of the line, which should read: *o o a y e e a.*

The following commentary on the poem should clear up any misgivings the reader may have about its intelligibility. The citation below is from an essay, soon to be published, by Aleksandr Parnis, to whom the translators wish to express their gratitude for permission to use this excerpt.

"Xlebnikov's poem *Kon' Prževal'skij* can scarcely be called 'trans-rational' in the precise Futurist meaning of the word, or, for that matter, 'nonsensical,' although it is one of the most elusive poems in the corpus of Xlebnikov's works (cf. K. Pomorska's analysis of the poem in *Russian Formalism and its Poetic Ambiance*). According to Nikolaj Stepanov, editor of the five-volume *Collected Works,* the title was in all likelihood Davyd Burljuk's invention, not Xlebnikov's. In fact it seems most probable that Xlebnikov himself gave the poem this title, since the image of the Prževal'skij horse appears in other poems, as well as in his polemical essays, where the Cubofuturists are identified with the "proud Prževal'skij horses," (cf. the poem *Serdce prozracnej čem sosud*).

"Besides the poem at hand, a whole cycle of poems by Xlebnikov were printed under the title 'The Prževal'skij Horse' in the Futurist miscellany *A Slap in the Face of Public Taste* (St. Petersberg, 1912). Among them were such well-known works as *Bobeobi. . .,* and *Krylyškuja zolotopis'mom tončajšix žil. . .* The title refers to a species of wild horses discovered by and named after Nikolaj Mixailovič Prževal'skij (1839-1888), a Russian explorer. It native habitat is Central Asia. In the poetics of Cubofuturism with its Asiatic orientation, the image of the Prževal'skij horse is associated with wildness and primordiality, and also symbolizes the swift, even flow of time.

"We can decipher the elusive semantics of the passage in question if we look at the whole context in which it occurs. The lines quoted metaphorically describe a rare species of orchid, *Orchis ustulata,* with unusual form and color. Here Xlebnikov uses a rare Ukrainian designation, *zozulyni čoboty* (cf. B. D. Grinčenko, *Slovar' ukrainskogo jazyka,* vol. II, Kiev, 1908, p. 177). The word *čoboty* appears in other poems as well (*Deti vydry, V lesu*). The comparative adjective "greener" and the epithet "blackeyed" correspond exactly to the flower in question.

"In interpreting this passage one should also bear in mind Xlebnikov's own interpretation of one of the lines, *šepot, ropot negi ston* ('whispers, murmurs, moans of languor'). In the essay "Conversation Between Oleg and Kazimir" (op. cit., vol. V, p. 191) he says in reference to this line, 'The self-sufficient word has a five-ray construction.' He has in mind, of course, the vowel scheme, where the vowel *o* is repeated five times."

The lifting of obligatory prohibitions on the combination of words into chains (sentences) is the basis for the artistic syntagmatics of lexical units.

Let us consider the lifting of semantic prohibitions as a fundamental case in point.

The combination of lexico-semantic units, forbidden (unmarked) in ordinary language and permitted in the language of poetry is the basis for tropes. Let us discuss metaphor, the basic form of trope, from this point of view.[2]

A linguistic metaphor and the metaphor of an artistic text are two different phenomena; one is marked in the natural linguistic context and in this sense can be equated with a usual word, whereas the other is tantamount to nonsense outside the given poetic context and has only an occasional meaning. Accordingly, if we were to analyze metaphors which have already moved from poetry and penetrated the language, and have become marked in non-artistic contexts ("the murmur of the trees," "diamonds were suspended from the blade of grass") we would obviously complicated our task by working with a semantic structure that has a dual function. The desire to commence our analysis with simple instances obliges us to examine metaphors which are transformed to a senseless combination of words outside a given text.

Let us conduct an experiment. We will take the sentence, "The armchairs were enveloped in soft female flesh," and ask our audience to determine whether or not the phrase is semantically marked. The author of this book conducted this and similar experiments. Excluding the answers of those aware of the quotation's source, the overall results were as follows: the subjects did not distinguish this sentence from other chains of words composed at random (grammatically marked, but semantically unmarked). The most frequent answer was, "In the general linguistic sense it is meaningless, but in a poetic text it would be perceived as meaningful."[3] Most interesting was the following response: "Before deciding whether it is semantically marked, one has to know if it is poetry." This brings us to the very essence of the conjunction of semantic units in poetry. In a non-artistic text we are dealing with semantic givens and the proper means for combining these elements into semantically marked phrases. In an artistic text words function as pronouns (in addition to their natural linguistic meaning), signs for designating an as yet unrevealed content. This content is constructed from their relations. While in a non-artistic text the semantics of the units dictates the nature of the relations, in an artistic text the nature of the relations dictates the semantics of the units. But since a real text has at

2 On the mechanism of metaphor see Ju. I. Levin, "Struktura russkoj metafory," *Trudy po znakovym sistemam*, vol. II (Tartu, 1965) and C. Brook-Roose, *A Grammar of Metaphor* (London, 1958).

3 On the linguistic conception of the marked phrase see I. I. Revzin, *Modeli jazyka*, op. cit., pp. 60-61.

once an artistic (supra-linguistic) and non-artistic (characteristic of natural language) meaning, both systems are projected onto each other; each, against the background of the other, is perceived as a "regular violation of a law," which is the condition for informational saturation.

The typical classification of metaphors, which goes back to Aristotle and is based on pure logic (substitution according to contiguity, analogy, etc.) describes only a single aspect of the problem.

The following would seem to be a more comprehensive approach. Consider the phrases:

> The wolf tore a lamb to pieces.

> The wolf tore a stone to pieces.

In grammatical terms both utterances are identically marked. Semantically the first can be regarded as marked, while the second cannot. If we view all the words of this utterance as sets of semantically distinctive features, the feature "tearing to pieces" enters into the concept "wolf" in conjunction with the grammatical feature of subject; and the concept "lamb" in conjunction with the grammatical feature of object. If the given semantic units are to be combinable, they must have a common semantic distinctive feature.

In poetry the reverse is true: the fact of combination determines the presumption of the presence of a common semantic feature. An extreme case—which for that very reason illuminates the way the mechanism works— is when the common element (in addition to grammatical markedness) is not semantic, but, say, phonological:

> . . .Tem časom, kak serdce, plešča po ploščadkam,
> Vagonnymi dvercami syplet v stepi. . .

> [That hour when the heart, plashing across freight-car platforms
> Pours like freight-car doors into the steppes. . .]
> (Pasternak)

In *Plešča po ploščadkam* ["splashing across freight-car platforms"] the shared phonological group *plšča* prompts the poet to combine these words, and proceeding as thought this were a fact, he creates a secondary meaning in which *pleskat'* and *ploščadka,* taken separately, are simply pronouns with occasional meanings.

Other less extreme instances are possible. The simplest way to form secondary meanings is to replace an expected semantic feature with its opposite. In the phrase "to spend" or "while away" an evening, the first verb signifies an activity whose aim is to fill a finite span of time, the second— to transform a long span ito a short one. In both instances the verbs are associated with a certain temporal demarcation. In the synonyms "evening," "hour," "time," or any other designation of a temporal segment, a measurable length of time is meant.[4] The common semantic distinctive feature entering into the opposition "measurable vs. immeasurable" as its first member semantically unites the words. Puškin plays on this expectatiion, but simultaneously defeats that expectation, replacing the first member of the opposition with the second (in a dialogue in Hell from the rough draft of a projected work on *Faust*):

[Ved'] my igraem ne ⟨iz⟩ (?) deneg,
A tol'ko b večnost' provodit'!

[[Isn't it true] that we are playing not ⟨because⟩ (?) money,
But only to spend eternity!]

The combining of the uncombinable, of "eternity" with its immeasurability and theverb "to spend," activates unexpected aspects of the meaning: eternity appears as an immeasurable chain of measurable periods of time (an eternity spent playing hearts!) In this secondary semantic series eternity is no longer simply an antonym of time ("time will be no more"), but also its synonym (they are interchangeable in an identical environment).

In the following text by Pasternak ("Disintegration") we find a more complex instance of this phenomenon:

Kuda časy nam zatesat'?
Kak skorotat' tebja, raspad?
Povolž'em mira čudesa
Vzjalis', bušujut i ne spjat.

[Where can we fit in the hours?
How should we while you away, disintegration?
Along the Volga the wonders of the world
Showed up—they rage and do not sleep.]

The phrase *skorotat'raspad* ["to while away disintegration"] sets a temporal limitation·on disintegraion, a feature that is not inherent to it in either direct or negative form (it is characteristic that when one is obliged to use the word in physics to mean a measurable length of time, the word *period* is added, forming a fixed phraseological form—*period poluraspada* ["half-life]. The word *raspad* as it appears here is imbued with the meaning of Hamlet's words at the end of Act I, where *raspad* is spoken of as an interval between previously connected ages (*raspalas' svjaz' vremen*).*

Thus we may define metaphor (and more broadly, tropes) as a tension between the semantic structure of art and that of natural language. The nature of tropes gives us a good indication of the semantic structure of

---

* Pasternak's translation of "The time is out of joint;" literally the line means "The bond of time has disintegrated."—Tr.

4 Cf. Gunnar Jakobsson's extremely interesting essay "Razvitie ponjatija vremeni v svete slavjanskogo čas'," *Scandoslavica* No. 4 (Munksgaard–Copenhagen, 1958); the essay explores the semantics of spatial duration in the Common Slavic *čas*.

poetic language as a special structure. This implies, on the one hand, that a writer's system of tropes is determined by the overall structure of his artistic and philosophical thought; on the other hand, its functional similarity to other types of artistic syntagmatics also determines its character. It is no accident that in those genres where metaphor is well developed (the plotless lyric, for example), the plot organization of the text (the syntagmatics of supra-phrasal units) is less strongly developed, and vice versa.

In this sense the difference between the frequently associated concepts of metaphor, on the one hand, and allegory and symbol on the other, is deeper than it is usually made out to be. Metaphor is constructed by bringing together two independent semantic units; allegory and symbol are constructed by deepening the meaning of one unit. The difference between them is the difference between the syntagmatic and paradigmatic axes of organization in an artistic text.

8. THE COMPOSITION OF THE VERBAL WORK OF ART

The Frame

Composition is usually understood to mean the syntagmatic organization of plot elements. Thus the paradigmatic elements of a given level must be singled out before we can make a study of their syntagmatic agreement. As we have seen, however, the articulation of plot elements depends on basic oppositions, and the latter, in turn, can be singled out only within a previously limited semantic field (it is possible to single out two complementary subsets only when there is a previously given universal set). From this it follows that the problem of the frame—the boundary separating the artistic text from the non-text—is one of fundamental importance. The same words and sentences which make up the text of a work are divided up into plot elements in various ways, depending on where one draws the line demarcating the text and non-text. What is on the outside does not enter into the structure of a given work; it is either not a work, or another work. In an eighteenth century theatre, for example, the stalls for especially privileged spectators were mounted on the stage in such a way that the spectators in the hall simultaneously saw both spectators and actors on the stage. But only the actors found themselves in the play's artistic space, the area situated within its frame of demarcation, and therefore the spectator saw spectators on the stage, but did not notice them.

A picture frame may be an independent work of art, but it is located on the *other* side of the line demarcating the canvas, and we do not see it when we look at the picutre. We need only begin to examine the frame as a kind of independent text in order for the canvas to disappear from the field of our artistic vision; it ends up on the other side of the boundary. A curtain especially painted for a given play enters into the text of the play; a curtain which does not change does not. The Moscow Art Theatre's curtain with its soaring seagull is used for every play staged at the theatre, and lies beyond the play's textual boundaries when we take it in isolation. But we have only to treat all the productions of the theatre as a single text (which is possible, given their conceptual and artistic similarity) and individual plays as elements of this unity, and the curtain becomes part of the artistic space of the text. It becomes an element of the text, and we can speak of its compositional role.

Titian's famous painting *The Repentant Magdalene,* located in the Hermitage Museum, is an example of a picture whose frame totally resists semantic ties. The painting is set in a frame, the work of a master, which depicts two half-naked men with twirled moustaches. The conjunction of the painting's subject and its frame creates a comic effect. The conjunction, however, does not take place, since we exclude the frame from our semantic field in viewing the picture; the frame is only the material boundary of the artistic space, which constitutes a whole universe. We need only turn our attention to the frame as an independent text for the picture to be transformed into the boundary of the frame, and in this sense it does not differ from the wall. The frame of a picture, the footlights of the stage, the borders of a film screen—all constitute the borders of an artistic world, self-sufficient in its universality.

This is related to certain theoretical aspects of art as a modeling system. Being spatially limited, a work of art is a model of an infinite universe.

The frame of a painting, the footlights in theatre, the beginning and end of a literary or musical work, the surfaces which mark the borders between a sculpture or an architectural edifice and the space artistically excluded from it—all these are various forms of a law that applies to all art: a work of art is a finite model of an infinite universe. Because a work of art is in principle a reflection of the infinite in the finite, of the whole within an episode, it cannot be constructed as the copy of an object in the forms inherent to it. It is the reflection of one reality in another, that is, it is always a *translation*.

Let us cite a simple example, one not taken from the sphere of art, which indicates the connection between the problem of boundaries and the arbitrariness of the language used to reflect one object in another.

The point of departure of Lobachevsky's geometry is a denial of Euclid's fifth postulate, which states that "only one line may be drawn through a given point parallel to a given line." The opposite assumption breaks completely with customary visual representation and cannot, it would seem, be depicted on a plane surface by means of "customary" (to use Lobachevsky's terminology) procedures of geometry. But if, like the German mathematician Klein, we draw a circle on an ordinary euclidian plane surface and look only at its interior, ignoring the circumference and the outlying area, we can construct a graphic model of Lobachevsky's proposition. We need only look at the drawing to be convinced that within the circumference (which in its demarcation represents Lobachevskian space, while the chords take the place of straight lines) Lobachevsky's postulate holds true: two lines can be drawn throught a point parallel to a third line (here a chord). It is the nature of the spatial demarcation which allows us to view ordinary geometry as a model of Lobachevsky's geometry within the circle.[1]

1 In the diagram one can see that between chords AD and CE one can draw a number of chords within the space of the circle which would satisfy the requirement of passing through point A without intersecting chord BC; this would be impossible if one were dealing with the unbounded space of a plane surface.

The example cited here is directly related to the problem of the frame in art. In modeling an infinite object (reality) by means of a finite text, a work of art substitutes its own space, not for a part (or rather not only for a part), but also for the whole of that reality, the aggregate of all its parts. Each individual text simultaneously models both a particular and a universal object. Thus the plot of *Anna Karenina* reflects, on the one hand, a certain narrow object—the life of the heroine, which we are fully capable of comparing with the lives of individuals who surround us in everyday life. This object, which has a proper name and all the other trappings of indiviuality, constitutes only a part of the universe reflected in art. In this sense we can set a vast number of other lives alongside the life of the heroine. But this same subject, on the other hand, is a reflection of another object which tends to expand without limit. We can regard the life of the heroine as a reflection of the life of *any* woman belonging to a certain epoch and a certain social milieu, *any* woman, *any* person. Otherwise the tragic vicissitudes of her life would only be of historical interest, and would simply be boring for a reader far removed from the special task of studying the life and manners of past epochs. Thus we can distinguish two aspects of plot (and more broadly, narration). One can be called mythological—when the text models an entire universe; the other, which reflects some episode in reality, may be called the story [*fabulnyj*] aspect. We might note that there are artistic texts which relate to reality only on the mythological principle. These are texts which reflect *everything* in the form of pure essences, and not through individual episodes. Myths are a case in point. But it is obviously impossible to construct artistic texts only on the "story" principle. They would not be perceived as models of some object, but as the object itself. Even when the "literature of fact," one of Dziga Vertov's documentaries, or *cinéma vérité* tries to replace art with slices of life, they inevitably create models of a universal nature. They mythologize reality, if only by virtue of montage or the *non-inclusion* of certain facets of the object in the movie camera's field of vision. Thus it is the mythologizing aspect of a text which is associated primarily with the frame, while the story aspect tries to destroy it. Contemporary artistic texts are constructed, as a rule, on the conflict between these tendencies, or the structural tension between them.

In practice this conflict most often takes the form of an argument between those who, like the Romantics and Realists of the nineteenth century, view art as a conventional reflection of the object (a "generalization") and those who regard art as that very object (a "thing"), the point of view taken by the Futurists and other representatives of the avant-garde in the twentieth century.

The exacerbation of these arguments, which are in fact arguments over the nature of conventionality in art, invariably exacerbates the problem of textual boundaries. A baroque statue which does not fit on a pedestal;

Sterne's *Sentimental Journey,* which ends with an explicit non-ending; the plays of Pirandello or Mejerxold's productions which carry the actor beyond the footlights; *Evgenij Onegin,* which comes abruptly to an end without any plot resolution; Tvardovskij's *Vasilij Terkin,* that "Book about a Soldier" which, like life itself, resists being pigeonholed because it never comes to an end:

Bez načala, bez konca—
Ne goditsja v "delo"!—

[Without beginning, without end—
It isn't fit for a filing folder!]

—all are different forms of conflict between the mythological and "story" aspects of the text.

The above is particularly important in connection with the problem of the frame in a verbal artistic text. The frame of a literary work consists of two elements: the beginning and the end. The particular modeling role of the categories of beginning and end is directly related to the most comprehensive cultural models. Such models, for example, will radically increase the markedness of these categories for a broad range of texts.

The heightened role of the beginning as the fundamental boundary is typical for many myths or texts of the early Middle Ages. This corresponds to the fact that the opposition "existence vs. non-existence" was viewed in terms of the opposition "created vs. not-created." The act of making, of creating, is an act of beginning. Therefore that which has a beginning exists. In this connection the claims made by medieval chronicles concerning the cultural, historical or political entity of the land, often takes the form of a narrative about the "beginning" of the land. Thus the Kievan Chronicle defines itself in the following manner: "Here are the tales of bygone years, from whence arose the Russian land, who was the first to rule in Kiev and how the Russian land arose." The *Tale of Bygone Years* is itself a story about beginnings. Not only lands, but also clans and families exist if they can point to their founding fathers.

The beginning has a defining and modeling function; it is not only evidence of existence, but also a substitute for causality, a category of later origin. To explain a phenomenon is to indicate its origin. Thus the explanation and evaluation of any fact, for example the fact that a prince has killed his brother, is carried out by pointing out *who first* committed the sin. A similar system of ideas is echoed in Gogol's "A Terrible Vengeance," where every new crime appears, not as the consequence of original sin, but as an extention of the very first act of murder. Therefore all the crimes of the descendants magnify the sins of the initiator of the events. We can find something comparable in Ivan the Terrible's assertion that Kurbskij, by fleeing abroad, destroyed the souls of his dead ancestors. It is significant that he was speaking not of Kurbskij's descendants, but about his ancestors.

The text reverts to the beginning, not the end. The fundamental question is not how it ended, but where it originated.

We should not assume that this sort of "mythologizing" is peculiar only to the *Tale of Bygone Years* or, say the *Tale of Sorrow and Misfortune** where the fate of the "stalwart lad" is anticipated by the introduction:

> ...And in the beginning of this corruptible age
> God created the heavens and the earth,
> God created Adam and Eve...
> ....
> But the human race is evil:
> From the start is was unsubmissive...

The endeavor to explain a phenomenon by pointing to its sources is characteristic of a very broad range of contemporary cultural models. One of them is the evolutionary-genetic stage of scientific research: on this stage, for example, the study of language as a structure was replaced by the study of the history of languages, and analyses of the functions of an artistic text in a society were replaced by investigations of the origin of texts. This does not cast doubt on the importance of such investigations, but only points to their ties with certain kinds of demarcations of cultural models.

Models of culture in which the beginning is a strongly marked feature are, in a way, correlated with the appearance of texts demarcated only at the beginning.

One can cite examples of texts which are considered to be "demarcated" if they have a beginning. The end is in principle excluded—the text demands continuation. Chronicles are of this type. They are texts which cannot end. If the text is broken off, someone must be found to continue it, or it will begin to look incomplete or defective. If it is given an "ending" the text becomes incomplete. Texts which in principle are open-ended include topical couplets like noels, which must continue in accord with the turn of events. Žukovskij's *A Bard in the Camp of Russian Warriors* and Voejkov's *The Madhouse* are constructed on this principle. We could also point to works published in chapter installments which are continued by the author after a part of the text has already become well-known to the reader— *Evgenij Onegin,* for example, or *Vasilij Terkin.* It is characteristic that at the moment when his "collection of motley chapters", published over the course of several years, was transformed into a book, a single text, Puškin did not give it a finished look, but weakened the function of the beginning as well by parodying the classical prologue to a narrative poem in the seventh chapter ("It may be late, but there's the prologue"). Puškin emphasized the "beginninglessness" of the novel in verse. *Vasilij Terkin* underwent an

---

* *Tale of Sorrow and Misfortune*—a seventeenth century tale with many folk elements (here organized, as often is the case, in rhythmic units) about the misadventures of a lad who did not obey his parents and, hounded by Misfortune, eventually fled to a monastery.—Tr.

analogous transformation. We can also see features of this structural principle in the composition of series of short stories, novels or films which are continued because the authors cannot resolve to kill off a hero who has caught the fancy of the reading public, or are exploiting the commercial success of the initial works.

Since it is indisputable that the contemporary literary journal is in some measure perceived as a single text, here too we are dealing with a construction that provides a fixed beginning and an "open end."

While the beginning of a text is in some degree associated with modeling the cause, the end activates the feature of the goal.

From eschatological legends to utopian teachings, we can trace a broad representation of cultural models with a marked ending, with the modeling function of the beginning sharply reduced.

The degree of markedness assigned to the beginning or end in various cultural models determines whether birth or death will be projected as the basic feature of existence, engendering such works as "The Birth of a Man," "Three Deaths," or *The Death of Ivan Il'ič.** It is the intensification of the modeling function of a text's end (the life of a man, like its description, is perceived as a special text which includes information of great importance) which entails a protest against viewing the end as the basic carrier of meaning. This gives rise to oxymoron (in the context of a given system) in expressions like: "a senseless end," or "a senseless death" and plots dedicated to the meaningless death and undivined destiny of their heroes:

> Spoj o tom, čto ne sveršil on
> Dlja čego ot nas spešil on. . .
>
> [Sing of what he did not accomplish,
> Why he hastened away from us. . .]
>   (Aleksandr Blok)

In a letter from Lermontov to M. A. Lopuxina, dated August 28, 1832, two poems are placed side by side. In one Lermontov speaks of his desire to turn away from the sensible and goal-oriented life of man in favor of the elemental life of nature:

> Dlja čego ja ne rodilsja
> Ètoj sineju volnoj?
> . . . .
> Ne strašilsja b muki ada,
> Raem ne byl by prel'ščen;
> . . . .
> Byl by volen ot rožden'ja
> Žit' i končit' žizn' moju!-

---

* "The Birth of a Man"– a story by Maksim Gorkij from the cycle *Around Russia* (1912); "Three Deaths"–an early story by Lev Tolstoj (1869); *The Death of Ivan Ilič*–a novella by the same author(1884).–Tr.

[Why was I not born
As this blue wave?
. . . .
I would not be afraid of the torments of Hell,
I would not be enticed by Paradise;
. . . .
I would be free from birth
To live and end my life!]

In the other we find an open polemic with the idea that the end of life is what gives it meaning:

Konec! Kak zvučno èto slovo,
Kak mnogo—malo myslej v nem!

[The end! How sonorous this word,
How much, how little it contains!]

We could compare this with the way the modeling function of the end is accentuated in each of the stories comprising *A Hero of Our Times* and the way it is muffled in the text of the novel as a whole. Pečorin's life "ends" long before the end of the text: we are informed of the death of the hero in the "preface" to his journal, that is, in the middle of the text, and the novel seems to end in mid-word: "I could get nothing more out of him; he does not, in general, care for metaphysical descussions." Lermontov's narrative poem *Saška* is consciously created as a fragment with no ending.

At the same time it is obvious that in modern everyday thinking, for example, the modeling function of the end is quite important (cf. the tendency to read books beginning with the end, or to "peek" at the end).

This is particularly important in connection with the problem of the frame in a verbal artistic text. The frame of a literary work consists of two elements: the beginning and the end. Let us give an example of how the end functions ·as a textual frame. In modern literary works certain plot situations are associated with the "end." Thus Puškin defined some typical "end" situations in the fragment "You advise me, friends, to take up *Onegin*. . . :':

Vy za "Onegina" sovetuete, drugi,
Opjat' prinjat'sja mne v osennie dosugi.
Vy govorite mne: on živ i ne ženat.
Itak, ešče roman ne končen. . .

[You advise me, friends,
To take up Onegin again in my autumnal leisure.
You say to me: he is alive and unmarried
So the novel is still not finished. . .]

This does not exclude the possibility that a text might have a blatant "non-ending" (Sterne's *Sentimental Journey*), and that certain ways of altering clichés might in turn be transformed into clichés. Let us examine

the most stereotyped idea of how a text should end, the "happy ending."
If the hero dies, we take the ending to be tragic. But if he marries, makes a
great discovery or helps to increase the production figures of the enterprise
where he works, we take the ending to be happy. It is interesting that when
we feel the end of a text to be happy or unhappy, completely different
indicators are involved than if we were dealing with a real-life phenomenon.
If someone recounting a real historical event that took place in the past
century tells us that the major figure involved is now dead, we do not take
the information as sad tidings: we know beforehand that a man who was
active a hundred years ago cannot be anything but dead. But we need only
make the same event the object of a work of art, and the situation undergoes
a fundamental change. If the hero triumphs at the end of the text, we feel
that the story has a happy ending; if the narrative continues to the point
where the hero dies our impression of the story likewise changes.

What is the point here?

In a work of art the course of events comes to a halt when the narrative
is brokent off. Nothing further takes place, and it is understood that the
hero, alive up to that moment, will not die, that the man who has found
love will not lose it, that the conqueror will not in the future be conquered,
for all further action is precluded.

This reveals the dual nature of an artistic model: while reflecting a
separate event, it simultaneously reflects a whole picture of the world; in
recounting the tragic fate of a heroine, it speaks of the tragic nature of the
world as a whole. That's why a good or bad ending is so significant for us:
it attests not only to the conclusion of some plot, but also to the construction
of the world as a whole.

It is revealing that in those instances where the final episode becomes
the initial episode of a new narrative (for a Christian the end of life is the
beginning of life beyond the grave; the happy ending of *The Barber of
Seville* becomes the opening dramatic situation in *The Marriage of Figaro*,
and so on) it is clearly recognized as a new story. It is no accident that
narrative plots frequently end with such phrases as "but that is another
story altogether," or "but more about that next time."

In contemporary narratives, however, the categories of the beginning
and end of a text play a different role. When a reader starts reading a book
or a spectator watches the beginning of a film or play, he may not know
for sure, or may not know at all, into what system the proffered text has
been encoded. He is naturally interested in getting a total picture of the
text's genre and style and those typical artistic codes which he should
activate in his consciousness in order to comprehend the text. On the
whole, he derives such information from the beginning. This process, of
course, is occasionally transformed into a struggle between the text and
cliché, and it may then stretch out over the entire text; the end often
assumes the role of an "anti-beginning," a *point* lending a new interpretation

to the whole system of the text's ending through parody or any other means. This, in particular, causes continual de-automatization of the codes employed and a maximum reduction of the text's redundancy.

And yet the coding fuction in contemporary narrative texts is relegated to the beginning, and the plot-mythologizing function to the end. It goes without saying that just as rules in art exist largely in order to be violated in an artistically meaningful way, so too in this case the standard distribution of functions makes possible numerous variational deviations.

The Problem of Artistic Space

We devote attention to the problem of artistic space because we consider a work of art as an area of space demarcated in some way and reflecting in its finitude an infinite object: the world which lies outside the work of art.

When we deal with the visual (spatial) arts, this becomes especially clear: the rules for representing the multi-dimensional and limitless space of reality within the limited, two-dimensional space of a painting become its specific *language.* For example, the laws of perspective as a means of representing three-dimensional objects in a two-dimensional image in a painting become one of the basic markers of the modeling system.

Visual art texts, however, are not the only ones which may be viewed as demarcated areas of space. The special character of visual perception inherent to man is such that in the majority of cases visible spatial objects serve as the denotata of verbal signs; as a result verbal models are perceived in a particular way. The iconic principle and a graphical quality are wholly peculiar to verbal models as well. We might perform a sort of mental experiment: let us imagine some extremely generalized concept, some sort of *all,* totally lacking concrete attributes, and try to determine its features for ourselves. It will not be difficult to ascertain that for the majority of people these features will have a spatial character; "boundlessness" (i.e. relation to the purely spatial category of boundary; in addition the word "boundlessness" in the everyday meaning it has for most people, is merely a synonym for something very large, an enormous expanse of something), the ability to have parts. The very concept of universality, as a number of experiments have shown, has an abstract spatial character for most people.

Thus the structure of the space of a text becomes a model of the structure of the space of the universe, and the internal syntagmatics of the elements within a text becomes the language of spatial modeling.

But that is not the full extent of the problem. Space is "the sum total of homogeneous objects (phenomena, states, functions, figures, variable meanings, and so on), between which relations exist which are similar to normal spatial relations (continuity, distance, and so on). In viewing a given sum of objects as space, we ignore all the properties of these objects except for those which are defined by the spatially similar relations which we are considering."[2]

Hence the possibility of spatial modeling of concepts which themselves are not spatial in nature. Physics and mathematics make broad use of this property of spatial modeling. Concepts like "chromatic space" and "phase space" are the basis of spatial models widely employed in optics or electrical engineering. This property of spatial models is extremely important for art.

Even on the level of supra-textual, purely ideational modeling, the language of spatial relations turns out to be one of the basic means for comprehending reality. The concepts "high-low," "right-left," "near-far," "open-closed," "demarcated-not demarcated" and "discrete-continuous" prove to be the material for constructing cultural models with completely non-spatial content and come to mean "valuable-not valuable," "good-bad," "one's own-another's," "accessible-inaccessible," "mortal-immortal," and so on. The most general social, religious, political, and ethical models of the world, with whose help man comprehends the world around him at various stages in his spiritual development, are invariably invested with spatial characteristics—sometimes in the form of oppositions such as "heaven vs. earth" or "earth vs. the nether regions" (a vertical tri-partite structure organized along the vertical axis), and sometimes in the form of a socio-political hierarchy with the marked opposition of "the height" to "the depths," and sometimes in a form that involves ethically marked oppositions such as "right-left" (expressions like *Naše delo* pravoe ["Our cause is *right*] and *pustit' zakaz nalevo* ["fill an order on the sly"]. Ideas regarding "elevated" and "degrading" thoughts, occupations and professions, the identification of what is "near" with what is understandable, one's own and familiar, and the identification of what is "distant" with what is not understood and alien—all these things are couched in models of the world invested with distinctly spatial features.

Historical and ethnical linguistic models of space become the bases of organization for the construction of a "picture of the world"—an integral conceptual model inherent to a given type of culture. Individual spatial models created by a text or group of texts become meaningful against the background of these constructions. For example, in a lyric by Tjutčev we find that the opposition "top vs. bottom" is interpreted not only in terms of the system "good vs. evil" or "heaven vs. Earth," as it is in a broad range of cultures, but also in terms of "darkness vs. light," "night vs. day," "silence vs. noise," "monochromatic vs. polychromatic," "greatness vs. vanity," "feeling of relaxation vs. feeling of fatigue."

A model of a vertically oriented universal system is created. In several instances the "top" is identified with "spaciousness" and the "bottom" with "crowding," or the "bottom" is associated with "materiality" and the "top" with "spirituality." The world of the "bottom" is the world of

2 A. D. Aleksandrov, "Abstraktnye prostranstva," *Matematika, ee soderžanie, metody i značenie*, vol. III (Moscow, 1956) p. 151.

everyday affairs.

> O, Kak pronzitel'ny i diki,
> Kak nenavistny dlja menja
> Sej šum, dvižen'e, govor, kliki
> Mladogo, plamennogo dnja!

> [O, how shrill and wild,
> How hateful for me
> Is the noise, the movement, the voices, the cries
> of the young, fiery day!]

In the poem "The soul would like to be a star. . ." there is an interesting variation on this theme:

> Duša xotela b byt' zvezdoj,
> No ne togda, kak s neba polunoči
> Sii svetila, kak živye oči,
> Gljadjat na sonnyj mir zemnoj,—
>
> No dnem, kogda, sokrytye kak dymom
> Paljaščix solnečnyx lučej,
> Oni, kak božestva, gorjat svetlej
> V èfire čistom i nezrimom.

> [The soul would like to be a star,
> But not when these heavenly bodies
> Like real eyes gaze down from the night sky
> Upon the sleeping mundane world—
>
> But in the daytime when hidden
> By the sun's burning rays, as though by smoke,
> They burn more brightly, like divinities
> In the pure and invisible ether.]

The opposition of "top" (the sky) and "bottom" (the earth) is given a primarily individual interpretation here. In the first stanza the only epithet relating to the semantics of the "sky" group is *živye* ["real"]* and the only one relating to that of the latter is "sleepy." If we recall that for Tjutčev "sleep" is always a synonym for death, for example:

> Est' bliznecy—dlja zemnorodnyx
> Dva božestva,—to Smert' i Son,
> Kak brat s sestroju divno sxodnyx. . .—

> [There are twins—for the earth-born
> Two deities—Death and Sleep,
> Like brother and sister amazingly alike. . .]

---

* *Živye glaza*—is a cliché meaning "bright eyes." Here the cliché is "de-automatized" (to use Lotman's term) in the context because the epithet refers to an inanimate object; and so the adjective reverts to its primary meaning "live, real"—Tr.

it is obvious that here the "top" is interpreted as the sphere of life, and the "bottom" as the sphere of death. This sort of interpretation is a constant in Tjutčev's poetry: wings rising up are always "real" or "live" ("O, if the living wings of the soul, soaring over the crowd. . ." or "Mother Nature gave him two powerful two living wings"). The earth is usually defined in terms of "dust:"

> O, ètot Jug, o èta Nicca!. . .
> O, kak ix blesk menja trevožit!
> Žizn', kak podstrelennaja ptica,
> Podnjat'sja xočet—i ne možet. . .
>
> Net ni poleta, ni razmaxu—
> Visjat polomannye kryl'ja,
> I vsja ona, prižavšis' k praxu,
> Drožit ot boli i bessil'ja. . .
>
> [O, the South, o Nice!
> O, how their brilliance troubles me!
> Life, like a wounded bird,
> Wants to rise—and cannot. . .
>
> There is neither flight nor spread of wings—
> The broken wings hang down,
> And the whole of my life, pressed to the dust,
> Trembles from pain and impotence. . .]

Here "brilliance," the brightness and color of the southern day, proves to be part of a synonymic series together with "dust" and the impossibility of flight.

The "night" of the first stanza, however, which encompasses heaven and earth, makes some contact possible between these opposing poles of Tjutčev's structure of the world. It is no accident that in the first stanza a verb of contact connects them, though the contact is one-sided ("They gaze down upon"). In the second stanza "day" on earth is not disseminated throughtout the whole universe. It envelopes only the "bottom" of the world. The "smoke" of the sun's burning rays shrouds only the earth. Far above, hidden from view ("invisible," with the possibility of contact thereby broken off) night reigns. Thus "night" is the eternal condition of the "top;" only periodically does it characterize the "bottom," the earth, and then only during those moments when the "bottom" loses many of the traits inherent to it: color, noise, movement.

It is not our aim to make an exhaustive study of Tjutčev's spatial composition of the world; here we are interested in stressing that the spatial order of the world in these texts becomes an organizing element around which its non-spatial features are also constructed.

Let us consider a lyric by Zabolockij, in whose works spatial structures also play a very important role. First of all we should note the important modeling role that the "top vs. bottom" opposition plays in Zabolockij's poetry. Here the "top" is always synonymous with "distance" and the "bottom" with "nearness." Therefore any movement, in the final analysis, implies movement up or down. Movement in essence is organized only along the vertical axis. Thus in the poem "A Dream," the author in his dream finds himself "in a silent country." The world which surrounds him is above all characterized by *distance* ("I sailed away, I wandered far...") and *remoteness* (strangeness).

But further on we find out that the distant world is infinitely *high:*

> Mosty v neobozrimoj vyšine
> Viseli nad uščel'jami provalov...

> [Bridges in the boundless heights
> Hung over the gaps of ravines...]

The earth is far below:

> My s mal'čikom na ozero pošli,
> On udočku kuda-to vniz zakinul
> I nečto, doletevšee s zemli,
> Ne toropjas', rukoju otodvinul.

> [I went to the lake with a young boy,
> He cast his line somewhere below
> And with his hand he leisurely pushed something aside
> That had flown up from the earth.]

This vertical axis simultaneously organizes the ethical space of the poem as well: evil for Zabolockij is invariably located below. In "The Cranes," for example, the moral aspect of the vertical axis is maximally bared; evil comes from below, and salvation is an upward surge:

> Černoe zijajuščee dulo
> Iz kustov navstreču podnjalos'
> . . . .
> I, rydan'ju gorestnomu vtorja,
> Žuravli rvanulis' v vyšinu.

> Tol'ko tam, gde dvižutsja svetila,
> V iskuplen'e sobstvennogo zla
> Im priroda snova vozvratila
> To, čto smert' s soboju unesla:
> Gordyj dux, vysokoe stremlen'e,
> Volju nepreklonnuju k bor'be...

> [A black, gaping muzzle
> Rose from the bushes to meet them...
> . . . .
> And their plaintive sobs resounding,
> The cranes rushed to the heights.

> Only there where heavenly bodies advance,
> In expiation for her own evil,
> Nature once again brought back to them
> What death had carried away:
> A proud spirit, high aspirations,
> An inexorable will to enter into the struggle. . .]

Associating height with distance, and depth with its opposite, makes the "top" the direction in which space expands: the higher one goes, the more limitless the expanse; the lower one goes, the more cramped it is. The ultimate bottom point combines within itself all vanished space. It follows that only upward movement is possible and that the opposition "top vs. bottom" becomes a structural invariant, not only of the antithesis "good vs. evil," but also of the antithesis "movement vs. immobility." Death, the cessation of movement, is movement downwards:

> A vožak v rubaške iz metalla
> Pogružalsja medlenno na dno. . .

> [And the leader in a shirt made of metal
> Sank slowly to the bottom. . .]

In "The Abominable Snowman" a spatial scheme common in twentieth century art—the atomic bomb as death from *above*—is destroyed. The hero— the "abominable snowman"—is carried upwards, and atomic death comes from below; in dying, the hero falls *down:*

> Govorjat, čto v Gimalajax gde-to,
> Vyše xramov i monastyrej,
> On živet, nevedomyj dlja sveta
> Pervobytnyj vykormyš zverej.
> . . . .
> V gornye uprjatan katakomby,
> On i znat' ne znaet, čto pod nim
> Gromozdjatsja atomnye bomby,
> Vernye xozjaevam svoim.

> Nikogda ix tajny ne otkroet
> Gimalajskij ètot troglodit,
> Daže esli, slovno asteroid,
> Ves' pylaja, v bezdnu poletit.

> [They say that somewhere in the Himalayas
> Higher than temples and monasteries,
> He lives, unbeknownst to the world,
> The primordial fosterling of beasts.
> . . . .
> Hidden in the mountains' catacombs
> He has no inkling that beneath him
> Atomic bombs are being piled up,
> Faithful to their masters.

The Himalayan troglodyte
Will never discover their secrets,
Even if like an asteroid,
He flies in flames into the abyss.]

The concept of movement in Zabolockij, however, often grows more complex in connection with the growing complexity of the concept of the "bottom." The point is that in a number of Zabolockij's poems the "bottom" as an antithesis to the "top," to space and movement, is not the lowest possible point. That withdrawal into the depths associated with death, depths which are deeper than the usual horizon of Zabolockij's poetry, unexpectedly brings out features which recall certain properties of the "top." Inherent to the top is the absence of petrified forms; movement here is interpreted as a *metamorphosis,* a transformation; unforeseen combinational possibilities exist here:

Ja xorošo zapomnil vnešnij vid
Vsex ètix tel, plyvuščix iz prostranstva:
Spleten'e form, i vypuklosti plit,
I dikost' pervobytnogo ubranstva.
Tam tonkosti ne vidno i sleda,
Iskusstvo form tam javno ne v počete. . .

[I remembered well the outward appearance
Of all these bodies floating in from space:
The plexus of forms, the convexes of slabs,
The wildness of primordial ornamentation,
There one sees no trace of sophistication,
The art of forms is clearly not upheld. . .]

This rearrangement of earthly forms is at the same time an introduction to more general forms of cosmic life. But the same rearrangement applies to the nether regions, to the posthumous fate of the human body. Addressing his deceased friends, the poet says:

Vy v toj strane, gde net gotovyx form,
Gde vse raz"jato, smešano, razbito,
Gde vmesto neba—liš' mogilnyj xolm. . .

[You are in that country where there are no finished forms,
Where everything is disjointed, confused, broken up,
Where in place of the sky, there is only a grave mound. . .]

Thus the earth's surface—*the ordinary space of everyday life*—is, in its immobility, opposed to the "top." Above and below movement is still possible. But this movement is of a specific sort. The mechanical shifting of immutable bodies in space is equated with immobility; mobility is transformation.

In this connection a new and essential opposition emerges in Zabolockij's works: immobility is equated not only with mechanical movement, but also with any movement which is totally and unambiguously predetermined. Such movement is perceived as slavery, and lies in opposition to freedom— the possibility of unpredictability (in terms of modern science this opposition could be represented as the antinomy "redundancy vs. information"). The absence of freedom and choice is a feature of the material world. The free world of thought stands in opposition to it. This interpretation of the opposition, typical for all of Zabolockij's early verse and a considerable number of works from the late period, explains why Zabolockij makes nature part of that lower, static world of slavery. The world of nature, full of anguish and lacking all freedom, is opposed to the world of thought, culture, technology and creation, a world which gives one a choice and the freedom to establish laws, where nature merely dictates servile obedience:

> I ujdet mudrec, zadumčiv,
> I živet, kak neljudim,
> I priroda, vmig naskučiv,
> Kak tjur'ma, stoit nad nim.

> U životnyx net nazvan'ja.
> Kto im zvat'sja povelel?
> Ravnomernoe stradan'e—
> Ix nevidimyj udel.
> . . . .
> Vsja priroda ulybnulas',
> Kak vysokaja tjur'ma.

> [And the wise man will go away, pensive,
> And live like a hermit,
> And nature, which immediately bores him,
> Stands over him like a prison.

> Animals do not have names.
> Who commanded that they should have names?
> The same suffering
> Is their invisible lot.
> . . . .
> All nature smiled
> Like a high-walled prison.]

The same images of nature are retained in Zabolockij's later works.

Culture, conscousness—all forms of spirituality belong to the top, while the animalistic, uncreative principle constitutes the bottom of the universe. The spatial resolution of the poem "Jackals" is interesting in this regard. The poem was inspired by a real landscape, that of the southern Crimean coast, and on the level of reality described by the poet, presents a particular spatial arrangement. The sanitarium is below, by the sea, and the jackals howl above, in the mountains. But the artist's spatial model conflicts with this picture and introduces corrections.

The sanitarium belongs to the world of culture—it is likened to a ship in another poem belonging to the Crimean cycle, of which the poet says:

> Gigantskij lebed', belyj genij,
> Na rejde vstal èlektroxod.
>
> On vstal nad bezdnoj vertikal'noj
> V trojnom sozvučii oktav,
> Obryvki buri muzykal'noj
> Iz okon ščedro raskidav.
>
> On ves' drožal ot ètoj buri,
> On s morem byl v odnom ključe,
> No tjagotel k arxitekture,
> Podnjav antennu na pleče.
>
> On v more byl *javlen'em smysla.* . . .

> [A gigantic swan, a white genius,
> The *èlektroxod* rose up on the roadstead.
>
> She rose over the vertical abyss
> In the triple consonance of octaves,
> Lavishly scattering snatches
> Of a musical storm out the windows.
>
> She trembled all over from that storm,
> She was in tune with the sea,
> But she gravitated toward architecture
> With an antenna erected on her shoulder.
>
> On the sea she was a *thing of meaning.* . . .]

Therefore the sanitarium by the sea is called "high" (cf. the *èlektroxod* "over the vertical abyss") while the jackals, though they are in the mountains, are situated below the top:

> Liš' tam, *naverxu, po ovragam.* . .
> Ne gasnut vsju noč' ogon'ki.

> [Only there, *above, along the ravines.* . .
> The lights (of their eyes) do not go out all night.]

But once he has placed the jackals in the ravines of the mountains (a spatial oxymoron!), Zabolockij furnishes them with "doubles"—the quintessence of brutishness—which are situated still further down:

> I zveri po kraju potoka
> Truslivo begut v trostniki,
> Gde v kamennyx norax gluboko
> Besnujutsja ix dvojniki.

> [But beasts along the edge of the stream
> Run timorously into the reeds,

Where deep in stone lairs
Their doubles rage.]

In Zabolockij's lyrics thought is invariably represented as the vertical ascent of liberated nature:

I ja, živoj, skitalsja *nad* poljami
Vxodil bez straxa v les,
I mysli mertvecov prozračnymi stolbami
Vokrug menja *vstavali do nebes.*

I golos Puškina byl nad listvoju slyšen,
I pticy Xlebnikova peli u vody.
. . . .
I vse suščestvovan'ja, vse narody
Netlennoe xranili bytie,
I sam ja byl ne detišče prirody,
No mysl' ee! No zybkij um ee!

[And I, alive, would wander *over* the fields,
I would enter the forest without fear,
And the thoughts of dead men, like transparent columns,
Rose up around me, *reaching to the heavens.*

And Puškin's voice was audible above the leaves,
And Xlebnikov's birds sang by the water.
. . . .
And all existences, all peoples
Preserved their incorruptible being,
And I myself was not nature's offspring,
But her thought! Her wavering mind!]

Creative work stands in opposition to all forms of immobility: material (in nature and in man's everyday life) and intellectual (in his consciousness). Creative work frees the world from the slavery of predetermination. It is a source of freedom. And it is in this connection that a special concept of harmony is always the product of human genius. In this sense the poem forms, but the creation of new and better correspondences. Therefore harmony is alsways the product of human genius. In this sense the poem "I do not search for harmony in nature. ." is Zabolockij's poetic manifesto. It is no accident that he made it the first poem in his collection of verse from 1932 to 1938 (violating chronological order). Man's creative work is an extension of the creative power of nature.

In nature too, a greater and a lesser spirituality are present: a lake has greater genius than the "thicket" surrounding it; it "burns up toward the night sky;" "a bowl of transparent water shone and thought a separate thought" ("A Lake in the Forest").

Thus the basic vertical axis is realized in these texts through a number of variant oppositions.

top	bottom
far	near
spacious	cramped
movement	immobility
metamorphosis	mechanical movement
freedom	slavery
information	redundancy
thought (culture)	nature
creation	absence of creation
(the creation of new forms)	(petrified forms)
harmony	absence of harmony

This is Zabolockij's general system. An artistic text, however, is not a copy of a system: it is formed of meaningful fulfillments and meaningful non-fulfillments of the system's requirements. It is precisely because the system of spatial relations we have described organizes the overwhelming majority of Zabolockij's texts that departures from the system become particularly meaningful. In "Mars in Opposition," a poem unique among Zabolockij's works in that the world of thought, logic and science is depicted here as something heartless and inhuman—we discover a completely different structure of artistic space. The opposition between thought or consciousness and daily life is maintained (as is the identification of the former with the "top" and the latter with the "bottom"). But then we find something absolutely unexpected in Zabolockij's work: "the spirit full of freedom and will" takes on a second meaning; it is "devoid of heart and soul." Intellect becomes a synonym for evil and the bestial, anti-human principle in culture:

> I ten' soznatel'nosti zlobnoj
> Krivila smutnye čerty,
> Kak budto dux zveropodobnyj
> Smotrel na zemlju s vysoty.

> [And the shadow of malicious intellect
> Distorted his cloudy features,
> As though a beast-like spirit
> Was looking at Earth from on high.]

The everyday domestic world represented in the forms of ordinary things and objects turns out to be near at hand, humane and good. The destruction of things—and this is almost unique in Zabolockij's work—proves to be evil. The outbreak of war and other forms of social evil are represented, not as an attack by the elements or nature against reason, but as the inhuman incursion of the abstract into the private material everyday life of man. The Pasternakian intonations here, it would seem, are not accidental:

> Vojna s ruž'em napereves
> V selen'jax žgla doma i vešči
> I ugonjala sem'i v les.

[War with its rifle at the ready
Burned houses and things in the villages
And drove families into the forest.]

The personified abstraction of war collides with the real, material world. The world of evil is a world without particulars. It is transformed on the basis of science, and all "trifles" are eliminated. Standing in opposition to it is the "untransformed," intricate, illogical world of earthly reality. Contrary to the semantic structures prevailing in his poetry, Zabolockij finds himself increasingly sympathetic with traditional democratic notions and uses the concept "natural" in a positive way:

Krovavyj Mars iz bezdny sinej
Smotrel vnimatel'no na nas.
. . . .
Kak budto dux zveropodobnyj
Smotrel na zemlju s vysoty.
Tot dux, čto vystroil kanaly
Dlja neizvestnyx nam sudov
I steklovidnye vokzaly
Sred' marsianskix gorodov.
Dux, polnyj razuma i voli,
Lišennyj serdca i dusi,
Kto ot čužoj ne straždet boli,
Komu vse sredstva xoroši.
No znaju ja, čto est' na svete
Planeta malaja odna,
Gde iz stoletija v stolet'e
Zivut inye plemena.
I tam est' muki i pečali,
I tam est' pišča dlja strastej,
No ljudi tam ne uterjali
Duši estestvennoj svoej.
. . . .
I èta malaja planeta—
Zemlja zloščastnaja moja.

[From the dark blue abyss, bloody Mars
Looked attentively at us.
. . . .
As though a beast-like spirit
Were looking at Earth from on high,
The spirit which built canals
For vessels unknown to us,
And glassy stations
Among Martian cities.
A spirit full of reason and will,
Devoid of heart and soul,
Who does not suffer when another is in pain,
To whom all means are good.

But I know that there is in this universe
One small planet,
Where from century to century
Other races live.
And there are sorrow and torment there
And there's food for passion there
But people there have not lost
Their natural soul.
. . . .
And this small planet
Is my ill-fated Earth.]

It is remarkable that in this text, one so unexpected in Zabolockij's work, the system of spatial relations changes radically. "High," "distant," and "spacious" are to "low," "near" and "small" as evil is to good. "The heavens" and "the dark blue abyss" have a negative meaning in this model of the world. Verbs which indicate downward movement have a negative meaning. We should note that in contrast to other texts by Zabolockij, the "upper" world is not represented as something fluctuating and mobile: it has grown hard and fixed in its logical inertness and immobility. It is no accident that Zabolockij not only ascribes balance, absence of contradiction and completeness to this world, but also a cruelly contrasting color:

From the dark blue abyss, bloody Mars. . .

The world of earth is a world of transitions and half-tints:

Tak zolotye volny sveta
Plyvut skvoz' sumrak bytija.

[Thus golden waves of light
Float through the dusk of existence.]

As we see, when the spatial structure of a text actualizes spatial models of the more general type (the works of a certain writer, of some literary school, the context of some national or regional culture) it always represents not only a variant of the general system, but also conflicts in some way with the system by de-automatizing its language.

Besides the concept "top vs. bottom," another essential feature which organizes the spatial structure of a text is the opposition "closed vs. open." Closed space is interpreted in texts in terms of various common spatial images—a house, a city, one's motherland—and is endowed with certain features: "kinship," "warmth," "security," and so on. It stands in opposition to open-ended, "outer" space and its features: "strangeness," "enmity," "cold," and so on. Opposite interpretations of "open" and "closed" are also possible.

In this case the *boundary* becomes the most important topological feature of space. The boundary divides the entire space of the text into two mutually non-intersecting subspaces. Its basic property is impenetra-

bility. The way in which the boundary divides the text is one of its essential
characteristics. This division can be between insiders and outsiders, between
the living and the dead, between rich and poor. What is more important is
that the boundary which divides space into two parts must be impenetrable,
and the internal structure of each of the subspaces must be different. For
example, the space of a fairy tale is clearly divided into "home" and "forest."
The border between them is clear-cut—the edge of the forest, or sometimes
a river (the battle with the snake almost always takes place on a bridge).
The personae of the forest cannot enter the home; they are allowed a
definite space. Only in the forest can terrible and miraculous events take
place

Certain types of space are very precisely allotted to certain personae in
Gogol's works: the world of the old-world landowners is fenced off from
the outside by innumerable protective, concentric circles (cf. the circle in
the story *Vij*) which are intended to reinforce the impenetrability of the
inner space. It is no accident that in the description of the Tovstogubs'
estate we find that words which convey the idea of circularity are often
repeated: "Sometimes I like to descend for a moment into the *sphere* of
this unusually solitary life, where not a single desire flies beyond the palisade
surrounding the small courtyard, beyond the wattle fencing of the orchard,
full of apple and plum trees, beyond the village huts *surrounding* it."[3]
The barking of a dog, the creaking of doors, the opposition of the warmth
of the house to the cold outside, the galleries surrounding the house and
protecting it from the rain—all these things create a zone of impregnability
against hostile outside forces. On the other hand there is Taras Bulba—a
hero of the open spaces. The narrative of his life begins with his *leaving
home* accompanied by the smashing of a jug and other domestic utensils.
His unwillingness to sleep inside the house is only the beginning of a long
series of descriptions which demonstrate that these characters belong to
the world of open space: "Deprived of house and home, man here became
dauntless." A *seč* [a Cossack military settlement—Tr.] has no walls, gates
or fences: the location constantly changes. "Nowhere was there a fence to
be seen. . A small rampart or abatis, guarded by absolutely no one, revealed
a terrible lack of discipline."[4] It is no accident that the walls appear only
as a force hostile to the Zaporozhian Cossacks. In the world of the fairy
tale or of the "old-world landowners" evil, destruction and danger come
from the outside, open world. Here one definds oneself by means of locks
and fences. In *Taras Bulba* the hero himself belongs to the outside world;
danger comes from the closed, internal demarcated world—the house in
which one may grow effeminate, and from homey comforts. The very
security of the inside world conceals a threat of this type for the hero; it
can entice him, lead him astray, and tie him down, which is tantamount to

3 N. V. Gogol', *Polnoe sobranie sočinenij*, vol. II (Moscow, 1937) p. 13.
4 Ibid., pp. 46, 62.

treachery. Walls and fences look less like a defense than like a threat (the Zaporozhian Cossacks "did not want to have anything to do with fortresses").

The simplest and most fundamental case is when the space of a text is divided by some boundary into two parts and each character belongs to one of them. But more complex situations are possible too in which different characters not only belong to different spatial areas, but are associated with different, occasionally incompatible, types of spatial division. The world of the text is divided up in different ways for different characters. There arises a sort of spatial polyphony, the play of different sorts of spatial division for each. "Poltava," for example, contains two non-intersecting and incompatible worlds: the world of the Romantic narrative poem with its strong passions, the rivalry of father and lover over Maria's heart, and the world of history and historic events. Some heroes (like Maria) belong only to the first world, others, like Petr, only to the second. Mazepa is the only character who enters into both.

In *War and Peace* the clash of various characters is simultaneously a clash between their respective ideas regarding the structure of the world.

Two other problems are closely related to that of the structure of artistic space: the problem of plot and the problem of point of view.

The Problem of Plot

We have ascertained that the scene of action involves more than a description of the landscape or a decorative background. The whole spatial continuum of a text in which the world of the object is reflected forms a certain *topos*. This *topos* is always invested with a certain "objectness," since space is always presented to man in the form of something concrete which occupies that space. In this case it is immaterial that sometimes (as for example in nineteenth century art) the filling of that space tends toward a maximal approximation of the everyday environment of the writer and his audience, while in other instances (the exotic descriptions in Romanticism, for example, or contemporary "cosmic" science fiction) it means a withdrawing from ordinary "object" reality as a matter of principle.[5]

More important is the fact that beyond the description of the things and objects which make up the environment of a text's personae, there arises a system of spatial relations, the structure of the *topos*. While serving as the principle of organization and disposition of the personae within the artistic continuum, the structure of the *topos* emerges as the language for

5 Since an "improbable" environment is created on the basis of the writer's profoundest ideas concerning the unshakeable foundations of the life around him, fantastic literature is precisely where we find those basic traits of everyday consciousness which the author tries to get rid of. When Xlestakov, indulging in unrestrained fantasy, describes the balls he gave in St. Petersburg ("The soup in the pot came right on board a boat from Paris. .") he gives the most exact description of the everyday life of a petty official (the pot of soup is set on the table and those seated around take off the cover themselves). In Gogol's words a man telling a lie "shows himself up to be the kind of person he really is." Thus the very concept of the fantastic is relative.

expressing other, non-spatial relations in the text. This determines the special modeling role of space within a text.

The concept of plot is closely linked with the concept of artistic space. At its foundations lies the concept of *event*. In his classically precise work *The Theory of Literature*, Tomaševskij writes:

> We use the word *fabula* to describe the sum total of interconnected events communicated in a work. . . . In opposition to the *fabula* stands the *sujet*, i.e. the same events, but in the form of their *exposition*, the order in which they are communicated in the work, the system of connections through which we are informed of the events in the work.6

We take an event to mean the smallest indivisible unit of plot construction, a unit which A. N. Veselovskij described as a *motif*. In searching for the basic features of the motif he turned to its semantic aspect: a motif is an elementary indivisible unit of narration correlated with an intergral model event on the extra-narrational (everyday) plane. "By *motif* I mean a formula which in its initial stages provides the community with answers to questions which nature everywhere poses, or which confirms those impressions of reality which are particularly striking, appear important or are repeated. The mark of a motif is its figurative, monomial schematism."7

This definition is indisputably profound. In emphasizing the dual essence of the motif—the verbal expression and the everyday idea-content— and pointing out its repetitiveness, Veselovskij clearly came close to determining the semiotic nature of the concept he introduced. But the attempt to apply a model thus constructed to the analysis of texts gives rise to certain difficulties; later we will see that the same everyday reality may in different texts either acquire or not acquire the nature of an event.

In contrast to Veselovskij, Viktor Šklovskij proclaimed another, purely syntagmatic way of defining the units of plot: "A tale, short story or novel is a combination of motifs; a song is a combination of stylistic motifs; therefore the plot and "plotness" [*sjužetnost'*] are form, just as rhyme is."8 It is true that Šklovskij himself did not abide by this principle as consistently as Propp in his *Morphology of the Folktale;* in fact it is not the syntagmatics of motifs, but rather the composition of devices, which lies at the foundation of his investigations. A device is viewed in terms of the general conception of "retardation," and the de-automatization of form as the relation between expectation and the text. Thus for Šklovskij a device is the relation of an element of one syntagmatic structure to that of another, and consequently it includes a semantic element. Therefore when Šklovskij asserts that "from the viewpoint of plot structure the concept of content is unnecessary in analyzing a work of art"9 we are witnessing a polemical attack rather

6 B. Tomaševskij, *Teorija literatury (Poètika)* (Leningrad, 1925) p. 137.
7 A. N. Veselovskij, *Istoričeskaja poètika* (Leningrad, 1940) p. 494.
8 V. Šklovskij, *Teorija prozy* (Moscow–Leningrad, 1925) p. 50.
9 Ibid.

than a precise interpretation of the author's position. That position is based on a desire to discover why all the automatic elements of an artistic text become meaningful from the viewpoint of content. Here we cannot fail to see that Šklovskij is attacking academic scholarship of the sort reflected in Veselovskij's criticism of Rode: "He treats poetic texts only as poetic texts," Veselovskij wrote, and further on, "A poetic work is just as much an historical monument as any other, and I see no special need for a mass of archeological props and checks before confirming its right to the title, to which it is born." The naive argument that follows is characteristic: "None of the troubadours' contemporaries denounced them for their lack of verismilitude."[10] No listener who aesthetically shares in the experience of a fairy tale denounces the narrator because the tale lacks verisimilitude, but does that mean that Baba Jaga and Zmej-Gorynyč* were everyday phenomena? It is precisely when the true thesis that a work of art is an historical monument is replaced by the notion that it is a monument "like any other" that we witness continued attempts in pseudo-scientific literature to see extinct dinosaurs in mythological monsters and the recollection of an atomic catastrophe and cosmic flights in the legend of Sodom and Gomorrah.[11] Veselovskij's profound basic principles were not fully realized in his works. But his view of the sign-motif as the primary element of plot, together with Propp's syntagmatic analysis and Šklovskij's syntactical-functional analysis, each in its own fashion, prepared the way for the present-day resolution of this problem.

What then is an event as a unit of plot construction?

An event in a text is the shifting of a persona across the borders of a semantic field. It follows that the description of some fact or action in their relation to a real denotatum or to the semantic system of a natural language can neither be defined as an event or as a non-event until one has resolved the question of its place in the secondary structural semantic field as determined by the type of culture. But even this does not provide an ultimate resolution: within the same scheme of culture the same episode, when placed on various structural levels, may or may not become an event. But since the general semantic ordering of the text is supplemented in equal measure by local orderings, each with its own concept-border, an event may be realized as a hierarchy of events on more individual planes, as a

* These are characters who recur in Russian folktales. Baba Jaga is an old hag with a large hooked nose and supernatural powers who lives in a hut on chicken legs; Zmej-Gorynyč is a monster similar to the hydra, in that he has many heads which regenerate as they are chopped off by the hero. — Tr.

10 A. N. Veselovskij, *Izbrannye stat'i* (Leningrad, 1939) p. 35.

11 Taking a naive realistic view of the correlation between literature and reality, Veselovskij is naturally puzzled by the fact that "Their hair is auburn; this is the favorite color of the Greeks and Romans; all of Homer's heroes, with the exception of Hector, are fair-haired" (*Istoričeskaja poètika,* p. 75). "Are we dealing here with the casual recording of ancient physiological impressions or with an ethnic feature?" he asks. But the physiology of sight and the ethnic type of Mediterranean peoples is hardly likely to have undergone such radical changes in the historical period under question.

chain of events, a plot. In this sense, that which on the level of the cultural text represents *one* event, may be transformed into a *plot* in some real text. One invariant construct of an event may be transformed into a series of plots on various levels. While constituting one plot link on the highest level, it may vary in the number of links, depending of the level of development of the text.

A plot thus viewed does not represent something independent, taken directly from life, or something passively received from tradition. A plot is organically related to a world picture which provides the scale for determining what constitutes an event and what constitutes a variant of that event communicating nothing new to us.

Let us imagine that a husband and wife have quarreled about the value of abstract art and go to the police station to have a report drawn up. The police inspector, having ascertained that no assault, battery or any other transgression of civil or criminal law has taken place, refuses to write up a report in view of the absence of an event. From his point of view nothing happened. For a psychologist, moralist, social scientist or art historian, however, the fact cited constitutes an event. The numerous arguments in the history of art concerning the comparative merits of various plots arise because the same event represents something essential from one point of view, something meaningless from another, and from yet another it does not exist.

This is not only true of artistic texts. It would be instructive from this point of view to examine the local news section in the newspapers of various epochs. An occurence, a meaningful departure from the norm, (that is, "news," since the fulfillment of a norm is not "news"*) depends on one's concept of the norm. From what we have said about an event being a revolutionary element opposing accepted classification, it follows that in the newspapers of reactionary epochs (e.g., during the "dark seven years" at the end of the reign of Nicholas I) the local news section regularly disappears. Since only those events take place which are foreseen, items having a plot disappear from newspaper accounts. When Herzen in a private letter to his father (dated November, 1840) reported an incident in the city (a policeman had robbed and killed a merchant), he was immediately banished from St. Petersburg by the Emperor for "spreading unfounded rumors." Here we find a characteristic fear of "incidents" and the belief that murder committed by a policeman is an event, and consequently that one should not acknowledge its existence; on the other hand, the reading of private letters by state agents is not an event (a norm, but not "news") and consequently is completely permissible. Recall Puškin's indignation on this count: for him the interference of the state in one's private life represented a scandalous anomaly and was "news." "What profound

* The word *sobytie* ordinarily means "event, occurrence." In colloquial speech it often means simply "news."—Tr.

immorality there is in the practices of our government! The police unseal a husband's letters to his wife and bring them to the tsar (a well-bred and honorable man), and the tsar is not ashamed to admit it."[12] Before us is a clear-cut example of a situation in which the qualification of a fact as an event depends on a system of concepts (in this case a system of moral concepts) and does not coincide for Puškin and Nicholas I.

In historical texts as well, the relating of a fact to events is secondary to the general world picture, This can easily be traced in the contrast between various types of memoirs or between historical studies written on the basis of an examination of the same documents.

This is still truer when applied to the structure of artistic texts. In a Norwegian chronicle of the thirteenth century an earthquake is described in the following manner: "The earth shook. . . at dinner, but others had already finished dinner." Here the earthquake and dinner are in equal measure events. This would clearly have been impossible for the Kievan chronicle. One could cite many examples where the death of a person is not an event.

In the *Heptameron* of Margaret of Navarre, the members of a party of socialites, broken up during a dangerous journey across flooded terrain in the mountains, safely come together again at a monastery. The fact that several servants died on the way (drowned in a river, eaten by bears, etc.) is not an event. It is only a circumstance—a variant of an event. In "Lucerne" Lev Tolstoj describes an historical event in the following manner:

> On the seventh of July, 1857, in Lucerne, in front of the Schweizerhof Hotel, where the richest people stayed, a poor wandering beggar minstrel sang songs and played the guitar for half an hour. Around a hundred people listened to him. Three times the singer asked them all to give him something. Not one person gave him a thing, and many laughed at him. . . Here is an *event* which present-day historians should record in fiery, ineffaceable letters. This event is more significant, more serious and much more profound than the facts set down in newspapers and histories.[13]

Love is an event from the point of view of a novel, but it is not an event from the point of view of a chronicle, which records important state marriages, but never takes note of the facts of family life (unless they are woven into the fabric of political events).

A chivalric romance does not record changes in the material status of the hero—from *its* point of view they do not constitute events—whereas the Gogolian school ceases to record love. As a "non-event" it becomes the basic aim of a scene from *The Inspector General:*

12 A. S. Puškin, op. cit., vol. XII, p. 329.
13 L. N. Tolstoj, *Sobranie sočinenij v 14-ti tomax,* vol. III, op. cit., p. 25.

> Marija Antonovna (looking out the window): What's that there
> that flew by? A magpie or some other bird?
> Xlestakov (kissing her shoulder and looking out the window):
>   A magpie. [14]

It is not love which constitutes an event, but rather actions whose goal is "rank, capital, a profitable marriage." Even the death of a hero does not constitute an event in some texts. In medieval chivalric texts death is an event if it is linked with glory or ignomy. In this case it is correspondingly viewed in a positive or negative light as either a good or bad event. In and of itself it is not regarded as a "striking impression of reality."

"Is it surprising that a common man fell in battle? The best of our ancestors fell in like manner," wrote Prince Vladimir Monomax. His son was of the same opinion: "If you killed my brother, that is not surprising, for in battle both tsars and common men perish."[15] The idea that glory rather than death constitutes an event was clearly expressed by Daniil of Galič when he addressed his troops in the following manner:

> Why are you horrified? Do you not know that there can be no
> war without the fallen? Do you not know that you went out
> against warriors and not against women? If a man is killed in
> battle, is that a marvel? Others die at home without glory, but
> these died with glory.[16]

The last example brings us to the gist of the matter. An event is that which did occur, though it could also not have occurred. The less probability that a given event will take place (i.e. the greater the information conveyed by the message concerning the event), the higher the rank of that event on the plot scale. For example, when a hero dies in a contemporary novel, it is assumed that he might not have died, that, say, he might have gotten married instead. The author of a medieval chronicle proceeds on the assumption that all people die, and therefore the reporting of a death conveys no information. But some die in glory, others "at home," and there he sees something worthy of mention. Thus an event always involves the violation of some prohibition and is always a fact which takes place, though it need not have taken place. For a man who thinks in terms of the categories of the criminal code, an event is an act of transgression; from the perspective of traffic laws, jay-walking is an event.

If we look at texts from this angle, we can easily divide them into two groups. those with plot and those without plot.

Texts without plots have a distinctly classificatory character; they establish a certain world and its mode of construction. Examples of texts without plots include the calendar, the telephone directory or a plotless

14 N. V. Gogol', op. cit., vol. IV, p. 75.

15 *Povest' vremennyx let*, vol. I (Moscow–leningrad, 1950) pp. 165, 169.

16 *Polnoe sobranie russkix letopisej* (hereafter *PSRL*), vol. II, Second Edition, (St. Petersberg, 1908) p. 822.

lyrical poem. Let us take as our example the telephone directory and examine certain characteristic traits of this type of text. Above all these texts have their own world. The universe of these texts is the world of denotata as represented in terms of natural language. The list of names in the text assumes the function of an inventory of this universe. The world of the telephone book constitutes the names of all telephone owners; the rest simply do not exist. In this sense that which *does not exist* from the point of view of the telephone book serves as the essential marker of the text. The world which is excluded from representation is one of the basic typological markers of texts as models of the universe.

Thus from the viewpoint of the literature of certain periods, base reality does not exist (Romanticism, for example), while from other points of view it is elevated poetic reality that does not exist (Futurism).

A second important trait of the plotless text is the fact that it insists on a definite *order* of internal organization of this world. The text is constructed in a particular manner and it does not permit its elements to move in such a way as to violate the established order. Thus, for example, in a telephone directory the names of subscribers are put in alphabetical order (in this case the order is stipulated by convenience; theoretically a number of other principles of organization could be applied). The shifting of any names in such a way as to violate the established order is not permitted.

If, instead of a telephone book, we take some artistic or mythological text, we can easily demonstrate that as a rule the principle of binary semantic opposition lies at the foundation of the internal organization of textual elements: the world is divided up into rich and poor, natives and strangers, orthodox and heretical, enlightened and unenlightened, people of Nature and people of Society, enemies and friends. In the text, these worlds, as we have said, almost always receive spatial realization: the world of the poor is realized in the form of a poor suburb, the slums or attics, while the world of the rich is realized as Main Street, a palace, or the dress circle of a theatre. Such notions arise as just and unjust lands, the antithesis of city and country, of civilized Europe and uninhabited islands, of the Bohemian forest and paternal castle. The classificatory border between opposing worlds assumes spatial features: Lethe, separating the living from the dead; the gates of hell with the inscription, "Abandon all hope, ye who enter here;" the worn soles which mark the beggar as an outcast, denying him access to the world of the rich; Olenin's long nails and white hands, which prevent him from blending in with the Cossack world.*

A text without plot makes these borders fast.

A text that possesses plot is built on the foundation of the plotless text as its negation. The world is divided into two groups, the living and the dead, and there is an impenetrable border between them. The living, while they are alive, cannot cross over to the dead, and the dead cannot

---

* The protagonist of Lev Tolstoj's novella *the Cossacks.—Tr.*

visit the living. The text that possesses plot, while maintaining this proscription for all personae, introduces a character or group of characters
freed from this proscription: Aeneas, Telemachus and Dante descend into
the realm of shadows; in folklore or in the works of Žukovskij or Blok a
corpse visits the living. Thus two groups of personae may be distinguished:
the mobile and the immobile.[17] The immobile submit to the general,
plotless type of structure. They are part of a classification which is thereby
consolidated. They are not permitted to cross the border. A mobile person
is one who has the right to cross the border. Here we find Rastignac making
his way from the bottom to the top; Romeo and Juliet crossing the border
that divides their warring houses; the hero breaking away from the home
of his fathers to take his vows at a monastery and become a saint; or a
hero breaking away from his social milieu and going to the people to make
a revolution. The movement of the plot, the *event*, is the crossing of that
forbidden border which the plotless structure establishes. It is not an event
when the hero moves *within* the space assigned to him. It clearly follows
that the concept of event is dependent on the structure of space assumed
by the text, or its classificatory aspect. Therefore a plot can always be
reduced to a basic episode—the crossing of the basic topological border in
the plot's spatial structure. At the same time, since a graduated system of
semantic borders is created on the basis of a hierarchy of binary oppositions
(in addition individual orderings arise which are sufficiently independent
of the base), possibilities arise for the individual shifting of proscribed
borders, for subordinate elements developed within the hierarchy of plot
movement.

Thus the plotless system is primary and can be embodied in an independent text. The system with plot is secondary and always represents a
layer superimposed on a basic plotless structure. The relationship between
both layers is always one of conflict: what the plotless text establishes as
an impossibility is the very thing that constitutes the content of the plot.
The plot is the "revolutionary element" in relation to the world picture.

If we interpret the plot as an expanded event, the crossing of a semantic
border, then the reversibility of plots becomes evident: the surmounting of
the same barrier within the limits of the same semantic field can be extended
into two plot chains running in opposite directions. Thus, for example, a
picture of the world which implies its division into man (the living) and
non-man (gods, beasts, dead men), or into "us" and "them," implies two
types of plots: a man crosses a border (a forest, the sea), visits the gods (or
beasts, or the dead) and returns with something he has taken from there.
Or one of "us," having crossed a border (climbed over a wall, crossed some
frontier, dressed or talked "the way they do," "cried Mohammed," as

17 For a further discussion of this phenomenon see S. Ju. Nekljudov's valuable
work "K voprosu o svjazi prostranstvennovremennyx otnošenij s sjužetnoj strukturoj
v russkoj byline," *Tezisy dokladov vo vtoroj letnej škole po vtoričnym modelirujuščim
sistemam* (Tartu, 1966).

Afanasij Nikitin advises, dressed like a Frenchman as Doloxov did) penetrates their world, or one of "them" penetrates "ours."

An invariant event in relation to the development of the plot may be viewed as a language, and the plot as a message in that language. However, as a text or a construct, the plot in turn emerges as a kind of language with respect to texts on the lower level. Even within the confines of a given level the plot gives the text only a typal resolution: for a particular picture of the world and for a particular structural level there exists a single plot. But in a real text it manifests itself only as a certain structural expectation which may or may not be fulfilled.

The Concept of Persona

Thus at the foundation of text construction lies a semantic structure and actions which always represent an attempt to surmount it. Therefore two types of functions are always given: Classificatory functions (passive) and the functions of the agent(active). A map is a good example of a classificatory (plotless) text. Other such examples are calendars, descriptions of signs and omens, texts designating normalized, regular actions—a train schedule, a code of laws, the *Domostroj;** in literature examples would include idylls or the celebrated *Golubinaja kniga.***

But if we draw a line across the map to indicate, say the possible sea or air routes, the text then assumes a plot: an action will have been introduced which surmounts the structure (in this case geographical).

By marking the movement of some concrete vessel on the map we get something which recalls the relations which arise in a text with a plot: the vessel may or may not depart; it may follow the route exactly or deviate from it (in a structural sense the same route traced on a map may represent completely different things, depending on whether it represents the fulfill-met or non-fulfillment of some normative task, or whether it represents a task accomplished independent of any correlation with the notion of typal obligation—in the first case each advancing "step" takes on the meaning of fulfillment or non-fulfillment of a norm, while in the second case it has no meaning whatsoever).

From the moment that a route is traced on a map—not a general route, but that of a single vessel—new evaluative coordinates are introduced. The map and the typal route are spatial and achronic, but as soon as the path of a ship is marked on them, one can pose questions about the time frame

* *Domostroj*—a sixteenth century guide to a pious, honorable life, be it religious, domestic or political, advising the proper attitude toward one's sovereign, one's wife, and one's subordinates.—Tr.

** *Golubinaja kniga*—a tripartite poem about a book of profound wisdom that fell from the heavens (hence the name which is derived from the word *glubina*—"depth"). It gives an apocryphal cosmogony, tells of the main objects of reverence for Christians (the Father of fathers, Mother of mothers, Tree of trees, etc.), and an allegory of the struggle between Truth and Falsehood.—Tr.

of its movement with respect to the time frame of the observer (whether the movement has ceased, is occurring now or will be completed in the future) and questions about the degree of reality of the path.

We can take the example of the map as a model of the text that possesses plot. It includes three levels: 1) the level of plotless semantic structure; 2) the level of typal action within the limits of the given structure; 3) the level of concrete action.

The interrelations of the levels change depending on where we draw the basic structural opposition:

code—message
1—2,3
1,2—3

Thus level two can be perceived both as code and as message, depending on the point of view.

Beginning with Propp's *Morphology of the Folktale* it has become evident that a persona represents an intersection of structural functions. Propp also recounted the basic functions (the hero, the helper, the adversary).

It follows from the above that the mandatory elements of any plot will include: 1) some semantic field divided into two mutually complementary subsets; 2) the border between these subsets, which under normal circumstances is impenetrable, though in a given instance (a text with a plot always deals with a *given* instance) it proves to be penetrable for the hero-agent; 3) the hero-agent.

Each of there elements has a certain set of features which come to light as they enter into plot relations with the other elements.

Thus the initial point of plot movement is the establishment of a relation of distinction and mutual freedom between the hero-agent and the semantic field surrounding him: if the hero's essence coincides with his environment, if he is not invested with the capacity to distinguish himself from that environment, the development of plot is impossible. An agent may not perform any act: the ship may not set out, the murderer may not murder, Pečorin and Bel'tov may idle about. But the nature of their mutual relations with their environment testifies to the fact that they are idle *agents*. The ship that does not sail and the stationary cliff, the murderer who has not murdered and the ordinary fellow who has not committed murder, Pečorin and Grusnickij, Bel'tov and Kruciferskij*—none of these represent structurally coincident figures, though none of them act.

The agent is the one who crosses the border of the plot field (the semantic field), and the border for the agent is a barrier. As a rule, therefore, all kinds of barriers in the text are concentrated at the border and structurally always represent a part of the border. It is immaterial whether it be the "adversaries" in a fairy tale, the waves and winds and currents hostile to

---

* Pečorin and Grušnickij are characters from Lermontov's novel *A Hero of Our Times;* Bel'tov and Kruciferskij are from Herzen's *Whose Fault?*–Tr.

Odysseus, the false friends in a picaresque novel or the false clues in a detective novel, for in a structural sense they all have an identical function: they make the movement from one semantic field to another extremely difficult, and altogether impossible for everyone except the agent in a single given instance (another variation of the plot event is also possible, wherein the agent perishes or for some other reason "drops out of the game" without surmounting the barrier). When the unified function of surmounting a barrier is stratified, as it is in some texts, helpers of the agent appear as a result.

Once the agent has crossed a border, he enters another semantic field, an "anti-field" vis-a-vis the initial one, If movement is to cease, he has to merge with the field, to be transformed from a moblie into an immobile persona. If this does not happen, the plot sequence is not concluded and movement continues. For example, the hero of a fairy tale in his initial situation is not a part of the world to which he belongs; he is pursued, he is not recognized, he does not reveal his true essence. Then he crosses the border separating "this" world from "that" world. It is the border itself (a forest, the sea) that is associated with the greatest dangers. But as long as the hero does not merge with his environment in "that" world (in "this" world he was poor, weak, the youngest brother among rich, strong older brothers; in "that" world he is a man among non-men) the plot does not come to an end; the hero returns and, changing his mode of existence, becomes a proprietor rather than an antipode of "this" world. Further movement is impossible. For this very reason as soon as a man in love gets married, as soon as insurrectionists are victorious or mortals die, the movement of plot comes to a halt.

Let us cite another example, this time a plot involving a god incarnate. A god takes on another form of existence in order to descend from the world of bliss to the mundane world (he acquires freedom with respect to his environment), he is born into the world (the crossing of the border), becomes a man (the son of man) but does not blend in with his new circumstances (a plot of the "Fedor Kuz'mič"* type exhausts itself at this point—the tsar becomes a moujik). While in the mundane world, he is part of another world. His death (the crossing of a border) and resurrection are related to this fact. The persona merges with his environment, and the action comes to a halt.

The identification of the agent and other plot functions (the environment, obstacles, assistance, the "anti-environment") with anthropomorphic personae seems so natural and ordinary that in generalizing our cultural experience to the level of a law, we suppose that any plot represents the development of relations between people simply by virtue of the fact that texts are created by people and for people. Here it might be useful to recall

* The author is referring to Lev Tostoj's story "The Posthumous Papers of Elder Fedor Kuz'mič"—Tr.

once again the map and the path of the ship. The agent is not a man, but a ship, and the obstacles are not people, but storms, currents and winds; the border is the ocean, the environment and anti-environment are the points of departure and arrival. In describing a text which marks the movement of a ship on a map as a kind of event (plot), we were totally spared the necessity of resorting to anthropomorphic personae. Why? The explanation is hidden in the nature of the classification system which determines the nature of semantic opposition and the border. It conditions the entire system, in particular the form in which plot functions will be realized. For example there are the well-known Chinese texts in which werewolves appear as agents and people are assigned the role of circumstances surrounding the action (environment, obstacle, assistance). The agent may be non-anthropomorphic, while anthropomorphic features may be attributed to the border or environment. Finally, the very anthropomorphization of personae does not signify their identification with our personalized, everyday notion of man. Thus, for example, when the punishment for murder involves taking vengeance on the male relatives of the murdered man, we are obviously not dealing with a desire to pay back the murderer by causing him grief (as the contemporary European is inclined to view such forms of veneance), but with the conviction that the clan is the agent (i.e., the murderer), whereas the actual murderer is only an instrument. Therefore it makes no difference which representative of the clan bears the answering blow.

In Medieval Russian chronicles there are accounts of the behavior of princes and other historical figures (their very division into historical and non-historical entities divides them into "agents" and "non-agents"). On closer examination, however, it turns out that the genuine agents are God, the Devil (Satan), demons, angels and good and evil counselors; the historical figures or people—the heroes of legends—are only instruments in their hands: "Satan entered into Cain and incited Cain to kill Abel." Or: "The names of these transgressors are Put'ša, Taleč', Elovit' and Ljaš'ko. Their father is Satan. For these servants are demons. For demons are sent to do evil, but angels are sent to do good."[18] The idea of man in the passive role of an instrument made God and the devil equal as agents. This embarrassed the chronicler and forced him to underscore the weakness of Satan and his helpers in further verbal descriptions: "When Jan was on his way home, on another night, a bear came, bit them [the pagan priests] and devoured them, and thus they perished through demonic instigation . . . for demons do not know men's thoughts . . . Only God can fathom human thoughts. Demons know nothing, for they are weak and vile to the sight." Action in the chronicle thus develops in a fashion similar to that of the *Iliad*, where a dual struggle is waged: one between groups of Gods, the other between the Acheans and the Trojans. From the viewpoint of the religious and ethical division, the agents are gods and the devil, while man is merely

18 *PSRL* ' vol. 1 (Moscow, 1962) pp. 89, 135.

an instrumental condition of the action. This is so obvious for the medieval reader that he sees no contradiction in a text of the following sort: "This year Metropolitan Ivan passed away; Ivan was a learned man. . . humble and gentle, taciturn and eloquent in the Holy Books."[19] "Taciturn" describes the man as agent, in his own right; "eloquent" describes the man, not in his own right, but as a bearer of higher wisdom, as its instrument. This is related to the idea that man is not the author of true (holy) books and icons, but an instrument for the realization of "God-inspired" action.

The personae of a chronicle, however, are included in other semantic fields with different, in this case political, characteristics (for example, "the Russian land vs. non-Russian lands" or "sound government vs. unsound government"). In this context princes themselves are agents, while prayers, saints or (in evil affairs) demons appear as helpers, the personified circumstances surrounding the action. Thus the personification of plot functions depends on the nature of the semantic classification.

The type of world picture, the type of plot and the type of persona are all dependent on each other.

Thus we have established that among personae, among the heroes of numerous artistic and non-artistic texts who are provided with human names and human appearance, we can distinguish two groups: agents, and the conditions and circumstances of the action. In order for both groups of plot functions to be "humanized," a special way of comprehending the world is required, in terms of which man is an active force and at the same time constitutes an obstacle to that force.

We have already shown that the personae of the first group are distinguished from those of the second by virtue of their mobility with respect to their surroundings. This very mobility, however, is the result of a single vital property: the mobile persona is distinguished from the immobile persona becuase he is permitted to act in certain ways forbidden to others. Thus Frol Skobeev's* norm of behavior is different from that of those around him: they are bound to certain norms of morality which do not restrict Frol Skobeev. From their point of view, Frol is a knave and a thief, and his behavior "knavery" and "thievery." From Frol's point of view (and that of the seventeenth century reader of this tale) the behavior of his victims reveals their stupidity, and this justifies his swindling them. The active hero conducts himself differently from the other personae, and he alone possesses this right. The right to behave in a special manner (heroically, immorally, morally, insanely, unpredictably, stragely, but always free from circumstances that are obligatory for immobile personae) is demonstrated by a long line of literary heroes, from Vas'ka Buslaev to Don

---

* *Frol Skobeev*—a late seventeenth-century tale in which the hero, a poor nobleman, contrives to marry the daughter of a wealthy courtier. He dresses as a woman in order to seduce the girl, marries her secretly and then tricks her irate father into forgiving both of them.—Tr.

19 Ibid., pp. 178-179, 208.

Quixote, Hamlet, Richard III, Grinev, Čičikov and Čackij.* To interpret this statement as merely an affirmation of the supposed necessity of conflict between the hero and his milieu is not only to narrow, but to distort the problem for the sake of accepted terminology. Not only persons, but also groups and classes of people (cf. *Taras Bulba*, for example) may be agents, and all of them must possess the properties of mobility with respect to some broader environment.

In order to understand how natural it is for a plot function to be transformed into a persona, a figure with human features, one must bear in mind yet another circumstance. If we compare the picaresque tale with the picaresque novel we will notice a curious difference. The picaresque tale is constructed according to a precise scheme: the hero-rogue acts within the semantic field of "wealth–poverty."[20] He is a poor man, but in contrast to other personae of his milieu, he is invested with mobility–with brains, initiative, the right to live outside the sphere of moral prohibitions. The barrier between poverty and wealth is impenetrable for the "fool," but it does not frighten the "rogue." Thus the plot of a picaresque tale is the history of successful roguery which makes the poor man rich and the spurned admirer a happy lover or husband. The plot-event may be unfolded in a plot-chain of events as, for example, in Frol Skobeev.

In the picaresque novel, however, we observe a typical complication, and not only because there are a large number of plot episodes instead of only one. If we were to analyze *Moll Flanders* or *The Comely Cook** we would be convinced that the persona who in one episode is an agent, in other episodes appears as an object of roguery, becoming for another rogue the embodiment of a "border," "an obstacle on the path toward wealth and happiness." The fact that the same elements of a text fulfill in turn various plot functions facilitates their personification, the identification of function with persona. An analogous effect is created as a result of changes in point of view.

On the Specific Character of the Artistic World

Everything said above about plot and event is equally applicable to artistic and non-artistic texts. It is no accident that we have attempted to

---

* Vas'ka Bus'laev is a freeman of medieval Novgorod who appears in a cycle of folk epics (*byliny*)–a rowdy, rebellious anti-hero; Grinev is the protagonist of Puškin's novella *The Captain's Daughter;* Čičikov is the purchaser of "dead souls" in Gogol's novel of that name; Čackij is the hero of Giboedov's play *Woe from Wit.* –Tr.

* *The Comely Cook (Prigožaja povarixa)*–an eighteenth century picaresque novel by Mixail Čulkov on the adventures of a fallen woman; only the first part is extant.–Tr.

20 Variants of this opposition will be "delight vs. non-delight." The corresponding opposition is "rogue vs. fool." Synonyms for the rogue are "wise," "cunning," and "young," and for the fool–"good-natured fellow," "old man," and "hypocrite." The hypocrite is most often a monk, the only person in a picaresque novel who makes references to the demands of morality. But if the features of a rogue are heavily underscored in the hypocrite, he can evoke sympathy.

illustrate our basic propositions with examples of both kinds. The specific character of the artistic plot, repeating on another level the specific character of metaphor, consists in the simultaneous presence of several meanings for each plot element, none of which annuls another, even when they are totally contradictory.

But since each simultaneity arises only on a certain level, forming strata of various mono-semantic systems on other levels or being "eliminated" in some abstract unity on the highest level, we may conclude that the "artistic quality" of a text arises on a particular level, the level of the authorial text.

Let us examine Lermntov's poem "Prayer" (1829):

Ne obvinjaj menja, Vsesil'nyj,
I ne karaj menja, molju,
Za to, čto mrak zemli mogil'nyj
S ee strastjami ja ljublju;
Za to, čto redko v dušu vxodit
Živyx rečej Tvoix struja,
Za to, čto v zablužden'i brodit
Moj um daleko ot Tebja;
Za to, čto lava vdoxnoven'ja
Klokočet na grudi moej;
Za to, čto dikie volnen'ja
Mračat steklo moix očej;
Za to, čto mir zemnoj mne tesen,
K Tebe ž proniknut' ja bojus',
I často zvukom grešnyx pesen
Ja, Bože, ne Tebe moljus'.

No ugasi sej čudnyj plamen',
Vsesožigajuščij koster,
Preobrati mne serdce v kamen',
Ostanovi golodnyj vzor;
Ot strašnoj žaždy pesnopen'ja
Puskaj, Tvorec, osvobožus'
Togda na tesnyj put' spasen'ja
K Tebe ja snova obraščus'.

[Do not accuse me, Almighty God,
And do not chastise me, I pray,
Because I love the sepulchral darkness
Because the stream of Thy living words
Seldom enters into my soul,
Because my mind in error
Wanders far from thee,
Because the lava of inspiration
Boils up on my breast;
Because wild emotions
Darken the glass of my eyes;

Because the mundane earth is too small for me,
I fear to force my way to Thee,
And often with the sound of sinful songs,
Thou are not the One to Whom I pray.

But extinguish this miraculous flame,
This all-consuming fire,
Turn my heart to stone,
Restrain my hungry gaze;
Free me, I pray, O Creator,
From the terrible thirst for poesy;
Then I will again return to Thee
On the narrow path of salvation.]

In examining the text of the poem we can very easily see that its semantic system is stratified into two layers:

I	II
God	the earth
eternity	transitoriness (corruptibility)
light	darkness
life	death
the good	sin
reality	shadow

The left column appears as the initial, marked member of the opposition. This is expressed in particular by the fact that it is chosen as the point of view (the direction of evaluation) and as the direction of action. The direction of evaluation is expressed above all in spatial categories. The use of "I" and "far from Thee" rather than "Thou" and "far from me," though the pairs are identical in their classificational structure, shows that "Thou" is taken as the point of semantic reference. The definition of the present world as "darkness" leads us to the antithetical concept of "light," and has a classificational structural character, being associated with a particular type of culture. The accompanying epithet "sepulchral" has a dual semantics. The code semantics entails the notion of earthly life as death, a counterpoise to "life eternal" beyond the grave. At the same time the epithet incorporates the spatial semantics of "the grave," a deep and closed space (the idea that the world is an abyss in contrast to paradise, and hell an abyss in contrast to the world; it is characteristic that for Dante one's degree of sinfulness corresponds to the degree of depth and closure, while the degree of holiness corresponds to the degree of elevation and openess). But this epithet also marks a point of reference, since the present world is an "abyss" only in relation to paradise.

There is also a definite orientation to verbs of action. The active *karat'* ["To punish, chastise"] indicates motion from left to right, while *molit'* ["to pray"] which implies no active process indicates motion from right to left. But the lines:

> ... I love the sepulchral darkness
> Of the earth with all its passions...

change the picture. They still fit into the general system of the cultural code described above, but they give the text an opposite orientation: instead of the "Almighty," the sinful "I" is selected as the point of view. And from this point of view "the sepulchral darkness of the earth with all its passions" can end up being an object of love.

But beginning with the ninth line the text ceases to be deciphered within the semantic system that has operated thus far. The nature of the "I" undergoes a decisive change. In the first part of the poem it is a mobile element whose value is determined by its relation to its surroundings: belonging to "earthly life," the "I" becomes transitory, mortal, wandering far from the truth, insignificant. Entering into the light and truth of the other world, this same "I" becomes important, not by virtue of its own importance, but through the value of that world of which it has become a part.

Beginning with the ninth line, the text, employing metaphors like "the lava of inspiration" which were already standard toward the end of the 1820's, made the reader conscious of another familiar cultural code, that of Romanticism. In this system the main opposition was "I—not I."

All those things that constitute "not I" are equated with each other; the worlds of heaven and earth become synonyms:

$$I \begin{cases} \text{the earthly world} \\ \text{God} \end{cases}$$

As a result the "I" does not become an element in the world (the environment) but rather itself becomes a world and space unto itself (hence the Romantic structure: the plot is eliminated). In addition, the "I" not only becomes immobile, but also enormous, equal to the whole world ("In my soul I created another world"). The "I" becomes an area for internal events.

In light of this system of concepts it is natural that the "I" should undergo spatial expansion: in lines nine and ten it is likened to a volcano (in a spatial sense as well, in contrast to Benediktov's metaphor "In the youth's breast there is a volcano"): the "lava of inspiration/ Boils up *on* my breast" (cf. a metaphor of the same type, "on the breast of the cliff-giant"). In lines eleven and twelve, even the eyes (a part) of the poet are likened to a stormy ocean.* This is followed by the words "the earthly world is too small for me," and simultaneously a rejection of the world of heaven. At first the "I" was a part of the world that stands in opposition to God; now the divine "Thou" is only a part of the world opposed to the "I". In this world composed of and oriented toward my "I" there is no object besides "me". Significantly, the object of prayer is not mentioned

---

* In Russian, the word *volnenie* ("disturbance", "emotion," "agitation") is linked to the word *volna* ("wave," "breaker").—Tr.

("Thou art not the One to Whom I pray").

In this context "sinful" ceases to be an epithet of censure since the world of the "I" is not judged by the extraneous laws of religion or morals. In the Romantic system the antonym of sinful is banal.

Lines seventeen to twenty are perceived as antithetical to the beginning; in the latter passions belong to the world of sepulchral darkness whereas here they are a "miraculous flame."

But line twenty already signals some other semantic system alien to Romanticism. These signals are related to the force with which the "I" acts on the object. In the Romantic system the "I" is the sole non-banal object of activity. And while the "heart not made of stone" (i.e., sensitive) is possible in the Romantic system (though far more often it is already turned to stone or "withered"), a "hungry gaze" very definitely drops out of the system. Even at the dawn of Romanticism the Masons were describing man as a being "whose eyes turned inward." In all likelihood the opposition "the earthly world (with "I" as a part) vs. the non-earthly world" once again fits this portion of the text. But it is earthly life which now proves to be bright and true, engendering a "terrible thirst" for action, attracting a "hungry gaze" and consequently lacking the features of transience, death, decay and dimness.

Finally the last two lines bring us back again (by means of such code signals as "narrow path" and "salvation") to the Christian code; but "narrow" is simultaneously perceived as an antonym of "spacious," which is not semanticized as in the Christian system ("the broad path is the path of sin, the path of life") but as a synonym for freedom and its reflexes in the cultural code of Romanticism.

We have been looking, not at the semantic structure of the text, but at the general cultural semantic field in which this text functions. We have demonstrated that the text is projected not against one, but against *three* different types of semantic structures. What would this mean if the text were not artistic, but, say, scientific?

In a scientific text the introduction of a new semantic system would signify the negation, the elimination of the old system. A scientific dialogue is such that one of the positions involved in the dispute is acknowledged to be false and is rejected. The other is victorious.

As we have seen, the semantic field of Lermontov's poem is constructed differently: it arises out of the *relation* of all three systems. That which negates does not annul that which is negated; rather they both enter into a relation of contrast and opposition. Therefore a scientific dispute provides proof that the point of view of the opponent lacks value. An artistic dispute is possible only with an opponent over whom absolute victory is impossible. The religious structure of consciousness in "Prayer" preserves both its attractiveness and grandeur, and for that very reason its refutation is poetic.

If "Prayer" were a philosophical tract it would be divided into several polemically opposing parts. As a poem it forms a single structure in which all semantic systems function simultaneously in complex "interplay." Baxtin pointed out this particular feature of art with great insight. Scientific truth exists in one semantic field. Artistic truth exists simultaneously in several fields within their mutual correlation. This circumstance greatly increases the number of meaningful features of each element.

We see what complex contradictions are created in systems that arise as a result of the creolization of languages of various cultures. But we should not therefore assume that if a text is maintained in one semantic field it cannot create the complex play of structural elements which also insures that semantic capacity which is inherent to art. We have seen that even within one cultural code system the same semantic elements are synonyms on one level and antonyms on another. What we have said is also applicable to the structuring of a work of art's plot. Let us examine Suxovo-Kobylin's dramatic trilogy from this point of view. In the play *Krečinskij's Wedding* there are two opposing camps: honorable people and dishonorable people. Muromskij, his daughter Lidočka and Nel'kin, "a landowner and close neighbor of the Muromskijs, a young man who has been an army officer," are varieties of the honorable type. Krečinskij and Raspljuev are varieties of the dishonorable type. The character of each one is a set of differential features revealed in relation to personae of the group he belongs to and personae of the other group. But since each of these groups is divided into subgroups (for example, the subgroup "Krečinskij" and the subgroup "Raspljuev") characterization is made up of additional differential features which arise in relation to subgroups. The second part of the trilogy, *The Case,* introduces a new opposition between individuals and the bureaucracy (non-human). The bureaucracy consists of personae of varying external appearance (cf. "Čibisov: decorous, presentable, fashionably dressed;" "Kas'jan Kas'janovič Šilo: the mug of a Corsican bandit, tousled hair, carelessly dressed"), but united in that they are set in opposition to people. These are the "authorities," "powers," "subordinates" (the terminology has an element of parody of the angelic hierarchy) and the "wheels," "pulleys," and "gears" of the bureaucracy (not people, but parts of machines). In this opposition Krečinskij ends up in the human camp and is an ally of the Muromskijs. Finally, in the third part, *Tarelkin's Death,* both members of the opposition belong to the non-human camp and a clash takes place between petty and big-time scoundrels who are all equally part of the inhuman, bureaucratic world. All three types of group divisions create their own exclusive, semantically distinctive features for their respective personae. But no system cancels out any other preceding system; rather it functions against its background.

Sučok, the serf in Turgenev's story "L'gov,"* stands out in our con-

---

* L'gov—the name of a village, here serving as the title for a story from Turgenev's collection *A Sportsman's Sketches.*—Tr.

sciousness as a set of semantically distinctive features. But different features in his character are activated in his antithetical relation to the landowner and in opposition to the peasant children. The image of Sučok is located on both these planes (and a number of others as well) simultaneously.

An artistic text is a complex system built on the combination of general and local orderings on various levels. This has a direct impact on the structuring of the plot.

As essential property of the artistic text is that it involves a relation of dual likeness: it is like that certain slice of life, that part of the universe, which it depicts, and it is like the whole of that universe. When we see a film we not only say, "That's what John Doe was like," but also "That's what all John Does are like," "That's what men are like," "That's what people are like," "Such is life."

In the first relation different texts are not homeomorphous; in the second they themselves are involved in a relation of likeness. But any text with a plot is more or less easy to divide up into segments, and this situation produces interesting results.

Let us take a text which most easily and visibly lends itself to segmentation—a play production. A theatrical production graphically illustrates one essential property of art: the paradoxical homeomorphism of the whole and the parts.

A play reflects certain phenomena in the outside world in its own language; at the same time it represents a closed world correlated with the outside world of reality, not in its parts, but in its universal integrality. The borders of real theatrical space are the footlights and the walls of the stage enclosure. This is the theatrical universe, which reflects the real universe. It is precisely in this sense that we clearly feel the *borders* of the stage world. It lends the play universality and does not permit us to pose questions about anything lying outside the theatrical area under the assumption that it is equally real.

A theatrical production, however, is broken up into distinct scene segments which constitute part of the text of the production and simultaneously flow within the same spatial borders as the play as a whole. Taken separately they are also homeomorphous to the world. But even scenes do not represent the ultimate segmenation of the text of the play: each new entrance provides a new model of the world, but within the same spatial framework. The borders of a screen play an analogous role in film: they establish a kind of homeomorphism for all shots and points of view reflected in separate frames. If the screen shows only a pair of eyes in a close-up, we do not perceive them as part of an enormous face whose borders extend beyond the spatial framework of the movie theatre. Within the limits of this frame the whole film world consists of these eyes. Being related in a certain way to the syntagmatics of the preceding shots (in this sense a shot is perceived as a part, and the close-up is not a relaevant feature; it is synonymous to verbal descriptions of the type "to gaze in horror" or "to look attentively"), it is simultaneously related to a particular reality, both partial (the eyes) and universal (the world). In the latter case it emerges as a self-sufficient whole whose meaning can be expressed approximately like this: "The world=the eyes." The eyes and their expression as recorded in the shot become a model of the universe. And this is achieved because the shot is isolated from the syntagmatic chain on a certain level, and because it is shot close-up, the range reflecting the relation of the screen's borders to the content of the shot. A play is broken up by scenes and entrances into synchronic slices, each of which divides the personae into two camps in a special way (if we are dealing with a monologue, an empty subset of elements is set in opposition to the hero, and in the framework of the *given* scene he fills the whole world). But in each successive segment these groups differ in their makeup and the correlation of elements. Consequently the border that is drawn in one way or another determines the principle whereby subsets of elements are differentiated, that is, it singles out their distinctive features. Thus the play (ignoring for the moment its syntagmatic structure) represents a sum of synchronic models of the universe.

But each segmentation is not only a principle of differentiation. The mutual superimposition of these binary segmentations creates bundles of differentiation. These bundles are identified with personae and become characters. The character of a persona is a set of all the binary oppositions between him and other personae (other groups) as given in the text, the sum of his inclusions in groups of other personae; in other words, it is a set of differential features. Thus character is a paradigm.

In its invariant form character enters into the basic opposition set forth in the plot. But individual oppositions of one sort or another create local orderings and additional plot possibilities. From this point of view we may interpret the opposition between the "aesthetics of identity" and the "aesthetics of comparison and opposition" as the difference between texts in which local orderings single out only one type of differential distinction, the type which coincides with the basic opposition, and texts in which local orderings single out a certain set of differentiations.

Persona and Character

The problem of character is of fundamental importance in general aesthetics. A full discussion lies outside the scope of this book, all the more so because there is a special and extensive literature dedicated to this problem. From the point of view of the questions that interest us it would make sense to examine only one aspect: the specificity of character in works of art as opposed to the way the typal essence of a man is treated in non-artistic literature.

G. A. Gukovskij, the author of many extraordinarily profound works on the history of Russian literature, devoted a number of studies to the problem of character typology in the systems of Classicism, Romanticism and Realism.

Gukovskij associated the Realist typification particularly with the idea of man's dependence on his social milieu, and illustrated this thesis with great insight, citing examples from the works of Puškin and Gogol. This view had widespread influence on Soviet literary criticism and was reflected in many subsequent works, including my own.

One cannot help but notice, however, that this particular formulation, while revealing the essential typological features of a number of artistic texts, underscores precisely that which links these features to those of a philosophical, political, social or scientific nature. It reveals typological traits of character at a specific stage of culture, but does not deal with those traits that distinguish artistic from non-artistic texts within that stage. If we ignore this difference, we inevitably conclude that a writer merely illustrates and popularizes a philosophical conception of man's nature. But since the idea of man's dependence on his social environment was expressed in philosophy already in the eighteenth century—long before it permeated nineteenth century Realistic literature—and since philosophers expressed the idea more fully, consistently and clearly than the writers of Realism, we are forced to conclude that for a man who already knows of the existence of this philosophical thesis, literature adds nothing new.

Besides defining the dependence of artistic typification on certain ideas common to all cultural phenomena during a given period, it would also be appropriate to dwell on the specifically artistic features of character structure.

An artistic image is constructed not only as the realization of a certain cultural scheme, but also as a system of meaningful deviations from that scheme; these are created by individual orderings. These deviations, which increase in proportion to the basic regularity of that scheme, on the one hand make that regularity more meaningful, and on the other hand reduce the predictability of the hero's behavior against its background.

These meaningful deviations create an unavoidably probabilistic "scattering" of the hero's behavior around the norm prescribed the the extra-artistic understanding of man's nature. That human essence which, in a culture of a given type, appears as the only possible norm of behavior, in an artistic text is realized as a definite set of possibilities only partially realized within its limits. This is not only a set of actions, but also a set of types of behavior permissible within the limits of a more general classification system.

The degree or amount of this "scattering" ranges from the almost total prescriptiveness of behavior couched in formulas for the hero in folklore or medieval texts to the deliberate unpredictability of behavior for heros in the theatre of the absurd. The amount of scattering itself is one of the indices of a writer's artistic method. We should distinguish between the "scattering" which exists for the reader who is well acquainted with the norm of a given artistic structure, and the unpredictability which arises when the norm is violated: the behavior of a saint in a medieval vita seems inexplicable to the contemporary reader, but for the author and his real audience it was strictly defined.

Let us examine how characters are constructed in Puškin's *The Stone Guest*. Each scene contains a unique system of persona oppositions.

> *Scene I*
> Don Juan—Leporello
>
> *Scene II*
> Don Carlos—Laura
> Don Juan—Laura
> Don Juan—Don Carlos
>
> *Scene III*
> Don Juan—Doña Anna
>
> *Scene IV*
> Don Juan—Doña Anna
> Don Juan—Knight Commander

The figure of Don Juan is always entering into new oppositions. Moreover even within the limits of one opposition the text is easily stratified into several synchronic segments in which Don Juan emerges as *a whole set of personae* (in terms of external appearance as well: for example, in front of Doña Anna at first he is a monk, then Don Diego, then finally himself). The figure of Don Juan is a kind of paradigm composed of the relations of all these unified and mutually contradictory segments.

The characters of personae must be comparable if they are to be set in opposition to each other. This breaks them up into a core common to all of them (the grounds for comparison) and meaningfully opposed elements. Personae may manifest their opposition to each other by speaking differently about the same thing. In Fonvizin's *The Brigadier,* for example:

> Councilor: We have so many industrious secretaries who compose legal resumes without grammar, it's a delight to behold! I have one in mind—when he writes something a learned man who knows grammar couldn't understand it in a hundred years.

> Brigadier: What is grammar good for? I've managed to do without it for sixty years and brought up children besides. Ivan, here, he's way over twenty—knock on wood—and he's never heard of grammar.

> Brigadier's Wife: Of course you don't need a grammar. Before you start studying it you've got to go out and buy it. You pay eighty kopecks for it, and God only knows whether you'll end up learning it.

Councilor's Wife: The devil take me if a grammar is good for
anything, especially in the country. In the city, at least, I
tore one up for curl papers.

Son: *J'en suis d'accord.* What good is grammar? I myself have
written a thousand *billets-doux,* and it seems to me you
can say "my darling," "my sweet" or *adieu, ma reine*
without looking into a grammar.

Similarly Puškin's Mozart and Salieri both express the same idea that
"Beaumarchais was not capable of poisoning someone," but this is the
means Puškin uses to reveal the opposing quality of their characters.

Salieri

I don't think so: he was too comical
To do such a thing.

Mozart

He was a genius,
Like you and me. And genius and villainy
Are incompatible—isn't that so?

Opposing personae can have a similar external appearance (the theme
of the double, the mirror image); they may be part of identical situations,
and so on.

Finally, an extremely important element is the fact that a persona
may be presented through the eyes of another persona, as he describes him,
that is, in his language. The way a persona is transformed when he is translated into the language of another's ideas characterizes both the language
bearer and the one whom he is describing. Thus Maksim Maksimovič's
description of Pečorin or Leporello's description of Don Juan serves to
characterize both the one who is speaking and the one being described. In
the case of Pečorin we saw how the character of a persona can be built up
by bringing such descriptions together in a single bundle.

It is nothing new to say that the features which set Don Juan in
opposition to Leporello are not those which set him in opposition to Don
Carlos, that different features set him in opposition to Laura and Doña
Anna, and still others to the Knight Commander, that in each of these cases
one could compile a very specific list of differential features and that all
these features together constitute the "character" of the persona.

What is really important is that Don Juan does not equal Don Juan.
The artistic consistency of his image takes the form of inconsistency (from
the viewpoint of character evaluations in the languages of non-artistic
structures). He is depraved and unscrupulous not only in the eyes of the
monk (the religious ethical explanation) but also for Leporello (the popular
plebian explanation). His faults are his virtues, and Puškin deliberately
makes it difficult to judge him according to a single standard—and we are
not only referring to oxymoronic descriptions like "My faithful friend, my

inconstant lover."

The hero's behavior is always unpredictable, first because his character is constructed, not as a previously known possibility, but as a paradigm, a set of possibilities unified on the level of the conceptual structure and variational on the level of the text. Second, the text unfolds along the syntagmatic axis, and although in the general paradigmatics of character the succeeding episode is just as natural as the one which is being realized at the present moment, the reader nonetheless has not yet mastered the whole paradigmatic language of the image. He "builds it up" inductively out of new pieces of text. But this matter does not only concern the dynamics which arise owing to the unfolding of the text in time and the reader's incomplete knowledge of the language of the image. At certain moments another structure begins to function alongside the existing paradigmatic structure of the image. Since the image does not disintegrate in the reader's consciousness, these two paradigms emerge as variants of a paradigmatic structure of the image of the second degree and, by entering into complex functional relations, guarantee that the hero's acts will be sufficiently unpredictable (while the unity of the image simultaneously guarantees the required predictability).

Thus the difference between the "peaceful" old Gypsy and the passionate Zemfira—the temperamental classification of the heroes according to the psychological opposition "gentle vs. willful"—is built on different foundations than the "Nature vs. Culture" opposition that is dominant in *The Gypsies*. But the intersection of these two different types of differentiation for personae makes them "individual" and their actions unexpected with respect to each of these conceptions in isolation, that is, with respect to extra-artistic interpretation.

Don Juan differs not only in his relation to different personae, but also in his relation to himself. Appearing before Doña Anna as a monk, as Don Diego and as himself, he behaves differently in each case. It is very important to recognize that he is not pretending: he really and sincerely transforms himself into another person. He believes his own words when he says to Doña Anna, "I did not love any of them."

The image, which is unified on one sufficiently abstract level, but which on lower levels is divided up into a number of substructures—perhaps not even mutually opposed, but simply independent and varied—creates the possibility on the level of the text for actions which are simultaneously regular and unexpected, that is, creates conditions for maintaining the informativeness and reducing the redundancy of the system.

We might make still another observation: the personae of Puškin's *The Stone Guest* are divided into two main groups according to the feature "mobility—immobility" or "variability—invariability." In the one camp we find Laura and Don Juan, in the second—Don Carlos ("Do you always have such thoughts?" asks Laura, astonished by his *constant* gloom) and the Commander, not even a man, but an immobile statue. Doña Anna *moves* from the second camp to the first. At first *faithful,* she *changes,* having betrayed her husband (she is unfaithful to faithfulness). The multifariousness, proteanism and artistry of Don Juan and Laura affirm the unity of love and art ("but love, too, is a melody. . .") as a mobile, multifarious essence. The opposition between mobile and immobile can be interpreted in different ways, depending on the cultural code system used by the information recipient. Gukovskij reduces it to the antitheses "happiness vs. duty," "personal vs. impersonal (family, customs, law)," and in the end, "the Renaissance vs. the Middle Ages." An abstract model constructed in this fashion will undoubtedly be true (the text lends itself to such interpretation), but it will neither be conclusive nor the only possible interpretation. For example, one need only compare *The Stone Guest* with *Mozart and Salieri* in order to see that Mozart has inherent traits of inconstancy and Salieri— inherent traits of constancy. Mozart removes the opposition "poetry vs. prose" (Don Juan vs. Leporello) in the architstructure of the persona, and on this structural level they are synonyms (they are not only compatible, but also coincide in one person: poetry—truth—prose).

As the archipersona develops into two persona-variants, these features are antithetical rather than identical, and are revealed through dialogue, in which the same content is poetic for Don Juan and prosaic for Leporello:

Don Juan

(pensively)

Poor Inez!
She is no more! Oh, how I loved her!

Leporello

Inez!—the black-eyed woman. . . I remember
For three months you paid court to her;
Hard-put, the Devil helped you out.

Don Juan

July. . at night. I found something strangely pleasant
In her sad gaze
And deathly pale lips. . .

To an equal degree Mozart removes the antithesis between the "Spanish grandee" and "the simple folk" in the archestructure of "man."[22] *Inconstant*

22 The possibility of bringing Don Juan and Leporello together in common opposition to the commander's camp, going so far as the creation of personae for whom the watershed between these two personae is completely irrelevant, does not alter the fact that simultaneously other contrasts and oppositions are at work. Don Juan and Don Carlos are together opposed to Leporello in that they are aristocrats (the play stresses that both are Spanish grandees) and he is a plebian, that they are brave and he is a coward. It would be interesting to trace the structural significance of bravery. In *The Stone Guest* it is not relevant since it is inherent to both antagonistic

as a man, he stands in opposition to Salieri, who is *constant as a principle.* Gukovskij (citing an unpublished work by Buxštab) interprets this as the antithesis between Classicism and Romanticism. Other interpretations are also possible: the opposition between man and dogma, between living man and an abstract idea (opening up the possibility of constructing an abstraction of a higher level which would unite this conflict with the one we find in *The Bronze Horseman*), art and theory, and so on. The entire sum of these interpretations distinguishes *Mozart and Salieri* from *The Stone Guest.* But in constructing a model of a higher level which would unite them in the archistructure, the opposition "inconstant vs. constant" may be interpreted, for example, as the antithesis between life and death. It is no coincidence that Don Carlos and the Commander are opposed to Don Juan as corpses to a living person (Laura: "Stop. . in the presence of the dead!;" Doña Anna: "O Lord! And here, beside this coffin. . .") and that Salieri is opposed to Mozart as a murderer. If variability and mobility are semantically interpreted as life, and only on more concrete levels deciphered as poetry (art in general), love, truth, freedom, humanity and integrity, then immobility is correspondingly seen as anti-life with the following interpretations: unambiguousness, dogmatism, grandeur, severity, duty and inhumanity.

With this sort of correlation of basic semantic groups it is natural that personae like Don Juan should be subject to structural inconstancy. Much more revealing is the fact that this law for constructing the verbal image of a man extends to other personae, whom the author consciously strives to make unambiguous, embodying in them an antithesis to the multifarious proteanism of life.

Firmness and immutability are underscored in the Commander's countenance. The mere fact that he is not a man but a statue deprives him, as it were, of the possibility of revealing various aspects of himself. But this given immobility becomes a background against which the most miniscule changes acquire no less relative significance than the radical shifts in the character and actions of other personae. The first mention made of the Commander introduces a decidedly humdrum image of a man belonging to the same social circle as Don Juan, but already dead.

> The dead man had good reason to be jealous.
> He kept Doña Anna under lock and key;
> None of us ever saw her.

Later he is referred to as "cold marble" and "this proud coffin." At

groups; in *Mozart and Salieri* only Salieri, a persona from the "non-variational" group, is endowed with bravery ("Although I'm not a coward. . ."). In him bravery is associated with so cardinal a trait as moroseness and a preference for death over life ("Although I'm not too fond of life. . ."). In Mozart's character bravery exists as a zero rather that negative trait: it is not mentioned. In *A Feast During the Plague* only Walsingham, a multifaceted hero, is brave, and bravery itself is the result of merriment, love of life and the desire to experience it in full measure.

this very point, in Scene III, a new problem arises: the image of the Commander is divided into that of an ordinary man, Don Juan's acquaintance, killed by him in a duel (also a very ordinary affair)[23] and that of a statue. Initially the thesis is advanced that it is impossible to unite them:

> What sort of giant does he represent here?
> What shoulders! What a Hercules!
> But the dead man himself was small and puny.
> If he were standing here on tiptoes
> He couldn't reach his own nose with his hand.

The point of Don Juan's joke is that he, as an atheist and free-thinker, knows the Commander and the statue are not one person, that only in joking about his dead enemy can he pretend they are the same. The first surprise in the image of the Commander is the knitting together of these two figures.

Don Juan is convinced that the Commander has died, that the statue is *not he*, that the statue is a thing and is incapable of action.

> Leporello
>
> And the Commander? What will he say about this?

> Don Juan
>
> Do you think he'll become jealous?
> Very improbable: he's a reasonable man,
> He's probably grown calm since he died.

The next step in the plot reveals the unity of these two images and the ability of the statue to act:

> Leporello
>
> . . look at his statue.

> Don Juan
>
> What?

> Leporello
>
> He seems to be looking at you
> And is angry.

23 Puškin creates an additional semantic effect by once again including the reader in two fields; he forces him to feel simultaneously the ordinariness of the murder during a duel, and the strangeness of this ordinariness. The personae behave like medieval Spaniards. But for medieval Spaniards "to be a medieval Spaniard" carries no information at all. In order to appreciate the poetic quality of medieval Spain, one must remember that it is strange to be a Spaniard. While transporting the spectator to the cultural epoch depicted, Puškin also leaves them in their own epoch (for the spetator of our day the binomial is transformed into a trinomial: medieval Spain—Puškin's epoch—the contemporary world).

Accepting the invitation, the statue of the Commander decisively reveals himself, not as the representation of a persona, but as a persona. This merging, however, represents a decided metamorphosis: the incorporeal —a spirit—is invested with the most corporeal—stone—and that which is by nature most immobile—a statue—acquires the features of what is most mobile—a phantom unconstrained by the mechanical laws to which all people and objects are subject.

The statue of the Commander which appears at the end of the play is not only that statue which experiences jealousy toward its living rival in the cemetery ("He seems to be looking at you/ And is angry. .."). It is no accident that the statue "eliminates" all of Don Juan's human relations, including his love for Doña Anna, as too inconsequential in comparison to what must now take place:

Don Juan

O God! Doña Anna!

Statue

Leave her,
It's all over. . .

And the fact that Don Juan collapses with the cry "Doña Anna!" shows that he does not accept the view that love (i.e., life) is insignificant in the face of death.

In Scene III, the statue's behavior is odd because it is acting like a human being. It is jealous. In the last scene its behavior is odd because it is simultaneously acting like a human being (responding to an invitation) and like something inhuman for whom all things human have no meaning.

Thus "immobile" personae are also subject to the law of the internal restructuring of the image; otherwise the description of their behavior would be totally redundant.

But this inconstancy does not go beyond certain limits, the transgression of which would make it impossible for the reader to identify various sections of the text with one persona, who would lose his wholeness and disintegrate, as it were, into separate personae.

This takes place when a culture's code system is lost: it is difficult for the modern-day observer to perceive as a single image the dynamism of the body and the static smile in many ancient, non-European sculptures; the "illogic" of a saint's vita astonishes the modern reader because he fails to see any unity in the behavior of the persona. Moreover the border between personae may run differently: the instigator and agent in medieval texts may have two names but constitute one persona. In twentieth century art one hero may be broken up into several personae.

Thus the reduction of various references about a person in a text to a single paradigmatic image always depends on a certain cultural code both for the author of the text and for his audience. Within this contour a persona breaks up into a series of mutually non-identical states; outside this contour there are other personae whose features are related to his features on the principle of complementarity, similarity, or some other principle.

When the cultural code of the author differs from that of his audience the borders of the persona may be realigned. Speaking of the difficulties the modern reader faces in *The Tale of Bygone Years,* I. P. Eremin wrote, "Something absolutely fantastic takes place: suddenly, for no apparent reason, Jaropolk is reincarnated as a saint under the chronicler's pen. . . The modern reader might somehow still have been able to reconcile himself to this new image of the "Blessed" Jaropolk if the chronicler had meant to show Jaropolk's "rebirth" at a certain stage in his life. But this is precisely the condition that is missing: the chronicle text provides no foundation for such an interpretation. It is absolutely obvious that the riddle of the chronicle account lies in the fact that before us is not *one* man at various stages in his spiritual development, but *two* men, *two* Jaropolks; although they exclude each other, the chronicle has them coexisting in the same narrative context."[24]

Different types of artistic codes have different ways of treating change and immobility in personae. The fairy tale or medieval hagiography divides personae into two distinct groups: one has the property of miraculous transformation, either external (someone ugly turns into someone beautiful, a beast turns into a man) or internal (a sinner is transformed into a saint), and the other—of immutability. Nineteenth century Realism may ascribe evolution to some personae and immutability, once again, to others. Classicism attributes immutability to all personae. But this does not signify the immobility of a persona on the level of the text—that would be simply impossible and would make not only the whole plot narrative, but the entire text, redundant. A persona is perceived as immobile if his various states in the text are identified with his general state on the structural level of the most abstract construction of the image. Thus in the text of *War an and Peace,* Nikolai Rostov changes perhaps no less than Andrej Bolkonskij or Pierre Bezuxov. But these changes do not constitute evolution: the immobile structure of the persona on the level of the general artistic conception of the novel corresponds to the mobile text. The mobile text with respect to Andrej Bolkonskij or Pierre corresponds to a definite sequence of persona structures for each of them. In changing, Rostov does not become "another person," that is, he does things which he previously did not do in the text, but which he could have done in correspondance with the structure of the type he represents. But in each case Andrej or Pierre becomes "another person," that is, they do things which were previously impossible for them. The structure of their type is a sequence which only on the second level of abstraction forms the unity "Andrej

24 I. P. Eremin, *Povest' vremennyx let,* op. cit. pp. 6-7.

Bolkonskij" or "Pierre Bezuxov."

The Cinematographic Concept of "Depth"
And the Literary Text

Let us now examine the specific nature of those connections which arise when the text is segmented into functionally identical parts: stanzas, chapters, etc. In order to elucidate this problem let us look at some examples from cinematography. The structure of cinematic narration is in general very interesting precisely because it lays bare the mechanics of any artistic narration, and we will turn to it from time to time to find graphic examples.

In film the unit of narrative segmentation is easily isolated. For the time being let us set aside the intriguing type of bond which Sergei Eisenstein described as follows: *Any two pieces set next to each other are inevitably united in a new concept, which arises as a new quality out of this conjunction.*[25] Let us examine cinematic narration as a sequence of cumulatively conjoined shots. The structure of the ribbon of film itself gives us an indisputable right to do so.

Shots segment the film into sections, making them strictly equal in respect to the frame—the borders of the screen (similarly, the scenes which are parts of a play have the same borders as the entire play—the footlights). Now a curious, purely topological property of part of an artistic narration manifests intself: it has the same borders as the whole. The same principle commonly occurs in prose: chapters have a beginning and an end, and in this respect are homeomorphous to the whole.

As we have remarked several times already, this leads to an increase in the role that differences play. In this connection it would be appropriate to say something about the compositional device which in the art of the film is called depth. The cameraman can bring the camera right up to the object being filmed or can shoot from a considerable distance. The same screeen can accomodate an enormous crowd or part of a face. The Japanese film *Woman in the Dunes* begins with a shot of slowly moving stones which then grow smaller until they turn out to be grains of sand carried along by the wind.

"Depth" is not simply the size of the depiction, but also its relation to the border (the range of depth in a tiny frame and on a large screen is the same). It is revealing in this sense that "depth" has never played a large role in painting where the dimensions of the canvas can be altered, and there is relative stability, in each genre, of the relation between pictorial space and figures and people.

But close and long range shots exist not only in film. They are clearly felt in literary narration when identical space or attention is devoted to phenomena whose descriptions vary quantitatively.

25 S. Eisenstein, *Izbrannye proizvedenija v 6-ti tomax*, vol. II (Moscow, 1964) p. 157.

For example, if successive segments of a text differ sharply from each other in terms of the quantitative aspect of their content—the number of personae, the magnitude of the whole and parts, the description of large and small objects; if in some novel a single chapter describes the events of one day, and another chapter whole decades; then we can also speak of different "depths."

In Part II of the third volume of *War and Peace,* in Chapter 20, we find Pierre in the midst of troops and the personae include "a mounted regiment with singers in the front," "a train of carts bearing the wounded," "peasant carters," and so on; in Chapter 22, besides Kutuzov's "mangificent retinue" and a crowd carrying an icon, there are seven dramatis personae— Pierre and Andrej Bolkonskij (soldiers and some unnamed general are also mentioned); in Chapters 24 and 25 we find Pierre and Andrej Bolkonskij (also mentioned are Timoxin, two officers from Bolkonskij's regiment, and Wohlzogen and Klausewitz, who are passing by). Clearly one can discern the relative close and long range (distance and proximity) of these "shots."

Let us cite another example—Nekrasov's poem "Morning:"

Utro

Ty grustna, ty stradaeš' dušoju:
Verju—zdes' ne stradat' mudreno.
S okružajuščej nas niščetoju
Zdes' priroda sama zaodno.

Beskonečno unyly i žalki
Eti pastbišča, nivy, luga,
Eti mokrye sonnye galki,
Čto sidjat na veršine stoga;

Eta kljača s krest' janinom p'janym,
Čerez silu beguščaja vskač'
V dal', pokrytuju sinim tumanom,
Eto mutnoe nebo. . . Xot' plač'!

No ne kraše i gorod bogatyj:
Te že tuči po nebu begut;
Žutko nervam—železnoj lopatoj
Tam teper' mostovuju skrebut.

Načinaetsja vsjudu rabota;
Vozvestili požar s kalanči;
Na pozornuju ploščad' kogo-to
Provezli—tam už ždut palači.

Prostitutka domoj na rassvete
Pospešaet, pokinuv postel';
Oficery v naemnoj karete
Skačut za gorod: budet duèl'.

Torgaši prosypajutsja družno
I spešat za prilavki zasest':
Çelyj den' im obmerivat' nužno,
Čtoby večerom sytno poest'.

Ču! iz kreposti grjanuli puški!
Navodnen'e stolice grozit. . .
Kto-to umer: na krasnoj poduške
Pervoj stepeni Anna ležit.

Dvornik vora kolotit—popalsja!
Gonjat stado gusej na uboj;
Gde-to v verxnem ètaže razdalsja
Vystrel—kto-to pokončil s soboj. . .

[Morning

You are sad, you are sick at heart!
I believe it—here it is hard not to suffer.
Here nature itself is one
With the poverty surrounding us.

Infinitely despondent and wretched
Are these pastures and fields and meadows
These sleepy wet jackdaws
Sitting on top of the rick;

This jade with its drunk peasant
Overtaxed, galloping
Into the distance covered with gray fog,
This dull sky. . . it makes you want to weep.

But the rich city is no better;
The same clouds race across the sky;
There they are now scraping the roadway
With an iron shovel, setting your nerves on edge.

Work is beginning everywhere;
They've shouted "Fire!" from the watchtower;
They've brought someone to the square of shame
Where the executioners are already waiting.

Leaving the bed, a prostitute
Hurries home at dawn;
Officers in a rented coach
Rush to the city's outskirts: there will be a duel.

Merchants wake up in concert
And hurry off to settle down behind their counters:
All day long they have to give false meansures
So that they can eat their fill in the evening.

Listen! Cannon shots just rang out from the fortress!
The capital is threatened by a flood. . . .
Someone has died; on a red cushion
Lies an Order of St. Anne, first Degree.

The yardman thrashes a thief—they've got him!
They drive a flock of geese to the slaughter;
From an upper story somewhere a shot
Rings out—someone's killed himself. . .]

Let us examine the text only from the point of view that interests us
at the moment. Both parts—the "country" (beginning with the first line)
and the "city" (beginning with the line "But the rich city is no better. . .")
are clearly segmented. In the first half syntactical parallelism divides the
text into sections to which structural equality is attributed. But on the
level of content (in the general sense of the word) we find "pastures and
fields and meadows" in one section and "sleepy, wet jackdaws/ Sitting on
top of the rick" in the other. In order to fill identical semantic space the
jackdaws have to be presented close-up, and their equality to the broad
landscape or the "dull sky" underscores the suggestive nature of the image:
wet jackdaws on the rick, the dull sky, the jade "with its drunk peasant"—
these are not only object sketches, but also models of the same sort of life
and in this sense they are equal to each other. To understand this it is
enough to imagine each of these syntactically parallel elements as a shot in
a film.

The same structure is maintained in the second half of the poem. Let
us try to imagine it as a film scenario. We see immediately that the shot
"Leaving the bed, a prostitute/ Hurries home at dawn" or "The yardman
thrashes a thief—they've got him!" differs in terms of the depth of the
shot from "Someone had died: on a red cushion/ Lies an Order of St. Anne,
First Degree."

When we look at the text as a scenario, the dual role played by its
syntactic connections is revealed: each separate picture is a part entering
into the overall picture of life in the capital (and on an even broader scale,
Russian life) in Nekrasov's time, and this whole is perceived as the result of
the combining of parts. But at the same time all the pictures—different
faces of one thing—are not parts of the whole, but modifications of the
whole. Life in its intergral essence is visible in each of them, and their
cumulation is the cumulation of *one thing in various ways* and with different
nuances. Once again we see that syntagmatic and paradigmatic connections
are realized in an artistic text in their unity and in their transmutations.

The comparison of individual "shot-segments" activates the multiplicity
of elements on the content plane, lending them the significance of differential
features and thereby suggesting the semantic content. The antithesis of
sound images like "They are now scraping the roadway/ With an iron
shovel, setting your nerves on edge" and "From an upper story somewhere
a shot/ Rings out. . ." to all the others which are visual; the antithesis of
immobility ("hurry off. . . to settle down") to mobility ("brought,"
"hurries," "rush about"); and the mutual opposition in the depth of the
"shots" in various "frames" of the text all create a considerable amount

of additional semantically distinctive elements.

It is precisely this sort of intersection between given types of constructions and relations which makes meaningless, redundant elements in one system meaningful in another (or rather, meaningful in different ways in others). In consequence the text remains consistently informative and prolongs that effect which we experience as an aesthetic effect.

The Viewpoint of the Text

Since only that which has an antithesis is meaningful,[26] any compositional device becomes semantically distinctive if it is included in an opposition to a contrasting system. Where the whole text is "shot" in one depth, the depth as such is not perceived. For example, it is not felt in epic narrations. The "rapid transitions" (Puškin) of Romantic stories are meaningful only in combination with sections of retarded narration. In exactly the same way "point of view" is perceived as an element of the artistic structure at that moment when the possibility arises for altering it within the limits of the narration (or projecting the text on another text from another point of view).[27]

The concept of "artistic point of view" manifests itself as the relation of the system to its subject (in this context the "system" may be linguistic, or of a different higher level). By the subject of the system (ideological, stylistic, and so on) we mean a consciousness capable of engendering a similar structure and, consequently, a consciousness reconstructed during the act of perceiving a text.

An artistic system is constructed as a hierarchy of relations. The very concept of meaningfulness implies the presence of a certain relation, that is, a certain orientation. But since an artistic model in its most general form reproduces an image of the world for a given consciousness, that is, models the relation between the individual and the world (in particular the perceiving individual and the perceived world), this orientation will be of a subject-object nature.

In Russian poetry of the period before Puškin, it was characteristic for all subject-object relations expressed in the text to converge in one fixed focus. In eighteenth century art, traditionally defined as Classicism, this single focus was extended beyond the limits of the author's person and coincided with the concept of truth, in whose name the artistic text spoke. The relation of truth to the world being depicted became the artistic point of view. The fixedness and unambiguousness of these relations, their radial

26 Cf. Niels Bohr's remark that the distinguishing trait of non-trivial truth is that a directly opposing claim is not manifestly absurd.

27 The concept of "point of view" can be traced to the works of Mixail Baxtin. At present this problem is being studied in detail by Boris Uspenskij, to whom I would like to express my gratitude for allowing me to read his study *Poètika kompozicii* (Moscow, 1970) in manuscript form.

convergence toward a single center, corresponded to the idea of the eternity, unity and immobility of truth. One and unchanging, truth was simultaneously hierarchical, revealing itself to each consciousness in varying degree. There was a corresponding hierarchy of artistic points of view, the basis for the laws governing genres.

In Romantic poetry artistic points of view also converge radially toward a firmly fixed center, and relations themselves are unambiguous and quite predictable (for that reason the Romantic style is easily parodied). This center, the subject of the poetic text, coincides with the person of the author and becomes his lyric double.[28]

But a text can also be structured in such a way that artistic points of view are not concentrated in a single center, but construct a sort of diffused subject consisting of various centers: the relations between them create additional artistic ideas. For example:

> Naprasno ja begu k sionskim vysotam,
> Grex alčnyj gonitsja za mnoju po pjatam;
> Tak nozdri pylnye utknuv v pesok sypučij,
> Golodnyj lev sledit olenja beg paxučij.

> [In vain I hasten to Zion's heights;
> Voracious sin follows at my heels,
> The way a hungry lion, his dusty nostrils buried
> In the shifting sand, follows the strong scent of the deer.]

Clearly it is impossible to select a single point of view to cover the expressions "dusty nostrils" and "strong-scented trail;" the subject of the first is the man observing the lion, and that of the second—the lion itself, since man cannot perceive the deer's trail as something that gives off a scent, let alone a strong scent. But the phrases "hungry lion" and "dusty nostirls" also lack a common subject center, since the first implies an observer who is not concretized in space, whereas the second implies that the lion is being comtemplated close-up, at a distance permitting the observer to make out the dust covering his nostrils. Even if we restrict ourselves to the last two lines, we observe not one focal center for the points of view, but a diffused field within which several points of view exist. The relations between them become an additional source of meanings.

Each element of an artistic structure exists as a possibility in the structure of language and, on a broader scale, in the structure of man's consciousness. Therefore the history of mankind's artistic evolution can be described with respect to any of these elements, whether it be the history of metaphor, the history of rhyme or of some genre. If we had sufficiently exhaustive descriptions of this sort, we could synchronize them in interconnected bundles and arrive at a picture of the development of art.

---

28 This phenomenon was described by G. A. Gukovskij in his study of Žukovskij's poetry (See *Puškin i russkie romantiki* [Saratov, 1945]).

However there are very few elements in the artistic structure so directly related to the general task of constructing a picture of the world as the "point of view" element. It is directly correlated with such problems in secondary modeling systems as the position of the creator of the text, the problem of truth and the problem of the personality.

The "point of view" gives the text a definite orientation with respect to its subject (this is particularly evident in cases of direct speech). But any text is pushed into some extra-textual structure whose most abstract level may be defined as the "type of world view," "the picture of the world" or the "model of culture" (the difference between these concepts is insignificant in this instance).

But a model of culture has its own orientation which is expressed in a certain scale of values, in relation to what is true and false, high and low. If we imagine a given culture's picture of the world as a text on a sufficiently abstract level, this orientation finds its expression in the point of view of this text. Then a question arises concerning possible correlations between the point of view of the culture's text and the points of view of some concrete text (a language text or a text expressed through other signs on the same level—a drawing, for example).

The relation between text and point of view is always a relation between creator and created. When applied to a literary text this involves a complex of general philosophical questions touching on the origin of the world and its rationality. Since the relation between the orientation of a cultural text and the points of view of the concrete texts entering into it is perceived as a relation of truth or falsehood, two possible relations immediately stand out: full coincidence and diametrical opposition.

The medieval system of thought, for example, built up this relation in the following manner. A general model of the world was conceived of as something previously existing, given, and possessing a creator. If one takes sacred texts to be the most authoriative in this system, then their point of view and the general orientation of the culture were united by virtue of the fact that they shared a creating agent. The creator of the world was simultaneously the creator of those "inspired texts" (or "icons not made by human hands"), and the human author was merely an intermediary, an executor, a copyist or scribe whose entire service consisted in faithfully repeating the authoritative text. Thus was truth achieved; this was the answer to the question, "What is the author's source for what he is describing in a literary work?"

In the medieval hierarchy of texts the chronicle occupied a lower position than hagiographic works, but here too one can observe a similar picture: there was a sort of static continuum, a model of the ideal norm for human history and human behavior into which the real text of the chronicle was entered. And once again the unity of point of view was achieved by virtue of the fact that the chronicler did not set forth his own personal position, but identified himself totally with tradition, truth and morality. Only in their name could he speak. That which did not belong to his personal position was regarded as truth; hence he strove to use legends and hearsay instead of his own stories. The chronicler associated himself with them as givens and, consequently, with the truth.

The notion of the text as something "uncreated" forces the author to introduce a large number of speeches in the first person, to present himself not as a creator, but as a stenographer. But this does not lead to a profusion of points of view. They can all be reduced to two: the "correct" one which coincides with the orientation of the text as a whole, and the "incorrect" one opposed to it. Let us examine a gospel text from this point of view:

> And as Jesus passed by, he saw a man which was blind from his birth. And his disciples asked him, saying, Master, who did sin, this man, or his parents, that he was born blind? Jesus answered, Neither hath this man sinned, nor his parents: but that the works of God should be made manifest in him. I must work the works of him that sent me, while it is day: the night cometh, when no man can work. As long as I am in the world, I am the light of the world.

And after the healing of the blind man:

> The neighbors therefore, and they which before had seen him that he was blind, said, Is not this he that sat and begged? Some said, This is he: others said, He is like him: but he said, I am he. (John 9:1-5,8-9)

Despite the fact that several personae and groups of personae figure in the text, in fact by its very structure only three positions are possible: the position of truth, the position of non-truth, and the position of transition from the one to the other (enlightenment and apostasy), that is, only two points of view are possible: truth and non-truth. This is apparent in the quoted text.

In this connection in the Old Russian chronicle there arises a dual "truthfulness" of direct speech. The chronicler introduces direct speech into his text as evidence that it is not something "made-up." In this sense the very fact of constructing a narrative in the form of direct speech is already perceived as proof of authenticity. But the content of these utterances also may be two-fold: it may be true (coinciding in its orientation with the texts' general "model of the world") or false (directly opposing).

In a *bylina* the breaking down of the text into first-person utterances distributed among the antagonists does not change its orientation, the one point of view governing the whole epos (Prince Vladimir calls Kalin-tsar a dog, but Kalin-tsar also calls himslf a dog);* in a chronicle direct speech

---

* Kalin-tsar is a "tartar" ruler who threatens to take Kiev by force if Prince Vladimir does not surrender to him. It is unfortunate that the author does not cite his source here, since there are many variants of this incident which do not manifest

COMPOSITION OF VERBAL ART 269

may be related to truth in two different ways: "If I have spoken the truth" and "If I spoke falsely."[29] It is precisely this divergence of two "points of view"—of the entire text and the given persona—which creates the possibility (only for negative characters) of speaking one's intentions—which are always *ill intentions.* This is the analogue to psychological analysis in texts of a later period ("for he was terrified, having guile in his heart").

Later in the history of the narrative artistic text we will often encounter different methods for correlating these two types of orientation.

Among the positions from which a picture of the world as a whole is oriented, we may find Truth (the novel in Classicism), Nature (the Enlightenment novel) or the People; finally, this general orientation may be of zero value (which means that the author refrains from judging the narrative). Čulkov, for example, takes this approach when he speaks of the signs of grief which his heroine manifests, but refuses to comment on the verity of her feelings, or on the inner world of his characters in general: "I am uncertain as to whether she was sorry for Vladimir or her father; for he did not tell me and I have no intention of writing what is untrue."

In Romantic narratives the points of view of the micro- and macro-text are combined in a single unmoving center of narration—the author's personality. The unity of the point of view becomes a synonym for Romantic subjectivism. In Russian literature *Evgenij Onegin* was the first work to take on the task of consciously structuring a text which would go beyond the framework of any single point of view and be built according to the laws of gree intersection of various subjective positions. Subjectively this was perceived as a movement away from the Romantic narrative poem toward the narrative genre of the novel.

The text's enslavement to one point of view is conceived of as the predominance of "expression" over "content," as "poetry." Opposing it is "prose," the dominion of "content," free of authorial subjectivity. But significantly, after the "poetry" of Romanticism laid bare the problem of "point of view" as the stylistic and philosophical center of the text, the movement toward "simplicity" was maintained, not by rejecting this accomplishment, but by complicating the issue, by affirming the possibility of many "points of view" operating simultaneously.

In Puškin's works *Evgenij Onegin* represented a new stage in textual construction. In 1822, in a well-known note conventionally titled "On Prose," Puškin clearly set content and expression in opposition to each other in a purely semiotic way.

Periphrastic prose (above all Karamzin's school) is condemned as lacking in truth. It is very interesting that the idea of constructing texts according

the same consistency. In one *bylina,* for example, the hero Il'ja Muromec who saves Kiev from Kalin-tsar is called a "dog" by Vladimir; Vladimir is called a "dog" by Il'ja in turn; and it is the narrator rather than the positive characters, who calls Kalin-tsar a "dog." (Gil'ferding, *Onežskie byliny,* No. 257)–Tr.

29 *PSRL,* vol. I, p. 260.

to certain (or any) conventional rules is repudiated. "Simple" content, conceived of as life itself, is opposed to a structurally organized text ("brilliant expressions"). But "life" in a literary work is non-aestheticized speech, a text that is not organized artistically and is therefore truthful. But naturally any text which enters into a work of art is an artistic text. The task, then, is to construct an artistic (organized) text which will appear to be non-artistic (unorganized), to create a structure which will be perceived as lacking structure. In order to evoke in the reader's mind a sensation of simplicity, of the colloquial naturalness of language, the true-to-life immediacy of the subject, the ingenuousness of characters, considerably more complex means of structuring were required than those known to the literature of the time. *The effect of simplifying was achieved by sharply increasing the degree of complexity of the text's structure.* Despite the obvious connection between the problem of point of view and truthfulness, their functional conjunction took place only at a definite historical stage. As long as the point of view of a given text was regarded as the only possible one, fixed throughout the text, that is, artistically inactive in general, the truth or falseness of an utterance was not connected with its particular orientation. It was supposed that certain personae were capable of creating only true texts, while others by nature were capable of creating only false texts. For example, the "enemy," "heretic" or adherent of a different faith in medieval texts always lies, regardless of the content of his utterance. The Devil is always the Deceiver; that is his constant quality.

The conjoining of the concept of truthfulness with a single previously fixed point of view is also encountered in contemporary literature. This sort of structuring is permissible in satire and in all emphatically conventional texts, as well as in journalistic writing. In realistic psychological prose it has a false ring. Here is one highly significant example. In L. Gumilevskij's story "The Fanatics" (1923) positive characters (*rabfak** students) clash with negative characters (Mr. Hower, director of the ARA* cafeteria). Mr. Hower speaks in broken Russian (*Zdès' nèt mèsto politikè** ["This is no place for politics!"]). But incorrect speech characterizes not only his monologues, but also his thoughts. His internal speech is conveyed as follows: "Tightening his belt, he looked into the mirror, wiped his lips with eau-de-cologne to remove the caked blood, and thought, 'This country is worthy of respect!' " [Etot strana dostojn uvaženija!] .[30] Incorrectness (here incorrectness in speech *when conversing with himself*) is not a relation of

---

* *Rabfak*–Literally *rabočij fakul'tet:* special courses organized in the first years after the Revolution to prepare children of workers and peasants for higher education establishments.–Tr.

* ARA–American Relief Administration, organized to help victims of the Volga famines in the early 1920's.–Tr.

* As an American, Mr. Hower has a hard time palatalizing his consonants and handling gender and aspect.-Tr.

30 L. Gumilevskij, "S vostoka svet," *Izbrannoe* (Moscow, 1964) p. 255.

several points of view, but an inherent trait of a negative character.

The problem of point of view crystallized at the intersection of several texts in the first person: several systems were formed, each with its own inner veracity. It is no accident that the possibility of several points of view existing in a work of verbal art made its earliest appearance in drama. In prose this conflict between several systems of direct speech as several points of view was clearly expressed in the epistolary novel of the eighteenth century. Choderlos de Laclos's *Les Liansons Dangereuses* was, in this respect, an innovative work.[31] The mutual imposition of texts of letters created what is in principle a new idea of truthfulness; it is not identified with any one position directly expressed in the text, but is created by the intersection of all of them. The textually fixed letters form several groups, each of which is a definite world, a system within itself, with its own inner logic and concept about truth. Each of these groups has a specific, inherent point of view. The givenness of behavior (temptation or warding off temptation, for example) and prejudicial evaluations are conceived of as something false. Truth means going beyond the limitations of each of these structures; it arises outside the text as an opportunity to look at each character and each first-person text from the vantage of another character (or characters) and other texts.

The next stage in the process of complicating the narrative point of view is clearly represented in *Evgenij Onegin*.[32] Instead of several personae narrating from various positions about the same thing, as in Choderlos de Laclos, an author appears who employs various styles as closed systems with a fixed point of view and sets forth the same content from several stylistic positions.[33]

Let us examine the stylistic structure of two stanzas from the fourth chapter of the novel:

XXIV

Poklonnik slavy i svobody,
V volnen'i burnyx dum svoix,
Vladimir i pisal by ody,
Da Ol'ga ne čitala ix.
Slučalos' li poètam sleznym
Čitat' v glaza svoim ljubeznym
Svoi tvoren'ja? Govorjat,
Čto v mire vyše net nagrad.

31 In a special lecture for a course on Gogol's prose that was given in 1948 (the lecture was not reproduced in his book on Gogol'), Gukovskij drew the attention of his students to the specific character of a purely semiotic formulation of the question of truthfulness. The question is reviewed in detail in Tzvetan Todorov, *Littérature et signification* (Paris, 1967).

32 See Ju. Lotman, "Xudožestvennaja struktura *Evgenija Onegina*," *Učenye zapiski Tartuskogo gosudarstvennogo universiteta*, issue 184 (Tartu,1966).

33 SS V. V. Vinogradov, *Stil' Puškina* (Moscow, 1941).

I vprjam', blažen ljubovnik skromnyj,
Čitajuščij mečty svoi
Predmetu pesen i ljubvi,
Krasavice prijatno-tomnoj!
Blažen... xot' možet byt', ona
Sovsem inym razvlečena.

XXV

No ja plody moi mečtanij
I garmoničeskix zatej
Čitaju tol'ko staroj njane,
Podruge junosti moej,
Da posle skučnogo obeda
Ko mne zabredšego soseda,
Pojmav neždanno za polu,
Dušu tragediej v uglu,
Ili (no èto krome šutok),
Toskoj i rifmami tomim,
Brodja nad ozerom moim,
Pugaju stado dikix utok:
Vnjav pen'ju sladkozvučnyx strof,
Oni sletajut s beregov.

XXIV

[A worshipper of freedom and fame,
In the agitation of his stormy thoughts
Vladimir would have written odes,
But Olga did not read them.
Have tearful poets
Read their works face to face
To their beloved? They say
There is no greater reward in this world.
And indeed, blessed is the modest lover
Who reads his dreams
To the object of his songs and love,
His lovely languid beauty!
Blessed... although perhaps she
May be distracted by something quite different.

XXV

But I read the fruits of my reveries
And harmonious fantasies
Only to my old nurse,
The friend of my youth,
Or after a boring dinner
I surprise a neighbour who has wandered in,
Taking him by his coat-flaps,

And stifle him with a tragedy in the corner,
Or (joking apart)
Overcome by depression and rhymes,
Wandering around my lake,
I frighten a flock of wild ducks:
Heeding the song of my sweet-sounding stanzas,
They fly up from the shore.]

These stanzas represent a frequent repetition of the same situation ("The poet reads his verses to a listener") in stylistically contrasting systems. Each of the three participants in the situation (the poet, his verses, and the listener) can be transformed.

I Vladimir	odes	Ol'ga
II Tearful poets	creations	beloved ones
III Modest lover	dreams	object of songs and love, lovely languid beauty
IV I	fruits of revery	old nurse
V I	a tragedy	neighbor
VI I	sweet-sounding stanzas	wild ducks

Correspondingly the act of reading verses is given a new name each time: "I read," "I stifle somebody," "I frighten." The reaction of the object of recitation also undergoes "transformation:"

Ol'ga did not read them. . .
They say
There is no greater reward in this world.
Blessed. . . although perhaps she
May be distracted by something quite different. . .
Heeding the song of my sweet-sounding stanzas,
They fly up from the shore.

The meaning of each of these verses is constructed according to a complex system: each separate lexical unit receives additional meaning depending on the nature of the structure in which it is included. Here the most immediate environment of the given work plays the central role. The action of the poet in instances III and IV is described in almost the same way:

Who reads his dreams. . .
But I read the fruits of my reveries
And harmonious fantasies. . .

But the fact that in instance III the action unites a "modest lover" and his "lovely, languid beauty," while in case IV it unites "I" and "my old nurse," lends the identical words a profoundly different stylistic meaning. The "dreams" in III are part of a conventional literary phraseological structure and are correlated with IV according to the principle of false expression and true content. In exactly the same way the "old nurse" is related to "lovely, languid beauty." But the antithesis "conventional poetry vs. true prose" is complicated by the fact that the old nurse is also "a friend of my youth," and this combination is given, not as an ironic junction of different styles, but as a monosematic stylistic group. Instead of the antithesis "poetry vs. prose" we have "false poetry vs. true poetry." The "worshipper of freedom and repute" and his "odes" take on a special meaning because "Olga did not read them" (here a bi-directional relation arises: Olga's indifference reveals the bookish nature of Lenskij's "agitation. . . of stormy thoughts" since the line "Olga did not read them" sounds like the voice of sober prose which, in the structure of the novel, is invariably associated with truth; but simultaneously the indisputable poetic charm of "freedom and fame"and "stormy thoughts" emphasizes Olga's down-to-earth quality). "They say/ There is no greater reward in the world," is a combination of two units that have been made equivalent, one conversational ("They say") and the other conventional and literary ("There is no greater reward in the world"), is accompanied by a "lowering" stylistic effect. But the meanings in these two strophes are formed not only through semantic connections. The words placed in each vertical column are perceived as variants (paradigms) of a single invariant meaning. Not one of them is related to another as content is to expression: they are superimposed on each other, thus forming a complex meaning. The very remoteness and apparent incompatibility of such concepts as "the object of songs and love," "old nurse," "neighbor," and "wild ducks" turns out to be an important means of semantic intensification when included in one paradigmatic series. The result is a unique semantic suppletivism in which different, remotely related words are felt to be variants of one concept. This makes each variant of the concept in isolation difficult to predict and consequently more meaningful. Another factor must also be mentioned: not only do individual lexemes come together in a complex archeunit, but also elements of different (and often opposite) stylistic systems prove to be part of a single stylistic structure. Theis equation of different stylistic planes leads to a realization of the relativity of each stylistic system in isolation, and hence to irony. The dominating role of irony in the stylistic unity of *Evgenij Onegin* is an obvious fact that has been noted in critical literature on the subject.

The mechanism of irony is one of the basic keys to the novel's style. Let us trace it in a few examples:

XXXVI

I tak oni stareli oba.
I otvorilis' nakonec
Pered suprugom dveri groba,
I novyj on prijal venec.
On umer v čas pered obedom,
Oplakannyj svoim sosedom,
Det'mi i vernoju ženoj
Čistoserdečnej, čem inoj.

On byl prostoj i dobryj barin,
I tam, gde prax ego ležit,
Nadgrobnyj pamjatnik glasit:
"Smirennyj grešnik, Dmitrij Larin,
Gospodnij rab i brigadir
Pod kamnem sim vkušaet mir."

XXXVII

Svoim penatam vozvraščennyj,
Vladimir Lenskij posetil
Soseda pamjatnik smirennyj,
I vzdox on peplu posvjatil;
I dolgo serdcu grustno bylo.
Poor Yorick!—molvil on unylo. . .

XXXVI

[And so they both grew old.
And finally the doors of the grave
Opened before her spouse
And he received his crown of glory.
He died an hour before dinner,
Mourned by his neighbor,
His children and his faithful wife—
More sincerely than some people.
He was a simple and kind barin,
And there, where his remains repose,
The tombstone reads,
"The humble sinner, Dmitrij Larin,
The Lord's slave and a brigadier
Savors peace beneath this stone."

XXXVII

Returning to his hearth and home,
Vladimir Lenskij visited
The humble tombstone of his neighbor,
And dedicated a sigh to his ashes;
And for some time his heart was sad.
"Poor Yorick!" he said despondently. . .]

Here the stylistic breaks are not formed by a system of transformations of the same extra-stylistic content, but rather by a consecutive shift of stylistic aspects. The first line, "And so they both grew old," is demonstratively neutral. What is marked here is the absence of features of any particular poetic style. With respect to style, this line has no point of view. The next three lines are characterized by a well sustained high style in the spirit of the eighteenth century, which creates a corresponding point of view: the periphrases ". . . the doors of the grave opened," and "he received his crown of glory" (instead of "he died"), as well as the lexicon ("spouse," "received") could not have evoked any other artistic experience for Puškin's audience. In the following line, however, the solemn periphrases are translated into another system: "He died." The style of the following lines is not at all neutral in its prosaic character. It is a conjunction of precise prosaisms which, in the system of the given structure of the text, lend the style a note of truthfulness, and consequently, a poetic quality, both of which are combined with elements that lower the style. The detail "an hour before dinner" in combination with "the doors of the grave opened" lend something of a comic note to the archaic naiveté of the country—the time of death is reckoned from mealtime:

> . . . My vremja znaem
> V derevne bez bol'šix suet:
> Želudok—vernyj naš breget.

> [. . . We know what time it is
> In the country without much fuss:
> Our stomachs are our faithful Bréguet.]

This same comic effect is created by combining the solemn "mourned" with "by his neighbor" since the image of the neighboring country landowner was sufficiently unambiguous for the reader of *Evgenij Onegin*, and moreover had already been delineated in other stanzas of the same chapter. In light of this the "children" and "faithful wife" mourning the deceased are perceived as an archaic, solemn cliché. All this throws light on the point of view in lines 2-4. The lofty poetics of the eighteenth century is perceived as a cliché behind which lies an archaic, naive consciousness, a provincial culture still experiencing and earlier phase of the nation's intellectual development with a simple heart. But the line "More sincerely than some people," though an antiquated cliché, discloses not a false phrase, but the substance of truth. While remaining a cliché whose presence is imperative in lofty epithets, and at the same time bearing the stamp of awkward provincialism, the text does not lose its ability to convey truth. The line "He was a simple and kind *barin*" introduces a completely unexpected point of view. Its semantic orientation implies the presence of a serf as the subject of this system. For the subject of the text, the object (Larin) is a *barin*. And from this point of view Larin looks simple and kind—which extends the contours of the patriarchal relations reigning in the Larin home. All these numerous stylistic semantic shifts are synthesized in the concluding lines, in the text of the epitaph, which is simultaneously solemn ("humble sinner," "savors peace") and comical (cf. "The Lord's slave and a brigadier," which puts Larin's relation to earthly and heavenly powers on a equal level).

In the next stanza we encounter a new group of shifts. The conventional poetic "returning to his hearth and home" (in the tradition of the friendly epistle) is followed by news about Lenskij visiting Larin's grave. The "tombstone of his neighbor" looks "humble," that is, prosaic ("humble prose") to Lenskij (from the naive point of view which finds its realization in the epitaph, the tombstone is imposing). "And dedicated a sigh to his ashes" leads us into the world of Lenskuj's ideas, which naturally culminate in the words "Poor Yorick!" Lenskij constructs his "I" on the model of Hamlet and recodes the situation into the system of the Shakespearian drama.

It is clear from this example (one could analyze any stanza of the novel in a similar fashion) that the sequence of semantic–stylistic breaks creates, not a focused but a scattered, multiple point of view, and it becomes the center of a supra-system which is perceived as the illusion of reality itself. For the realistic style, attempting to exceed the boundaries of subjectivism of semantic–stylistic "points of view." and to create an objective reality, there was great import in the specific interrelation of these multiple centers, these varied (adjacent or mutually superposed) structures. Each one does not replace the others, but correlates with them. As a result the text means not only what it means, but something else as well. The new meaning does not supplant the old, but correlates with it. As a result the artistic model reproduces a very important aspect of reality–the fact that there is no exhaustive, finite interpretation.

We can see from the examples cited above that already in *Evgenij Onegin* Puškin not only arranges points of view in a complex structure, employing the device of narration on one theme from various stylistic positions, but also resorts to other, more complex means.

The device of retelling the material from various points of view was convenient because for the as yet unprepared reader it laid bare the essence of the writer's method. But it was too polemical, too demonstrative to become the basis of a style after it had been established as a norm. Later the montage of points of view that took hold in narrative art involved shifts in the objects described. A clear example of this sort of construction is *War and Peace* which closely approximates the montage techniques of modern film. The organic quality of this kinship can be seen in "The False Coupon,"* a story with a distinctly cinematographic structure involving changes in point of view, montage, and so on.

Finally, we must consider yet another device in the structuring of point of view which also is best illustrated through film. Let us suppose that the cameraman is obliged to shoot the film through the eyes of some persona. This problem frequently arises in the process of making films, both in theory and practive. One example is Alfred Hitchcock's sensational attempt to film a suicide from the perspective of the subject in *Spellbound*: at first he turned the muzzle of the revolver directly at the audience and

---

* "The False Coupon"–another story by Tolstoj (1905)–Tr.

then flashed a sequence of red, white and black across the screen.[34]

Numerous experiments have shown that the long stretches of film shot from the vantage of some persona result not in an increase of the feeling of subjectivity, but, on the contrary, in its loss: the viewer begins to perceive the shots as an ordinary panoramic view. In order for a film text to be presented in such a way that it realizes the point of view of some persona, shots taken from his special vantage point must be alternated (juxtaposed in editing) with shots that fix the persona from without, from the spatial vantage point of the viewer ("no one's point of view) or other personae.

Similarly the reproduction of any point of view in a narrative text of the post-Puškin period is constructed as a sort of amalgam, where linguistic means of expressing the point of view of the hero are juxtaposed with the points of view of the author and other personae. Thus in *Belkin's Tales,* each story has three narrators: the person telling the story to Belkin (though their names may be coded in initials, they are concretized socially and psychologically[35]), Belkin himself, and Puškin. Moreover personae figure in the text who often seriously deform the narrative's point of view through their direct speech. Each story is constructed in such a way that each of these points of view is accented in different ways in different parts of the text. Different points of view may emerge within a single phrase. In this way the specific character of subjective positions and objective "super-position," a construct of reality, are both accentuated.

Because of the special role of artistic space in the creation of a text— a model of the represented object—the point of view often is spatially embodied in a work. The point of view emerges as the *orientation* of artistic space. One and the same spatial scheme—the opposition of inner, closed (finite) space to external, open (infinite) space can be interpreted in different ways, depending on the orientation. The line

> Nas malo izbrannyx, sčastlivcev prazdnyx. . .
>
> [We are the select few, the idle lucky men. . .]
>   (Puškin)

combines the point of view of the narrative with inner (closed) space. The line

> Mil'ony—vas. Nas—t'my, i t'my, i t'my. . .
>
> [You number in the millions. We—an innumerable host. . .]
>   (Blok)

forms a system in which the speaker is combined with the outside, open world. In this connection it becomes clear that a point of view can remain

34 The attempt produced a shocking effect. But we should remember that in literature the attempt to describe death from the viewpoint of the dying is by no means a recent phenomenon. Tolstoj attempted it in *Sevastopol Stories,* Hemingway in *For Whom the Bell Tolls,* Vladimov in *Big Ore,* and so on.

35 See V. V. Gippius, *ot Puškina do Bloka* (Moscow—Leningrad, 1966).

artistically active only while its anti-system, the diametrically opposite point of view, is also active.

The problem of point of view brings a dynamic element to the text: each point of view aspires to truthfulness and strives to assert itself in the struggle with opposing points of view. But if, in its triumph, it annihilates the opposing system, it destroys itself as something of artistic interest. When Romanticism died the polemic against it also ceased to exist artistically. Therefore in its battle with opposing systems, the point of view not only damages, but also resurrects and activates these systems. Hence the complex "polyphonic" structure of points of view that lies at the foundation of the narrative in modern literature.

The Juxtaposition of Heterogeneous Elements
As a Compositional Principle

The syntagmatic structuring of the artistic text differs in essence from the usual form of syntagmatics we find in primary modeling systems.

In natural language structures we are dealing with sequences of signs or elements of signs on a certain level. This allows us to stratify the natural linguistic structure into individual layers, each with a completely immanent function.

By analogy with non-artistic sign systems there is a tendency to distinguish individual levels in literary texts as well—phonological, grammatical, lexico-semantic, micro-syntactic (phrasal) and macro-syntactic (supra-phrasal). This is no doubt necessary, and without a preliminary description of these levels it is impossible to construct a precise model of the artistic text. But we must understand that this marking of levels makes sense only as a preliminary and heuristic operation. The real functioning of an artistic text is connected with the interaction among levels, which is more vigorous than in non-artistic structures.

The composition of an artistic text is structured as a *sequence of functionally heterogeneous elements*, a sequence of *structural dominants on various levels*.

Let us imagine that in analyzing some film we can compose a structural description of the depth of the shots and show the compositional organization of their sequence. We can do this with respect to the sequence of camera angles, the acceleration and deacceleration of the frames, the structure of personae, the sound-track system, and so on. In the actual functioning of the text, however, the slices that are shot close up will give way not only to their opposite, but also to shots where the primary bearer of meaning is the camera angle. At this moment the depth of the shot does not cease to be meaningful, but remains as an almost imperceptible structural background. Thus in an ordinary non-artistic text we are dealing with the dynamics of communication within the limits of one language, while in an artistic text we are dealing with several languages, and the loudest voice is constantly changing. The very sequence and correlation of these languages constitute a unified system of artistic information which the text conveys. In constituting a unified structure on a certain level, this system contains unpredictable intersections, which guarantees that the flow of information will not decrease. That is why the more complex the organization of a text and of each of its levels, the more unexpected will be the points of intersection of individual substructures; the greater the number of substructures in which a given element appears, the more "random" it will seem. Hence the familiar paradox that arises only in an *artistic text:* the more it is structured, the less predictable it becomes.

But we are speaking here not only of elements of heterogeneous levels which are combined in a single compositional whole. Within each level as well sequences are constructed according to a comparable principle: heterogeneous elements are combined in such a way as to create, on the one hand, definite perceptible structural sequences and, on the other hand, the continual violation of those sequences as a result of the imposition of other structures and their "disruptive" influence. This leads to the creation of an extremely flexible mechanism with incalculable semantic energy. Thus elements of structure known to be unequal, which are organized on various levels of the general linguistic plane of content and various levels of the plane of expression ("persona" and rhyme, the violation of rhythmic inertia and the epigraph, the shifting of depth and points of view and the semantic breakdown in a metaphor, and so on and so forth) emerge as elements of equal value in a single syntagmatic construction. A description of this unified sythetic level of structural dominants should probably be submitted for judgment to those readers who are interested in how a work is structured, not how the study of the work is structured. The preliminary task of giving the fullest possible description of all levels remains the province of a comparatively small circle of specialists who are less interested in the results of the study than its mechanics. It is important to stress this point, since as complete a description as is now possible of all levels of a comparatively small artistic text would fill an enormous number of pages, and one could lose sight of what is most important—the functional unity of the text.

We can summarize the above remarks as follows: one of the basic structural laws of an artistic text is its *unevenness*—the concurrence of structurally heterogeneous segments.[36] In his studies on the principles of perspective in Russian icon painting, B. A. Uspenskij has shown that, in

36 We find an interesting example of the unevenness of a text's structural organization in Botticelli's illustrations for Dante's *Divine Comedy*. The drawings are done in a sustained "realistic" (relative to the Renaissance) manner. The figures of Dante and Virgil, as well as the figures in the background are executed in direct three-demensional perspective. But in the same illustration the figures of Dante and Virgil are repeated several times along the axis of their movement against the unrepeated background. Thus in relation to the background figures the observer must see the entire illustration, but in respect to the central characters only one part. The "density" of orderings in various places of the drawing varies.

conformity with the structural principles of medieval Russian art, the perspective at the periphery of the painting differs from the perspective at the center. One could extend this observation: in a very large group of extremely diverse texts we can observe the alternation of segments in which the same principles manifest themselves with a varying degree of condensation, or organized segments of the text are placed together in different ways.

This juxtaposing of heterogeneous elements is manifested on all levels— from the lowest levels connected with the plane of expression in the structure of natural language, to the highest levels belonging to the level of content in the general linguistic system. Thus, for example, in *War and Peace,* the personae not only submit to a basic conceptual artistic opposition (personae representing *hoi polloi* and those representing the beau monde, static personae and active personae, etc.), but also to more individual, though very important, orderings. This being the case, we find that different norms of behavior operate for different personae, even for those who enter into the same group as defined on a more abstract level. Thus if one describes the behavoir of Doloxov and Anatolyj Kuragin as a system of permission and prohibition, it is obvious that although on a certain level they may be viewed as variants of a single type, in the real text of the novel these personae are governed by different norms of behavior. But we run into different norms of behavior not only when we move from persona to persona; special rules and norms of behavior are also indigenous to certain areas of space. Nikolaj Rostov behaves differently in the regiment than at home, and differently in the country than in Moscow. When a persona finds himself at a ball or on the field of battle, his behavior is regulated not only by the norms of his character, but also by the general norms of the *place.*

The clashes between various points of view, various types of behavior, various ideas of what is possible and impossible, important or unimportant, intersect the text of the novel and force us in each section to experience the new view of the world and the new construction of human behavior in that section. Galloping back to Brünn, the site of the Austrian emperor's court, with news of the victory over Mortier, Andrej Bolkonskij is convinced of the extreme importance of this event, which he sees through the eyes of a direct participant (his horse was shot down under him and he himself was grazed by a bullet) and from the point of view of the Russian Army. He considers this the only possible view of the matter, and expects the Austrians to have a similar reaction to the event: "All the details of the battle once again arose vividly in his mind, no longer vague, but specific, in that concise exposition which he imagined himself setting forth before the Emperor Franz." But in Brünn his view clashes with another view—not the view of the army, but of the court, not the Russian, but the Austrian view, evaluating the events from a distance instead of at close range. We are not surprised by the fact that the view at Emperor Franz's court differs from that at Kutuzov's headquarters. What is remarkable is that Andrej does not accept this point of view, which is hostile to him. But the very fact of its existence alters his own attitude toward the battle: "His whole way of thinking changed in an instant; the battle now seemed to him a long-past, distant recollection."[37]

At the ball Nataša "neither noticed nor saw any of those things which interested everyone at that ball. She not only failed to notice how the sovereign spoke for a long time with the French ambassador, how he spoke most graciously with some lady... She did not even see the sovereign, and noticed that he had left only because after his departure the ball became more animated."[38] Nataša and the "others" have different norms for determining what is "important " and "unimportant," but their proximity forces us to perceive each system of evaluations in its uniqueness. At the same ball Nataša "was gayer than she had ever been in her life," but Pierre "for the first time felt himself offended by the position his wife occupied in higher circles." He was "morose and absent-minded." The ball scene is immediately followed by the episode in which Bolkonskij visits Speranskij, and those norms which govern Nataša's behavior at the ball come into conflict with "official" behavior. We can observe how, in the development of the narrative, unilinear plots are replaced by multi-linear plots, how the presence of many personae and several plot lines entails a structure in which each chapter transfers the reader from one plot line to another, how the structure of the text is complicated by shifts in points of view. All these things are varying manifestations of one principle: adjacent parts of the text must be organized in different ways. This ensures that there will be a constant resistance to predictability, a constant flow of information, in the artistic structure.[39]

Neighboring textual segments enter into various constructional systems on the level of the text; on a higher level, they are incorporated into a single structure (the author concentrates on the first aspect of the question, whereas the reader first takes immediate note of the second aspect). This dual (or rather, multi-leveled) inclusion of textual elements in both opposing and common structures, this constant struggle between the tendency towards unification and the tendency towards the dissimilation of structural principles gives rise to the constant informational activity of the artistic structure throughout the entire text—a fairly rare phenomenon in communication systems.

The effect of juxtaposition (the montage effect, in Eisenstein's terminology) is organically connected with the switchover to another structure. Consequently at the moment when one segment gives way to another, at

37 L. N. Tolstoj, *Sobranie sočinenij v 14-ti tomax*, vol. IV, op. cit., pp. 186, 188.
38 Ibid., vol. V, pp. 207-208.
39 In a structural sense we find an analogous phenomenon in the shifting comic and tragic sequences in Shakespeare, and also in those numerous instances where a varying degree of conventionality is assigned to different parts of the text. The textual "breaks" which we have investigated in *Evgenij Onegin* could be similarly interpreted.

least *two* possibilities must confront the author (and the audience, in the structure of its expectations): the continuation of an already familiar structural organization or the appearance of a new one. The artistic information that is generated consists precisely in this *choice* and the mutual projection of text and expectation (structural inertia). Thus, for example, when a film is shot completely in black and white or completely in color, the color of each shot is unambiguously predetermined by the color of the preceding shots, and the choice of color or black-and-white cannot convey meaning. But imagine a film where some shots are in color and others in black-and-white. Then choice, expectation and the juxtaposition of shots according to the principle of color relations becomes a carrier of meaning. Modern film goes even farther, introducing a fundamental ordering of bichromatic and polychromatic shots, which within themselves are divided into subgroups (light blue–dark blue, brown–yellow, etc. in the former, and the polychromatism of various color dominants in the latter). It is then possible to adjoin bichromatic and polychromatic frames, and the variants within each group, to form a complex system. The director may create an association between a color and a certain hero, creating an analogy to a musical theme, or identifying certain kinds of coloration with "points of view" or emotional intensity (as the correlate of intonation), in order to create additional information.

Juxtaposed units that are incompatible in one system force the reader to construct an additional structure in which the incompatibility is eliminated. The text is correlated with both, and this leads to an increase in the number of semantic possibilities. Let us look at the conjunction of segments in Pasternak's poetry from this point of view:

> Možet molnija udarit',–
> Vspyxnet mokroju kabinkoj.
> Ili vsex ščenjat razdarjat.. ,

> [Lightning may strike–
> It will light up like a wet cabin,
> Or they will give away all the pups. . .]

The montage of statements that "Lightning may strike" and "They will give away all the pups," representing two possible and *equivalent* misfortunes, reveals their semantic incommensurability and therefore the "incorrectness" (illogic) of such a syntagmatic construction. However against the background of this feeling of "incorrectness" (which must be preserved for the structure to work) another ordering takes shape–the connection of concepts inherent to the world of children (and in a more restricted sense, the world of "summer places"). In this world the disappearance of pups is a great misfortune, and the forces which bring it about ("grown-ups") are just as powerful and incomprehensible as the forces of nature. But the world of children is not only juxtaposed with the "logical" world (the general structure of linguistic content). In the succeeding lines it is joined by the cozy phrase "praises the art of keeping house," conjoined, in turn, with the unconjoinable subject "the storm" ("The storm praises the art of keeping house [!]"). The Romantic "waterspout of melancholy" "strains" toward an ordinary well, and all this is combined with the familiar, intimate phrase, "What else do you want?", which proves to be equivalent to the romantic ironic *Mein Liebchen, was willst du noch mehr?* in the title of the poem:

> I kogda k kolodcu rvetsja
> Smerč toski, to mimoxodom
> Burja xvalit domovodstvo.
> Čto tebe ešče ugodno?

> [And when the waterspout of melancholy
> Strains toward the well, the storm in passing
> Praises the art of keeping house.
> What else do you want?]

"Strange affinities," as Puškin put it, are the law of syntagmatics of the artistic text.

The increase in information that results when the only combinations possible in receding structures are provided with an alternative, is a phenomenon clearly manifested in painting. In medieval works there is a strictly fixed system of poses and gestures, and each persona has *one* such pose allotted to him. Classicism retains the fixed pose, but broadens the assortment available. For each figure the artist can *choose* one of several interpretations "appropriate" to the meaning and setting of the figure. The Realistic art of the nineteenth century repudiates this "conventionality" as well. The range of possible poses from which the artist makes his selection is determined by his everyday experience in visual observation, which here plays the same role that the structure of the content of natural language plays in poetry. Of course verisimilitude is sporadically violated in this system as well (metaphor in poetry, the conscious violation of accepted norms of perspective, elements of the grotesque, and so on). By allowing itself to make use of combinations forbidden by everyday experience (as Majakovskij and Pasternak do in poetry), twentieth century art significantly increases the information load of the text.

In this connection it would probably be interesting to trace the conflict between the languages of painting and the cinema and their mutual attempts to place each other in a subordinate position in a single structure encompassing the artistic culture of the twentieth century. The mutual influence of various arts is a manifestation on the highest level of the general law of conjoining various structural principles in artistic works.

9. THE TEXT AND EXTRA–TEXTUAL ARTISTIC STRUCTURES

The Relativity of the Opposition Between The Text And Extra-textual Structures

Given what we already know about the structure of a text, the fact that if some element is not expressed in signs on a given level this does not necessarily imply a break in the text (to solve such a problem we must establish just what corresponds to the given section in structures on other levels)–it is obvious that the concept of text is not absolute. It is correlated with many attendant historical, cultural and psychological structures.

We can view a poem from a poetic cycle as a text; in this case its relation to the cycle will be extra-textual, the relation of a text to external structures. But the unity of a cycle's organization permits us to examine *it* as a text on a certain plane. Similarly one might consider as a text all the works that a given author wrote in a clearly marked period of time (Puškin's works written in Boldino; Belinskij's essays in *Sovremennik* [*The Contemporary*]; Mickiewicz's *Crimean Sonnets;* Picasso's rose and blue periods), or works which we perceive as having a certain unity (stylistic, thematic, and so on). Finally, there can also be such texts as the works of Shakespeare, the artistic legacy of Ancient Greece, English literature, and, ultimately, the art of mankind. It would be impossible to raise strict objections to the contention that any of the aforementioned can be examined as a text.

We could cite many examples of texts created as individual works which later function as *parts* of a more extended text of the same author, other authors, or anonymous authors. This constantly occurs in folklore. The chapters of *A Hero of Our Times* were both composed and printed as separate novellas; later they were transformed (in the first separate publication) not into a cycle of novellas, but into a novel. Chapters of *Evgenij Onegin* or *Vasilij Terkin*, printed in separate publications with large chronological gaps between them at times, seemed more independent of each other to their contemporaries who read each section as it came out, than to later readers holding one book with a single title and successively numbered chapters and pages. In this sense the publication of a novel in periodicals or even newspapers in installments with the note "to be continued," naturally occasions a special perception of the text. In such cases there can be no doubt that the text of the installment may have a dual correlation: the chapters of a novel as part of a novel, and the chapters of a novel as part of the structural, conceptual whole of one issue of a periodical. Since both these concepts are possible one must acknowledge that the word "text" means different things in each case.

On the other hand we are equally familiar with cases where a part of a text functions as an independent, wholly autonomous artistic unit. A ready example is *Manon Lescaut*. Jurij Tynjanov extracted "David's Lament for Jonathon" from Kjuxel'beker's long, difficult narrative poem *David* and published it as a separate piece, thus *creating* a magnificent work of art, one of the finest examples of the Russian political lyric of the early nineteenth century; and it is no longer possible to end the independent existence of this poem by "stuffing" it back where it came from.

The question of whether a work is a text or part of a text is not a scholastic dispute. Karamzin's *The Island of Bornholm* perplexed his contemporaries, who could not decide whether it was a novella or a fragment, due to a different conception of the meaning and nature of a work of art. Is the first volume of *Dead Souls* a work or part of a work? The question is hardly an idle one. Belinskij felt it extremely important that the public accept it as a separate finished text; but for Gogol, the work would have been terribly impoverished in that case.

When Nicholas I requested that A. A. Ivanov "supplement" *The Appearance of the Messiah* with a second picture, a *pendant* on *The Christening of Russians in the Dnieper,* he saw the picture as *part* of a text due to ideological considerations and his conviction, inculcated by the symmetry of barracks life, that "paired" decorations should be hung on the walls. But for Ivanov the moment of spiritual transfiguration of humanity, the transformation of Greeks, Jews, slaves, and patricians *into brothers,* was *an integral text* and could not be supplemented with a *pendant*.

Thus we conclude that one must take into account the possible difference between what the author considers a text to be, what the audience regards as a primary artistic whole, and finally the perspective of the scholar, who perceives the text as a useful abstraction of artistic unity.

The Typology of Texts
And the Typology of Extra-textual Relations

Any artistic text can perform its social function only when aesthetic communication is present in the collective in which it operates. Since sign communication requires not only a text but a language, the artistic work which is taken by itself, outside a given cultural context and a system of cultural codes, is like "an epitaph written in an incomprehensible tongue." But since the act of artistic communication, like any communicative act, implies the presence of a collective communicating through sign systems, there may be two possible relations between the text and the code: synthesis and analysis. Here we appear to be dealing with instances that do not merely reproduce a situation analogous to that studied by linguists.

In natural language, both the speaker and the listener, despite the difference in the operations they carry out, remain within one system, be it Russian, English, Czech or any other language. Naturally one can study the same problem in art as well if one operates with an artificially constructed receiver of information that is culturally, intellectually, and emotionally equal to the author of the text. This problem, while essential to the description of the psychology of creative work and the psychology of the perception of art, does not concern us at the moment. We are speaking of a situation much closer to the daily practive of artistic communication and specific to this type of communication, when the sender and receiver of information use code systems that are not identical. This is a particularly important problem, for our studies of poetry and prose have shown that the presumption of a particular type of organization is often a decisive structural factor, for after we attribute some structure to a text we perceive the absence of certain features as "minus-devices," as deliberate silence. Therefore if the text is to function in a given manner, it is not sufficient for it to be organized in a given manner; the *possibility* of such organization must be provided for in the hierarchy of codes of the given culture. We all know how difficult it is to determine in every case whether or not a text is artistic. No sooner does one make a rule than the living history of literature reveals so many exceptions that nothing is left of it. The attempt to answer this question is an independent and fairly complex task and we cannot attempt to solve it here. But we can try to approach it differently by asking, "In what instances is the act of artistic communication possible?" Let us imagine a civilization that does not know what art is (for example, a computer civilization). Naturally if an artistic text is introduced into such a society and circulated it may convey a certain amount of information but it will not be artistic.

If one assumed the rather improbable existence of a culture knowing only artistic communication, here too there could be no question of the *distinction* between artistic and non-artistic texts. Thus a necessary preliminary condition for determining which text is artistic and which non-artistic, is the presence of the opposition between artistic and non-artistic structures in the very code of the culture. Then we can easily list the possibilities of a text's functions in relation to this opposition.

There are obviously four possibilities:

1) The writer creates a text as a work of art and the reader perceives it as such.

2) The writer creates a text that is non-artistic, but the reader perceives it aesthetically (for example, the modern perception of sacred, historical texts of ancient or medieval cultures).

3) The writer creates an artistic text, but the reader is not capable of identifying it with any of those forms of organization which satisfy his definition of art, and so he perceives it as non-artistic information.

4) A non-artistic text written by the author as such is perceived as non-artistic by the reader—a trivial case.

This elementary streamlined scheme covers only final, extreme cases, which for certain purposes is very convenient. But the true picture presented by literature at various stages in its development is far more complex. The boundary between artistic and non-artistic texts may be drawn so differently from the way we are accustomed to perceiving it today that we may be inclined to overlook it, believing that it is not characteristic of a given type of culture. The nature of this boundary is vital to the typological description of a culture: it may be stable or extremely mobile. It may relate to other boundaries in extremely different ways, dividing texts into sacred and worldly, high and low, valuable and worthless. At extreme opposite poles we find: 1) systems attributing so great a structural difference to art and non-art that it is impossible to use the same styles or even the same natural languages in creating these texts, and 2) systems that regard this opposition as purely functional. In twentieth century art, for example, a newspaper text can in principle be incorporated into poetry; non-artistic texts can be made to function as artistic texts in various other ways.

But the relation of the opposition "artistic vs. non-artistic text" in the consciousness of author and reader is only the first aspect of the problem. Far more complicated are those cases where both participants in the act of artistic communication perceive the text as artistic, but the structure of that concept is profoundly different for both of them. This is the central problem in the relation between the text and extra-textual structures.

The perception of an artistic text is always a struggle between audience and author (in this sense we can apply mathematical game theory to the study of the perception of art). The audience takes in part of the text and then "finishes" or "constructs" the rest. The author's next "move" may confirm the guess and make further reading pointless (at least from the perspective of modern aesthetic norms) or it may disprove the guess and require a new construction from the reader. But the next "move" made by the author once again poses the two possibilities. This continues until the author wins; he outplays the artistic experience, aesthetic norms and prejudices of the reader, and thrusts his model of the world and concept of the structure of reality upon him. This moment is the end of the work, and it can occur before the end of the text if the author uses a cliché-model whose nature becomes apparent to the reader at the beginning of the work. The reader, of course, is not passive; he *has an interest* in mastering the model that the artist presents to him. With its help he hopes to explain and conquer the forces of the outer and inner world. Therefore the artist's victory is a source of joy to the vanquished reader.

Here is an example. On your way to the movies you already have a certain expectation based on advertisements, the name of the studio, the director and the actors, the film's genre, and opinions of your acquaintances who have already seen the film, and so on. When you define the as yet unseen film as a mystery, a psychological drama, a comedy, a work produced by Kiev's Dovženko Studios, a film directed by Fellini, a film starring Igor Il'inskij or Charlie Chaplin, you are defining the contours of your expectation, whose structure is based on your previous artistic experience. You perceive the first shots of the projected film in relation to that structure, and if the entire work fits the *a priori* structure of your expectation, you leave the theatre with a profound sense of dissatisfaction. The work brought nothing new to you; the author's model of the world proved to be a cliché. But there is another possibility. At a given moment the real course of the film and your idea of its necessary course enter into conflict; in essence, this conflict destroys the old model of the world, which is sometimes false, sometimes merely familiar, representing knowledge that has been gained and transformed into a cliché. A new, more perfect model of reality is created. The capacity of art to model reality (a point repeatedly discussed here) leads each spectator to project shots in the film not only onto the structure of his artistic experience, but onto the structure of his life's experience.

Thus it would be apropros here to introduce the concept of the relation of the real structure of a work (the real code) to the structure expected by the audience; this concept is essential to the construction of generative models and the solution of problems arising in the course of translation. This is the primary and broadest level in the construction of generative models. The relation may be of two types.

In this discussion we can divide all types of literary works and works of art into two classes which are typologically correlated, although from a historical point of view they are most often sequentially related.

The first class consists of artistic phenomena whose structures are given beforehand; the audience's expectations are met by the entire construction of the work.

Throughout the history of art, artistic systems that associate aesthetic worth with originality are the exception rather than the rule. The folklore of all nations, medieval art (an inevitable, universal historical stage), *commedia dell'arte,* Classicism—these are only a few of the artistic systems which judge a work according to its observation of certain rules rather their violation. The rules governing word choice and the construction of meta- phors, rituals of narration, strictly defined possibilities for plot combinations that are known in advance, and *loci communi* (whole pieces of frozen text) all form a very special artistic system. Most importantly, the audience is armed not only with a set of possibilities, but also a set of impossibilities standing in paired opposition to the first set on each level of the artisitc construction. If the author were to choose a situation that was "impossible" from the viewpoint of the code rules within a given system of artistic perception, the structure expected by the audience would be destroyed, and as a result they would regard the work as inferior and the author as unskilled and ignorant, or even a blasphemer of sinful audacity.

But despite the similarities between this sort of artistic system and language, we cannot help but notice the profound difference between the nature of the language code and that of the artistic structures given above.

Since the code of a langauge is given beforehand, its application becomes automatic. The speaker does not notice it. Only when the rules of the code are broken or have not been properly mastered does the code cease to be automatic; then our attention is drawn to the structural aspect of language.

In folklore and artistic phenomena of the same type, the relation to structural rules is different—they are not automatized. The explanation would appear to be that here the rules of the author and of the audience are not one, but two phenomena in a state of mutual identity.

Artistic systems of this type are based on a sum of principles which may be defined as the *aesthetics of identity*. It is based on the total identification of depicted phenomena of life with model-clichés that are known beforehand to the audience and operate according to a system of "rules." "Cliché" is not a bad word as applied to art, but rather a phenomenon which is negative only in certain of its historical and structual aspects. Stereotypes (clichés) of consciousness play a great part in the process of cognition and, in a broader sense, in the process of information transfer.

The epistemological nature of the aesthetics of identity is such that various phenomena of life are perceived through their equation with certain logical models. The artist deliberately discards all "nonessential" elements, those that give the phenomenon its individuality. This is the art of identification. Confronted with different phenomena: A', A'', A''', A''''... A^n. it does not weary of repeating A' is A; A'' is A; ... A^n is A. Consequently in such an aesthetic system repetition is not like a dialectically complex analogy, but absolute and unconditional. This is the poetry of classification. At this stage there are no song refrains repeated each time in a different way, but rather *loci communi*—folk tale introductions and epic repetitions. Understandably, the poetry that adheres most consistently to this type is not rhymed.

But variety is necessary for the existence of identification. In order to tirelessly repeat "This is A," A' must be followed by A'', and so on to infinity. The force of artistic cognition here lies in the fact that the artist identifies abstract model A with phenomena that are most unexpected and least resemble A for the non-artistic eye (A', A'', A''', and so on). The monotony of the identification at one pole is compensated by unbridled variety at the other. No wonder the most typical examples of the aesthetics of identity manifest a frozen system of characters, plots and other structural elements at one pole, and at the other pole an extremely fluid dynamic form like improvisation. The freedom of improvisation and the fetters of rules are interdependent. For these types of art improvisation creates the necessary entropy. If we dealt only with a rigid system of rules, each new work of art would be only a copy of its predecessor; redundancy would suppress entropy, and the work of art would lose its informational value. To illustrate this, we can point to *commedia dell'arte,* whose structure is very interesting in this respect. The principle of identity is the basis for the construction of characters. The images of the comedy are only stable costumes. The artistic effect relies on the spectators' knowledge of the characters of such personae as Pantalone, Harlequin, the Captain, and the Lovers. If an actor violated the set rules of behavior for his costume, the spectator would condemn him and regard it as a sign that he has not mastered the role. The actor's art is praised as a skillful execution of the canon of actions of his image. The spectator should not have a moment's doubt of the persona's nature, and for this reason they are not only provided with typical costumes and makeup (corresponding to the given image), but each speaks in a different dialect and has his own vocal timbre. A Venetian dialect, a red jacket, red trousers, black cloak and a characteristic hook-nosed, bearded mask are signals to the spectator that the actor's actions should be projected onto the type Pantalone. The same is true of a Bolognese dialect and black mantle for the Doctor, a Bergamese dialect for the Zanni, and so on.

But if the aesthetic of identity is not to lose its nature as a means of cognition and information, the creation of a given model of the world, the fixed clichés of concepts must express diverse living material. It is revealing in this sense that *commedia dell'arte* has, at one pole, a strict set of images and clichés with certain possibilities and certain prohibitions, while at the other pole, it is constructed as the freest sort of improvisation to be found in the history of the European Theatre.[1] Thus the improvisation itself is not an unrestrained flight of fantasy, but a combination of elements known to the spectator. In 1634, N. Barbieri described the art of improvisation as follows: "Comedians study and memorize a great mixture of things: maxims, ideas, love speeches, reproaches, speeches of despair and delirium; they keep these ready for use; their training corresponds to the style of the persona they portray."[2] This combination of extreme freedom and extreme restriction characterizes the aesthetic of identity as well. To varying degrees the same principles are manifested in most folklore genres and in medieval art.[3]

Anyone who has watched a child running ecstatically from one fir tree to another, never tiring of repeating, "That's a fir, and that's a fir," or from a birch to a maple and a fir, exclaiming, "That's a tree, and that's a tree," can easily understand why the expression of different real phenomena in one given conceptual cliché is an act of cognition, which, because of its importance, can evoke great emotional tension. This is the way the child perceives a phenomenon, discarding the features peculiar to a given fir or type of tree, and including them in one common category. This is essentially

1 The basic literature on *commedia dell'arte* is cited in A. K. Dživelegov, *Ital'janskaja narodnaja komedija* (Moscow, 1954) pp. 292-295.

2 From S. Mokul'skij (ed.), *Xrestomatija po istorii zapadnoevropejskogo teatra*, vol. I, 2nd ed., (Moscow, 1953) p. 239.

3 On the meaning of poetic ritual in medieval Russian art see D. S. Lixačev, *Čelovek v literature Drevnej Rusi* (Moscow–Leningrad, 1958).

the same principle that we confront when we encounter the motif of naming in folklore.

The other class of structures we find on this level are systems whose code is unknown to the audience before the act of artistic perception begins. This is the aesthetic of opposition rather than identity. The author sets his own, original resolution, which he believes to be the truer one, in opposition to methods of modeling reality that are familiar to the reader. In the first instance the act of artistic perception involves simplification and generalization; here we are dealing with complication. But this complexity is not the same as decorativeness. Realistic prose is stylistically simpler than Romantic prose, but the rejection of Romantic clichés expected by the reader in *Belkin's Tales* created a more complex structure built on "minus-devices."

The efforts of the author and his audience to destroy a system of familiar rules can subjectively be perceived as a rejection of all structural norms, as creation "without rules." But creation independent of rules and structural relations is impossible. This would contradict the nature of a work of art as a model and a sign; it would make it impossible to understand the world with the help of art and to convey the results of that understanding to an audience. In the struggle against self-conscious, pretentious writing, an author or a school may turn to essays, reportage, the use of genuine, clearly non-artistic documents or newsreels; this represents the destruction of a *familiar system,* but not the *principle of system-ness.* Any line from a newspaper when transferred word for word to an artistic text (if that text does not lose its artistic qualities in the process) *becomes a structural element.* From the viewpoint of mathematical game theory, such art is not "a game without rules," but a game whose rules must be established in the process of play.

The aesthetic of opposition has a long history, and the appearance of such dialectically complex phenomena as rhyme is undoubtedly related to it. It is, however, most vividly expressed in Realistic art.

As we have seen, the division of artistic phenomena into two classes, based on the aesthetic of identity and the aesthetic of opposition, results in larger units of classification than the concept of "artistic method." But this division is by no means useless. We are obliged to confront it at close range in attempting to construct generative models of artistic works, and accordingly in working out many important problems.

This should be an object of special study. Even now one can state *a priori* that the construction of generative models for works reflecting the aesthetic of identity is not all that complicated; but even the possibility of such a construction for works classed as part of the aesthetic of opposition has yet to be demonstrated. It would be naive to presume that if one described all possible variants of iambic tetrameter and calculated the statistical probability of their alternation, that the results could be a code for constructing a new *Evgenij Onegin*. No less naive is the supposition that the most detailed structural description of the "old" *Evgenij Onegin* could become a generative model for the writing of a new one. To estimate how many states a computer capable of creating a new *Evgenij Onegin* would need is tantamount to estimating how many states would be required of a computer about to make a new, magnificent discovery.

Generative models can be practically applied in two ways: to reconstruct lost texts (parts of myths that have not survived, lost pages of medieval manuscripts) and to reconstruct artistic texts in a given language that already exist in another language. Clearly the task and methods of resolution will differ in these cases.

In working with phenomena classed under the aesthetic of opposition we must distinguish cases when the destroyed cliché-structure exists in the reader's consciousness due to his habits and a certain amount of inertia, but are not expressed in the text. Then the conflict between the aesthetic of the cliché and the new aesthetic represents a conflict between textual and extra-textual structural constructions. This is true, for example, of Nekrasov's lyrics or Čexov's prose. Such texts are the most difficult to model.

Things become simpler when an author uses certain elements in the construction of the work to evoke in the reader's consciousness a structure which will then be destroyed, as in Puškin's *Belkin's Tales* or the places in *Evgenij Onegin* where the style abruptly changes. The most telling text in this respect is parody. True, in destroying a structural cliché, parody does not place another sort of structure in opposition to the first. This other structure, which is true from the author's viewpoint, can be assumed to exist, but it is expressed by purely negative means. Parody is a curious, rare example of a construction where the genuine, innovative structure is outside the text and its relation to the structural cliché is an extra-textual one, only the author's attitude to the textual construction. One cannot, therefore, agree with the formalist interpretation of parody, which is so broad that it includes Gogol's tales or Puškin's "The Shot," works having a clearly expressed "positive" authorial structure within the boundaries of the text. It follows that parody can never be a central artistic genre and is not the one that initiates the struggle against clichés. If parody is to be perceived in full as an artistic phenomenon, literary works must exist and be known to the reader which, in destroying the aesthetic of clichés, create a truer structure, one opposed to parody and more accurately modeling reality. Only when the reader is aware of such a new structure can he supplement the destructive parodical text with an extra-textual constructive element; only the presence of this structure conveys the author's point of view on the parodied system. Therefore, being a vivid and, in a certain sense, laboratory genre, parody always plays a secondary role in literary history.

The concepts of the "aesthetic of identity" and "aesthetic of opposition" serve yet another purpose, permitting us to attempt to apply more precise criteria in the more subjective spheres of art studies—the evaluation of the quality of a given work, for example. As we pointed out earlier, one can *a priori* state that the artificial modeling of a work in the class of the aesthetic of identity requires significantly less data (and the data are far simpler) than in a work of the opposing class. In addition the observation of canons, norms and clichés characteristic of the aesthetic of identity does not annoy us or strike us as an artistic fault in the text of a folk epic or fairy tale. On the other hand when we come across the same structural features in a modern social novel we feel that we are dealing with an artistic failure, a falsification of the living truth. The formula "I predicted the whole structure" is deadly for the second type of work, but has no effect on our evaluation of the first type.

This may be explained by the fact that the reader prepares himself for the reception of a work of art, and part of this preparation is the awareness that a work belongs to the aesthetic of identity or opposition. Signals which tell him how to classify the work include the opening formulas, names, references to genre in the title, and even the reputation of the theatre or publication presenting the work to the audience. It is clear that when the spectator knows he is about to witness a performace of *commedia dell'arte* and not a play by Čexov, his system of values will correspond with that knowledge. If we are dealing with a bad, hackneyed novel, this is what happens: when the author says that we are dealing with a novel and uses that term in the sense it came to acquire in the 1830's, he forces us to expect a new structure, a new explanation of reality. But in fact the work is constructed on the aesthetic of identity, through the realization of clichés. This is what creates the impression of artistic inferiority. Consequently, while it is extremely difficult to conceive of a computer able to create good poetry on the basis of the aesthetic of opposition, bad works of this type could probably be created very easily. The possibility of artificially modeling a poem that belongs to the currently dominant aesthetic class, and the facility with which such a model could be constructed can serve as an objective—and negative!—criterion of artistic quality. One may wonder whether it is worth artificially creating bad works when there is no need for them. Upon reflection, however, it should be clear that the possibility of modeling bad, hackneyed poetry and articles with computers would do a great service to human culture. Art and anti-art are complementary concepts. In introducing precise criteria for anti-artistic phenomena and learning how to model them, the scholar and critic would acquire an instrument for measuring genuine art. At a certain stage in scholarship, the criterion for the genuine "artisticness" of contemporary art might be formulated as "a system which cannot be mechanically modeled." For many texts, even popular ones, it would be clearly fatal.

The author's text enters into a complex system of extra-textual connections; by virtue of the hierarchy of non-artistic and artistic norms on various levels that are generalized by the experience of the artistic past, these connections create a complex code that permits us to decipher information contained in the text.

But the specific nature of artistic communication is such that the code of the receiver always differs to some degree from the code of the sender. The differences may be comparatively slight, based on the individual's cultural experience or his specific psychological makeup; but they may also be profound, socio-historical, cultural differences which either prevent or reinterpret the artistic perception of the text. The reader tries to confine the text to familiar conceptions, selecting those extra-textual structures from his artistic experience that seem to him to be most appropriate for the given instance.

The features of extra-textual structures are determined by the same socio-historical, national, anthropological and psychological factors that form artistic models of the world. But it should be noted that the communicative nature of art makes a deep imprint on it, and among those textual or extra-textual structures that determine the forms of art, some are more in the "interests" of the audience's position in the act of communication, others are more in the "interests" of the author.[4]

We can state *a priori* that those principles governing the construction of an artistic code which are closer to the structural principles of the natural language are more "convenient" for the audience; those farther from the natural language are more convenient for the author. The author creates a text that functions simultaneously within several code systems. Each new part must awaken an awareness of already existing codes and be projected onto them; this correlation lends it new meanings and gives new meanings to parts of the text that previously seemed comprehensible. The reader is inclined to view an artistic text as a normal speech message, extracting information from each episode and reducing the composition to a temporal sequence of separate events. Naturally enough, a text with a plot gravitates toward the "reader's" position, and a plotless text to that of the author.

The reader wishes to acquire the necessary information with the least effort (pleasure in prolonging the effort is a typically authorial position).[5] While the author strives to increase the number of code systems and complicate their structure, the reader is inclined to reduce them to a minimum that seems sufficient to him. The tendency to complicate characters is an

4 This idea was first expressed and substantiated in detail by Boris Uspenskij in a series of lectures on "point of view" in art which he read in 1966 at Tartu State University.

5 One should bear in mind that the "author–reader" scheme is derived from an analysis of the act of communication. In real life it manifests itself only as a more or less spontaneous tendency. In each real author and real reader, both "author" and "reader" exist in varying proportions, which is what we are referring to here.

authorial tendency; a black-and-white contrasting structure is the tendency manifested by the reader.

Finally, the author tends to increase the complexity of the extra-textual structure, simplifying the text, creating works that seem simple but cannot be adequately deciphered without complex assumptions and a wealth of extra-textual cultural connections. It is most convenient for the reader when the maximum part of the structure is manifest in the text. It is readily apparent that the "reader's" tendencies triumph in texts whose plots are most evident and whose construction is most clearly contrastive and exposed: folklore, medieval art, picaresque novels, Romantic narrative poems. We must acknowledge that there is a tendency (though not a rule) for the "reader's ' position to be more characteristic of popular forms of art and, in particular, what we call "popular culture."

CONCLUSION

The artistic text, as we have ascertained, may be viewed as a specially organized mechanism which can contain an exceptionally high concentration of information. If we compare a sentence of colloquial speech with a poem, a set of paints with a picture, or a scale with a fugue, we immediately realize that the second element of each pair can contain, store, and convey a volume of information that is beyond the capacity of the first element.

Our conclusions are in full agreement with the fundamental idea of information theory which states that the volume of information in a message should be seen as the function of the number of possible alternative messages. The structure of an artistic text has a practically infinite number of boundaries which divide this text into segments that are equivalent in certain respects, and consequently may be regarded as alternatives.

The writer can choose not only between alternative segments, but also between types of organization of alternatives; not only between equivalent elements of his artistic language, but also between types of artistic language. When the choice is made for the writer by the natural language in which he writes, an epoch where the choice of artistic means is so firmly established that there can be no alternative, or the circumstances of his life; whenever the text does not realize one of at least two possibilities, but automatically follows one, it loses its capacity to convey information. Therefore the *increase of the possibilities of choice* is the law of an aritistic text's organization. Everything that is automatic and unavoidable in natural language is realized as a choice of one of equivalent possibilities in an artistic text. We find an analogous relation between the material of real life located outside the text and the artistic text itself; when something that is realized as the *sole* possibility in life becomes a plot element, it appears as the result of the author's choice (since he could choose another plot or another variant of the plot).

But we have seen that the relation between writer and reader creates additional alternative possibilities. In the transition from writer to reader, the measure of indeterminacy grows (although certain purely personal alternatives are irretrievably lost) and accordingly the information contained in the text increases.

Extra-systemic, structurally unorganized material cannot store and convey information. Therefore the first step toward the creation of a text is the creation of a *system*. When elements are not organized and there is an equal probability of the appearance of any one, when there is no structure but simply an amorphous entropic mass, there can be no information. So when a writer, in the heat of literary dispute, condemns the art of the preceding period for its limited possibilities and its conventional language, and proposes a new art with *unlimited possibilities,* we should realize that we are dealing either with sheer rhetoric or a mistake, which is more often than not sincere. Unlimited possibilities, the absence of all rules, total freedom from limitations imposed by a system are not the ideal for communication, but a death blow. Moreover, as we have seen, the more complex the system of rules, the freer the transmission of content: the grammar and vocabulary of traffic lights are simpler than those of natural language, and this creates considerable difficulties in the transmission of content any more complex than the direction of traffic. If we assume that freedom and variety of communication in a Realistic text are related to the absence of rules governing its language ("the writer is free from conventions," "he is bound by nothing," "he takes both form and content from life"), we are taking a naively realistic view of things, belied by the history of literature as well as by information theory.

The creation of a structure, however, is not an act of communication but only the condition for such an act. In non-artistic texts, it is the message and not the language that is informative. This aspect of communication is also present in art, but here the entire system of relations acquires a considerably more complex character.

A structure governed by unified constructive rules is not informative, since all of its groups are unambiguously predetermined by the system of construction. This is connected to Wittgenstein's contention that nothing is unexpected in logic. But within the artistic text langauge also becomes a carrier of information. This is achieved in the following ways:

1. The author of a text can *choose the language* in which he will construct the text; the nature of this choice is not immediately apparent to the reader. Thus in art two tendencies are simultaneously at work: the tendency to demarcate languages (the language of poetry and prose, the language of various genres, etc.) and to overcome these demarcations. One of these tendencies predominates in any historically given text, but it does not eliminate the opposing tendency. In this sense victory in an artistic text is equivalent to defeat because it cancels the alternative to the proposed resolution. When elements structurally opposed to a system penetrate that system, the reader is forced to hesitate in the choice of a deciphering code. The more complicated the choice (including emotional complexities), the greater amount of information it carries. One cannot argue with Wittgenstein if one believes that only one kind of logic is possible. But if one allows for several equivalent systems of this type, then each remains predictable within its own boundaries, but in relation to corresponding groups of parallel structures each system creates the possibility of choice. The structure will regain its informativeness.

2. The text belongs to *two* (or several) languages *simultaneously.* Not only do the elements of the text take on a dual (or multiple) meaning, but the entire structure becomes a carrier of information, for it functions by

projecting itself onto the norms of another structure.

3. An important means for the informational activization of a structure is *its violation*. An artistic text does not merely represent the implementation of structural norms, but their violation as well. It functions in a dual structural field consisting of the tendency to establish order and to violate it. Although each tendency tries to dominate and destroy the opposing one, the victory of either would prove fatal to art. The life of an artistic text depends on their mutual tension.

a) The structure of artistic language can be violated in a text when it is not totally implemented—when the work is made to look incomplete, broken-off or fragmentary (for example, the stanzas deliberately left out of *Evgenij Onegin*). A portrait with a carefully drawn face and hands lightly sketched in is a text whose conventions differ at the center and the periphery of the canvas. But there are well-known cases where the fact that the text is *unfinished* can artistically activate its structure. This feeling is so strong that it forces us to perceive texts that were accidently left unfinished as consciously organized in a particular way.

b) Very often a structure is violated in order to activate it, to introduce extra-structural elements. These may belong to another structure, in which case we would be dealing with the instance discussed in point 2. But they may be elements of an unknown structure, and here we must work out a corresponding code system.

4. Each type of culture is characterized by a set of functions which are served by corresponding objects of material culture, ideological establishments, texts, and so on. Certain sets of functions are also inherent to arts of different epochs. On various levels these include the functions of "being literature," "being poetry," "being lofty art," or "being comic." Social functions are served by mechanisms suitable to them. For literary functions such a mechanism is the text. It is not without interest, however, that under normal circumstances it is considered most effective to use a mechanism or text especially designed for a given function; but during certain periods in the development of a culture we notice a tendency not to use the ready mechanism. A bogatyr, for example, overcomes his opponent without a weapon: Ilja Muromec "grabbed the bogatyr by the legs/ And began to swing the bogatyr around." Samson defeats the Philistines armed with the jawbone of an ass. The image of the club—a "non-weapon" in the context of late nineteenth century military equipment—is not unmotivated; Lev Tolstoj equates it with a people's war.

In certain historical literary situations there is a tendency to use a text in undesignated ways, so that the function and the text contradict each other. A poetic text may be made to function as a prosaic text, or a mystery novel as a psychological one (Dostoevskij); non-artistic texts (whose inner structure is opposed to that of artistic ones) may function as works of art.

A contradiction between a text and its function in the extra-textual structure of art makes the structure of the artistic language a carrier of information.

When an artistic text simultaneously enters into many intersecting extra-textual structures and each element of the text enters into many segments of the intra-textual structure, the artistic work becomes the carrier of meanings whose correlations are extraordinarily complex. The fact that an artistic text conveys a large amount of information is connected in particular with such structural features as the shift of structural dominants; at the moment when a structural element can be automatically predicted it retreats into the background and the structural dominant is transferred to another level that has not yet been automatized. It is quite understandable that rhyme should appear at the end of lines, the structural position with the greatest accumulation of rhythmic entropy (and in this sense it is also telling that the freer the meter, the greater the demands made on the rhyme and vice versa). We could show that in certain types of poems metaphors gravitate toward the end of the line.

Our study of the artistic text as a structural whole demonstrates, on the one hand, that those things which are original and unique in a work of art are not uninvolved in any structure and therefore accessible only to impressionistic "empathy" and not precise analysis. On the contrary, they occur at the intersection of many structures and belong to them simultaneously, "playing" with the many meanings that arise in the process.

On the other hand, any description of one structural level inevitably impoverishes the rich semantics of a text. Such descriptions should, therefore, be regarded as a purely heuristic stage in the study of a text, engendered by the wholly legitimate desire first to work out methods for the precise resolution of simple problems, and then to approach more complex structural descriptions; they are not intended to reduce the artistic text to unambiguous systems and then provide the ultimate interpretation of a work of art.

The comparison between art and life is not a new one. But we are only beginning to realize how much truth is contained in this once striking metaphor. We can declare with certainty that more than anything else created by man, the artistic text most clearly manifests those properties which draw the cybernetician's attention to the structure of living tissue.

For this reason, the study of the structure of the artistic text is significant for all scientific disciplines.